John
► ◄ ► ◄
von Neumann

John
▶▶◀◀◀
von Neumann

▶◀ Norman Macrae

A Cornelia & Michael Bessie Book
Pantheon Books New York

All rights reserved under International and Pan-American Copyright Conventions. Published in the United States by Pantheon Books, a division of Random House, Inc., New York, and simultaneously in Canada by Random House of Canada Limited, Toronto.

Permissions acknowledgments may be found on page 384.

Library of Congress Cataloging-in-Publication Data

Macrae, Norman, 1923–
John von Neumann / by Norman Macrae.
p. cm.
"Cornelia & Michael Bessie books."
Includes bibliographical references and index.
ISBN 0-679-41308-1
1. Von Neumann, John, 1903–1957. 2. Mathematicians—United States—Biography. I. Title.
QA29.V66M33 1992
510'.92—dc20
[B]   91-50891

Book design by M. Kristen Bearse

Manufactured in the United States of America
First Edition

To Stephen White,
who started this project, gave me his research,
and urged me to complete it.

Contents

Introduction

► ◄ *T*wo aspects of John von Neumann's career were very controversial. Awkwardly, I find myself on his side in both controversies. First, he was more hawkish than most of his friends in framing nuclear deterrence in 1949–55 against Stalin and his immediate successors. I think that some hawkishness at that stage saved the planet. When the draft of this book was circulated to people whom I respect, several scholars and Johnny's contemporaries resented this conclusion. I hope that I have not anywhere been rude to the great and good men who held a more pacifist view, as Johnny himself carefully was not.

Second, Johnny grabbed other people's ideas, then by his clarity leapt five blocks ahead of them, and helped put them into practical effect. I think that is one of the things very clever people exist to do. Because Johnny thought his computers would allow "research teams to tackle one hundred times as many projects one hundred times more quickly," he thought that by now we would have made great scientific advances, such as providing limitless energy through nuclear fusion and controlling the world's weather. Today such views are regarded as irresponsible. I think that, over the next twenty years, they will come back more into fashion. But I launch this book when I know many eminent reviewers will disagree with me.

N. M.

John

▶◀▶◀▶◀

von Neumann

▶◀▶◀▶◀ *1*

The Cheapest

Way to Make the World Richer

▶◀*H*e was born Neumann Janos on December 28, 1903, in Budapest, the capital of his native Hungary. He died John von Neumann on February 8, 1957, of a tragically early cancer in Washington, D.C., the capital of his adopted United States. To friends and even acquaintances in America he was always known as "Johnny," as in Hungary he had been "Jancsi." He is called Johnny throughout this book because it is part of the unpompous measure of a man who changed all our lives, although nine-tenths of humankind has never heard of him. The cheapest way to make the world richer would be to get lots of his like.

He was a prodigious child and a prodigious student, and through his brief fifty-three years grew steadily more prodigious. The most startling young innovator among the pure mathematicians of the 1920s, he surged on to leave his mark on theoretical physics and then on dramatically applied physics, on decision theory, on me-

3

teorology, on biology, on economics, on deterrence to war—and eventually became, more than any other individual, the creator of the modern digital computer and the most farsighted of those who put it to early use. He marked up nearly all his achievements while he was mainly engaged in something else.

In each century there are a handful of people who, grappling with problems in their lonely brains, write a few equations on a few blackboards, and the world changes. Johnny was among the most consistently effective of the mathematicians in our century —which possibly means in any century hitherto, because we can now do such extraordinary things so quickly once these men have worked out their sums.

If Johnny had not lived, the development of America's nuclear, thermonuclear, and certainly missile-borne deterrent would have been slower, maybe fatally so. Without him, the computer revolution would not yet have reached its present foothills, from which so many new roads will go. In his last decade the often-terrifying clarity of his mind was at the service of the Truman and especially Eisenhower administrations, and a lot of people were scared stiff by that. Fortunately, those who were scared included the Russians.

The world in these nicer 1990s is probably escaping with rather surprising intactness from the consequences of the mad and even-tually nuclear-armed Stalin in 1945–53. At a crucial stage of this escape, Johnny played a successful and therefore hawkish and in-itially reviled part. He helped restore self-confidence among those who saw the need to deter the spread of Stalinist tyranny and secret police because he articulated with total intellectuality, if sometimes also with rather inappropriate wit, the shocking things that some cruder hard-liners were used to shouting only emo-tionally. Hawks like the banker-turned-admiral Lewis Strauss were grieved at being treated by some of the world's other clev-erest professors as if all deterrers of Stalin were blimpish genocides and intellectual slobs. They found in Johnny a calmly rational strengthener of their determined views. Near to the time of John-ny's death, said Strauss, there was a meeting at the Walter Reed

Hospital where "gathered round his bedside, and attentive to his last words of advice and wisdom, were the Secretary of Defense and his deputies, the Secretaries of the Army, Navy, and Air Force, and all the military Chiefs of Staff." The central figure, wrote the admiral, was the young mathematician who not so many years before had come to the United States as an immigrant from Hungary. "I have never witnessed a more dramatic scene or a more moving tribute to a great intelligence."

The tersest and probably truest assessment of how Johnny attained this influence was given by a very clever man on the unlikely medium of then-communist Hungary's usually wholly untruthful state television. When the Nobel laureate Eugene Wigner visited his native Budapest a decade after Johnny's death, the interviewer asked whether it was true that in the early and middle 1950s the scientific and nuclear policies of the United States were largely decided by Hungary's Neumann Jancsi. Wigner replied in his precise manner: "That is not quite so. But after Dr. von Neumann had analysed a problem, it was clear what had to be done." Because blood is thicker than heavy water, even communists in Hungary liked the reply.

◄►◄►

Much earlier, Johnny had been a young mathematics prodigy at the century's biggest and most nervous scientific breakthrough— the birth of quantum mechanics (i.e., the theory underlying so much of modern technology, including the whole electronic revolution, but awkwardly also helping forward the atom bomb)— in dangerous Germany in 1925, less than a decade before Germany went crazy. "Quantum mechanics," said one physicist at Johnny's death, "was very fortunate indeed to attract, in the first years after its discovery in 1925, the interest of a mathematical genius of von Neumann's stature. As a result, the mathematical framework of the theory was developed and the formal aspects of its entirely novel rules of interpretation were analyzed by one single man in two years (1927–29)."

Although that judgment was far too optimistic (see chap. 6),

Johnny's useful initial formalization required some tact because in 1927 he was a twenty-three-year-old east European Jew, in a Germany of hierarchical Herr Professors, at a time when mathematicians and physicists won some applause within their separate mysteries by sneering at each other. Johnny's essential niceness and convincing clarity meant that—as nearly throughout his life —he became the one mathematician admired by most scholars outside his own discipline. This was quite an important ingredient of what happened later in 1941–45 when he helped work out oblique shock waves and the implosion lens for the atom bomb (A-bomb) for America in the second world war, and then in 1945–55 when he mobilized computers and rockets and much else for the deterrence of a third one. Mercifully, the mathematician respected by the top physicists and military and government men —and also a man who achieved clarity at astonishing speed—was after 1930 located in the thitherto rather unmathematical United States.

Johnny's professional and social success as early as 1926–29 was the more startling because the precocious youth, in those years moving with playboy enthusiasm in and out of Weimar Berlin's horrid nightclubs and worse, was—once again—really mainly interested in something else. He wanted in the 1920s to become the supreme mathematical logician, establishing in infinite dimensions (but preferably on a single sheet of paper) a modern version of the axioms by which the ancient Greeks and others had managed for twenty-three hundred years to make mathematics seem entirely rigorous. "Rigor" means obeying rules that this calculation follows certainly from that one, which follows undeniably from that one, allowing mathematicians to follow a line of thought that is absolutely guaranteed, thus establishing mathematics' claim to be the foundation of all rationality. Johnny in his German youth wanted to return math to the role of leading all intellectual progress, instead of so much of it being ad hoc. He wanted, by axiomatization, to rescue the then most modern part of math (set theory) from its alleged contradictions.

This was an objective in which (by his own estimation) he

fortunately failed, because Kurt Gödel proved by mathematical means that such total axiomatization is impossible. Johnny's response was unusual for a scholar. After reading Gödel's paper in 1931, he instantly accepted his argument, called him the greatest logician since Aristotle, and (storing his own early experience as a German logician to architect the modern computer) turned to doing something else. He had plenty else to turn to, and left much half-rummaged-through baggage when he died.

◀▶◀▶

Because the reader will live with Johnny von Neumann for the next few hundred pages, it is time to introduce him physically and temperamentally. In his final and most effective years he was a "plump, smiling man, with the mildly distracted air of a professor." His "glittering brown eyes were set in a face always ready to break into grin." These descriptions are from the Hungarian of an interviewer on America's Radio Free Europe; Johnny's fellow professors felt he looked like a banker instead. He nearly always wore a business suit, even when riding up a Colorado mountain on a mule. One of his colleagues urged him to "buy an old jacket, sprinkle chalk on it, and look more like us."

Three usual descriptions are that Johnny exuded self-confidence, had the world's best memory, and could multiply eight-figure numbers by other eight-figure numbers in his head. All these descriptions are half wrong. Deep down, this apparently confident man was self-critical and rather shy. He hated arguments with anybody less intelligent than himself (i.e., almost all mankind), especially when he could crush that person with indisputable facts. He felt that crushing people was hurtful and rude and (most important) always resented. He was puzzled that most other thoughtful people had not noticed that resentment by anybody—from a Nobel Prize–winning colleague, to the president of the United States, or to a waiter—would usually hamper whatever thoughtful people wanted next to influence or do.

He had therefore jovially thought through some deliberate tactics for avoiding rifts in personal relations. As a favored one, he had accumulated an inexhaustible stock of dirty rhymes and stories with which he would turn aside boring conversations that could degenerate into wrath. If somebody tried to get him to take sides in some emotional academic or political controversy, he would say the problem made him feel like the aged bishop of Chichester, who unwisely felt his breeches stir—or (when ladies were present) reminded him of some abstruse and humorous and not really relevant incident in ancient Babylon. Or else he would say, "Have another drink."

His powers of memory were awe-inspiring, but only about matters on which he had fearsomely concentrated his mind. He could recite verbatim pages and pages from books such as Dickens's *Tale of Two Cities* which he had read fifteen years before, or from entries on subjects revealingly chosen from the *Encyclopaedia Britannica*. This was because he had concentrated hard when first reading them—in these two cases when he was trying to get a feel for proper English syntax before emigrating to the United States. If a person or subject bored him, he could switch right off. This explained his occasional bewildering absentmindednesses and the many times when he plainly did not recognize a quite eminent person he had met the previous day.

The deliberate, fact-remembering parts of his memory were far better than the photographic parts of it. Although he was particularly awful at remembering boring people's faces, this shy man hated being hurtful even to them. His obituary in *Life* magazine in 1957 recalled his famous cocktail parties at Princeton ("those old geniuses got downright approachable at the von Neumanns' ") and continued that Johnny's "talents as a host were based on his drinks, which were strong, his repertoire of off-color stories, which was massive, and his social ease, which was consummate. Although he could rarely remember a name, von Neumann would escort each new guest around the room, bowing punctiliously to cover up the fact that he was not using names when introducing people."

The most important use to which he had put his memory was that he had stuffed an unprecedented number of mathematical constants and equations into it. Most of us have very few mathematical constants in our mind, perhaps only the up-to-twelve-times multiplication table. Johnny had put in his mind layers and layers of algebraic verities. These were the explanation of his extraordinary powers of mental calculation. He was not actually better than many other mathematicians—or indeed than some vaudeville freaks—at multiplying one eight-digit figure by another. But he used his accumulation of mathematical constants and equations to become a startling problem-solver and extraordinary concept-expander. When scientific groups at Los Alamos and elsewhere heard von Neumann was coming, "they would set up all of their advanced mathematical problems like ducks in a shooting gallery. Then he would arrive and systematically topple them over."

His ability at concept expanding mattered more. If you took a suggestion to Johnny, said one of his assistants, Julian Bigelow, "he was in a short while five blocks ahead of you." A graduate student sometimes felt he was "riding a bicycle after an express train in which Dr. von Neumann was carrying away . . . more and more wonderful expansions of [other people's] original ideas." Quite a lot of Johnny's best work sprang from concept expansions like that, and they caused difficulties with the originators at times.

◄►◄►

Johnny had engaging mannerisms when doing these sums, although he changed some in later life after he was told about them. When calculating a problem while sitting, he was apt to stare at the ceiling muttering, with an almost frighteningly blank face. He did this when the Rand Corporation asked whether his computers could be modified to tackle a particular problem, which—as Rand staff explained to him for two hours on blackboards and with graphs—would understandably be beyond computers in their present state. For two or three minutes (see that obituary in *Life* again), Johnny

stared so blankly that a Rand scientist later said he looked as if his mind had slipped his face out of gear. Then he said "Gentlemen, you do not need the computer, I have the answer." While the scientists sat in stunned silence, von Neumann reeled off the various steps which would provide the solution. . . . Having risen to this routine challenge, von Neumann followed up with a routine suggestion: Let's go to lunch.

At one research establishment, it had been decided to remit a problem to Johnny's mental mathematics, but in the intervening period a staffer with a calculating machine spent the best part of a night and solved it. When the question was put to Johnny, he stared at the ceiling and said "the first step is to calculate . . ." While he was in mid-mutter, the staffer suggested that the right answer was such and such. Johnny went on muttering and then said with surprise, "That is correct." Later, it was explained to him that the staffer had spent several hours on what took him five minutes. Otherwise, claimed his friends (probably libelously, for he really was not petty), Johnny might have sulked for weeks.

When he was given a problem while standing, Johnny at one stage would dance from foot to foot. Although this practice caused some spills at his crowded cocktail parties, it forms one of the best stories half against him: his reaction to the fly puzzle. Two bicyclists are 20 miles apart and head toward each other at 10 miles per hour each. At the same time a fly traveling at a steady 15 miles per hour starts from the front wheel of the northbound bicycle. It lands on the front wheel of the southbound bicycle, and then instantly turns around and flies back, and after next landing instantly flies north again. Question: What total distance did the fly cover before it was crushed between the two front wheels?

The slow way of answering is to calculate the distance that the fly travels on its first trip to the southbound front wheel, then the distance it travels on its next trip to the northbound wheel, and finally to sum the infinite series so obtained. It is extraordinary how many mathematicians can be fooled into doing that long sum. The short way is to note that the bicycles will meet exactly an hour after starting, by which time the 15-miles-per-hour fly must have covered 15 miles. When the question was put to Johnny, he danced and answered immediately, "15 miles." "Oh, you've heard the trick before," said the disappointed questioner. "What trick?" asked the puzzled Johnny. "I simply summed the infinite series." It is worth adding that, when ribbed on this later, Johnny said "the figures actually put to me were not so simple."

When he was asked a question on the hoof, Johnny would put his hands behind his back and work out sums while moving forward in a strange waddle—"moving in small steps with considerable random acceleration, but never at great speed." He once calculated how much heat would have been absorbed into a square meter of earth, apparently when there was a question of whether it would be safe to pick up a metal object that had been left in the sun most of the day. "Well," said Johnny, waddling toward it, "the sun's heat at its surface is . . ." He had calculated before he reached the object that it had better not be picked up. We will meet several such quick Johnny calculations in this book, some of them stretching toward matters that, in one of his favorite phrases, could "potentially jiggle the planet."

◄► ◄►

If Johnny had lived a normal scholar's life span, to just about now, would he have brought further big changes in the way we live? This is a fair question for a biographer, and my honest answer is, I would guess so. The ways in which he would have changed it depend on what ideas others would have brought to him, and on how many multitudes of five blocks he would then have jumped ahead of them. But some guesses can be made from his sometimes-unpublished jottings in his last years.

Johnny himself expected that scientific progress in 1957–92 would be faster than it has been. Near his death he was groping toward possibilities around which other scientists' imaginations have not yet begun to furl. These included his approach (or what he called his "somewhat systematized set of speculations on how an approach ought to be made") to the lessons to be learned from the human nervous system for his computers. He felt the whole concept of numbers had to be reoriented for the computer age, and feared it had not been.

He drew up models in which groups of mechanical cells might start to act somewhat like a living entity, retaining their identities while moving about or standing still in active or inactive states, and causing neighboring groups of cells to take on similar states to themselves. He pondered how we might theoretically get an eventual automaton of the complexity and speed of the human brain, but operating for a hundred years with the expectation of about one error. He discussed the possibility of constructing computers and robots that would manage to build other computers and robots with self-improving artificial intelligence. The advance to a human brain from that of a jellyfish had been attained by Darwinian evolution, and he pondered whether his computers might be given some of the same attributes. With proper calculation it could be possible to get each successive generation of computers and robots automatically to be more efficient in responding to their changing environments, and then to pass on to the next self-reproducing generation of computers the proper rules for survival of the fittest and for evolution of the computer species.

Today in 1992 this does not sound as strange as it sounded then. The latest fashions in the search for artificial intelligence are "neural networks" that learn how to solve problems by adjusting the strengths of layers of computer units until the desired solution is secured. In the later 1990s, at least one main function of the brain, but not yet of the computer (probably vision), may be simulated on a computer before it is understood by it or us.

Johnny had actively participated in the biggest scientific breakthrough of the first half of the twentieth century—scientific understanding of the atom. He had helped to mathematize that and to develop computers in the electronic revolution that followed from it. I think his last lectures and jottings suggest that he hoped to play similar roles in the next three likely big breakthroughs: after scientific understanding of the atom, then forward—in uncertain order—to scientific understanding of the brain, of the cell (or gene), and involvement of his computers in conquering the great remaining problems of the physical environment (such as controlling the world's weather). To these four challenges—the atom (pressing on to secure virtually free energy via nuclear fusion), the brain, the gene, and the physical environment—he sometimes added his hopes for the introduction of mathematical rigor (i.e., proper science) into the worthy but twittering faculties of economics and their even weaker sisters in today's social half-sciences.

He had expected great advances in all these fields by 1992. Sadly, only in the understanding of the gene have really big steps (by Johnny's standards) been made, and even in that pretty unmathematically. As he had expected, human genes turned out to be simple information-storage devices like his computers, but he did not know at death that the cipher they read could be so tersely written (and rewritable) in three-letter words in a four-letter alphabet. He would have been delighted that by 1992 we can identify and rewrite many of the fifty or sixty genes that tell a fly's egg how to turn itself into a fly. He would have wanted to give all the help that a mathematician can provide to press on to a complete genetic recipe for the makeup of a human being. I asked two of his friends what they thought Johnny would be doing if he had lived to 1992 and got almost the same answer from both: "Johnny would have become as excited by molecular biology as he was by quantum mechanics," they said in very similar words, "and he would have longed to help mathematize it." Intriguingly, his only grandson is now a molecular biologist on Harvard's medical faculty.

My own guess is that, once he had completed the modernization of America's deterrent under Eisenhower, he would have wanted to go back to help mathematize lots of other people's subjects. Mathematics has proved a marvelous tool for guiding developments in physics, but it is aggravating that nobody has yet managed to make such activities as psychiatry and stimulation of the human learning process into mathematically respectable professions. Johnny was worried that too few of his fellow professors could, in their own subjects, like economics, show that one thing will always follow from another.

In the book he wrote on his deathbed, *The Computer and the*

Brain, Johnny suspected that this was because we did not yet have enough sorts of mathematics. He had always recognized that math was too specialized a language, one that he could comprehend as instantly as he could English or German, but it was tiresome that when he talked math other people looked as puzzled as if he were talking Japanese. The languages we use, he said, are clearly a historical accident, as is shown by the multiplicity of them. "Just as languages like Greek or Sanskrit are historical facts and not absolute necessities, it is only reasonable to assume that logics and mathematics are similarly historical, accidental forms of expression." He thought that "when we talk mathematics we may be discussing a secondary language, built on the primary language truly used by the central nervous system." He was trying to grope toward that primary language, and toward useful secondary languages that might be developed from it, when he died.

All his life Johnny was searching for new notions or notations that could marvelously increase man's power to push forward scientific revolutions. He hoped his computers could help move toward them in lots of subjects. He knew that existing professors in those subjects might then be rather cross. When he was writing *The Theory of Games and Economic Behavior* with Oskar Morgenstern, he waxed rather rude (unusual for him) about the "ignorance" of modern economics. He snorted that "economic problems are often stated in such vague terms as to make mathematical treatment appear a priori hopeless because it is quite unclear what the problems really are." He found economics and much other social science to be incomparably cruder than physics was in the seventeenth century—before "God said: let Newton be," and so mechanics and the scientific and industrial revolutions began.

Newton's breakthrough to the mathematization of physics, said Johnny, "brought about, and can hardly be separated from, the discovery of the infinitesimal calculus. . . . It is therefore to be expected—or feared—that mathematical discoveries of a stature comparable to that of calculus will be needed in order to produce decisive success in this field [economic and other social science]. . . . It is unlikely that the mere repetition of the tricks which served us so well in physics will do for social phenomena too." More optimistically, he told another audience that "a considerable segment of chemistry could be moved from the laboratory field into the mathematical field if one could integrate the applicable equations of quantum theory." It is probable that in the thirty-five years since his death software has advanced by less than he had hoped. But, thanks to the miracle of the chip, the improvement and fall in price and miniaturization of computer hardware have exceeded anything of which he dreamed. At his death in 1957 the most advanced of his computers, although filling a large room, had less computing power than has a fairly smart pocket calculator (perhaps a $250 one) in 1992. Remember that when Johnny plotted how to control the world's weather, and to do so many other things, he was operating with the equivalent of a pocket calculator like that.

◀▶◀▶

Nearer to his own field, the trick that was then (in the early 1950s) most needed in physics was the readier solution of nonlinear partial differential equations (PDEs). These equations are the brutes where, with each move you make to try to solve them, all other factors within those equations may change. You start to walk out of a maze but, with each of your forward steps, the walls may rearrange themselves. Such equations are especially important in fluid dynamics—that is, studies of the strange things that happen with movements of gases (such as air) and liquids (such as water).

Johnny had delved deep in them when he became one of America's leading experts in conventional explosives in the 1941–43 part of the war. He had noted physical and mathematical regularities in the nonlinear equations that rule fluid dynamics. He was excited because the patterns appearing there could dominate so many things from aerodynamics to nuclear fusion and hurricanes. Johnny envisaged his computers as machines that would allow some of these scientific problems to be solved by systematically applying a weight of analysis tens of thousands times greater than had ever been applied to them before.

In aerodynamics, his belief has proved right. It is now possible to design on computers a new aircraft or a rocket carrying a man to one spot on the moon. We do not have to kill so many test pilots to find what happens when we go through the speed of sound. The same is true in so many other fields of design and construction. But on at least two other matters Johnny's last writings have infuriated some modern experts: the meteorologists and researchers on fusion. Johnny believed that sometime after the 1950s scientists should have made sufficient advances in meteorology to start to control the weather, not merely to forecast it. And he thought we would discover a manageable sort of nuclear fusion. "In a few decades" the release of energy from storage in matter ("the transmutation of elements, alchemy rather than chemistry") would bring mankind a new sort of energy that would be as free as "the unmetered air."

He saw, before wailing about it became fashionable, that the release of carbon dioxide through the burning of coal and oil was liable to bring "a general warming of the world by about one degree Fahrenheit" in little more than his own generation. This would presumably increase exponentially, and "another fifteen degrees of warming would probably melt the ice of Greenland and Antarctica," bringing flooding and semitropical climates to areas that did not expect them. Less fashionably, but more worriedly, he calculated that, if the dust from the eruption of the volcano Krakatau in 1883 had stayed in the stratosphere for fifteen (instead of its actual three) years, and so reflected sunlight away from the earth, it might have sufficed to lower the world's temperature by 5° F. He noted that "the last Ice Age, when half of North America and all of northern and western Europe were under an icecap like that of Greenland and Antarctica, was only 15° F colder than the present age." We will have more Krakataus, although nobody can yet say how many and when. Johnny would be worried that forty years' use of his computers has not done more to find out the odds.

It was typical of Johnny that he reacted in the early 1950s to these interesting thoughts, about the greenhouse effect and potential Krakataus, not with despair but with a determination to turn them to man's advantage. His antennae bristled with his usual suggestions for seize-the-opportunity projects, such as painting the ice caps a different color. "The persistence of large icefields," he said, "is due to the fact that ice both reflects sunlight energy and radiates away terrestrial energy at an even higher rate than ordinary soil. Microscopic layers of colored matter spread on an icy surface, or in the atmosphere above one, could inhibit the reflection-radiation process, melt the ice and change the local climate." He thought that by the 1990s people would have moved toward doing such things: maybe not to turn every Iceland into a Hawaii but probably seizing the chance that "temporary disturbances—including the invasions of cold polar air that constitute the typical winter of the middle latitudes, and tropical storms (hurricanes)—might be corrected or at least depressed." Modern scientists will say that trying this would be very irresponsible, but he would have been on the side of testing on computers how far and why. He foresaw horrid problems such as possible nasty forms of climatic war (perhaps the Soviet Union might threaten to fasten an ice age on North America), but he did not expect computational difficulties.

If Johnny returned now, he would be delighted that his computers had increased so much in number and power. He would be astonished that they were used so widely, but depressed that they were not used with greater scientific success. To quote his daughter, the distinguished economist Dr. Marina von Neumann Whitman: "If anyone had ever told him that the company I work for, General Motors, would produce and utilize literally millions of computers every year (each of the roughly 8 million vehicles we produce each year contains several, not to mention the ones in our plants and offices), I think he would have been startled. And the notion of adults fulminating against computers as corrupters of youth in the form of video games would have amused and perhaps secretly pleased the playful, childlike aspect of his personality."

Against that, this biographer would guess, he would be stunned into more of his familiar dawn-to-midnight working days because so many researchers, even in the precise sciences, still do not work with models through which statistics can be coherently applied; while some imprecise sciences (including economics and club-of-Rome-type ecology) use too many models that stench ludicrously of garbage in and therefore garbage out. He would be worried that computers were being used to back up emotional viewpoints rather than to find out facts. But he would also want computers to help fight pessimism and despair, which he regarded as scientific sins.

Since Johnny's death, the fashion in very clever mathematics has swung back to saying that matters are infinitely more complicated than some precomputer mathematicians thought, that the movement of a butterfly's wings over Beijing today can affect next month's storm patterns over New York, that a beautiful chaos rules where old-fashioned calculators assumed there should be order. Johnny's whole bent, from about age nine, was to try to restore order where other people saw chaos. He would want to work out the functional equations, new languages, and moments of escalation into chaos, to show how and where to flutter those butterflies' wings. He would be happy to reduce forecasters' aims to predicting not exact outcome, but outcome on the average. This division—between those who find the unfathomable inevitable and beautiful, and those who find it irrational and thus needing to be changed—has been a usual split, or perhaps cycle, among mathematicians for twenty-five hundred years.

"From the earliest times," said E. T. Bell, a leading historian of mathematics, writing before Johnny or certainly modern chaos theorists had been heard of, "we meet these two distinct and antagonistic types of mind: the justifiably cautious who hang back because the ground quakes under their feet, and the bolder pioneers who leap the chasm to find treasure and comparative safety on the other side." Bell's example among the ancient Greeks of a cautious man who refused to leap was Zeno of Elea (494–435 B.C.). Zeno worried even Aristotle with his mathematical proof that Achilles could never overtake a crawling tortoise that set out ahead of him. Achilles must first reach the place from which the tortoise started. When he reaches that place, the tortoise has departed and so is still ahead at position A. When Achilles then reaches position A, the tortoise has departed and therefore must still be ahead, so . . . Johnny exuded a genuine bewilderment that minds like Zeno's cannot see that infinitely many quantities such as one, one-half, and one-fourth can add up to a finite quantity, including the position where the tortoise is.

Bell's example of an ancient Greek mathematician who, like Johnny, did dare to leap chasms was Archimedes (287–212 B.C.). By calculating the value of π, discovering the science of hydrostatics, and nearly discovering calculus, Archimedes did even more for his generation of mathematicians than Johnny did for ours. Archimedes ended his life by hurling stone shots, each weighing over a quarter of a ton, from his supercatapult to destroy a Roman fleet. Like Johnny, he thus ended as his country's most mathematical armorer.

Both the cautious and the chasm leapers are needed, but the leapers matter more. In the long sweep of history, Bell's judgment was that the cautious ones generally "committed but few mistakes and were comparatively sterile of truth no less than of error"; whereas darers, like Archimedes and Johnny, have "discovered much of the highest interest to mathematics and rational thought in general, some of which may be open to destructive criticism, however." This is a fair epitaph on Johnny. It confirms why we need to get many more of his like again. He discovered much of the highest interest to rational thought, some of which may be open to destructive criticism, however.

◄►◄►

Happily, and this is not sufficiently realized, it should be possible to get more like him. Because a mind like Johnny's needs to be financed only into having a pen and paper, the appearance of Johnnies is the cheapest way of increasing man's material prosperity very fast. When Johnny's Princeton colleague Albert Einstein was asked, "Where is your laboratory?" he pointed to his head; when then asked, "Where is your expensive equipment?"

he brandished his fountain pen. Johnny resembled his colleague Einstein in this respect, although (see later) some people who remember 1945–56 will say we are lucky that he resembled gentle and generous and dreamy Einstein in no political way what ever. The great glory from Einstein's dreaminess, which can also be called his closer touch with the cosmos, was that he had marvelous flashes of irrational intuition that changed the direction of scientific progress; Johnny amiably envied these because Johnny could never be irrational himself.

"For von Neumann," said his assistant Paul Halmos, "it seemed impossible to be unclear in thought or expression." Although "we can all think clearly, more or less, some of the time, von Neumann's clarity of thought was orders of magnitude greater than that of most of us, all the time." Halmos was probably thinking of Einstein when he likened some scientists to the creator of the Great G-minor Fugue, while adding in his next sentence that by contrast "von Neumann's greatness was of the human kind."

A big advantage to mere humans is that one can develop them from the nursery on. Among the several million babies born this month, it is plausible that there will not have been any Einsteins or creators of the Great G-minor Fugue. But it is genetically almost certain that there will have been some who could become capable of thinking at the towering level of Johnny's concentration, intellect, and mind.

Unfortunately, most of them will not go on to coinvent the digital computer or to accomplish the other things Johnny did in his spare time. This is because various accidents or mishandlings will get in their way. Some of the mishandling will be parental, some educational, some will come from a shattering of self-confidence in the teens and twenties, some from later blockages by bosses, spouses, or friends. There are not enough studies of how such minds operate, so neither they nor those who encounter them are very skilled at dealing with the original (therefore controversial) things they think and sometimes say.

This book is a study of an exceptionally well-balanced man who—without pushfulness or expenditure on public relations—

became the most quietly effective mathematical mind of this century. That mind was shaped in four tumultuous environments: defeated Hungary in 1903–21, Weimar Germany in the 1920s, depression-era Princeton in the 1930s, hot- and cold-war Washington in the 1940s and 1950s—through which Johnny successively passed.

◄►◄►

In the first of these, Budapest, we will see that Johnny had exactly the right (successful but relaxed and rather jolly) parental upbringing, and went through the early twentieth-century Hungarian education system that (this book will argue) was the most brilliant the world has seen until its close imitator in post-1945 Japan. Still, it was also a Hungary which lost two-thirds of its territory and all its previous boom by being on the losing side in the 1914–18 war, and which then (when Johnny was fifteen) had a brief communist revolution. From these communist shambles it passed straight into long rule by an initially anti-Semitic admiral who rode into the capital of his landlocked country on a white horse. If he stayed in his native country, Johnny had no great hope of success. He therefore had to do his profound thinking (the ordinary mind boggles at this) in three different workaday languages in succession.

Johnny then spent his next decade as an ennobled Jew in a brilliant intellectual atmosphere—with academic colleagues making scientific breakthroughs almost every month—in taut Weimar Germany, where he could tangibly feel the approach of national madness and holocaust.

Johnny was then invited to the United States at the time of the 1929 stock-market crash, which brought in the decade of the Great Depression. Yet, says his companion on nearly the next boat over, Wigner, Johnny "fell in love with America on the first day. He thought: these are sane people who don't talk in those traditional terms which are meaningless. To a certain extent even the materialism of the United States, which was greater than that of Europe, appealed to him." A liking for material wealth possibly is a usual characteristic of men with effective minds (which Johnny was), although not of saints (which Johnny was not).

Johnny then spent his last decade soberly calculating that a mad Stalin, who had gotten from traitors of Johnny's acquaintance the secret of a nuclear bomb Johnny had helped to invent, was rather likely to use it to incinerate or enslave the planet unless firm deterrents were put in his way. This incineration was an unpleasantness that Johnny helped to avert, although he offended a lot of other scientists' susceptibilities as he determinedly, yet calmly and wittily, did so.

Two problems of this book are, first, a danger of being rude to various scholars who were slightly less clever than Johnny but much cleverer than you or me; and, second, a danger of praising Johnny too glutinously. One check on the first fault is that Johnny himself was excessively polite to everybody, except perhaps to the one-half of humankind who are women. His politeness did not keep him from staring at young women's legs even when he was a fat fifty-year-old. Most people would sympathize with his two long-suffering wives. A check on writing too many glutinous sentences about Johnny is the knowledge that he would have shouted, perhaps, "Nebbitch two!" against any overpraise. "Nebbitch" was his own spelling of the Yiddish word "nebbish," meaning something like "That's a loser," and he had a useful if disconcerting pastime of quantifying as "nebbitch one" or "nebbitch two" or "nebbitch three" or "nebbitch four" (the worst) the degrees of meaninglessness in scientific statements that proved pompously misleading, including, in retrospect, some of his own.

Johnny was amazingly free of amour propre, in a profession where many top mathematicians up to and including Sir Isaac Newton (1642–1727) had been as sick as peacocks with it. Newton spent his early life denying he had plagiarized anything from anybody (although he fortunately had), and then spent part of his middle life appointing supposedly impartial commissions (whose reports he himself wrote) to declare quite wrongly that Gottfried Leibniz (1646–1716) had plagiarized everything from him. Actually, Newton had thought of some of the things that led Leibniz to discover differential calculus but had not published them in any form that Leibniz could have read.

In contrast, Johnny borrowed (we must not say plagiarized) anything from anybody, with great courtesy and aplomb. His mind was not as original as Leibniz's or Newton's or Einstein's, but he seized other people's original (though fluffy) ideas and quickly changed them in expanded detail into a form where they could be useful for scholarship and for mankind. He rightly deemed that this was clever people's duty and their great fun, so he was not worried that he was not credited with all his due by the general public and the newspapers (the latter he held in what sometimes seemed Prussian disdain). One of the professional ways in which he wrung more than twenty-four hours' work out of a twenty-four-hour day was to get the boring research on some projects done by collaborators whom he enthused by gasping that they were famously expanding their own original ideas.

A curious consequence is that Johnny's contribution when he worked with proud but rather upper-second-rank colleagues is still often underrated. By contrast, when he influenced top men who were more nearly his intellectual peers, those peers gushed. "He was the incomparable Johnny von Neumann," wrote one Nobel Prize winner in economics. "He darted briefly into our domain, and it has never been the same since." Von Neumann was the author of "the greatest paper on mathematical economics ever written," wrote a second professor of economics in 1983, surprising a lot of other professors in his subject who even by then had not actually read it.

I lectured on Johnny to a London seminar of professors and lecturers in philosophy, and we were all surprised at the first question from a professor of philosophy at the University of Amsterdam (John Dorling). He asked whether Johnny thought of himself as a philosopher, because it was arguable that he was the most versatile philosopher of the century. "In about six areas of philosophy, von Neumann made very substantial contributions . . . turning vague problems into ones that could be precisely formulated mathematically. Six areas are much more than any well-known philosopher this century has made a similar contribution to." In 1990 a thirty-five-year-old professor told me that "von Neumann took the fear out of learning math for all the professors who taught me."

In the 1950s the physicist Hans Bethe, who won the Nobel Prize for exploring the energy of the sun and stars and who was thus Johnny's senior in rank at Los Alamos, wondered quite seriously whether "a brain like von Neumann's does not indicate a species superior to that of man." From Princeton came the reply that Johnny was admittedly not human but a demigod "who had, however, made a detailed study of humans and could imitate them perfectly." That other Nobel Prize winner, Eugene Wigner, had a devoted inferiority complex toward Johnny right from their Budapest school days when Wigner was twelve and Johnny eleven. Eleven-year-old Johnny taught him set-theory math during Sunday afternoon walks.

◄► ◄►

All this might make Johnny sound like the professor's professor. There is more than a whiff of this in the answers he gave when America's National Academy of Science asked shortly before his death what he thought were his three greatest achievements. Remember that he was by then regarded as the main brain behind the modern digital computer and behind numerical meteorology. He was coordinator of America's deterrent, which was persuading Soviet Russia to turn from Stalinism to the less appalling Khrushchevism. He was thought by some to be the most effective clever man in the world.

Johnny replied to the academy that he considered his most important contributions to have been on the theory of self-adjoint operators in Hilbert space, and on the mathematical foundations of quantum theory and the ergodic theorem. The reader can be excused a resounding "er?" The writer and the readers of Johnny's story face an initial daunting problem, but then get thrills and lots of fun. The daunting problem about these geniuses is that at first perhaps only about three hundred people understand what on earth they are saying. Archimedes can initially have been understood by only a few hundred—that is, by all the broadly educated people within earshot in ancient Greece. When undergraduate Johnny wrote his papers "Zur Einführung der transfiniten Ordnungszählen" (Toward the Introduction of Transfinite Ordinal Numbers) and "Eine Axiomatisierung der Mengenlehre" (An Axiomatization of Set Theory) in the early 1920s, only about three hundred would have understood him—that is, Johnny's older, astonished, and sometimes resentful mathematical peers.

Between the 1920s and his death, this situation worried him by growing worse. He himself lamented near to his last year that "whereas in the 1920s a mathematician could grasp all of mathematics, that is now impossible." Somebody asked him "what percentage of all mathematics might a person aspire to understand today?" Johnny went into one of his characteristic ten-second trances and replied: "About 28 percent."

This reply was probably unfair to himself. It is true, now even more than in 1955, that no mathematician can conceivably follow the thousands of new mathematical theorems that appear in mathematical publications each year. But Johnny's especial skill was to pick out work that seemed surprising and therefore interesting. He was bored with mathematical discoveries that he assumed should have (and perhaps had) been made long ago. After politely muttering "nebbitch" only inaudibly during other people's meaningless lectures, he somewhat undercut his politeness by snoring as he dropped asleep. But he pounced with lion's claws on the new mathematical ideas of other people that did look interesting, and he pummeled them into a shape that was more precise. In subjects other than mathematics, he pounced on more surprising arguments still and helped them to become detailed.

◄►◄►

Most people nowadays assume he was a right-wing Republican. Actually, he voted in each presidential election with the majority of the American people: for Roosevelt and Truman each time and for Eisenhower in 1952. It may therefore be right to deal now with the one charge most frequently made against him: that he was a warmonger and a toady to those with military power—a man who called crassly for what would have been a globe-destroying preventive war against the Russians in 1945–53. The truth is that he stuck remorselessly to cold logic and in favor of human freedom throughout.

Johnny was a European Jew who got his immediate family out to America in time. He had in the 1930s foreseen the full horror of the holocaust to come. He had known from life in Berlin what would occur. "If these boys [the Nazis] last long, which is unfortunately probable," he wrote on Hitler's accession in 1933, the consequences will be fearful. By the later 1930s he was writing to Rudolf Ortvay in Hungary that there was going to be a European war, and that those Jews caught on the German side of it could be faced by the same horrors as were Armenians subjected to Turkish genocide in 1916.

Many of his fellow scientists during that 1930s decade of despair tried to see a workers' paradise in Stalin's Soviet Russia. The cure for that was to go to Soviet Russia. Johnny went there during Stalin's purges, and he had also known Russian-backed communism during Bela Kun's putsch in Budapest in 1919.

During 1941–45 Johnny said to friends what in 1954 he would say publicly to the Gray Committee. He believed that America, as leader of the free world, was "engaged in a triangular war, where our two enemies [Germany and Russia] are doing the nice thing of fighting each other." Earlier, in 1939–40, he had said that the Germany he knew would quickly overwhelm the inconsequential France that he had lectured in.

Among people who wanted to believe optimistic nonsense about western Europe or Soviet Russia, this sort of statement made him unpopular. Among more thoughtful people, it gave him a reputation for prescience. He was sought out by them, and they included the military and political leaders of the United States. He enjoyed being thus sought out and liked the "thump of the helicopter on his lawn." He did have a rather German respect for officialdom. When he was transforming meteorology, one of his colleagues accused him of "showing almost Chinese politeness even to the US Weather Service."

The one time when his prescience fortunately went wrong was in 1945–53, when he thought that an eventual war between the United States and Stalin's Russia was very probable. He deemed it his duty to think out ways in which, despite such a catastrophe, his United States and some other parts of the planet could be saved from destruction.

The A-bomb, at whose "adulterous conception and agonised delivery" he had helped officiate, could clearly soon be expanded into something a thousand times more deadly than the bomb dropped on Hiroshima. Johnny guessed what was being done by some of the dreamy Left he knew at Los Alamos. Klaus Fuchs, out of genuine idealism, was seeking to give the power to destroy the planet to Stalin, whose suitability for getting it was not well advertised by his desire at the time to murder his doctors because they did not make him feel better on the increasingly frequent occasions when he went to bed mad roaring drunk. But Johnny was not as neurotic about spies as were most of those who understood Stalin. He thought Russia would find that the secret of the A-bomb was an easy one for educated men to work out.

Because this awkward danger existed, Johnny turned his mind to ways to meet it. In 1945–49, communism was being spread by force across much of the Eurasian landmass. In this period Johnny did declare that America would eventually have to say to Stalin, "Go no further." Everybody eventually agreed. He also said that it would be preferable to say this before more countries, like his Hungary, were swallowed up and before Stalin got the A-bomb (which he guessed would be soon).

This view has often been interpreted as meaning he favored a preemptive strike against Soviet Russia. I cannot find anything in his papers that suggests that he advocated that, although a lot of honest people thought that he did. In the pre-Eisenhower (pre-1952) period he was not greatly affecting government action anyway but will have sounded consensual with hawks. By the time he was invited into the inner councils of government, Russia had got the bomb, and resistance to Russia had become American foreign policy. Within those inner councils Johnny acted not as a hawk but as a determined owl, which still meant showing claws.

One possibility was that, if war with Russia looked inevitable, America should resort to first conventional or first nuclear strike. Johnny did not shrink from contemplating that, and with the coldest of mathematics he worked out with what weapons a first strike would be most effective. Another possibility was that Russia would edge toward making a first strike; in that case America must have the power to threaten a quite devastating return strike, which is why Johnny was one of the men who, with Edward Teller, urged and helped forward the development of the thermonuclear bomb. He also worked out, again coldly and mathematically, how deployment of this would be most effective. He was clear about what needed to keep on being said.

When Hitler told his generals in 1938 that he intended to go to war, only a few of those generals objected. The rest calculated (to some degree logically) that the weakness of France meant they should quickly win. Their reaction would have been different if all of them had known that in the early minutes of a war they themselves would certainly be killed by a nuclear device homing on to them. Johnny was concerned in all his utterances after 1945 that all the top decision makers in the Soviet Union should be kept totally aware of this. By the time Johnny died in 1957, Stalin had been dead four years, and Russia had become a better place rather than a place ruled by Lavrenty Beria.

Johnny was one of the most thoughtful of the men who delivered us.

Many of his fellow scientists advocated policies that showed they did not understand either how fragile freedom then was or the nature of the struggle for succession in progress in Russia. This pacifism within his profession grieved Johnny because most of the near-pacifists were nicer men than his allies the hawks. He did not argue with many appeasers of Russia. Here again he showed the characteristic that he did not like to argue with anybody. He much preferred to give advice to those who asked for it, not to quarrel with those who did not.

At first this made him a bad chairman of committees, which may sound strange to those who regarded him as the Eisenhower administration's master committee chairman in his last three years. The difference came when he could pick his committees' membership himself. He would then set very specific questions—such as, what weight of explosive power will we need for an effective deterrent, and can we get a rocket to carry it? He kept discussion tied to these hard facts. Said Strauss, "He had the invaluable faculty of being able to take the most difficult problem, separate it into its components, whereupon everything looked brilliantly simple, and all of us wondered why we had not been able to see through to the answer as clearly." When he chaired vaguer committees picked by other people, he let blatherers blather too long, being too shy—especially when frankness might hurt the pride of people—to contradict them.

It is usual to call this a weakness, but is it really? Laura Fermi, the historian wife of Enrico Fermi (one of the scientists who disagreed with Johnny and opposed development of the thermonuclear bomb), wrote that, among all the scientists then arguing about how not to destroy the world, "Dr. von Neumann is one of the very few men about whom I have not heard a single critical remark. It is astonishing that so much equanimity and so much intelligence could be concentrated in a man of not extraordinary appearance." This equanimity was one of the ways in which Johnny quietly got things done.

Enough has now been said to suggest that Johnny was a figure of extraordinary importance in our century. He was also a good man and a good friend and a good citizen. An attempt to tell his story fairly and analytically is now, thirty-five years after his death, overdue.

► ◄► ◄► ◄ *2*

A Silver

Spoon in Budapest, 1903–14

►◄ *I*f you are to beget a genius, a boom area in *belle époque* will serve you best. The booming Budapest of 1903, into which Johnny was born, was about to produce one of the most glittering single generations of scientists, writers, artists, musicians, and useful expatriate millionaires to come from one small community since the city-states of the Italian Renaissance. In much of 1867–1913, Budapest sped forward economically faster than anywhere else in Europe, and with the delights that a self-reliant plutocracy (rather than a self-questioning democracy) temporarily brings.

Budapest surfed into the twentieth century on a wave of music and operetta down the blue Danube, as an industrializing city that "still smelt of violets in the spring," pulsing with mental vigor in its (by 1900) six hundred middle-class coffeehouses and its brilliant elitist educational system. It was the twin city where clever rich little boys in Pest (like Johnny) had a cosmopolitan choice of governesses before age ten, and after age ten (provided they could pass exams and pay) a choice between at least three of the world's best high schools. Across the river, "horse-drawn droshkies carried silk-gowned women and their Hussar counts in red uniforms and furred hats through the ancient war-scarred hills of Buda," with a marvelous life-style for anybody above the middle-middle class.

Most of Budapest's beckoning high schools were run by the churches, but the majority of their most successful scholars were at birth Jews. Five of Hungary's six Nobel Prize winners were Jews born between 1875 and 1905, and one was asked why Hungary in his generation had brought forth so many geniuses. Nobel laureate Wigner replied that he did not understand the question. Hungary in that time had produced only one genius, Johnny von Neumann.

Hungarians less modest than Wigner would see signs of genius in far more of his contemporary countrymen than that. We will be tripping at various stages of this book over so many Hungarians of Johnny's generation who changed the world's and especially America's experience in math, medicine, technology, science, music, art, entertainment, economics. Remember, as we do, from what a small constituency of upper-middle-class Budapest males —in one fifty-year period and mainly from three great schools— this tribe of world changers came.

Ten of the most distinguished were physical scientists. Three of these were in fields separate from Johnny's and Wigner's: George Bekesy, who elucidated the workings of the inner ear; Albert Szent-Gyorgy, the physiologist who worked in the fields of physics and medicine; Dennis Gabor, the Nobel Prize–winning pioneer of holography. The other seven participated more directly in mathematical physics in the quantum age.

Six of the seven were born Jews. The seven, in order of birth, were Theodore von Karman (who entered Budapest's Minta School in 1893), George de Hevesy, Michael Polanyi, Leo Szilard, Wigner, Johnny, and Edward Teller (who entered the Minta School in 1918). When Teller arrived in America in the 1930s, he was told that the popular rumor about his fellow Hungarians was that they were not really from Hungary, but men come from Mars to dominate American science. Teller assumed the right worried expression. "Von Karman must have been talking," he said.

Searchers for the secret of Budapest's generation of geniuses—the men from Mars—may find the reasons in three comparisons with simultaneously prospering New York. Two of the comparisons show similarities: surging self-confidence in a national boom plus wise freedom of immigration. One shows a contrast: Hungary was in no sense a democracy. It teetered between a feudal society and a meritocracy, which devised a brilliant education system purely for the elite.

Start by understanding the self-confidence. In the three and a half decades before Johnny's birth in 1903, Budapest had been the fastest-growing big city in Europe—next to New York and Chicago, possibly the fastest in the world. New York and Chicago had gained in confidence in 1865 as the biggest cities on the winning side in a civil war, in a food-producing prairie country that knew it could emulate and then surpass antique Europe. Hungary felt the same surge by winning home rule within Austria-Hungary in 1867, in a food-surplus prairie country that felt it could emulate and then surpass antique Austria. Actually, Hungarian home rule was gift wrapped by Bismarck, who had humiliated Austria in a war of a few weeks in 1866, but the magic still worked.

There are no reliable figures for expansion of real gross national product (GNP) in Europe in the last third of the nineteenth century, but it is clear that Hungary's was just about the fastest. According to the historian John Lukacs, freight traffic on Hungary's railroads rose from 3,000,000 tons in 1866 to 275,000,000 tons in 1894, and passenger traffic multiplied nearly seventeenfold. Hungary's wheat production more than doubled in 1870–1900. So did its other grain yields per acre and the number of its cattle. Its exports trebled. In the 1890s Budapest was the largest flour-milling area in the world, before surrendering the top spot to Minneapolis. In the 1880s Hungary had suddenly become the biggest exporter of flour to countries as far off as Brazil. Manufacturing was rising fastest around the period when Johnny was born. The number of industrial workers in Budapest grew from 63,000 in 1896 to 177,000 by 1910.

At home rule in 1867, Budapest's total population of 280,000 meant that it was Europe's seventeenth largest city. By Johnny's birth in 1903 its population of over 800,000 made it Europe's sixth largest, behind only London, Paris, Berlin, Vienna, and St. Petersburg. It had passed Rome, Madrid, Naples, Hamburg, Lisbon, Liverpool, Birmingham, Manchester, Glasgow, Brussels, and Amsterdam on the way up. In 1866–1905 Budapest's population trebled, and its numbers of buildings doubled despite some of the tightest town-planning rules in Europe (which allowed few buildings of more than five stories).

The feature in which Budapest differed from New York is that booming Hungary was in no way a democracy. In the 1906 elections shortly after Johnny's birth, only 5% of Hungarians got to vote. In 1871–72 Budapest moved from rule by aristocracy to rule by ingenious plutocracy. Legislation that year decreed that half of the four hundred Budapest city deputies should be the two hundred payers of the highest taxes on the city rolls. This sort of plutocracy was quickly modified and has been castigated as wicked ever since. Embarrassingly for us democrats, its results were magnificent in the short term.

Within a booming city, where the biggest taxpayers were a progressively changing group, Budapest acquired rather nationalist and sometimes nouveaux riches city fathers who wanted to spend what was largely their families' own money on making Budapest a more cultured and more beautiful city than Vienna. Admittedly, as some aesthetes winced, the rich city fathers in 1871–1910 did incline to a giantism that only people as vulgar as nouveaux riches and emperors and tourists really like. At Johnny's birth, Budapest had the largest parliament building in the world and the largest stock exchange building in Europe. It was quite unnecessarily expanding the often-empty royal palace. In 1897 the visiting Kaiser Wilhelm from Germany said the city looked wonderfully prosperous, although there were too few statues about.

The council spent the next decade erecting statues in almost every square. But these were modernist as well as ambitious guardians of a plutocracy.

In the 1890s they built beneath Andrassy Avenue (Budapest's Champs-Élysées) the first underground electric subway line in Europe. Budapest replaced its horse buses (and their disease-breeding horseshit) with electric tramcars earlier than almost any other city. In 1903 the Elizabeth Bridge over the Danube was the longest single-span bridge in the world. Budapest's opera house had two hundred fewer seats than Vienna's, but the acoustics had been scientifically planned to be far better. Budapest's "orpheums" (a mixture between nightclub and *café chantant*) gave the city the same air as Paris, and so did its intellectual coffeehouse set. The atmosphere is caught best in John Lukacs's book *Budapest 1900*, and so are many of the above facts and figures. From the most literary of those coffeehouses, unsurprisingly called the Café New York, Gyula Krudy wrote lyrically of his Budapest in Lukacs's translation:

Here the dancing in the theaters is the best, here everyone in a crowd may think he is a gentleman even if he left jail the day before, the physicians' cures are wonderful, the lawyers are world famous, even the renter of the smallest rooms has his bath, the shopkeepers are inventive, the policeman guards the public peace . . . the streetlights burn till the morning . . . the tramcars will carry you to the farthest places within an hour . . . the women are well-read from the theater magazines . . . the salesgirls swear your wife is the most beautiful of women, other girls in the nightclubs and orpheums hear out your political opinions politely . . . and the undertaker shows his thirty-two gold teeth when you take your leave of this city forever.

Krudy claimed that even Budapest's prostitutes "were pretty and young enough to be princesses in Berlin." In addition to free-lancing and in the orpheums, some prostitutes were chosen for health-inspected brothels, which caused a scandal in Britain's

House of Commons. In 1907 a group of British M.P.'s were invited to Budapest to report favorably on Hungary's plutocracy. Some assumed that their evening at the best of the brothels could be charged to the host government. When the indignant brothel owner published her list of unpaid bills, the wives of the M.P.'s were not amused, but parts of the British press were.

Because many of the bubbling writers at Budapest's Café New York were left-wing Dickensian in their politics and romanticism and compassion, it is now accepted historical wisdom that this 1867–1913 system of Hungarian rule—aristocracy in the countryside, plutocracy plus aristocracy in Budapest—bore down wickedly on the poor.

In Budapest, as distinct from the countryside, the figures (most of them again drawn from Lukacs) do not support this. In 1869–1900 infant mortality in Budapest dropped by half, to become healthier than Vienna's, despite Vienna's famous doctors. Illiteracy in Budapest dropped to below 10%, although among Hungary's rural Romanians and Ruthenians it was nearer 70% even by 1910. Crime rates, fire risks in the poorer areas, killer diseases in Budapest—all moved in 1867–1913 from dreadful eastern European to much better western European averages. Budapest's working classes ate better than Vienna's—a fact that became emotive in Austria-Hungary when Vienna starved at the end of the 1914–18 war. Foreigners in Budapest in 1900 remarked on the high and rather formal standard of clothing of the ordinary people.

What was jarring about Budapest was its aggravating class system. In the late nineteenth century a middle-middle-class family in Budapest would have twice as many domestic servants as a similar family in Vienna, three times as many as in Berlin. If a Budapest family in 1910 was rich enough to rent an apartment of more than three rooms, it was statistically likely to employ a maid. Snobbery permeated all classes, although with one great saving grace, which provided the second and most surprising similarity between Budapest and New York.

In 1870–1914 Budapest and New York were the two cities in the world to which the brightest Jews seemed wisest to immigrate.

In them—but in few other places—an intelligent Jew of the 1890s could rise in income and status nearly to the level permitted by his ability. In Budapest Jews quickly became the professional (doctor and lawyer) as well as merchant class.

The qualities of immigrant Jews were marvelously suited for the 1890–1914 stage of the entrepreneurial revolution, just as the qualities of immigrant East Asians probably are for the 1990s. These qualities (both for 1890 Jews and 1990 East Asians) included family traditions of togetherness and hard brain work and hunger for education, a willingness not to annoy host communities by turning very political, general classlessness in not aiming for the most prestigious life-styles but going instead for the main chance. By 1903 Budapest's second- and third-generation Jews had turned—with servant-pampered variations that we will discuss—into a sophisticated, arts-and-music-loving, gently humorous, civilized, and usually liberal middle class, much as the Jews in New York.

It was into such a fortunate family and society that Johnny was born.

◄►◄►

On that third day after Christmas in 1903, Johnny was the firstborn son of Neumann Miksa and the former Kann Margit, which is not as lucid a statement as it might be. In Hungarian, the last name is given first as in a telephone book. The conversion of Hungarian names to their equivalents in other languages is not succinctly straightforward. Miksa becomes Maximilian and sometimes Max, but Miksa's best friends among his contemporaries called him Maxi, which is closest to the original Hungarian. Margit is clearly Margaret, but it was familiarized to Gitta or (by Margit's husband and sons) to Gittush, both of which are a good deal closer to Kitty, in sound if not in intent. Johnny, we will say in a book that is in English, not in Hungarian, was the son of Max Neumann and the former Margaret Kann.

Max (born 1870) had arrived in Budapest at the end of the 1880s from the small town of Pecs near what is now the Yugoslavian border. It is a little old Roman town that had its brief hour on European television screens in 1990, when its local soccer team surprisingly won Hungary's knockout soccer cup and thus qualified to entertain Manchester United.

Max was a debonair, fourth-generation-or-earlier, nonpracticing Hungarian Jew, with a fine classical education in a Catholic —probably Cistercian—provincial gymnasium (one of Hungary's superb senior high schools). He was well attuned to fin de siècle Austria-Hungary and indeed to being a lively intellectual in any age. His party piece was to compose two-line ditties about the latest vicissitudes of his personal or business life, and about national and international politics. He sang them to the lilts of Strauss and Schubert, or (when being especially ironic) to German marching tunes. They were just sufficiently outrageous to be almost highbrow, like Edward Lear and Monty Python.

Max passed his law examinations (indeed became a doctor of laws) with some ease and prospered as a lawyer for a bank. He made friends, particularly with another young doctor of laws of his own age: Dr. August Alcsuti, who later became his brother-in-law. This Alcsuti was from a better-off family than Max. He had been educated at Budapest's finest gymnasium (the Minta or "Model" School), which demanded fairly high tuition fees. He was as contemplative as Max (whom he was the first to call Maxi) was energetically active, and he was to give some interesting twists to our story.

First, this Alcsuti became a judge. Indeed, he was eventually the president of a senate at Budapest's court of appeals. Competent jurists say that he could have become Hungary's chief justice, but the Hungarian government of the 1930s disliked his Jewish connections. He survived the Nazi period in forced retirement, but then the incoming communists branded him an enemy of the people and deprived him of the last cent of his pension. His daughter got him out to the United States, where he died an American citizen aged ninety-two in 1963. He therefore outlived Johnny, and saw his dazzling nephew reach the peak of his international fame. But Alcsuti insisted to the end that Max (Johnny's father) had been the most brilliant man he had ever met. Alcsuti's daughter says her father may have excluded Johnny ("we all knew Johnny was a genius, and perhaps geniuses don't count"), but Max's glitter beside the blue Danube of the 1890s impressed all his gifted contemporaries. It is clear that Johnny, in addition to getting a superb upbringing, inherited some darling intellectual genes.

Second, Alcsuti knew from his school and university days the rich young set of Pest. They included the two unmarried daughters of Jacob Kann, and Alcsuti introduced debonair Max to them. Max quickly wooed, won, and wed the calmer and elder daughter Margaret (born 1880). The younger daughter Vilma, always known as Lily, conceived in her teens a passion for Alcsuti. She pouted and went into sulks until he married her. Later, when the Alcsutis became poor immigrants to America after 1945, this Vilma was to turn from a spoiled brat into a heroine who lightened Alcsuti's old age. "I've never known a woman who changed so much," Alcsuti somewhat ambiguously said.

From the beginning, however, it was clear that Max had made a very good marriage when he wed Margaret, including in the worldly sense. Jacob Kann, his father-in-law, was a distinctly prosperous man. With a partner, he had built up in Budapest a thriving business in agricultural equipment that grew even faster in 1880–1914 than Hungary's then-soaring GNP. One special early line was millstones, which were useful when in the 1890s the area around Budapest became the biggest milling center in the world. A more important innovation was that the firm of Kann-Heller (K.H.) learned from what Sears was doing in the United States. It turned itself into a big seller by catalogue to Hungary's large farms. However provincial Max's own origins had been, with marriage he became a member of a Jewish family of substance.

In all central Europe at that time the fact of Jewishness made a difference of one kind or another, generally a pretty unpleasant one. In turn-of-the-century Hungary, as we have seen, it was not unpleasant. Some people assume that this was because Hungary was most liberal. The real reason is the reverse. Of all the countries of central Europe, Hungary remained must stubbornly feudal for as long as a feudal system could possibly be maintained.

Even in 1913 half the land area of the country was held in estates

of over 60 hectares. Hungary possessed a proud land-holding nobility and a gentry known as the "sandaled nobility," who had
managed in one way or another to lose title to inherit lands. Because anything else was considered beneath their dignity, they
came to form a swelling government bureaucracy. Indeed the
translation "sandaled nobility" is too polite. The Hungarian word
bocskoros referred to the old peasantry who could not afford even
sandals but had to handicap themselves by binding their feet in
rags attached with string.

Until 1848, many of Hungary's population were virtually serfs,
tied to the land. After 1848 they were free citizens but often did
not notice it. They remained bound to the land, in the outer regions
pulling a surly forelock to the rich squire. The nobility, sandaled
or not, had military obligations but managed to avoid most taxes.
There was need for an entrepreneurial class who would spur the
country to industrial greatness after 1867 and who would pay taxes
and be doctors and lawyers and ballet choreographers, and useful
things like that.

Up to 1867 the Jewish population was small and of no great
importance. Those Jews who moved into Hungary were minor
merchants who were perceived neither as threats by the nobility
nor as oppressors by the peasants. They were accordingly tolerated
by both. Then, as the nineteenth century wore on, the Jews became
the nobility's allies. An actual majority of the people in rural areas
did not speak Hungarian as their first language but regarded themselves as Croats, Romanians, Ruthenians, Serbs, Slovaks. Outside
the central plain these polyglots were unwilling to be Magyarized,
and began to mutter in revolt. The Jews in the towns were willing
to be Magyarized, and were not accustomed to muttering in revolt.
They had their reward when in 1867 Hungary got its semi-
independence.

The institution of the dual monarchy of Austria-Hungary in
1867 provided Hungary with freedom in internal affairs. In the
next year the few discriminatory laws against the Jews were re-
pealed. They did not reappear until after 1919. As a consequence,
there was a flood of Jewish immigration into Hungary in the 1880s
and 1890s as there was simultaneously into New York.

By the beginning of the twentieth century towns such as Pecs (in which Max Neumann was born), on one of the main immigration routes for Jews into Hungary, were as much as 40% Jewish. Even Budapest, with its swelling Magyar bureaucracy, was more than one-fourth Jewish. Of Hungary's total population of over nineteen million, only 5% were Jewish, but that was because there were few Jews in the rural areas. In the towns the Hungarian Jews had come to constitute an important middle and upper middle class—a distinction toward which the nobility still evinced no interest and the peasantry no aspirations.

By 1910 Jews made up around 60% of Budapest's doctors and lawyers, as well as of its bankers. They did not in those days move into Hungarian politics (which were not democratic) or the civil service (which was the preserve of the sandaled nobility). But they played a full part in the artistic, literary, musical, and cinematic surges of what their detractors called "Judapest." The world, and especially America, was to be changed by the last two. In music this Hungarian generation produced many of America's famous conductors: Fritz Reiner and George Solti in Chicago, Eugene Ormandy in Philadelphia, George Szell in Cleveland, and Antal Dorati in Dallas—an extraordinary record from this small constituency.

The American word "movie" probably derived from the Hungarian *mozi*. Budapest's movie surge, said cynics, allowed 1913–43 Hungarians to create America's Hollywood before 1943–53 Hungarians less destructively created America's H-bomb. On-screen, most people might recognize as Hungarian Zsa-Zsa Gabor and Paul Lukas, but perhaps not those born as Vilma Banki and Laszlo Steiner (later that apparently quintessential English gentleman Leslie Howard). Offscreen, many of Hollywood's earliest moguls (Fox and Zukor), visionaries (Korda), producers (Curtiz, producer of *Casablanca*), and many scriptwriters came from Budapest's first movie houses (*mozi*) and movie discussion groups in the area around the Café New York. In his early days the ditty-singing Max Neumann was part of this social set. Later, as a banker, he helped to finance cinema and theater business.

The next great Budapest surge in 1910–30 was a burst of creativity in science and mathematics, to which Jews appear to be drawn wherever they are found, and for which they may possess special talents. Jews often are in circumstances when it is easier to deal with rational statistical figures than with irrational human ones—to escape, as Einstein (who regretted this) said, from the You and the Us to the It. There has been much speculation on why Budapest in Johnny's youth produced so many famous mathematicians and scientists. Most of the scientists concerned were Jewish in origin and a parent-selected group. Their parents were the Jews who in the 1890s preferred to go to Budapest rather than to New York.

One can see why an intelligent Jew in 1870–1910 could well pick Budapest rather than entry through Ellis Island into America. Old Budapest at the turn of the century was a more sophisticated place than East Side New York. Budapest was creating the best high schools in the world, which New York was not. In Budapest immigrating Jews would soon employ domestic servants, which in New York they would not. They would be able to create an amusing dinner-table culture. There was no need of a long sea voyage to get to Budapest from the ghettos and pogroms of czarist Russia—or from Jews' still-inferior citizenship in imperial Germany and even Dreyfus-era France.

To America, after sea voyages became no longer frightening in the 1890s, fares suddenly became very cheap, but for the lowest classes only. The price wars between steamship companies in the 1890s were like those between airlines eighty years later: lots of bargain offers for the masses but not for the business classes. In these price wars the Hamburg–New York steerage steamship fare in the 1890s was halved from $20 to $10, but nonsteerage fares remained expensive, especially on unsinkable ships like the *Titanic*. More steerage-class Jewish families settled on New York, and more upper-class strivers on Budapest. In ideal high school circumstances, the latter bred the generation of geniuses.

◄►◄►

There is a danger in overemphasizing Johnny's Jewish origins. Except for a Jewish sense of humor—which he kept all his life—

Jewishness never meant much to him. His daughter says she did not know of her Jewish heritage until her teens. This was not only because Johnny formally became a Catholic when he married her mother in 1930. As is generally the case when families move into the middle class, there was no disposition in the Neumann family, even in Johnny's childhood, to exercise any fundamentalist religious belief. Johnny and later his two brothers went placidly through the ritual of the bar mitzvah, but when they were in the nursery religion imposed no dogmatic limitations. Jacob Kann and his wife did not seek to impose any brand of Judaism on their daughters or grandchildren. His brand consisted of going to Temple about once a year. Hers consisted of fasting on the Day of Atonement, after which the whole family joined her in eating cake and drinking chocolate with thick whipped cream. Two of their four daughters had married Christians anyway.

When one of Max's sons asked why the Neumanns still called themselves Jewish since they did not follow even the practices that Grandfather and Grandmother did, Max replied, "tradition." The Alcsutis converted early, and with religious conviction, to Christianity. Max did not, although Alcsuti's daughter says that even by 1910 "wise Max foresaw Hitler." Max said to Alcsuti that anti-Semitism was likely to rise, and he felt that respected and successful people such as themselves might be able to help their coreligionists if they stayed with them. None of the Neumann family converted to Christianity until Max died in 1929, after which all did.

Johnny often made Jewish jokes to his fellow mathematicians. "Die Goim haben den folgenden Satz bewiesen" (The Goys have proved the following theorem), he once said to Stan Ulam in Princeton about some non-Jewish mathematicians' results—implying that, as Jews, Ulam and he should have got to it first. This showed a sense of togetherness with Ulam rather than religious conviction. But Johnny was also the great logician and less eagerly agnostic than lesser logicians are. "There probably has to be a God," he said to his mother late in life, "because it is more difficult to explain many things if there isn't." At the very end, on his deathbed, when the cleverest man in the mathematical world faced imminent and early extinction, Johnny made a rather surprising religious decision. The reader will find in chapter 15 what it was, but let him ponder through the next thirteen chapters what it might be.

All that was so many years later. For this account of 1903–13, what was significant was that Johnny was born into easy circumstances, which was a great deal more than most central European Jews born in 1903 could say. He could expect to be well educated, to be admitted into the university, to make for himself the career of his choice, whatever that choice might be. He could not count on escaping anti-Semitism entirely, but he would not suffer the psychic damage that cruel and crude anti-Semitism produced elsewhere. He was a member of a culture that had great respect for scientific and mathematical achievement, and indeed for intellectual achievement of any kind, and that appeared to possess particular qualifications for those sorts of achievements. There was, in short, a silver spoon in his mouth and a cuisine entirely to his liking.

Back there in 1903–13 Max and Margaret Neumann, for historical reasons and on their own account, had contrived a rich endowment for the first ten years of their firstborn's life. How rich that endowment was they could not have immediately guessed.

◄►◄►

The firm of Kann-Heller (K.H.) occupied much of the ground floor of what was then 62 Vaczi Boulevard but was in 1945 renamed 62 Bajcsy-Zsilinszky Street after a resistance hero who was murdered by the Germans' Hungarian-Nazi allies in World War II. At one stage in Johnny's youth it was called Kaiser Wilhelm Street after Hungary's German ally in World War I. Vaczi Boulevard was, and under all its names has remained, a broad avenue making its way out of central Budapest toward the city of Vacz, lined on both sides with three- or four-story buildings, solidly constructed, in which are to be found business establishments below and apartments above. Despite the street's air of commercial bustle, it was at the time a distinctly upper-middle-class residential district, a cut above what the young bride and bridegroom, Max and Margaret, might have enjoyed on the bridegroom's own wages. Jacob Kann was rich enough even in the 1890s to be offered as a bargain a nobleman's old house in the town park, Budapest's poshest address. He turned it down as too grand for a working Jew like himself. So Johnny, like Margaret Thatcher two decades later, grew up over the shop. It has proved a useful, because commercially involved, environment for children through the ages.

As the salesrooms of Kann-Heller spread over the ground floor of what was virtually a half block of Vaczi Boulevard, the families of Kann and Heller took up residence in the three floors above. The Hellers eventually occupied the whole of what Americans call the second floor but Europeans regarded as the piano gentile. The second Mrs. Kann (who died in 1914) rather resented this. Kann had originally owned a large apartment with his first wife, who was a relative of the Hellers. When she died, Kann, his second wife, and his four daughters—as they came along—took over the building's top two floors.

When each Kann daughter married, the newly created family made its home in the building. The family Molnar (of Jacob's eldest daughter) and the family Aldor (of the second daughter) were already there when the Neumanns and Alcsutis arrived. Kann also bought an apartment house around the corner, and various relatives rented apartments in that, but the center of the family was the house called "sixty-two." Ultimately the Neumann family, grown to include Johnny and Michael and Nicholas, occupied a spacious eighteen-room apartment—if you count bathrooms and such as rooms—on the top floor. The Aldors had the other apartment there. The Alcsuti family with their daughter had an apartment on the floor below, as did the Molnars. Jacob Kann appeared to wander in and out all the four families' apartments pretty much at will. The ties between the Neumann and the Alcsuti families, as might be expected when two friends marry two sisters, were particularly close, and in effect they shared their halves of the top two floors.

It was into this warren of comfortable domesticity that Johnny was born in 1903 and his brothers after him (Michael in 1907 and Nicholas in 1911) and where shape began to be imposed on his future. By 1905 Max was advancing rapidly both in Budapest society and in the world of banking. He moved to a more impressive institution than the bank in which he began and became a partner, a man of substance and achievement. He was also, by instinct, a great educator.

"Father," said his son Nicholas in his perceptive book *John von Neumann as Seen by His Brother*, "believed in the life of the mind." This was manifested first in his choice of governesses and preschool teachers for his family; and second, and more important, in the way he ran mealtimes. Max turned the family lunch table and supper table into formidable seminars on every conceivable intellectual and topical subject, enlivened by his wit and by his singing of his Edward Learish ditties, in which the children and Margaret delightedly joined.

Nursemaids, governesses, and preschool teachers were an integral part of upper-middle-class European households in those days, especially in countries where (as in Hungary) children did not start school until age ten. As the Kann grandchildren and some of Johnny's second cousins came along, the building on Vaczi Boulevard became an educational institution in its own right. There was an especial early emphasis on learning foreign languages. Max thought that youngsters who spoke only Hungarian would not merely fail to prosper in the central Europe then darkening around them. They might not even survive.

Johnny's earliest nursemaid was jovially called Mary of Cibakhaza. As a Mary she had to be distinguished from the Kanns' dignified and beloved old servant whom the children called Aunt Mary, and Cibakhaza was this dry nurse's home village. She was succeeded by a young lady from Breslau who came to help the children learn German and to take care of them generally. This Marthe Otto enjoyed the household hugely enough to call in her sister Helene as aide. Both Marthe and Lene later emigrated to America, and kept touch with the von Neumann and Alcsuti families there. In the 1950s both returned to a liberated West Germany to die.

Mlle. Augustine Grosjean (called Aunt Titi) came to the house to teach Johnny French from about age six. She was a cultured woman who had also taught Alcsuti from about age six. There were a Signora Puglia to teach Italian, and a Mr. Thompson and a Mr. Blythe as independent teachers to teach English; Max joined Johnny in these English lessons and helped the two men with internment problems in the 1914–18 war. During that war it was thought (originally by the Aldors) that the best way to get a French teacher who was not an enemy alien was to bring in a teacher from Alsace, which until 1919 was incorporated into imperial Germany. This proved awkward because she was even more emotionally and nationalistically French than an ordinary Frenchwoman, and the silences between her and the German governesses tended to be profound. This happened even at Christmas, which the Neumann children celebrated in the jolly German way, with trees and presents and goodwill. In Johnny's preschool days, before 1914, there were also a succession of elementary schoolteachers who provided a conventional primary education and who changed the world by introducing Johnny to arithmetic.

Max, by around 1910, was still debonair, dark, mustached, and given to wearing spotted bow ties; Kann wore only black ties, and Alcsuti black and white. But Max's short body was becoming slightly stout, which worried him more than encroaching stoutness worried Johnny twenty years later. Max therefore became keen on healthy exercise, which Johnny never did. So a fencing master was summoned to sixty-two. Its spacious entrance hall was cleared of furniture so that energetic Max and the young Neumanns, one by one, could learn to thrust and parry. The fencing master was, of course, called Professor. He conferred on Johnny no skill with the épée. Johnny later claimed that all he did acquire was a lifelong aversion to being called, in his own turn, Professor.

There was also a music teacher to teach piano, but she, too, failed somewhat with Johnny. An attempt to teach him the cello proved bizarre. The family was disappointed that he never appeared to move beyond practicing scales. It turned out that he had learned to prop a math or history book on the music stand. He was devoting his full attention to his reading while his fingers moved routinely through the exercises. He was dangerously apt to do the same thing later while driving an automobile. But Nicholas defends Johnny against the charge of being *botfulu* (Hungarian for "a stick-eared or antimusical clod"). Some Hungarians say the word's etymology is from *bojt*—the tuft of hair in a dog's ear— and no Neumann deserves that. Johnny joined almost tunefully in the singing of Max's ditties and, like any Austro-Hungarian, hummed or sang major themes from popular operas. At Princeton he was accused of playing loud German marching tunes on his gramophone, even when he and neighbors such as Einstein were trying to work. The tunes may have reminded Johnny of ironic Max.

Max instilled in him a love of two other subjects that would play an important part in Johnny's contribution to computer technology—namely, Latin and Greek. One of Max's hobbies, besides music and poetry and banking and being a fin-de-siècle Austro-Hungarian gentleman, was his love of the language, literature, and history of ancient Greece and Rome. Johnny later told Princeton colleagues that as a precocious six-year-old he liked to converse at the lunch table with his father in a way that mystified the rest of the family. The two males were chatting each other up in classical Greek. It has to be said that the rest of the family denies this.

Latin was then the major subject at Hungary's fine high schools: one hour a day, six days a week, for the eight years of the gymnasium. Greek became a required subject from age fourteen. Because people had been learning how to teach Latin for many centuries, instruction in it in Hungary's provincial high schools was nearly as good as in the finest high schools of Budapest. In subjects where new knowledge was appearing all the time, like physics and to some extent math, the gap was wider. It therefore became a habit for the very brightest students from provincial high schools to say that Latin and Greek were the most essential grounding for all modern education. Max had this habit to a marked degree. He looked on Latin as the axiomatization of language and was displeased that languages in current use had lost the purity of Latin rigor. The infant Johnny—who later helped to create the language called computer, which is (apart from math) perhaps the most expandable new language that man has created for fifty thousand years—usefully inherited this view.

The role of Latin as a tidy axiomatization of language has been best explained by a contemporary of Max's who hated it. Winston Churchill (1874–1965) was told at Harrow School in the 1880s that Mr. Gladstone got his greatest pleasure when reading Homer for fun. This son of Gladstone's tartest parliamentary opponent replied that it served the old fool right. But Churchill later pondered in his autobiography:

In a sensible language like English important words are connected and related to one another by other little words. The Romans in their stern antiquity considered such a method weak and unworthy. Nothing would satisfy them but that the structure of every word should be reacted on by its neighbours in accordance with elaborate rules to meet the different conditions in which it might be used. There is no doubt that this method both sounds and looks more impressive than our own. The sentence fits together like a piece of polished machinery. Every phrase can be intensely charged with meaning. It must have been very laborious even if you were brought up to it; but no doubt it gave the Romans, and the Greeks too, a fine and easy way of establishing their posthumous fame. They were the first comers in the field of thought and literature. When they arrived at fairly obvious reflections upon life and love, upon war, fate or manners, they coined them into the slogans or epigrams for which their language was so well adapted, and thus preserved the patent rights for all time. Hence their reputation. Nobody ever told me this at school. I have thought it all out in later life.

Max and Johnny belonged to the group of rather Germanic scholars who always thought it good that "the structure of every word should be reacted on by its neighbours in accordance with elaborate rules to meet the different conditions in which it might be used." In this information-processing age, that belief is suddenly useful again. Children and even some adults still sometimes ask, "What is the use of learning Latin?" Henceforth the answer should be: it could give you a sufficiently tidy mind to grow up and invent something logical like the modern computer.

During young Johnny's upbringing there also proved to be an educational side to Grandfather Kann, a small bearded figure, with light blue eyes, dressed either formally or in a velvetlike jacket, usually with gold watch and chain. When Grandfather entered any of the four apartments, he tended to head straight for the nursery. The younger children remember him for his love of classical music, which he played lovingly on their gramophones and discussed with them. Johnny was entranced by another of his characteristics: Grandfather Kann had gone straight from commercial high school into founding his business, but he proved to be demonic in his capacity for arithmetic manipulation. He could add in his head monstrous columns of numbers or multiply mentally two numbers in the thousands or even millions. The six-year-old Johnny would laboriously perform the computation with pencil and paper, and announce with glee that Grandfather had been absolutely on the mark. Later Johnny himself was known for his facility in mental computation, but he had long before persuaded himself that he could never match Jacob's level of multiplication skill. He recalled it with delight and a certain jolly exaggeration.

In this atmosphere, Johnny's Greek-plus-Schubert multilingual and multidenominational education proceeded expeditiously and without any intolerable expenditure of effort. But, still not quite ten years old, he was beginning to move into territory that few adults explore. The simple numbers of arithmetic, he found, had a kind of structure that transcended tedious calculation. They possessed characteristics such as oddness and evenness and primeness and squareness that were interesting in their own right. One could say things about numbers that went far beyond $2 + 2 = 4$, and those things increasingly fascinated him. Max noted this, and the subsequent schoolteachers he hired to visit the house tended to possess considerable mathematical skills. Max did not push his oldest son, but he quietly saw to it that the path ahead was clear.

In a more relaxed fashion, Margaret was equally supportive. She was a family woman, a good deal less rigorous than her husband, artistically inclined, a wafer-thin and later chain-smoking enthusiast for comporting oneself with what she called "elegance" (which later became Johnny's highest term of praise for neat mathematical calculations, such as the ones that made the H-bomb possible). Above all Margaret was a mother hen tending her children and protecting them. Her second son Michael recalls, with great affection, that she always loved most the child who most needed her, and as a practical matter that subordinated Johnny in her attention. But Johnny was emotionally closer to his mother than to his formidable father. After Max's death, Margaret came to join Johnny in America when life in Budapest had become impossible for her. She lived to see Johnny through all the years of his great achievements and, sadly, to watch over his decline toward early death. She died in the summer of 1956 when she knew he would soon be dead, too. Possibly it was better for her that way.

There are few now who remember the Johnny of those early years, 1903–14. When he began school, he made some friends who remained attached to him throughout his lifetime, and there are some in whom the memory of a young Johnny is still alive. But if he had neighborhood or playground preschool friends, they were quickly forgotten when he moved into the wider world, as such friends generally are. Because Vaczi Boulevard was a rather Jewish area, a tragic number will have been murdered in their forties during the Holocaust. Those who can speak of those years recall indications that even as a child Johnny stood a bit outside ordinary social relationships. His mind moved too fast to make him a useful participant in infants' parlor games. Even children appeared to have an uneasy sense that Johnny was observing them more often than he was acting as one of them. In that respect, too, the child was father to the man. The mature Johnny had at least his share of devoted friends, but he often did not handle very personal relationships easily or well, even within the family, and the manner in which he made efforts to do so was not in line with the rest of his personality.

That he became a mathematician not very long after he was weaned seems certain, but he was also a good deal more than that. Those who knew him early recall he seemed driven to suck understanding from all that surrounded him and a good deal that did not. When his mother once stared rather aimlessly in front of her, six-year-old Johnny asked: "What are you calculating?" By age eight, he was absorbed in history. As soon as he could read with any kind of facility, he demanded history books. His father, quick to recognize the kind of son he had bred and delighted with the course the child seemed to be following, hastened to comply.

Max had always been a voracious consumer of books. An opportunity arose during his business to purchase an entire library from an estate of a family named König. The Mr. König concerned had gone blind. The library's centerpiece was the forty-four volumes of a universal history—*Allgemeine Geschichte*—by Wilhelm Oncken, a German historian of renown. In the room at sixty-two, in which this and the family's other books were housed, Max had bookshelves installed up to the ceiling. The König library, as the room was called, then became the reading room and center of family studies.

The older of Johnny's brothers, Michael, recalled that Johnny ploughed through all forty-four volumes of the universal history with almost ferocious methodology. Later Michael had his own turn at the bookcase. He found a trail of paper slips that Johnny had scattered through volume after volume. Michael was also confounded by the fact that what Johnny read, Johnny remembered. Decades later friends were startled to discover that he remembered still. He could recite whole chapters verbatim. The love of history never left him, and he continued to learn and to remember. When Johnny arrived in the United States as a man of twenty-six, he possessed an acquaintance with the Civil War that few of his American friends could match. As quickly as he could, he set out to visit the battlefields so that he might add another dimension to his book knowledge. In political conversations from the 1920s to the 1950s he would sometimes avoid controversies by reminding people how unexpectedly some political events had turned out in 500 B.C.

Nicholas was particularly impressed by the minilectures that Johnny gave at the supper table after reading Oncken and other books, sometimes only recording what he had read but often throwing up new thoughts that had occurred to him while reading. For example, Johnny suggested that the giant reptiles must have had some brain centers near their huge leg joints, in order to operate them. He noticed that the retina of the eye really does not operate in the same way as grains on photonegative film, or other man-made devices that some textbooks teach are modeled on it. The retina takes samples, which are then processed along nerve paths that exit forward through the eye as the optic nerve, before bending back in a completely transparent medium—while in most man-made panels wire bundles exit toward the rear. Johnny was also worried that, while there is clearly multichannel or area input to the eye, there seemed to him to be single-channel or linear input to the ear. He wondered whether the spiral cavity inside the ear was not recording a sequence of changing frequencies, but might be recording an overall wave form or other incidentals of the sound waves around us. All through his life Johnny remained excited by the difference between the central nervous system's working technology and the artificial technology that engineers try to put into machines and automata.

These mealtime ponderings reached their peak after Johnny had gone to school at age ten, but they are worth recording in this chapter because Max's mealtime seminars were an important feature of all his children's development almost from the nursery. Once again Nicholas Vonneuman's book paints the picture best —of an educational instilling that modern households have most often lost. Families in those pretelevision and precommuting days met for a relatively full and lengthy late lunch. Then father would go back to the office, but the children would not return to ordinary school. Schooltime afternoons in Hungary were for sports or private tuition or study. The whole family would then have a similar lengthy dinner in the evening.

The mealtime habit that Max encouraged was that the members of the family, including himself, should each present for family analysis and discussion particular subjects that during the day had interested them. Nicholas early went to the König library, and introduced a discussion of Heinrich Heine's poems, which led on to frank analysis of how far anti-Semitism was likely to blight their prospects. Margaret impressed on the children the achievements of their grandfather Kann, who had risen from poverty to found a great business in K.H. by each day "doing the impossible." Nicholas shrewdly links this to Johnny's lifelong determination and ability to find mathematical solutions to problems that others said were not amenable to mathematical treatment.

Another argument propounded by Nicholas sprang from investigations which suggested that the *Titanic* disaster would have been avoided if only certain tiny details had gone right. Rational Johnny snorted all such if-only arguments into derision. All Nicholas could logically say, Johnny declared, was that there would have been another set of random circumstances, some (although not all) of which might have made the disaster even worse. Michael was tickled by a professor of structural engineering who demanded safety factors so that, if possible, a new bridge should not "collapse even once in its first five years." Johnny calculated the financial problems of multiplying safety specifications by a factor of 5 and then 10. He said one could always secure nearly 100% probability from statistical formulas, but sometimes only by making the spread of ranges too hideously expensive for anybody to attempt anything that moves humanity forward at all.

Johnny's own contributions to the mealtime seminars were often on his own subject of science. He would talk patiently down on the level of the least qualified listener for a few minutes and switch tactfully to another subject only if he was plainly above his audience's head. But these talks allowed him to express puzzlement, which is often difficult for a brilliant elder son. Outside a warm family atmosphere, an infant prodigy might feel too competitive to say when he is bewildered, although bewilderment is a clever boy's quickest way to puzzle through something about which he is unsure. Johnny asked, What do most people think is the brain's primary language, because Hungarian babies seem to learn to speak Hungarian in about the same amount of time that Japanese babies learn to speak Japanese? He was worried that he had learned to ride a bicycle, a most complicated process, through some subconscious process—without having used his powers of logic and reasoning at any stage. When he saw his first talking movie he was bewildered that the voices seemed to be coming out of the actors' lips, although they surely were coming via some unseen microphone out of a loudspeaker that was not on screen?

Despite Johnny's power to scintillate, the star of these seminars (as the sometimes present Alcsuti insisted) was the governing Max. He would bring his workaday banking decisions back to the family. He asked the children how they would have reacted to particular investment possibilities or balance-sheet risks, weighing social responsibility in helping worthwhile sponsorable projects against the obligation to make money for all connected with the firm, including the shareholders but the workers too. He discussed which activities he had delegated to which of his staff. He asked whether the children thought he should have reserved more or fewer of the difficult decisions for himself.

He brought back samples or models of the new industrial ventures he was financing, which by coincidence once included the Hungaria Jacquard Textile Weaving Factory. It was in Napoleon's France in 1805 that Joseph-Marie Jacquard attached to looms punch cards with cunningly distributed holes. Hooks would then push up through the holes and pull down variously colored threads, enabling the moving shuttle to go over one thread and under another and thus weave the pattern that Jacquard had thought up. The irascible genius Charles Babbage (1791–1871) invented the first computer by noting in his diary that "the Jacquard loom is capable of weaving any design that the imagination of man may conceive." Babbage concluded that he could therefore devise an analytical machine that consisted of two parts: a store (or computer memory) and a mill. Within the computer memory, "when any formula is required to be computed, a set of operation cards must be strung together which contain a series of operations in the order in which they occur." Under these cards Babbage's steam-driven hooks would go, and the hooks would "call in the variables into the mill, in the order in which they are required to be acted upon."

Schoolboy Johnny would have been introduced to all this over a Budapest lunch, because his father was financing the entry into Hungary of Jacquard looms. Johnny was also introduced to banking as a romantic occupation. Unlike so many modern scientists, one part of his brain from school days was taught always to assess anything he did in terms of potential yield to the community, as measured against what could otherwise be too escalating a cost.

From an early age Max allowed his sons to sit in on what would now be called his business lunches and business dinners at home. These were not three-martini affairs, but some of Max's customers among visiting businessmen from Germany and England must have found them even more taxing to the brain. Conversation flowed over public affairs in an intelligent but not political manner, because Max was aware that he sat in the middle of a central Europe that was moving bumblingly toward the 1914 war. "What's new in the universe?" Johnny would whisper as the Munich accountants or Manchester mill owners or Marseilles shippers or Viennese theater impresarios thronged through the Neumann dining room. He would later summarize the performance of the more disappointing as, "I don't know, I'm not coming from there."

The Budapest visitors to that dining room rarely were disappointing, because Max attracted the stars. A frequent visitor (who married Alcsuti's sister) was the psychoanalyst Sandor Ferenczi, one of the big five associates of Sigmund Freud. (Johnny's later probing into the relationship between the computer and the brain was sometimes criticized as too Freudian, and he will have taken aboard penetrating analysis of inhibitions while young.) Other guests at Max's table included the physicist Rudolf Ortvay and the Budapest University professor of mathematics Leopold Fejer;

Max did not use these meals to show off Johnny to such men, but did draw out their minds for Johnny to observe. He did this even more relaxedly with members of the artistic community. Max's bank financed one of the Hungarian theater chains. This led to interesting first nights and to fascinating conversations about the influence of Max Reinhart in Vienna and of the plays of Ferenc Molnar—a Hungarian who in the 1920s had two or three of his plays running on New York's Broadway at the same time. It also made the boys very aware of what sort of art does not please the box office and the banker. "The proscenium is the interface between illusion and reality," said youthful Johnny who was a bit apt to talk that way. But he saw that some modern playwrights and directors were not making it so.

The Neumann dinner table glittered with especial brilliance after 1910 because Max—although still a relatively young man—was becoming a major figure in Budapest society and an adviser to the Hungarian government on the booming Hungarian economy. He was a particular adviser to Minister Kalman Szell. In 1913 the forty-three-year-old Max was rewarded with hereditary nobility, so that in German he and his descendants could be called "von Neumann." Ennoblement was not an unusual reward for prominent bankers and industrialists during those last years of the Austro-Hungarian empire. Many of the 220 Hungarian Jewish families who were ennobled in 1900–14 (versus just over half that number in the whole century before) hastened to change their names. Ennoblement was a way through which one could seize the chance to call oneself something less Jewish. Max Neumann deliberately did not change his name. Some Americans say that European titles were too often handed out to people who had subscribed to politicians' expenses. Max did not, and anyway this accusation tastes to Europeans like inverted American snobbery. Rich men who give money to the governing party in the United States are apt to be rewarded with ambassadorships. This sale of jobs seems more dangerous to public efficiency than does the handing out of handles to people's names. Johnny, at any rate, relished the "von." He said that in America it brought him attention in shops. His brothers, once they had arrived in the United States, were more sensitive to criticism. Nicholas subordinated the von and made it simply Vonneuman; Michael usually called himself Michael Neumann, both in America and in the old country.

Somewhat concealed in Max's change of status lay a tale of affection. The name "von Neumann" is a Germanized version of the title Max actually assumed. What nobility gave him, in the old landholding tradition, was the privilege of attaching a place-name to his family name. He chose the Hungarian town of Margitta, with which he had no connections of any kind, and became margittai Neumann Miksa, or Max Neumann of Margitta. While at Zurich Johnny called himself Johann Neumann von Margitta, and Margaret called herself Frau Dr. Maximilian Neumann von Margitta on formal occasions in her early widowhood. There was a Margitta building in Pecs that might be ascribed as the symbolical baronial castle, but the name of Margitta clearly tickled the husband of the former Margit Kann. Max was called on to devise a coat of arms. He summoned up no lions rampant. His coat of arms bore three marguerites (daisies) on a field of green. Margaret was not often out of the mind of her husband.

There remain near Budapest today distinct signs of Max's advancement. A few miles out from the center of town are two homes that the family occupied during the summers of those years: country homes, or villas, they were called in those premotorized years. The first consists of two houses in a single garden; it was bought and owned by Kann. The second is Max's far more elegant country home high in the hills, with a fine stone staircase leading up 30 feet to a grand entrance. The coat of arms with its marguerites surmounts it all. On either side of the entrance is a bay with three windows, and over the windows of each bay there appear in turn, carved in relief, a rooster, a cat, and a rabbit. Those were Max's affectionate names for his three sons. Johnny was the rooster because he did sometimes crow. Michael was the cat because he looked rather like one. Nicholas was the rabbit because he was the youngest.

A short distance from one of these homes Mariette Kovesi spent her summers. She, too, entered into the intimacy of the family. Some twenty years later, in 1930, she and Johnny were married. When this marriage broke up, he returned to Budapest to marry another girl from next door. His childhood left him with happy memories of his sort of Hungary throughout his life.

The summer house was built to be a home in which children played, and it remains so today. It has become a recreation place for the children of suburban Budapest. The coat of arms and the household pets carved in relief have lost their significance. All that is known in the neighborhood is that the house was built, a long while back, by a wealthy banker. Max would have known the appropriate Latin tag.

At just about the time that Johnny became von Neumann in 1913 he was preparing to begin his formal schooling. He was about to be ten years old and demonstrating every sign of becoming a scholar. Indeed he could not unreasonably be called that at once. He was about to enter into competition with others of his age for the first time. The first result of that competition was to indicate that young Neumann Jancsi was a prodigy.

►◄►◄►◄ **3**

At the

Lutheran Gymnasium, 1914–21

►◄ *T*here was never much doubt that Johnny would one day be going on to university. The direct road to the university began at the gymnasium, which can be a startling statement if one is not prepared to pronounce the word in the central European fashion, with a hard *g* and a broad *a*. To the ancient Greeks, a gymnasium signified a building in which young men, unclothed, engaged in or prepared for athletic competition. The Germans adopted the word to signify a secondary school of high standards, brought into being to train young men, fully clothed, to strive for entry into university. The dynamic beneath many a good German gymnasium was that it competed to get the brightest children in its district sent to it. Then it competed to bring them the most excellent university entrance results, so that the (preferably fee-paying) parents of the next generation of bright children would be attracted to send their sons or (sometimes) daughters to it rather than to a neighboring school.

That usage of the word "gymnasium" was borrowed by most of German-speaking Europe, including Austria-Hungary, and by any countries that looked to Germany for educational leadership. Bigger European countries chose their own names for their competitive secondary schools. France called its version a lycée, and Britain called its version either a grammar school (if it was mainly publicly financed) or a public school (if it was almost wholly financed by private fees, just to be muddling). The modern Japanese—who have adopted an extreme, and extremely successful, version of the gymnasium system—call their schools for eleven-to-eighteen-year-olds junior high schools and senior high schools, as if they were just like open-to-all American high schools, which they are not.

The disadvantage of the gymnasium system is that children are firmly and too often finally divided into two streams at the age of ten or eleven. In some schools are potential university material; in others are all the rest. There have intermittently been elements of such a system in America, but it goes against the grain of a country that prides itself on equality of opportunity.

The advantage of the gymnasium system is that, in the best gymnasia, students can be pressed toward the limits of their capacities. They are exposed to an intellectual rigor that is not usually reached in more democratic countries' high schools. In particular, the gymnasium system gives dignity to those who provide instruction in top secondary schools. A scholar or scientist who knows that his talents lie in pedagogy rather than in research does not feel he is falling back if he spends his whole life teaching in such a school. A fine teacher retiring at the age of sixty from the old Minta School in Budapest or from Winchester College in England would find many of the most famous men in Hungary and Britain in his debt because they had passed through his hands.

Enthusiasts say that the most democratically successful of these gymnasium systems in history has been the one in post-1945 Japan. From a low start, it has achieved the most effective educational standards ever known in any country anywhere for nine-tenths of that nation's eighteen-year-olds. They may not be the most relaxed or happy kids, but they are awesomely efficient. The most elitely successful of these gymnasium systems in history was arguably the one in little Hungary from about 1890 to nearly the 1930s. Hungary did not give much help to the nine-tenths of its children who were intellectually below the soaring top tenth, but it turned its young soarers into a genuine elite.

Both post-1945 Japan and pre-1939 Hungary succeeded by carrying competition for excellence to extremes. In today's Japan there is lauding on television of the high school that has won the most places that year at Tokyo University. Parents in each district know which one or two local schools have the best recent record in university entrance. They also know which has the best record in giving a start to less intellectual careers—down to which local high school is most likely to get your nonscholarly child a blue-collar job with which particular big local business corporation. If a Japanese school does not find a successful niche, it closes. That is why Japan has fewer schools than the West, but nearly all good ones, with what Westerners regard as grossly overlarge classes of forty or more pupils. Yet most parents in Tokyo send their children to commercial pre–high school crammers (called *juku*) in desperate competition to pass the entrance exam into the high school of their choice.

The most successful of these features of booming post-1945 Japan have unconsciously mirrored those of booming pre-1929 middle-class Budapest. At his Budapest high school in 1914–21, Johnny had an overlarge average of forty-eight fellow pupils in his class. His preschool tribe of governesses and tutors played the role of Japanese *juku*. Many of Japan's post-1945 education reforms were driven by a nationalist desire to emulate triumphant America. Many of Hungary's post-1890 education reforms were driven by a nationalist desire to surpass resented Austria.

The importance of producing visibly high performance has concentrated modern Japanese education a bit too much on "measurable subjects" such as mathematics. The same happened in old Hungary. The average Japanese eighteen-year-old is today more advanced in math than all except the top 1% of American eighteen-year-olds. The same would have been true of gymnasium pupils in Budapest in 1914. Japan grades competition in excellence between schools by university entrance results. Hungary could not do that, because its brightest high school graduates dispersed to universities all over Europe. So Hungarian schools entered their brightest graduate eighteen-year-olds each year for an Eotvos Prize in mathematics and an Eotvos Prize in physics. These were named after the barons Eotvos, father and son, who were reforming figures at the University of Budapest post-1890. Eotvos Prize–winning Johnny was later to suggest that it might be wise for other countries—indeed perhaps each American state—to have such prizes.

A difference between old Hungary and new Japan was that a successful candidate for a gymnasium in Hungary entered it at age ten, and stayed in the same school until age eighteen. Another is that the best Hungarian gymnasia had often been started by religious foundations, but that did not bring the religious discrimination you might expect. Jewish Johnny in 1914–21 went to what was generally called Budapest's Lutheran Gymnasium, although its full name was more elegant: the Evangelical School of the Augustine Faith—with "Augustine" meaning in honor of Martin Luther's home town of Augsburg. A search of its rolls shows that in Johnny's last year in 1921 it had 653 pupils. Of these, 340 (over half) were listed as Jewish. Only 198 were Lutherans. Fifty-four belonged to other protestant churches and sixty-one were Roman Catholics. Before 1919, any discrimination was financial. The Lutherans paid the lowest school fees, the Catholics higher ones, and the Jews most of all. After 1919, other restrictions against Jews crept in. Johnny and his brothers remained Jewish, but received religious instruction from both the school's rabbi and its Christian clergymen. Max wanted them to make a choice. A lot of their contemporaries found it convenient to embrace Christianity. Although the Lutheran's 1921 rolls suggest that only 52% of its pupils were Jewish, over 70% may have been originally born into that culture and faith.

The answer to "the huge mystery of 1890–1930 Hungary's educational achievement" lies largely in those figures. Hungary's post-1870 willingness to import middle-class Jews—because of its Magyar aristocracy's contempt for its majority of non-Magyar peasants—attracted the brightest and most educationally ambitious of Europe's Jews to Budapest. From Russia's steppes, from Bismarck's Germany, from Dreyfus's France, and from Hungary's own mountain villages they came: a cultured and upwardly mobile group, intent on giving their sons (sadly, more than their daughters) the education that some of them had never had. Many arrived in the 1890s when Hungary's counts and barons and monks and pastors had a new ambition: to produce more brilliant scholars and generally cultured young men than Vienna did. A discriminately excellent supply streamed into a competitively excellent schools system.

◄►◄►

At the moment when Johnny was ready for high school in 1914, Budapest housed three gymnasia of recognized excellence from which his family might choose. All called for the payment of tuition fees, which was no problem for a banker's son. Any one of them would be able to turn a clever little boy into a scholar who would be welcomed by any European university he might choose.

Of the three, the most notable in 1914 was the Minta (or Model) School. It had been created a generation earlier by an ennobled Jew, Dr. Mor von Karman, who had strong ideas about the manner in which a gymnasium ought to be organized and run, most of them concerned with discipline and tight rigor. He could ultimately point to his own son as a sample of work done at the Minta. Theodore von Karman (born 1883) was senior to all the famous Hungarian scientists who made their way to the United States, where he pioneered the science of aerodynamics, enjoyed a long and productive career at California Institute of Technology (CalTech), and was accused of inventing consultancy.

Close behind the Minta in 1914 was the Lutheran Gymnasium. It was older than the Minta but had begun to model itself on the Model, which was what the elder von Karman had intended.

Thirdly, there were the Real gymnasia, the word "Real" being pronounced in two syllables and signifying urban or practical rather than genuine. There were several such schools in Budapest, which provided comparatively little Latin and less Greek. They concentrated more on modern languages and such mundane courses as engineering drawing. Jacob Kann had worked his way through the Commercial High School, which was a sort of Real. By 1914 one of these Real schools was considered a cut above the rest, and it enjoyed a status comparable to the Minta and the Lutheran. It was designed to produce candidates for technical institutions rather than classical universities—in American terms, for MIT and CalTech, rather than for Harvard and Stanford.

For Johnny, Max von Neumann chose the Lutheran. It could be relied on to deliver a serious education in Latin and Greek, which was no small matter to Max. To his father, Johnny was not so inevitably a mathematician as he might appear to others, and avenues should not be closed when a child is nine or ten. The boy's clear affection for history needed to be taken into account, and he had an affinity for languages. Max intended his son to receive a thoroughly humanistic education, which narrowed the choice to the Minta or the Lutheran. Max's brother-in-law Alcsuti cast a vote against the Minta. He had attended that gymnasium himself and had thought it too experimental, too progressive, and too casual about textbooks. The selection was made on grounds such as those.

Johnny entered the Lutheran in 1914, when the scholastic achievements of Budapest gymnasia were at their height. This has helped to breed a darling American myth. It is the myth of four extraordinary young Hungarian Jews, born at much the same time in more or less the same district of Budapest, who attended the same school together, became brilliant scientists there, and emigrated en bloc to the United States where they created, with only modest assistance, the A-bomb.

As with most myths, there are only strands of truth in this. There were indeed four Hungarians of much the same age who made significant contributions to America's nuclear bomb, along with a large number of scientists who never saw Budapest.

The eldest of the Hungarian four was Leo Szilard. He entered the Real Gymnasium in 1908 and graduated in 1916. He always was (said Johnny) the archetype of the Budapester who could enter a swing door behind you and come out in front. Because his graduation was in 1916, Szilard was drafted into Franz Josef's Austro-Hungarian army in the unlikely role of a cavalry officer. He managed to report himself ill before his unit went to be massacred at the front. Critics said this was typical of him, but really it was typical of his being first in almost every bizarre thing. His illness in 1916 was genuine, and almost historic. He was nearly the first to contract the Spanish flu, which three years later was to kill millions in Europe.

It is Szilard who appears in the fine first paragraph of Richard Rhodes's book *The Making of the Atomic Bomb*, where he steps off a sidewalk in Southampton Row in London on a gray depression morning in 1933. "As he crossed the street time cracked open before him and he saw a way to the future, death into the world and all our woe, the shape of things to come." While Szilard was in mid-street, it occurred to him that if scientists could find an element which, when split by neutrons, would emit two neutrons where it absorbs only one, so that those two would emit four, and those four emit eight, and . . . well, then a nuclear chain reaction could be set in being, which could make it possible to "liberate energy on an industrial scale, and to construct atomic bombs." Szilard hurried to patent the idea of a chain reaction and assigned the patents to the British admiralty for safekeeping. It is not clear whether in wartime he intended to tell Hitler or Los Alamos that blowing up the world was a breach of his private patent. He thought it was important to stop other people from patenting the idea.

Szilard was closely associated in 1943–45 with the making of the A-bomb in America's Manhattan Project, much against the better judgment of Major General Leslie Groves, who was supposed to run it. Groves described Szilard as "the kind of man any employer would have fired as a troublemaker." At one stage he tried to get Szilard interned as an enemy alien—on the view that this eccentric might be a Jewish Nazi spy. The unfortunate FBI agents tracking the absentminded Szilard had what they did not sufficiently appreciate was a hilarious time. In commenting on Richard Rhodes's book, which brilliantly describes all this, Wigner said, "I was particularly impressed by his realisation of the importance of Leo Szilard's contributions which are almost always underestimated but which he fully realises and perhaps even overstates." Wigner's judgments were usually right. He regarded Johnny as the one true genius at Los Alamos.

Wigner was the second oldest of these four Hungarians. He enrolled in the Lutheran Gymnasium in 1913, a year before Johnny. He made important theoretical contributions at Princeton and Tennessee's Oak Ridge to producing the esoteric materials that went into the nuclear bomb. He was awarded the Nobel Prize in physics in 1963.

Johnny was the third of the four Hungarians behind the bomb. Edward Teller (who joined the Minta School in 1918 and graduated from it in 1926) was the fourth. Teller was a hugely important figure in leading America into the possession of the thermonuclear bomb and into firmness in foreign policy. Unfortunately he often managed to rub even the nicest people the wrong way, whereas Johnny was skilled at smoothing even the most tiresome people's ruffled feathers.

These four Budapesters were as different as four men from similar backgrounds could be. They resembled one another only in the power of their intellects and in the nature of their professional careers. Wigner, still (1992) at Princeton, is shy, painfully modest, quiet. Teller, after a lifetime of successful controversy, is emotional, extroverted, and not one to hide his candle. Szilard was passionate, oblique, engagé, and infuriating. Johnny, as we shall see, was none of these. Johnny's most usual motivation was to try to make the next minute the most productive one for whatever intellectual business he had in mind.

◄►◄►

The Lutheran School still stands next to the church that brought it into being. When Hungary escaped from communism in 1989, it reopened as a school. Portraits of Johnny and Wigner have been commissioned for places of honor in it. During the communist years, it was taken over by Hungary's Ministry of Education to be an institute for educational research. Professor Rubik, inventor of the Rubik cube, was at one time on its staff. But even under communism, on the first landing as one mounts the stairs to the second floor, there remained a large plaque commemorating Laszlo Ratz, instructor in mathematics in Johnny's 1914–21.

The plaque keeps the memory of the man alive as much as any plaque can do. At least one of his students keeps it alive in even more convincing fashion. A visitor to Wigner in the late 1970s asked, "Do you remember Ratz?" Wigner was by then nearly sixty years away from the Lutheran School. "There he is," Wigner replied and pointed to a picture of Ratz on his office wall. During my own interview with Wigner in 1989, he mentioned Ratz's name six times. In his address on receiving the Nobel Prize in the Stockholm town hall in 1963, Wigner gratefully listed Ratz and Johnny as among his earliest influences.

Schoolmaster Ratz was a mathematician in his own right, known at Budapest University and respected there, although he produced on his own no mathematics of great distinction. He also supervised the athletic program at the Lutheran. This is an arrangement not unknown in the United States, although it is otherwise stated there: often the football coach also teaches mathematics.

Wigner and others recall that Ratz's recognition of Johnny's mathematical talents was instant. The youngster knew more than he had any right to know. Once Ratz had satisfied himself that the knowledge ran deep, he acted. He paid a visit to Max. It would be nonsense, and perhaps sinful, to provide the boy with no more than the conventional education in mathematics that the Lutheran, and Ratz himself, could offer, excellent in its own terms as that might be. Ratz proposed instead to make it his responsibility to see that a great deal more was provided, if there was no parental objection. There was no educational price to be paid. Jancsi would continue to receive all the benefits of the ordinary curriculum.

Max was at once agreeable. He may well have expected something of the sort. Ratz turned his student over to the mathematicians at Budapest University, themselves men of no small renown. Professor Joseph Kurschak soon wrote to a university tutor, Gabriel Szego, saying that the Lutheran School had a young boy of quite extraordinary talent. Would Szego, as was the Hungarian tradition with infant prodigies, give some university teaching to the lad?

Szego's own account of what happened was modest. He wrote that he went to the von Neumann house once or twice a week, had tea, discussed set theory, the theory of measurement, and some other subjects with Jancsi, and set him some problems. Other accounts in Budapest were more dramatic. Mrs. Szego recalled that her husband came home with tears in his eyes from his first encounter with the young prodigy. The brilliant solutions to the problems posed by Szego, written by Johnny on the stationery of his father's bank, can still be seen in the von Neumann archives in Budapest.

Tutor Szego was later to become one of the half dozen most distinguished Hungarian mathematicians of the twentieth century. He was professor at Königsberg until the Nazis threw him out in 1933. He then came to Stanford University in America. As chairman of the math faculty he made a first-class department there out of what had been rather little. In 1940 Stanford also attracted Hungary's George Polya, and some part of the story of Silicon Valley springs from that.

After Szego had done the initial coaching in 1915–16, tuition of schoolboy Johnny was taken over by other prominent mathematicians at Budapest University. He had contact with Kurschak, some with the brilliant Alfred Haar, and a little with the internationally known Frigyes Riesz. He was taught more directly by Michael Fekete (whose surname in Hungarian means "black") and Leopold Fejer (*feher* is Hungarian for "white"). Fejer had been born with the Jewish surname Weiss. When his candidacy as a professor was proposed, a "Christian" anti-Semitic professor had asked sneeringly, "Is this candidate related to our colleague on the faculty of divinity, Father Ignatius Fejer?" "Illegitimate son," flashed back Eotvos, who knew how to put that sort of thing down.

Before he finished high school, Johnny had been accepted by most of the university mathematicians as a colleague. Johnny's first published paper was sent for publication when he was seventeen. It was a note, signed jointly with Fekete, on a subject that would not have appealed to the average seventeen-year-old: about the zeros of certain minimal polynomials and the problem of the transfinite diameter, aiming for a generalization of Fejer's previous theorems on location of the roots of Tschebycheff polynomials. It appeared in the *Journal of the German Mathematical Society* in 1922: "Über die Lage der Nullstellen gewisser Minimumpolynome." After being prompted by the seventeen-year-old, Fekete later devoted to this subject much of his scientific life.

In the rest of Johnny's education Ratz was every bit as good as his word. Johnny learned his Latin and his Greek and his history in the gymnasium classroom along with his fellows. Ratz went so far as to insist that Johnny scrupulously attend the courses in mathematics provided in the gymnasium curriculum, and Johnny dutifully put aside the work with which he was engaged at the university to direct his attention to beginner's algebra and the like. William Fellner, one of his schoolmates, recalled with admiration that Johnny not only clearly enjoyed those classes but also was in his own fashion working to learn from them, although what he was learning was not what the courses were designed to teach. He had understood that already, before the age of ten.

◄►◄►

Two of Johnny's friends among his schoolmates were to remain close to him all through his life. Nobel Prize winner Wigner was a year ahead of him at the Lutheran School. Fellner was a year behind and was with Johnny at the Institute of Technology at Zurich. Fellner then went to Berlin, where he took a degree in economics. Returning to Budapest, he embarked on a career in business. In 1938, for sensible reasons, Fellner came first to the University of California at Berkeley and subsequently to Yale, where he became a professor of economics. His career in the United States was distinguished and more than simply academic. He was a member of President Ford's council of economic advisers (CEA). By one of history's coincidences, which shows how small is the world of the higher mind, his immediate predecessor at the CEA was the much younger Professor Marina von Neumann Whitman, Johnny's daughter, who was born in 1935. Fellner stayed active in government. At the time of his death in 1983 he was resident scholar at the American Enterprise Institute in Washington, which was a powerhouse of the return to freer-market economics in the Reagan-Bush years.

Both Wigner and Fellner knew Johnny uninterruptedly from the time when they were classmates. Johnny spent his summers in Budapest when Fellner was partner in a Budapest manufacturing firm. Wigner speaks of Johnny still with great warmth and devotion as a friend, and with awesome respect as a mathematician and physicist and every other sort of scholar. In a 1963 interview with Thomas Kuhn for the Quantum History Archives, the year he won his Nobel Prize, Wigner seemed almost to have an inferiority complex toward the dead Johnny. "You have a good memory?" asked Kuhn. "Not like von Neumann's," replied Wigner. Kuhn was soon saying that "it must have been a shattering experience to have grown up with von Neumann however bright one is."

Fellner was no less admiring and affectionate. Steve White— who, with Ulam, researched a biography of Johnny's first twenty years but never finished or published it (see Notes)—interviewed both Fellner and Wigner on their memories of Johnny as an adolescent. The following summary, like so much in the early part of this book, was mainly written by White.

Throughout his school days, Johnny desperately wanted to be a companionable boy. He did not seek to stand apart from his fellows, although both Wigner and Fellner saw that in certain respects he clearly was apart, and it could have been no secret from lesser classmates. By the age of twelve he had moved far beyond his two friends, but he made no great matter of it. Johnny was never overbearing, Fellner said. Wigner adds that he was never so absorbed in his own intellectual concerns as to be thoughtless of the concerns of others.

Johnny liked his classmates. He was anxious to feel easy with them but never achieved the ease he would have wished. Johnny was on the outside looking in, not in shyness or in envy, but he always felt himself more an observer than a participant. He had not yet added the weight he put on in later years, but he was not at all athletic. There at least Ratz failed. The less physical games that boys play—the riddles, the mental gymnastics, the puzzles and problems and all the range of challenges of that general sort —interested him a good deal, but he spoiled the game for others. He was no less assertive as a boy than as a man. When he knew the answer, he gave it. The most that can be said, if the inferences hold, is that it would have been easy for Johnny to have made himself disliked, and he was not. But neither was he sought out. Johnny was not one of the boys—and, although as man and boy he tried, he never really became one.

One of Wigner's recollections of those early teenage days said a good deal about Johnny. Wigner had happened on a theorem in number theory, a branch of mathematics that is at once fascinating and frustrating. Wigner spoke of the theorem to Johnny (who, remember, was one year younger than Wigner). He was not surprised to learn that Johnny was familiar with it. "But can you prove it?" Wigner asked. To do so, said Johnny, it would be useful to invoke certain other theorems of number theory. Did Wigner, to begin with, know such-and-such theorem? Wigner did. Did he also know such-and-such theorem? Wigner did not. The catechism continued. Wigner, it turned out, knew quite a few of those useful theorems but was ignorant of others. Johnny paused for a few moments of deep thought. Using only the subsidiary theorems with which Wigner was acquainted, he then provided a proof of the theorem with which the discussion had begun. It made the proof a good deal clumsier than it had to be, but Johnny's view appeared to be that if Wigner wanted a proof, he was entitled to have one.

When Johnny concentrated on a problem, Wigner remembers, his concentration was fierce. He would move to a corner of the room and bury himself in it, his back to the room itself. Staring at the intersection of two walls, he would begin to mutter under his breath. What he was muttering was never quite distinct. Minutes would pass. Johnny did not turn, and only rarely suspended the dialogue he was having with his own synapses. When he eventually did turn, it was to report. The report was often formidable.

On one such occasion Wigner spoke of a demonstration he had witnessed in which two five-digit numbers were multiplied mentally, without so much as a pencil or scrap of paper. Johnny reported that his own grandfather had that sort of capacity but that he himself had never tried it. It would be amusing to try. Wigner selected the two numbers and set himself to totting up their product in the conventional way while Johnny marched into his corner. Several minutes of muttering ensued; it was not proving to be easy. But Johnny eventually turned and delivered his answer. Wigner congratulated his friend warmly; he was impressed. Was his answer correct? Johnny asked. Wigner was obliged to reply that it was not. "Then why on earth," Johnny asked, "are you congratulating me?" Wigner was not to be shaken. Johnny, he said, had come remarkably near.

The story conflicts with the notion that Johnny was a mental calculator without peer. The uninformed view has always held that mathematicians are the very devils at multiplying and dividing. Some are, some are not, and there are always idiots savants here and there who are better at it than even the very best mathematicians. Johnny became interested in the matter, as he became interested in anything that smacked of mathematics, and discovered that he could do extraordinary things by fixing lots of mathematical constants in his mind and exploiting certain algebraic verities there. That was the manner in which Johnny eventually did it, but it was not the way of Grandfather Kann. Johnny's methods brought some problems. Because complications usually disappeared before him, he would sometimes go the more complicated way around. In one lecture he once got lost while scribbling on the blackboard. "Um," he said, "I know three ways of proving this point but I have unfortunately chosen a fourth one."

Many modern mathematicians think in terms of odd shapes. They use Johnny's computers to conjure up even odder ones. Johnny would not encourage such thinking. If mathematics was not quickly brought into terms of equations, he thought it could quickly become insufficiently rigorous, insufficiently logical, very liable to mislead. Ulam later defined Johnny's mind percipiently:

> In many mathematical conversations on topics belonging to set theory and allied fields, von Neumann even seemed to think formally. Most mathematicians, when discussing problems in these fields, seemingly have an intuitive framework based on geometrical or almost tactile pictures of abstract sense, transformations, etc. Von Neumann gave the impression of operating sequentially by purely formal deductions. What I mean to say is that the basis of his intuition, which could produce new theorems and proofs just as well as the naive intuition, seemed to be of a type that is much rarer. If one has to divide mathematicians as Poincaré proposed into two types—those with visual and those with auditory intuition—Johnny perhaps belonged to the latter. In him the auditory sense, however, probably was very abstract. It involved, rather, a complementarity between the formal appearance of a collection of symbols and the game played with them on the one hand, and an interpretation of their meanings on the other. The foregoing distinction is somewhat like that between a mental picture of a physical chessboard and a mental picture of a sequence of moves on it, written down in algebraic notation.

The reader will have most fun tracing Johnny's achievements through the rest of this book if he or she grasps that they sprang from a brain that operated in this way. In almost everything he did, from inventing new sorts of pure mathematics to calculating how best America could deter Stalin, he was moving shorthand algebraic notations in rigorously permitted directions across the moving chessboard of his mind.

This mode of operation can make some men extremely cross. Among a different constituency it can inspire great confidence. Johnny's bosom companions throughout life were those who were privately awestruck at his efficiency but were jovial and joke-making, instead of sycophantic or jealous, about it. To be surrounded by such companions can instill confidence in oneself as well as in them. At the gymnasium Johnny's self-confidence was more subdued than it later became, but he possessed it. And he clearly engendered that confidence in the cleverest people around him: in Ratz to begin with, in the mathematicians at the university, and in the brightest fellow schoolboys such as Wigner.

Ratz contributed a lot to Johnny's career, in this time before it budded. It would not have been difficult for Johnny to have gone off the rails as a boy and as a young man. Many other infant prodigies among mathematicians have done so and are not always remembered with the affection that embraced Johnny in most of his doings. Johnny had firm roots in his home life, and at the remarkable dinner table of Max, but he needed somebody to guide him also into the real world. In 1914–21 Ratz did this.

Whatever schoolboy Johnny might be doing at the university, within the gymnasium every attempt was made to treat him as an ordinary student—at the head of his class, to be sure, but still subject to the discipline of the gymnasium, which was a good deal more than minimal, although also not bureaucratic. Johnny's surviving school reports show him winning the citation "excellent" on every line, with three usual exceptions. In handwriting, physical exercise and music, the mark could be the rather rude "satisfactory," nearly the lowest pass mark. Conduct was more usually marked "good" than "excellent." His brother Nicholas recalls that the teachers said Johnny was always brilliant on any topic but did not always know what the topic of yesterday's homework was. Johnny did the homework very quickly and then dived into something else. There was much else to dive into.

◄►◄►

The rich family life of the Kann clan continued unabated during those gymnasium years at the house on Vacsi Boulevard and at the summer home in the hills. That family life was an integral part of Johnny's existence. Even after he started to conduct his professional life in other cities in other countries, he returned each summer to Budapest and, for as long as he could, renewed his way of life there. During his school days he became more and more deeply immersed in mathematics, but much of that mathematics was done in the bustle of rooms full of younger children, who appeared to amuse rather than distract him. His powers of concentration were enormous and remained so, yet he appeared to be aware of all that was going on around him, which was often a good deal.

As a teenager he was amiable, except in matters of the mind, where that amiability occasionally gave way. The conversations at Max's dinner table became more important to him and also more intellectual and wide-ranging. As his father was expert at chess, the competitive boy immersed himself in the game. He devised a system that was constructed, in the true style of the Johnny yet to come, from first principles and proceeded inexorably to necessary conclusions. At regular intervals he tested his changing system against Max. Fortunately and regularly, his father dispatched even fourteen-year-old Johnny tidily, leaving the system in ruins for the moment at least.

During the summers, the family traveled to Venice and Semmering and Karlsbad and wherever. Johnny was generally along. Then, too, there were costume parties and parlor games and a wide variety of family delights, and he was at the center of these. For the most part he was happy to be learning. Mathematics, of course; he was in fact doing mathematics. But the younger children's teachers were in and out, and he picked up more French and English and Italian from them. His voracity for knowledge could be as amusing as it was terrifying. A cousin struggles with considerations of decorum, and then she recalls an occasion when Johnny went to the lavatory and took two books with him—for fear he would finish the book he was currently reading before he was ready to emerge.

The placidity of the gymnasium years 1914–21 was the more surprising because the political backdrop was not placid at all. In

1914–18, when Johnny was ten to fourteen, Hungary was engaged on the losing side in a savage European war. In 1919, when he was fifteen, Hungary suffered 133 days of a revolutionary communist government, which was replaced by a right-wing, and partially anti-Semitic, one. In 1920, when Johnny was a sixteen-year-young Hungarian, the Treaty of Trianon took two-thirds of Hungary's territory from it. In his final gymnasium year (1921) this loss of land hit hard at Grandfather Kann's business of selling things to people on the land. And it caused Max's bank to run into local financial difficulties, so Max transferred quickly to a more international bank with a slightly lesser job. How did infant prodigy Johnny continue so calmly through all this?

◂▸◂▸

The 1914–18 war affected the von Neumanns relatively little. The holiday trips to Austrian lakes continued pretty unabated. Hungary was the breadbasket of Austria-Hungary, and wartime shortages hoisted the price of bread sufficiently for businesslike Hungarians often to grow richer.

Austria-Hungary did not send great armies to the western front. Its main war was on the eastern front against Russia in southern Poland—with separately dated other wars against Serbia, Italy, and Romania. The usual result of battles on the main eastern front was that the Kaiser's Germans beat the Russians, while the Russians beat the Austro-Hungarians, but nobody was able to advance very far. Both the Russians and Austrians sent steaming up to railheads trains full of soldiers, equipment, heavy guns, shells, and too many horses. Even when the Russians won the battles after much bloodshed, they could not quickly send trains over the desolate Polish land they had conquered, so they became too far from railheads again. Cities such as Budapest were never really under threat.

The political atmosphere in loose Austria-Hungary was not as repressive as one might expect in total war. Einstein's schoolmate and benefactor, Friedrich Adler, walked into Vienna's Hotel Meissel und Schadn in 1916 and shot the Austrian Prime Minister,

Count Sturgkh, dead. Adler explained that he hoped this would initiate debate on whether Austria should continue in the war. After he was immediately condemned to death, his sentence was commuted to the rather more Austro-Hungarian one of eighteen months' imprisonment. Adler's father, who was a founder of the social democrats, pleaded in mitigation that his son must be mad because he had recently written a paper agreeing with Einstein's theory of relativity. The young Adler's imprisonment was spent in pleasant conditions in a fortress. He wrote to Einstein in 1918 that in these difficult times life was better inside prison walls than outside them.

In Budapest the von Neumanns felt that victory in the war would put Hungary too much under German influence but that defeat in it would be more awful. It would allow anti-Semitic czarist Russia to spread further into central Europe. Max at his dinner table composed ribald rhymes about the Emperor Franz Josef and about the Austro-Hungarian army's troubles in battles such as mining-area Tarnopol, where it advanced too far from the railhead so that shells and even food for the soldiers did not arrive. To a Schubert tune Max and Johnny sang Max's composition: "Unsere Truppen stehen schon vor Tarnopol, Tarnopol. Unsere Truppen sind keine Puppen, essen Suppen und nicht Kohl." In English this sounds awful: "Our troops are advancing to Tarnopol, Tarnopol. As they aren't dolls; they'll need to eat soup rather than coal." In logistics it was probably wiser than the Austrian high command.

The ten-to-fourteen-year-old Johnny followed the war closely, moving pins around war maps. He played with his family some complicated war games that he had made up himself, with fortifications and highways drawn on graph paper. The winner was the one who devised the right strategies, sometimes copied from ancient battles. One brother says there was no emotional feeling about which side won, but Catherine Pedroni (née Alcsuti) remembered with amusement that Johnny, Mike, and a boy cousin sometimes wore mock German uniforms during them.

Toward the end of the war, even Hungarian politics turned

serious. There were two general strikes in Budapest in the first half of 1918, with some looting and riots. Fourteen-year-old Johnny walked to school through them. At the armistice in November 1918 a revolutionary Hungarian government was installed under Count Michael Karolyi. "We can't have a revolution without a count," said Hungarian wags, quoted in Rhodes's book. Karolyi had thought the victorious allies would welcome a democratic Hungary with open arms and a kindly peace treaty. A mob that supported Karolyi murdered one of his political opponents (Count Tisza, who in Hungarian style had remained prime minister for part of the war, although personally against it). Karolyi ostentatiously sent a large wreath to the Tisza family. Equally ostentatiously the family threw the wreath on the garbage heap. It soon became apparent that the victorious allies were making the same gesture to Karolyi's pleas for a generous peace. In March 1919 his ramshackle administration collapsed into the waiting arms of Bela Kun's communist party, which looked much nastier.

Bela Kun was a nonpracticing Hungarian Jew who had been a prisoner of war in Russia, where he had become a fanatical and therefore ignorant disciple of Lenin. Lots of rebellious workers and soldiers (who had not been disarmed because the eastern front's war had ended in such chaos) drove around Budapest in early 1919 in trucks, singing the *Internationale* and proclaiming that a new 1789 had arrived. Groups of thugs known as the Lenin boys gathered for such purposes as preparing to attack rich bankers. The von Neumann family was rich enough to depart with some promptness by night train to a holiday home on the Adriatic, while Max went to Vienna to contact counterrevolutionary forces under Admiral Horthy, which soon (August 1919) came marching back in.

The Horthy government did not go the conciliatory way that Max had wanted. It killed five thousand people in its vengeful White Terror, after about five hundred had been killed in Bela Kun's Red Terror. The Red Terrorists, said a Hungarian historian, "revealed the primitive cruelty of coarse and ignorant men"; the worse tortures imposed by the Whites were the deliberate actions of elegant officers. These officers came from the Magyar aristocrat class, and their rage turned against the Jews. Bela Kun had been turfing the frightened sandaled nobility out of government posts. His fellow Jews were the only available educated people who could take their place. Around thirty-five of Bela Kun's fifty-five top political commissars were Jews. So the Horthy government in 1920 brought in Hungary's first specifically anti-Semitic measures in over fifty years. Entry admissions into university, it ruled, should "correspond as nearly as possible to the relative population of the various races and nationalities."

This meant that only about 5% of university entrants should be Jews, which was absurd in a country where Jews made up 50%–80% of the lawyers, doctors, and other learned professions. Johnny was always going to be among that top 5%, for whom any university would compete, but the anti-Semitism was a shock to him. Teller was an eleven-year-old Jew who stayed in Hungary through the communist regime. His family had to give up some of its apartment's bourgeois excess of floor space to two soldiers, who looted for hoarded money and pissed in the potted plants. Teller's parents were worried that Jews were so prominent in the commune. "I fear what my people are doing," his mother said. "When this is over there will be a terrible revenge."

Bela Kun and his immediate lieutenants had been trained for revolution while they were Russian prisoners. Their instruction had been meticulous but inefficient. Professor Peter Lax of New York University, who has kindly purged this book of some of its most horrible original mathematical errors, tells me a 1919 story. His father, then a rising young doctor, cured a Red Army commissar, General Meszaros (a name embarrassingly meaning "butcher"), of typhoid fever during the commune. This did not greatly aid the commissar, who recovered just in time to be executed by the Whites. But he gratefully gave Dr. Lax a commissar's most precious possession. This was a letter from Lenin on how to run revolutions. Lenin's broad lines were, "Make these promises to the peasants. . . . Make these pledges to the proletariat. . . . Give these assurances to the bourgeoisie. . . . Do not feel in any way bound by these promises, pledges or assurances." When the Lax family emigrated from Hungary to the United States in pre–Pearl Harbor 1941, they had to pass through wartime Nazi Germany to Lisbon. The Germans respected their visas punctiliously, but Dr. Lax felt that a personal letter from Lenin on how to run revolutions might be an unfortunate part of a traveling Jew's baggage through the Nazi empire in that year. He destroyed the envelope before leaving Budapest. This is a pity. If the letter had been posted to America from an ordinary postbox in Budapest, without the sender's address being attached, it would almost certainly have gotten through. Hungarian attitudes even in 1941 were more relaxed than most people suppose.

Johnny was later to ascribe to many Hungarians of his generation "an emotional fear and dislike of Russia." His detractors say his firmness in the cold war sprang from similar feelings in himself. They forget that the word "emotional" was a pejorative one to logical Johnny. He was far too much ruled by the mind rather than by the emotions to be a fanatical hater of anybody or anything. Theodore von Karman, who had some social democratic pretensions, became undersecretary for the universities during Bela Kun's regime. He remained Johnny's friend throughout life.

A main point that was brought home to Johnny by the 1919 Budapest commune was that communism does not work. Arthur Koestler, as a poor fourteen-year-old in 1919 Budapest, was at first in favor of communism, but his family found it hard to buy most food with the Bela Kun regime's ration cards and worthless paper money. The only food that was plentiful that summer was vanilla ice cream, presumably because it was not price controlled. Koestler's family ate it even for breakfast.

This economic and administrative nonsense was a shock to Johnny. For the first fifteen years of his life he had lived in a country with fast-increasing prosperity, where bourgeois decencies of human behavior were observed. This had been true even in wartime 1914–18. Now a set of illogical fools had pushed themselves to the top, waving chrysanthemums (a symbol of the Hungarian revolution) but also the Lenin boys' guns, chanting that they were going to make things better for the poor, while quite obviously making things most especially worse for them. As so often in socialist revolutions, the "intellectual leaders of the workers" were rich incompetents. George Lukacs, the supposedly great Marxist historian and Kun's commissar for cultural affairs, was the son of a bank director like Johnny—and long identifiable as fairly dotty.

Then, after Kun and Lukacs, another group of governing people had come in to depose these fools. They had taken revenge with measures that were even more uncivilizedly brutal and that sometimes (e.g., in the discrimination against the Jews) were bound to make the economic slowdown even worse. A lot of Hungarians who had been active in the commune fled to Russia after August 1919. Almost every prominent Hungarian extended family had some such departed sheep. At first they wrote freely to them. After a while, messages crept back that anybody in the Soviet Union who received regular letters from abroad was at risk for his life, so please do not send any. This became a main reason for post-1919 Hungary's righteous horror against Soviet Russia.

The Kun and Horthy regimes had put Hungary in a doghouse, and the 1920 Treaty of Trianon stripped Hungary of much of its territory. This was not of enormous emotional moment to the von Neumanns, who were internationalists rather than nationalists. But there was reason to worry about the effects on business. As suppliers of agricultural equipment, the firm of Kann-Heller faced slump. Kann had patriotically invested quite a lot in Austro-Hungarian war loans just before 1918, so his personal fortune was also impaired.

Business affairs at Max's Magyar Jelzalog Hitelbank were not going well, and there were arguments with some of Max's fellow directors. Fortunately Max was enough of a catch for any investment institution to want him, so he transferred to the more internationalist house of Adolf Kohner's sons. He celebrated with one of his ditties: "Leer gebrannt ist die Statte und gemein die Forderung/Als er, der sie auferwachte, zu die Kohnersöhne gung." This can be roughly translated, "The store is burned empty and the liabilities weigh like tons/As he who once awoke it goes off to Kohner's sons." Max, like Johnny, generally appreciated his own worth.

Still, there were some financial clouds as Johnny sat for the final examination at the gymnasium, the *matura*, in June 1921. There was a certain distinction in being first to finish. Johnny achieved it, to his almost immediate regret. As he left the classroom he realized that on two of the questions he had done less than his best.

It was no matter. Aside from those two questions, it was an almost perfect paper. He also sat for the exam for the Eotvos Prize, which he won. Theodore von Karman had been an earlier winner of an Eotvos Prize, as had Szilard. Teller was to win one a few years later. By getting the Eotvos, Jancsi von Neumann finished his secondary schooling with the same flourish that had characterized it from the start.

►◄►◄►◄ 4

An Undergraduate
with Lion's Claws, 1921–26

►◄**D**uring Johnny's final year at the Lutheran School the question of his further education had to be resolved, and Max sought counsel. He talked, among others, to Dr. Theodore von Karman, for whom—despite von Karman's comic ministership in Kun's communist government—Max had great respect. After a banker-type weighing of the prospects, it was decided that Johnny should be educated for a career in chemical engineering. The successes of German chemists during the 1914–18 war had generated for chemistry the same glamour as came to nuclear physics one war later. Johnny had not revealed among his many talents any particular affinity for chemistry or engineering, so the decision looked odd. There were two reasons for what was decided, one defensive and one aggressively wise.

The defensive reason was that most of poor Hungary's brightest scholars were being dragooned into chemical engineering at this time. When Wigner was seventeen, a year earlier than Johnny, he

was asked by his father what he proposed to make of his life. He
had it in mind to become a theoretical physicist, the young Wigner
replied. "And exactly how many jobs are there in Hungary for
theoretical physicists?" his father inquired. "Four," replied young
Wigner. The discussion more or less ended there, and Wigner was
sent to Berlin University to be educated as a chemical engineer.
Later Fellner was sent to Zurich to become one. Neither he nor
Wigner stayed long in this field.

Nor did Johnny, who in 1921 was sent to become a chemical
engineer first to Berlin University and then to Zurich. There was
a flavor of the Wigner family's search for security in the account
Johnny gave of his early job prospects before the Gray Committee,
convened in 1954 in Washington in order to harry J. Robert Oppenheimer. During the questioning in that preposterous persecution (where he talked the greatest sense), Johnny was asked why
he had not stayed in Hungary. "I first intended to become a chemical engineer," he answered, "and if I had become a chemical
engineer I might have returned to Hungary. Since I decided to
become a mathematician and the outlook in Hungary was not at
all promising, whereas in Germany then it was promising indeed,
I decided to go to Germany."

In short, a career in engineering was a practical choice, and Max
was a practical man. And Johnny, even at that early age, had a
well-developed taste for good living, which was not likely to be
gratified in a career as a Hungarian lecturer in mathematics. His
father brought home a fine income, but there was no family fortune and—now that his bank had run into troubles—no likelihood
that one would be forthcoming. It would do no harm to have an
anchor to windward.

The second, and successful, decision made about young Johnny's career that summer was more ambitious. While casting his
anchor to windward, Johnny was also allowed to drift a kite toward the stars. Before leaving to become a chemical engineer in
Zurich via Berlin, he enrolled at the Budapest University as a
candidate for an advanced doctoral degree in mathematics. The
academic progression in Europe has never been as formalized as

that in the United States, but what seventeen-year-old Johnny proposed was not an ordinary program. He planned to carry on his undergraduate and graduate education simultaneously, in two distinct disciplines and in three cities several hundreds of miles apart. To cap this cheek, the schoolboy's project for a Ph.D. thesis was to attempt axiomatization of Georg Cantor's set theory. This was the most contentious subject in contemporary mathematics and had already driven some great professors around mountainous bends. The seventeen-year-old seemed to suggest that he would try to jog up Everest in gym shoes, although only as a part-time gig.

Meanwhile there was the more boring project to become a chemical engineer. The main decision made in 1921 was that Johnny should take a leisurely two-year nondegree course in chemistry at the University of Berlin, and then in the fall of 1923 take the entrance exam for the second year (i.e., omitting the first year) of the prestigious four-year course in the chemical engineering department of the famous Eidgennossische Technische Hochschule (ETH) in Zurich. This brought an interesting contrast with another great mind.

Einstein had taken the entrance exam to ETH in the fall of 1895 and had failed it—although he passed in the next year after twelve months in a crammer. It was partly because of his disappointing early ETH results that young Einstein was initially deemed too dumb to get a research grant. He had to go off first to be an ill-paid clerk in the Swiss patent office. From there he thought through the shattering truth of the special theory of relativity while in furnished lodgings, cut off from communion with academic minds. Einstein explained his failure at the 1895 ETH entrance exam by the fact that his father had told him "to choose a practical profession, but this was simply unbearable to me." Johnny never appreciated any academic yearning for the impractical. There was a clear, and for the world eventually important, difference between Johnny's and Einstein's attitudes to business competence and welfare dependency. The difference probably stemmed from the different images that the two men's fathers had passed on.

Johnny's father had been formidably efficient and helped to build up large businesses with interestingly large national results. He made enough money to succor, in the extended family tradition, sisters and cousins and aunts. Einstein's father had tried to build up a succession of small businesses, all of which went fairly bust. So he had to borrow money from cousins and uncles and aunts, including the money for what Albert demanded should be his nonpractical education.

Johnny saw a romance in successful business. Einstein's instinct was to regard profitable business as other people's vulgar bad joke. Johnny saw the earning of a competence as essential for self-respect. Einstein thought that the helping of lame dogs over stiles was every lame dog's right. Yet both Johnny and Einstein knew early that they themselves would not be lame dogs. They saw with fair assurance that they could advance man's knowledge. Johnny felt confident about this by age seventeen, because his first thoughts on axiomatizing Cantor's set theory were coalescing excitingly well.

On that September 1921 train to Berlin he was accompanied by his father. A future Wall Street banker met him on it and said, "I suppose you are coming to Berlin to learn mathematics." "No," replied the seventeen-year-old, "I already know mathematics. I am coming to learn chemistry."

Some commentators on Johnny have assumed that he came to Berlin to study attentively at the feet of Berlin's Nobel laureate in chemistry, Fritz Haber, Germany's much-loved main inventor of poison gas. Haber could be called, together with Computer Johnny, one of the handful of little-publicized people who have hugely affected the twentieth century. If Haber had not found a way to fix nitrogen from the air to make nitrates for explosives, blockaded Germany would have had to surrender from the 1914–18 war in about 1915. Haber justified his invention of poison gas in 1915 with an argument also heard at Los Alamos thirty years later. "If this shortens the war," he said, "it will save many young lives."

It is unlikely that Johnny was a personal student of Haber's, because Johnny's aims in chemistry in Berlin were limited to the rather simple one of getting what his first-term report at ETH called his "Matrikelauszug von der Universität Berlin." Indeed Fellner contended to White that Johnny hardly studied chemistry in Berlin at all. Fellner had names and addresses in the Plattenstrasse in Zurich where Johnny as early as 1922 came and shared accommodations with him while looking at what was being taught in the first-year course at the ETH, before sitting the second-year entrance exam himself. Some people have therefore called 1921–23 Johnny's "lost two years."

The mystery can be lightened, and that charge refuted, by remembering what Johnny needed to do between September 1921 and September 1923, and what was happening to the world then. As the least of his worries he had to prepare to pass the entrance exam that Einstein had failed, and the ETH reports that in September 1923 he did this "with an outstanding result." This was an achievement because chemistry was not a subject that Johnny had done much at school, and most of his school-learning in it will have been in Hungarian. He therefore had to do some reading in German of chemistry and chemical engineering in 1921–23, even though he hardly needed a teacher on the level of Haber. Something more like a correspondence course out of Berlin might have sufficed, with only occasional appearances in class.

Also, it could have been sensible for a banker's son in 1921–23 to operate partly out of Switzerland, especially as the last year wore on. The Weimar Republic's great inflation was in progress, so that you could hold a middle-class bank account in German marks at the beginning of the day, and by the evening it would not buy a bunch of carrots. By contrast, if you held your money in foreign exchange, you could in 1923 travel right across Germany on a first-class railroad fare for the equivalent of one penny. "It is not enough for a European to be rich," said Johnny later. "He also needs a bank account in Switzerland."

Threats of civil war were rising in Germany, and so was anti-Semitism. Unsuccessful putsches exploded: the black Reichswehr's in Berlin and Hitler's in the Munich beer hall. Germany may have seemed no place for a bright young Jewish boy whose chemistry studies did not require him to be permanently there, in his first years away from home. Sex in Berlin in 1921–23, for a young foreigner with foreign exchange, was cheap and plentiful and commercial and salacious, and some worrying stories may have filtered back to 62 Vaczi Boulevard. And, much more important than all of this, cramming for an entry exam in chemistry was not in 1921–23 the most riveting feature of young Johnny's life. Whatever the ambiguity of the entry of his name onto the rolls of three separate institutions of higher learning for two quite separate subjects at the same time, there is no doubt that very soon after leaving school in 1921 Johnny realized that he was going to be a mathematician with exhilarating world fame.

"Mathematicians at the outset of their creative work," wrote Ulam, "are often confronted by two conflicting inclinations. The first is to contribute to the edifice of existing work—it is there that one can be sure of gaining recognition quickly by solving outstanding problems. The second is a desire to blaze new trails and to create new syntheses. . . . In his early work Johnny chose the first of these alternatives." Indeed Johnny chose this banker's son's course, to be the solver of outstanding problems of the day, all through his life until near the end, when his computers were changing his concept of what the future of life ought to be.

In 1921–23, his teenage eyes were fixed shorter-term on the main intellectual chance, on the most hotly argued question in pure mathematics. There was no doubt what that was. Johnny had to come out either on the side of Göttingen's Professor David Hilbert (1862–1943), the grand old man of German mathematics, or else for the school around the Dutch mathematician L. E. J. Brouwer. Broadly, Hilbert wanted to reaxiomatize modern mathematics—including all of Cantor's set theory—so as to make it more rigorous and useful. Brouwer thought that some parts of set theory were too unrigorous to be safely used at all. Johnny came out on the side of Hilbert.

Hilbert was one of the last great men who itched to hope that rigorous mathematics should eventually be able to solve nearly every problem. He came from the German tradition of Leibniz, who had trusted that in another three centuries or so (i.e., just about now in 1992): "there might be no more need of disputation between two philosophers than between two accountants. For it would suffice to take their pencils in their hands, to sit down to their slates, and to say to each other (with a friend as witness if they liked): let us calculate." By "philosophers" Leibniz wanted to mean all rational men. He seemed to hope that by about 1992 we would be solving all our political arguments, all our marital dilemmas, most questions of beauty and art, as well as all questions for scientific progress, by sitting down at our slates and calculating. He would have been thrilled if he could have envisaged those slates being replaced by Johnny's computers.

Hilbert did not have hopes as rigid as this, but he thought that mathematics should again take the lead in scientific progress. A chief requirement for this was that modern mathematics should itself become more scientific and axiomatic. By axiomatic, he meant that mathematicians' calculations should keep showing that this will follow from this from this—not just sometimes but every time. Johnny in his early German period thought a bit in this Germanic way.

In 1900 Hilbert had listed twenty-three problems for mathematicians in the new century. They included the need to make Cantor's mathematics more rigorous, so as to extend axiomatization in mathematics and in natural sciences. Without more axiomatization—without rational explanation of why this always follows from this from this—Hilbert feared that the influence of mathematics might "continue to diminish." "I neither expect nor hope for this," Hilbert said, "because mathematics is the foundation of all exact knowledge of natural phenomena. So that it may fulfil this high destiny, may the new century bring it gifted prophets and disciples . . . masters of genius." Hilbert thought that young mathematicians of the new century would have marvellous new tools. They should use them to introduce new axiomatization not only in mathematics, but also in physics and all other "sciences in which mathematics play an important part."

With these means he trusted that his school of mathematicians would prove the consistency of both classical and modern (set theory) mathematics, and the "freedom of both from contradictions." Only in this way, he believed, would all sciences be able to continue accelerating on and on.

By 1921, alas, mathematics was not proceeding neatly in that direction. It was becoming untidily more controversial instead.

◆►◆►

Much of the controversy had been created by Cantor (1845–1918), who had a turbulent career right from his childhood in St. Petersburg, through his lectureships at minor European universities such as Halle (he was too infuriating to get preferment at major ones), down to his death in a German lunatic asylum during Kaiser Wilhelm's war. Stefan Banach (1892–1945) said that this professor with constant nervous breakdowns was "the sort of Jew who does like to turn respectable people's established assumptions upside down: Jesus, Marx, Freud, Cantor." E. T. Bell called the final chapter of his history, *Men of Mathematics*, "Paradise Lost?" He feared that Leibniz's dream had collapsed and that "the controversial topic of Mengenlehre (theory of sets, or classes, particularly of infinite sets) created in 1874–95 by Georg Cantor . . . typifies for mathematics the general collapse of those principles which the prescient seers of the nineteenth century, foreseeing everything but the grand debacle, believed to be fundamentally sound in all things from physical science to democratic government."

To be fair to Cantor, he was not as revolutionary as that.

Set theory, in its earliest forms before Cantor, had its origins in physics and chemistry. During the nineteenth century both physicists and chemists had become concerned with the behavior of individual particles in things such as gases, but it was not really possible to count how many there were. It therefore became useful to consider their behavior wholesale, as it were. The mathematics that came into being to organize and simplify that kind of manipulation took on a life of its own.

If there is an uncountably large number of boys and girls in a room, set theorists said, strike up the band, and ask each to take a partner in a dance. The odd numbers left over would then be analyzable and manageable. More prosaically, if all the chairs in a vast conference hall are occupied, and nobody is left standing, it is reasonable to say that the number of chairs is the same as the number of people, even if you have not managed to count either of them. This correspondence in sets became a useful concept, and so did other terms such as the union of sets and intersection of sets and subsets. Because all of this was done without counting in terms of actual numbers, there was already a departure from decently rigorous mathematics. There was not proper axiomatization, in the sense that scientists were not saying with precision that this followed from this.

Cantor seized on set theory when it was becoming the most important part of modern mathematics and extended it into contemplation of the infinite. This was annoying to conventional scholars because it created contradictions. As a simplistic example in geometry, there are an infinite number of points in any straight line, but it sounds odd to say that there are therefore as many points in the next tiny hyphen as in a line of infinite length. When you talk of extending that line in infinite dimensions, you can become even more infinitely confused. As a simplistic example in arithmetic, half of all numbers are even, but if you have an infinite set of even numbers, it sounds contradictory to say either that it is or that it is not only half as large as an infinite set of all numbers. Some eminent scholars, such as Bertrand Russell, as we shall see, nearly went crazy over this. Cantor suggested that there are different sorts of infinity and invited contemplation of numbers beyond infinity.

There is a danger that exasperated readers will think that this biography has at this point gone as crazy as Cantor himself eventually was, by worrying about these German professors who shouted at each other eighty years ago as they danced on the head of a pin. Einstein called their debate the frog-mouse battle. But the professors were not just dancing. Some of them were threatening to withdraw mathematics from being of full use in technology's forward march.

Just when analysts were discovering that, as a practical matter, pure mathematics has to deal with concepts that smack of infinity more often than it has to deal with the merely finite, a group of mathematicians around Brouwer and Hermann Weyl said that such dealings with infinity were trafficking with the devil. They complained that impossible problems were being created by the careless acceptance of the concept of the infinite as an arithmetical tool. They maintained that no proofs reached after involvement with considerations of the infinite, however plausible, should be acceptable to decently rigorous mathematicians. They urged that nothing could be said about the infinite with any degree of confidence and that logicians had only entrapped themselves when they sought to suggest otherwise. Their attitude had a certain stern scholastic attraction but also a considerable disadvantage. It ruled out much of modern mathematics as improper and unsound.

From Göttingen Hilbert declared war on these fainthearts. He believed that Cantor was a genius and that people such as Brouwer and Weyl would cripple mathematics if they were allowed to start "jettisoning everything which does not suit them and setting up an embargo. The effect is to dismember our science and to run the risk of losing part of our most valuable possessions." Boomed Hilbert, "We shall not be ejected from the paradise Cantor has created for us." He called on young mathematicians to make sensible use of new notations and to prove that Cantor's math was rigorous and axiomatizable and usable.

By 1921, the seventeen-year-old Johnny was eager to respond to this call. He had already worked out that he should be able to do so.

◄►◄►

The second of Johnny's published papers had been prepared while he was still in high school in 1921, although it was not published until 1923 as "Zur Einführung der transfiniten Ordnungszählen" (Toward the Introduction of Transfinite Ordinal Numbers). Ordinal means numbers expressing order—first, second, third— which cardinal numbers (e.g., one or nine or seven) do not necessarily do. A transfinite cardinal number was already the name for the size of an infinite set.

The opening sentence of "Zur Einführung" was in true Johnny style: "The aim of this work is to consider concretely and precisely the idea of Cantor's ordinal numbers." He says it is necessary to turn the somewhat vague formulations of Cantor himself into more precise definitions. One of Johnny's definitions is that each ordinal number is the set of all smaller ordinal numbers, which is rather a good avoider of some complications when the concept of infinity starts muddling you up. Johnny points out proudly that throughout "Zur Einführung" vague notations such as "et cetera" are never used. Old East Prussian Hilbert and his school were delighted by this formalism, as Johnny knew they would be.

On arrival at the University of Berlin as a student chemist in 1921, Johnny therefore probably did not make a beeline for the great poison-gas-inventing professor of chemistry Haber. He made a beeline instead for the professor of mathematics Erhard Schmidt, who had been Hilbert's pupil twenty years before. Schmidt was also a friend of Ernst Zermelo, who had made some of the most thoughtful advances in axiomatizing set theory so far. Although Zermelo's work lacked Johnny's later precision, it helped Johnny because it did show the need for what mathematicians call an "axiom of choice." Some people say that Zermelo had also made approaches to the problems Johnny rendered precise in his *Theory of Games*. Johnny later earned a reputation for imbibing vague ideas from younger people and within a few minutes darting five blocks ahead of them. As a young man he also imbibed ideas from more distinguished older professors and dashed those same blocks ahead.

By 1922 Johnny had a first draft of his own thesis. We know the early history of this because, some years after Johnny's death, Professor Herbert Fraenkel of the Hebrew University in Jerusalem wrote to Ulam:

Around 1922–23, being then professor at Marburg University, I received from Professor Erhard Schmidt of Berlin a long manuscript of an author unknown to me, Johannes von Neumann, with the title "Die Axiomatisierung der Mengenlehre" [The Axiomatization of Set Theory], this being his eventual doctoral dissertation. . . . I was asked to express my views since it seemed incomprehensible. I don't maintain that I understood everything, but enough to see that this was an outstanding work and to recognise "ex ungue leonem." While answering in this sense, I invited the young scholar to visit me in Marburg and discussed things with him, strongly advising him to prepare the ground for the understanding of so technical an essay by a more informal essay which should stress the new access to the problem and its fundamental consequences. He wrote such an essay under the title "Eine Axiomatisierung der Mengenlehre" [An Axiomatization of Set Theory], and I published it in 1925 in the Journal für Mathematik of which I was then associate editor.

Ex ungue leonem—spotting a lion from the claw—was the phrase Daniel Bernoulli had used about Newton two and a half centuries before. Bernoulli had been sent a mathematical paper that was at that stage anonymous, but he instantly recognized it as Newton's work.

The opening of "Eine Axiomatisierung der Mengenlehre," Johnny's third published work, was again in Johnny's style: "The aim of the present work is to give a logically unobjectionable axiomatic treatment of set theory. I would like to say something first about difficulties which make such an axiomatization of set theory desirable." This did sound a little like a sophomore undergraduate in theology stating in a paper that he intended to give a logically irrefutable proof of the nature of the existence of God.

If an inexperienced theology student produced such a paper, it would almost certainly be wrong. Unfortunately, inexperienced Johnny's axiomatization of set theory also led him and some others along a wrong path. Two sets of sets of conclusions should probably be drawn from "Eine Axiomatisierung." The longer of them will be discussed in the next chapter. We will try there to put Johnny's early contribution as a logician into the whole and sometimes illogical twenty-five hundred years' history of logics and mathematics. We will hope dimly to perceive not only where he went wrong but also why this gave him the background he needed when he went on to help invent the computer.

The shorter set of conclusions, of course, is that it made old Hilbert very happy indeed. "Eine Axiomatisierung" was passed among the mighty before its publication in 1925, and it sent the reputation of the young undergraduate up through the roof. Hilbert's biographer suggests that it was then that young Johnny became Hilbert's frequent visitor. "The two mathematicians, more than 40 years apart in age, spent long hours together in Hilbert's garden or study." As K. O. Friedrichs later told Lax, some of Göttingen's other old-guard mathematicians were not pleased by this. They regarded cherubic Johnny as a flash in the pan. But in 1924 Hilbert's acclaim was the greatest a young mathematician could have.

For years Hilbert had said that the axiomatization of set theory was needed to put mathematics back in the driver's seat of new technological advances. Now the axiomatization appeared to have been carried forward by a young man who had not yet sat even for his first degree. If these were Johnny's two lost years of 1921–23, they appeared to his early contemporaries to be about as lost as the two years of the Great Plague in the 1660s when Newton had dragged himself away to rural Lincolnshire, where he more or less invented modern science.

◄►◄►

In September of 1923 Johnny arrived at Zurich's ETH and passed his entrance exams in chemical engineering with some ease. His report card for his first semester in the winter of 1923–24 showed him with a perfect mark of six in every subject: organic chemistry, inorganic chemistry, analytical chemistry, experimental physics, higher mathematics, and even the French language (which was an obligatory course for German-speaking Swiss).

In later terms at the ETH he made his way doggedly if rather less spectacularly through the engineering curriculum. It rarely commanded his full attention, although his contemporary Fellner recalled brief spells of intense concentration during which he invested all his efforts in the task directly before him. During these spells Johnny said he feared he might fail his final examinations, but Fellner knew of nobody who shared those fears. Johnny's other achievement seems to have been a bill for broken laboratory glass that for some years remained a Zurich record. He was apt to be thinking of something else while doing laboratory experiments, as he also was while driving an automobile.

In another part of the ETH the professor of mathematics was Weyl, who was a founding member of the Brouwer school of mathematical thought, which Johnny was helping Hilbert to try to destroy. Magisterial "heiliger Hermann" Weyl, who was later to join Johnny in Princeton, welcomed him in 1923 as into a second intellectual home. During Weyl's absences from Zurich, undergraduate Johnny took over the teaching of some of his classes. Hungary's Polya was also a professor of mathematics at the ETH at this time. Polya said that he referred in one lecture to an unsolved problem. Johnny came up privately at the end, and solved it. A legend is that Weyl announced that in two future lectures he would tackle a particular issue that Johnny then solved in one page full of equations. It should be said that Johnny denied this second story, but he clearly enjoyed his days as an undergraduate chemist the more because he was already a mathematical lion.

There were other diversions in Zurich, in neighborhood taverns where students gathered to lift a glass or nine. In the taverns another talent bloomed: for ribald stories and dirty limericks, at which, according to Fellner, Johnny was better than he was at engineering but not nearly as good as he was at mathematics. He did not reach his father's standards as a troubadour.

Meanwhile, he was passing courses in Budapest that he never attended. From time to time he paid a quick visit to Budapest University when some institutional requirement called for his actual presence. He also went home for the summer vacations. He polished up his dissertation while at Zurich, completed it, and took final examinations in Budapest to become a Ph.D. with highest honors in 1926. This was also just after his graduation in Zurich. He was not yet twenty-three years old.

Then, with his two degrees in hand, he went to Göttingen on a grant from the Rockefeller Foundation, his first debt to the United States. At Göttingen Hilbert and others had been waiting for him for some time. The arrival there in 1926 was useful for him and the rest of us. It was a university where there was sufficient competition (especially from great physicists) to ensure that a young mathematical genius such as Johnny did not grow too leonine, arrogant, abstract, or insane.

►◄►◄►◄ **5**

Rigor Becomes

More Relaxed, 500 B.C.–A.D. 1931

►◄ *T*his book is meant to be a biography of the mind of John von Neumann, so in this chapter we pause from the chronological in order to probe three reasons for Johnny's effectiveness: what by 1926 he owed to Max; what methods of choosing and rationing his mathematical work he gradually developed; and what lessons he drew from the twenty-five hundred years of mathematical history since the ancient Greeks whom he so admired.

Johnny's debt to Max and his family was that he was brought up to think relaxedly, instead of being turned taut in childhood as so many other infant mathematical prodigies are. If a family finds it has bred a precocious little genius, the most important qualities to encourage are—as Max saw—(*a*) a sense of calmness and humor, (*b*) an inquiring mind that finds inquiring to be fun.

The sorts of father or mother who unexpectedly breed geniuses are usually bad at this. Some of them want aggressively to push the bright brat—and thus often make him nervy, unstable, unliked. Other parents resent that the infant so soon becomes obviously brighter than his siblings and themselves.

Among the great mathematicians and physicists of his time, Johnny apparently intimated to contemporaries that he found a relaxing sense of humor mainly in Fermi and the young Richard Feynman, although also among more personal friends such as Ulam. "But," said one Nobel Prize winner, "from people like Leo Szilard, or Robert Oppenheimer, or even Albert Einstein, he tended to distance himself (this is my impression)."

The eventual distancing from Einstein sprang partly from political exasperation. Churchill's scientific adviser, Sir Frederick Lindemann, told his biographer that his friend Einstein's towering intellect made him the greatest scientific genius of the century, but he then snorted that Einstein "in all matters of politics was a guileless child, and would lend his great name to worthless causes which he did not understand, signing many ridiculous political or other manifestos put before him by designing people."

Johnny saw this happen to two politically opposite groups of colleagues in succession. First, among good Göttingen scientists who after 1926 started saying silly things on the way to accepting and eventually serving Nazism. Then, among respected American friends who after 1933 declaimed equally silly things on the way to excusing Stalin. A common feature of clever men who occasionally supped on too-short spoons with Nazism or Communism was that as kids they had never adequately learned to laugh.

At the beginning of his career (when he was trying to axiomatize set theory) and at the end (when he was trying to learn for the computer from the brain), Johnny's intellectual path crossed that of two brilliant men who were shattering examples of the danger of not having witty troubadours like Max as their father. Although Johnny had real affection for one of them, he saw in both the passions that can turn great mathematicians practically nuts. The two men concerned were both born before Johnny and died after him. Both had at birth as great an inborn capacity for superb math as Johnny had. While Johnny got his steady and witty and stimulating upbringing under Max in troubled and war-defeated Hungary in 1903–21, the other two were reared in what should have been the calmer atmospheres of England and America. Through their lives they were recoiling from exactly the wrong sort of childhood, which had put their powers for doing greater good in emotional twist. It is right to be brutal in analyzing this, even at the risk of annoying their many admirers and pupils and friends, because similar great minds are being ruined in upbringing now. The handicap does not always lie in financial underprivilege in youth. Our two examples of geniuses turned emotionally too dotty had as their childhood guardians a right-wing former British prime minister and a left-wing Harvard professor. They were Britain's Bertrand, third Earl Russell (1872–1970), and America's Norbert Wiener (1894–1964).

Bertie Russell is the more important for this stage of our story because he was the man before Johnny who was trying to axiomatize set theory. Russell axiomatized it at enormous length, but went mulish when he found he had done so in essence inadequately. Johnny axiomatized it with sharp brevity, but quickly admitted when he found he had also gone wrong. The reaction of the two men when their hopes were punctured speaks volumes to those who want to hear.

Bertie Russell had arrived on the news pages of the worst newspapers at the age of three because of his brother's randy tubercular tutor. "Apparently upon grounds of pure theory," wrote Russell later, "my father and mother decided that although he [a Mr. D. A. Spalding] ought to remain childless on account of his tuberculosis, it was unfair to expect him to be celibate." On the father's earnest urging, Bertie's society beauty of a mother therefore had sex with the delighted weedy tutor as a regularly rationed dollop of noblesse oblige, although "there is no evidence that she obtained any pleasure from doing so."

When both Russell's young parents died suddenly, the father's will nominated Spalding and another atheist to be the guardians of his two little sons, so as "to protect them from the evils of a religious upbringing." After sensational litigation before goggling

Victorians the two Russell boys were made wards in chancery. They were sent in 1876 to live with their horrified, suing grandfather, who (hence the headlines) was an earl and a former British prime minister. He had been regarded as a promising young conservative politician at the time of Waterloo. Grandfather's effect on his son (Bertie's father) suggests that the problems of a generation gap festered after Napoleon's war as grimly as they did after the kaiser's—and after Hitler's and Ho Chi Minh's.

Clever and inquiring little Russell therefore moved into a grandparental home where his questions on philosophy met such answers as "What is matter? Never mind. What is mind? No matter. Heh, heh, heh." Bertie later began his autobiography: "Three passions, simple but overwhelmingly strong, have governed my life: the longing for love, the search for knowledge, and unbearable pity for the suffering of mankind. These passions, like great winds, have blown me hither and thither, on a wayward course over a deep ocean of anguish, reaching to the very verge of despair." That is not a good mood in which to do calm mathematics.

One time when this brilliant manic-depressive was feeling manically happy was when, in his twenties, he was trying to axiomatize set-theory mathematics. Russell described his initial success in 1900 in words that Johnny might have been tempted to use early in 1922:

> The time was one of intellectual intoxication. . . . For years I had been endeavouring to analyse the fundamental notions of mathematics, such as ordinal and cardinal numbers. Suddenly, in the space of a few weeks, I discovered what appeared to be definitive answers to the problems that had baffled me for years. And in the course of discovering these answers I was introducing a new mathematical technique, by which regions formerly abandoned to the vagueness of philosophers were conquered for the precision of exact formulae. Intellectually, the month of September 1900 was the highest point of my life.

It is therefore a pity that Russell was in the next few months to be plunged into what he called "the deepest despair I have ever known." In February 1901 this despair was the result of a harrowing incident with an attractive small boy (which Freud could have explained). But then, said Russell,

In May I had an intellectual setback almost as severe as the emotional setback which I had had in February. Cantor had a proof that there is no greatest number, and it seemed to me that the number of all the things in the world ought to be the greatest possible. Accordingly I examined his proof with some minuteness, and endeavoured to apply to it the class of all the things there are. This led me to consider those classes which are not members of themselves, and to ask whether the class of such classes is or is not a member of itself. I found that either answer implies its contradictory. At first I supposed that I should be able to overcome the contradiction quite easily, and that probably there was some trivial error in the reasoning. Gradually however it became clear that this was not the case. . . . There was an affinity with the ancient Greek contradiction about Epimenides the Cretan, who said that all Cretans are liars. A contradiction essentially similar to that of Epimenides can be created by giving a person a piece of paper on which is written: "The statement on the other side of this paper is false." The person turns the paper over and finds on the other side: "The statement on the other side of this paper is true." It seemed unworthy of a grown man to spend time on such trivialities, but what was I to do?

What Russell eventually did emotionally was to go off into a life of continuous social revolt against anything that seemed to be calmly succeeding, like in the 1950s Eisenhower's United States. In the post-1945 period he was leader of the British movement for unilateral nuclear disarmament. By 1961 he was calling President Kennedy and Prime Minister Macmillan "much more wicked than Hitler . . . the wickedest people in the history of man." At a time when he was still supposed to be teaching young people, gentle Russell was shouting at them, at sometimes-violent demonstrations, things that people much less brilliant than he knew to be logically perverse.

◄►◄►

One of Russell's pupils at Cambridge in 1913 who made him most irascible was, as Russell wrote to a lady professor at Bryn Mawr, "an infant prodigy named Wiener, Ph.D. Harvard, aged 18. . . . The youth has been flattered and thinks himself God Almighty. . . . There is a perpetual contest between him and me as to which is to do the teaching."

Here was our second misparented genius, Norbert Wiener (1894–1964). Steve J. Heims's biography *John von Neumann and Norbert Wiener: From Mathematics to the Technologies of Life and Death* takes a diametrically opposite view to mine on the two men's legacy to our times. But Professor Heims's biographical facts are impressive. He describes how Norbert's dominating father had immigrated into America in 1881 at the age of nineteen, with the intention of founding a vegetarian, humanitarian, and socialist community. Because the father landed with only 25¢ in his pocket, he became a Harvard professor instead. While Bertie Russell's grandparents had rather discouraged book learning, Norbert Wiener's father gave a press conference at his birth in 1894 to announce that the child was to be turned through forced book reading into a genius. So Wiener was put at age nine into a high school class where the average age was sixteen; he graduated from university at age fourteen; and then went to Harvard graduate school. He was driven from the age of one by lessons at home that, Wiener recorded in his autobiography, began

in an easy conversational tone. This lasted exactly until I made the first mathematical mistake. Then the gentle and loving father was replaced by the avenger of blood. The first warning he gave of my unconscious delinquency was a very sharp and aspirated "What?" . . . By this time I was weeping and terrified. . . . My lessons ended in a family scene. Father was raging, I was weeping and my mother did her best to defend me, although hers was a losing battle. She suggested at times that the noise was disturbing the neighbors and that they had come to the door to complain.

With that sort of upbringing the brilliant Wiener immatured with age, right from his terror in the nursery to his death at sixty-nine (in Stockholm, which his enemies said he was visiting to lobby to get the Nobel Prize).

When the twenty-two-year-old Johnny reached Göttingen in 1926, the thirty-one-year-old Wiener had just flounced out of it, after having accused his professors (especially the great Richard Courant) of plagiarizing from his work. Young Johnny would have regarded any plagiarism by such a professor as flattery. Wiener wrote a novel, fortunately and naturally never published, about an old professor, meant to be Courant, who stole young men's ideas as his own. His autobiography had to be emaciated by libel lawyers. He accused so many of so much.

Because Johnny had a genuine admiration for Wiener's mind, which he suspected might be intrinsically better than his own, he cooperated in the latter's cybernetics initiatives after 1945, which had obvious implications for the ways computers might go. But Johnny wanted to point out his belief that biology was soon likely to advance through the study of cells (i.e., Johnny foresaw the decoding of DNA), so he prepared a long letter in the late 1940s to explain where he thought Wiener was in one respect going wrong. He agonized over sending this letter because a mutual friend gave warning that Wiener's boiling resentments made him "utterly unsuited to meticulous step by step analytical-experimental staircase procedures." The letter was dispatched and had the feared result. Wiener doodled ostentatiously during Johnny's subsequent lectures on the subject and pretended to fall asleep.

Almost inevitably Wiener reacted to free men's victory in 1945 in a way that got Johnny's goat. Wiener wished that the nuclear bomb should be instantly disinvented, and the world stopped so that he could get off. He was especially horrified that the next war might be with the Soviet Union. "I have no intention of letting my services be used in such a conflict," he said in October 1945. Two days later he wrote a letter of resignation to the president of MIT, in which he stated his intention "to leave scientific work completely and finally. I shall try to find some way of living on my farm in the country. I am not too sanguine of success, but I see no other course which accords with my conscience." The letter, although written and preserved, was of course never acted on because Wiener had soon moved on from this depressive stage into a new manic one about his next brilliant intended project.

None of these sadnesses should be taken by anybody, except shallow Blimps, as aspersions on the intellectual brilliance of Russell or Wiener or the many other mathematical scientists of similar genre. But it is more restful to have thoughtful scholars who are driven by calm observation of current facts rather than by passions like great winds, blowing hither and thither, on a wayward course, over a deep ocean of anguish, reaching the very verge of despair.

◄►◄►

Johnny was not waywardly wafted by such winds. Although many contemporaries regarded him as a warmonger, history will more logically say that Johnny was just about the only great mathematician of the twentieth century whom most people might reasonably have elected to have a considerable say in running a superpower (or, indeed, a whelk stall). From the beginning Johnny saw mathematics as a road into logic. He believed, with others, that mathematics really began when our primitive ancestors turned from merely counting how many beans made five to realizing that "two of anything plus two of anything else equalled four, not just usually but all the time." This was the crucial advance in human reasoning power. Dogs, gorillas, dolphins, and the sorts of politician you and I vote against have not noticed it even yet.

Once people saw that two plus two always equals four, the notation existed for very clever people to find what other things always happen: in other words, for advances to other abstract proofs. Unfortunately, those clever people too often hasten to escape from us grosser folk, and to make their subject as nearly as possible a free construct of the human mind. Even when a problem is suggested by happenings in the real world of external events, or the real world of throwing dice, a brilliant mathematician's urge can be to cut the tie as quickly as possible. He or she seeks to deal with the problem as totally abstracted from real events as it is possible to make it. Some mathematical economists have ruined their science in the same way.

Johnny always wanted to resist that urge. He preached that there were three stages in the history of a mathematical idea. They might be called the practical, the aesthetic, and healthy recognition of the absurd.

◄►◄►

In the first stage, he argued heretically, "all mathematical ideas originate in empirics, although the genealogy is sometimes long and obscure." Empirical means based on observation and experiment, not on abstract proof. Some pure and abstract mathematicians were angry when he said that. So were scientists in other disciplines who thought they had advanced into making their sciences properly mathematical, but were constantly told by Johnny that they had not. Johnny came closest to explaining his early obsession with axiomatizing—or rendering mathematically rigorous—everything he touched when he expostulated in what he called an "improvised and unsystematic" contribution during a 1949 seminar on aerodynamics:

> This subject [aerodynamics] has been considered, in the classical literature as well as in the more recent literature, on widely varying levels of rigor and of its opposite. . . . It is quite difficult ever to be sure of anything in this domain. Mathematically one is in a continuous state of uncertainty, because the usual theorems of existence and uniqueness of a solution, which one would like to have, have never been demonstrated and are probably not true in their obvious forms. . . .

He continued by quoting some of the things said by eminent people in aerodynamics ("this argument sounds convincing, but it is wrong"). He concluded, "There probably exists a set of conditions under which one and only one solution exists in every reasonably stated problem. However we have only surmises as to what it is and we have to be guided almost entirely by physical intuition in searching for it. It is therefore impossible to be very specific about any point. And it is difficult to say about any solution which has been derived, with any degree of assurance, that it is the one which must exist in nature."

Because aerodynamicists were just then getting jet aircraft to fly through the speed of sound, some of them were rather cross. But Johnny's interest in this subject has helped to save lives even into the 1990s. Today aircraft are designed on his computers, with rigorous mathematics and usually without test pilots having to be killed. And we are less liable in the computer age to spend billions on devising an aircraft that cannot actually fly.

Johnny was helped in his urge to make mathematics practical because his first postgraduate home was in Göttingen, where there were (see chap. 6) so many brilliant physicists around. They were not, initially, welcoming physicists. A British chancellor of the exchequer once said that an economist is a man who "can tell you 394 ways to make love, but has never actually met a woman." Physicists at Göttingen in 1926 were a bit inclined to regard mathematicians the same way, and Johnny had a certain sympathy with them. But he soon saw—and in later years insisted—that in one respect physicists are lucky. Top theoretical physicists, he said, are almost always engaged in trying to solve certain specific problems—usually only a small number of them, often arising from a need to resolve a difficulty or exploit an opportunity when empirical experiments in physics have thrown up some interesting or puzzling results. This gives them exhilarating opportunities for togetherness. We will see this when we turn to Johnny's part in developing the A-bomb in 1943–45.

By contrast, mathematicians are rarely in the position of having a specific common problem to solve, of joining together in a jolly hunt for some targeted truth. Johnny thought he was leading such a long-established joint hunt when he was trying to axiomatize set-theory mathematics at the beginning of his career, but later he saw he was wrong. More usually, said Johnny, a mathematician "has a wide variety of fields to which he may turn, and he enjoys a very considerable freedom in what he does with them." In musing how a mathematician makes his lonely choices, in this second stage of the development of a mathematical idea, Johnny came to the relaxed and very Johnny-ish conclusion that the decisions "are mainly aesthetical."

He explained his own motivations when making his big advances in pure mathematics in the 1920s and 1930s with a calm man's excitement springing from each sentence:

One expects a mathematical theorem or a mathematical theory not only to describe and classify in a simple and elegant way numerous and a priori disparate special cases. One also expects elegance in its architectural, structural make-up. The ease in stating the problem, great difficulty in getting hold of it and in all attempts at approaching it, then again some very surprising twists by which the approach, or some part of the approach, becomes easy. . . . If the deductions are lengthy or complicated there should be some simple general principle involved, which explains the complications and details, reduces the apparent arbitrariness to a few simple guiding motivations. . . . These criteria are clearly known to any creative art, and the existence of some underlying empirical worldly motif in the background—often in a very remote background overgrown by subsequent developments and followed into a multitude of labyrinthine variants—all this is much more akin to the atmosphere of art pure and simple than to that of the empirical sciences.

One reason why Johnny remained cheerful and practical is that even in the early 1920s he was getting aesthetic relaxation as he roamed fancy-free through pure mathematics. He enjoyed precisely those fields (such as Cantor's contradictions) that worried some more obsessed people sick. Johnny recommended that pure mathematicians feel patient rather than guilty. For example, he said, many parts of differential geometry and group theory were "certainly conceived as abstract, non-applied disciplines and almost always cultivated in this spirit. After a decade in one case, and a century in the other, they turned out to be very useful in physics."

But Johnny had helpful braking signals, because of his sensitive antennae for—and sense of—the absurd. He was always ready to mutter "nebbitch one" or "nebbitch two" or "nebbitch three" against his own work. So, in discussing the third stage of any mathematical idea, he annoyed a lot of his cleverest colleagues when he wrote:

As a mathematical discipline travels far from its empirical source. . . . it is beset with very grave dangers. It becomes more and more purely aestheticising, more and more purely l'art pour l'art. This need not be bad if the field is surrounded by correlated subjects which still have close empirical connections, or if the discipline is under the influence of men who have an exceptionally well-developed taste. But there is a grave danger that the subject will develop along the line of least resistance, that the stream so far from its source will separate into a multitude of insignificant branches, and that a discipline will become a disorganised mass of details and complexities. In other words, a great distance from its empirical source, or after much abstract inbreeding, a mathematical subject is in danger of degeneration. At the inception the style is usually classical. When it shows signs of becoming baroque, then the danger signal is up. It would be very easy to give examples, to take specific evolutions into a baroque and very high baroque. . . . Whenever this stage is reached the only remedy seems to me to be the rejuvenating return to the source: the re-injection of more or less directly empirical ideas.

In 1926 the physicists in Göttingen—then thrillingly involved in the discovery of quantum mechanics—were about to help him in such a reinjection.

◄►◄►

We turn now to this chapter's third gulp in assessing Johnny's effectiveness: to discussing what he carefully learned from history: starting with ancient Greece and ending with his own account of the frog-mouse battle, into which he soared with such strong young wings in 1921–26 and so spectacularly crashed.

This will involve galloping breathlessly through the past twenty-five hundred years in the next dozen pages, and making comparisons between Johnny and men as towering as Aristotle, Galileo, and Newton. Neither Johnny nor even this biography would pretend he had the brainpower of such as those three. But he interestingly did make study of their processes of thought, the reasons for their effectiveness, and their public-relations mistakes. Pioneering mathematicians at the frontiers of their science, such as Johnny, do feel some glee that they are daily adding ideas that were not quite thought of by the most remarkable minds of the past two and a half millennia. As a classical scholar, Johnny felt this to high degree, but he was also intrigued at the pitfalls into which his greater predecessors sometimes fell.

According to verbal tradition, the very words "mathematics" (meaning that which is learned) and "philosophy" (love of wisdom) were first used in about 500 B.C. by Pythagoras, who also proclaimed, "all is number," and thus asserted the importance of arithmetic (meaning to do with numbers) over geometry (meaning measurement of the earth), even though it is for his geometrical theorem about the hypoteneuse that every schoolchild hears of him. Johnny accorded with Pythagoras in finding it easier to calculate in numbers instead of shapes, and was admiring because these ancients did not really have manageable numbers in which to think. It was not easy for a Roman to multiply in his head CCLXV by XLIV, still less to manipulate Egyptian numbers where the symbol for one hundred was a coiled rope, for one thousand a lotus blossom, for ten thousand a pointed finger, for one hundred thousand a tadpole, and for one million a man stretching his arms to the heavens in astonishment. For the Egyptians 3,456,789 would not be a nice round and divisible number, but would be shown by three amazed men, four tadpoles, five pointed fingers, six lotus blossoms, seven coiled ropes, eight circles, and nine vertical lines. An economist analyzing the current (1992) U.S. budget deficit would have to start by drawing around four hundred thousand pictures of amazed men.

Pythagoras has been variously described as mathematician, astronomer, philosopher, liberal, fascist, saint, worshipper of black magic, scholar, charlatan, prophet, propagandist, and extraordinary nut. Like a number of later and often-unorthodox mathematicians, he was a strict vegetarian, but for an unusual reason. He believed in the transmigration of souls and did not want to eat the body of an animal that might be the abode of the soul of a dead friend. The American historian Carl Boyer says that after the Pythagoreans "mathematics was more closely related to a love of wisdom than to the exigencies of practical life; and it has had this tendency ever since." Johnny regretted this part of the Pythagorean influence. He had his share of Pythagorean colleagues at Princeton when he started to build what some said would be his noisy computing machine.

Socrates, who was made to kill himself with the hemlock a century after Pythagoras in 399 B.C., had little regard for mathematics, which he regarded as a muddling factor in his search for all that is good. In the hours before his death he pondered whether the language called mathematics had yet evolved into its most useful form, which is what Johnny also pondered on his deathbed 2,350 years later. But Socrates' student and admirer, Plato, wrote above the door of his academy, "Let nobody ignorant of geometry enter here," and Plato and his younger contemporary Aristotle (died 322 B.C.) were makers of both mathematicians and philosophers. To some extent Aristotle invented pure mathematics by seeing that mathematicians' primary question needs to be: not What do we know? but How do we know it? Johnny deeply admired Aristotle. He was trying to be nice when in 1931 he called his own conqueror Gödel "the greatest philosopher since Aristotle."

The four Greeks mentioned so far (plus Archimedes) had more deeply inquiring minds than the rigorous Euclid, who came to the University of Alexandria just before 300 B.C. not as a researcher, not as an administrator, but as a good teacher—which too few universities still have. Euclid masterfully codified the teaching of others on How do we know it? in the thirteen chapters of his *Elements*, a book that arouses envy among us authors even today. It has remained a textbook from which geometry has been taught to the young for twenty-three centuries, which this book will not. *Elements* has gone through more editions and printings than any other book except the Christian Bible, and has survived the usual gross mishandling by subeditors, including a particularly annoying one in about A.D. 400. It helped establish the rigorous and axiomatic methods on which teaching of logic since the Greeks has most often been based.

In a method still faithfully followed by Johnny in his papers in the 1920s, Euclid began by defining what he intended to deal with. Then he put forth certain assertions about the universe in general, and about mathematics in particular, with which he felt confident that nobody was likely to argue. Euclid then developed by logical definitions and axioms the whole of geometry as it was understood in his time, and a bit more. He thereby asserted that the most extravagant of theorems, remote as they might be from direct perception or intuition, derived their validity from his bare-bones axioms and were thenceforth imposed on the belief of any man.

Critics still thunder that the Euclidean system is arrogant, dictatorial, cramping, blinkered, and restrictive in tying us to Euclidean notions of space and time, some of which have unsurprisingly proved to be as wrong as most other notions held in 300 B.C. Because Euclid liked shapes formed by straight lines, since these and circles were the easiest to write axioms about, anti-Euclideans say most of us still live too rigidly in cubes and rectangles, in square rooms in rectangular houses in square city blocks. We anchor our minds in thinking that is too straight-line and two-dimensional. We suppose that everything we experience stems from logical cause and effect, although poets and artists know that it does not.

Johnny had no sympathy with such anti-Euclideans. He himself could adapt theorems so that he did not need to think in two-dimensional terms when using Euclid's axioms. He could play with them while thinking in terms of infinite dimensions, and was rather rude to those who could not. And he was very serious when he said several times why the mathematics inherited from the classical Greeks had been crucial to the development of civilization. The great virtues were that mathematics remained rigorously free from emotional content, free from ethical content, and free from political content. It allowed people to try to rise to the top by being reasoning scientists and scholars, instead of being bullying politicians or priests.

The Euclidean system of axiomatic search for truth really is a main reason why countries from the European tradition (including the United States) were the first into continuing technological revolution, the first into fast-rising standards of living, the first to escape from tyranny and tribal societies to some tolerance and scientific manner. There are big advantages in having a tradition passed down from revered ancients that clever men should think axiomatically, in terms of "if we do this, the logical result should be this, and then this."

Most other early societies missed this. Even the ancient (well, pre-European) Chinese inventors of gunpowder, printing, and compasses never tried to attain philosophical understanding of why their inventions worked; that is one reason why their progress faltered. In cruder tribal societies that do not have Euclidean traditions the cleverest people do not aspire to become scientists and scholars, but to be witch doctors and voodoo tribal kings. Later versions of such unmathematical societies then make frightened and superstitious people believe that wisdom equals their present private dogmatism (whether called Christ's Holy Inquisition or Marxism-Leninism or letting sleeping dogs lie). Leaders of such societies then rely on that fear and superstition to get rid of more inquiring minds who might otherwise take these tribal dictators' places.

Johnny always preferred to put his pro-Euclid views in gentle jokes, rather than in assaults on either bishops or bolsheviks, but he knew his European history well. Various religions, ending with Christianity, did have too much influence through Europe's dark ages, from A.D. 400 to nearly 1400, when knowledge did not advance much. Christian bishops did not deal kindly with minds brilliant enough to challenge conventional common sense. The Middle Ages' brightest British scientist, Roger Bacon (circa 1220–92), was groping toward discovering some of the Newtonian secrets of light and also (as Johnny did) toward making the killing of people more economic, through his formula for gunpowder; Bacon was briefly imprisoned for dabbling in black magic. But mathematics did win through to have the main influence in Europe's eventual technological revolution, which can plausibly be dated from an evening in 1583 when a nineteen-year-old mathematical monk (later to breed lots of illegitimate children) went to prayers in Pisa Cathedral.

Galileo Galilei was born in Italy in 1564 (the same year that William Shakespeare was born in England), and he died in 1642 (the same year that Newton was born in England). From his Pisa pew in 1583, through measuring time against his pulse, it is said that Galileo noticed that an erratically swaying lamp above the altar completed both its wider and narrower swings in the same time. He thereby saw that the time taken by a pendulum's swing varies not with the distance it covers but with the pendulum's length. This discovery made it possible to invent accurate clocks. Within three decades after Galileo's death the average error of the best clocks was reduced from at least fifteen minutes a day to under ten seconds a day. Daniel Boorstin (the former librarian of Congress) is right to say that clocks were the mother of machines. They brought the first precision machine tools, such as the screw and the gear or toothed wheel. They enabled time to enter into technology as a new dimension and thus switched science from statics to dynamics.

Like Archimedes and Johnny, Galileo became a professor of mathematics and then the most scientific armorer of his adopted country. Just after the year 1600 some Dutch spectacle makers noticed that by looking simultaneously through convex and concave spectacle lenses, held at different distances from the eye, the weather vanes atop their Dutch churches were extraordinarily magnified, up to three times. In 1609 they were trying to sell this technology to Venice because it would help it to ward off naval attacks. If from the top of the Campanile you could identify a ship that was two hours' sailing away, this was also of use to speculators against Shylock on the Rialto. Venice asked Galileo whether the Dutchmen's spyglass could be improved, and Galileo instantly rearranged the lenses so that they would magnify objects up to ten times. The analogy is irresistible with the army ordnance department's electronic computer in 1944 before and after Johnny looked at it.

Galileo then turned his new telescope on to the heavens and espied the moons of Jupiter. Behold, they moved. And Galileo soon calculated why the Earth also did. This was not what he had expected. A prominent mathematician had recently and apparently reasonably declared, as Daniel Boorstin recorded:

Nobody in his senses, or imbued with the slightest knowledge of physics, will ever think that the Earth, heavy and unwieldy from its own weight and mass, staggers up and down around its own center and that of the sun; for at the slightest jar of the Earth we would see cities and fortresses, towns and mountains thrown down. . . . If the Earth were to be moved neither an arrow shot straight up nor a stone dropped from the top of a tower would fall perpendicularly but either ahead or behind.

It therefore did not seem unscientific to most of his contemporaries that Galileo (who had annoyed the church in other matters anyway) was eventually shown the awful instruments of torture of the Inquisition and was required to kneel in the Vatican and recant: to apologize for his heresy that "the sun is the center of the world and immobile and that the Earth is not the center and moves."

Would Johnny have similarly recanted if some dictator had shown him instruments of torture, and asked him to deny his latest tenets in von Neumann algebra? My impression is that he would have recanted like a shot, while some of the mathematicians to whom this chapter has been ruder (like Russell and Wiener) would not have. But I also think this would have been entirely logical of Johnny. He would have argued that Galileo's truths were already written down, and that bright minds would soon carry them further. This argument proved correct. On Christmas Day of the year that Galileo died, Newton was born.

◄►◄►

Even more than Galileo, and certainly more than Johnny, Newton was a mathematician who hugely changed history. So, for this biography, the comparisons with Johnny intrigue, particularly because astrologers would say they were both Christmas babes.

Newton had no Max to give him a happy and educated childhood. Newton's mother dumped him in infancy in a remote Lincolnshire farm with her own mother. Shortly after the death of Isaac's illiterate father, she was marrying a clergyman whom the infant would annoy. She wanted Isaac to leave school to earn his living at the age of eleven, but he found a local schoolmaster to champion him (some rural Ratz?) and went to Cambridge as a poor working scholar in 1662.

Like the equally rural Lord Rutherford (1871–1937), Newton was sufficiently practical to cut delays by making his own equipment, which Johnny was not. Like Johnny, Newton was conservative in politics and enjoyed holding dignified government posts. Indeed Newton—whose illiterate father could not have become a "von"—pretended to have aristocratic ancestors, whom he had simply invented. Like Johnny from ages seventeen to nineteen in 1921–23, Newton from ages twenty-two to twenty-four in 1665–67 had two relaxed years that he turned immensely productive. The Great Plague hit Britain in the year of his Cambridge graduation (1665), and he went to his family's remote farm to avoid it. While there, he started on his three greatest discoveries: the laws of gravity and motion, the mathematical nature of color (the poet Keats complained that Newton destroyed all the poetry of the rainbow), and his part in the infinitesimal calculus.

Would Johnny, if he were isolated in Lincolnshire in 1665–67, have stumbled or reasoned his way to such discoveries? On one of them, that seems to me plausible. Johnny's mind was the sort that could in 1665–67 have begun to think through toward the secrets of gravity. Or, at least, if some lesser minds had suggested the subject, he could have leaped five blocks ahead of them toward the solutions. Johnny's picnic trick (see chap. 1), in quickly calculating the heat per square foot of nearby earth outside the shade, had some similarities with Newton's calculations when theorizing about that famous falling apple. Indeed Johnny and Newton used some of the same favorite mathematical constants. Newton hypothesized that if the apple was being attracted toward the center of the earth and was crashing down, while the moon (which was a known distance from the earth) fortunately was not, then it should be possible to work out the equations of forces acting on them. If the moon was sixty times as far from the center of the earth as the apple was, his inverse-square laws suggested that the moon should have one-thirty-six-hundredth of the acceleration of the apple (thirty-six hundred is sixty squared).

Although Newton's original figures got the radius of the earth wrong, his eventual correction of them worked so well that his equations accurately explained the motions of planets (including planets discovered since his day), of flying bullets, spinning tops, and moving machinery. It was therefore possible to carry through quite an industrial revolution on the basis of the mathematics that Newton worked out. Once the calculus to formulate his concepts was in place, his work provided the language and the tool for most subsequent branches of physics, including electricity, acoustics, optics, and even (see next chap.) Erwin Schrödinger's version of quantum mechanics. It would therefore be nice for all the world (except those who had to meet Newton—a nasty man) if we could get lots of his like again.

Johnny was always aware that he could not show even a fraction of the originality that enabled Newton to do all these things, but he hoped at the end that his computers might issue in an age when more Newtons could come. He thought the time could soon be ripe for them. Physics in 1660–1950 had been very lucky that the mathematics appearing in Newton's day had been so suitable for it. One day, Johnny believed, the equivalent of infinitesimal calculus would arrive to make social sciences such as economics less ignorant than they are now. At least one of Newton's contemporaries, Germany's Baron Gottfried Wilhelm von Leibniz (1646–1716), was moving toward discovering the calculus at about the same pace as Newton.

The axioms that Euclid had passed down made insufficient contribution to analysis of the movement of an object. By 1667 we had need of a math which dealt with the idea of change and which could describe quantitatively all the rates of change: such as velocity, which is the rate at which distance traveled is changing; acceleration, which is the rate at which velocity is changing; curvature, which describes the rate at which slope is changing; and lots more. This is what calculus provided. The trick was to devise mathematical notations for any change of any sort in the tiniest possible next moment of time and to give intellectual rigor to that.

A lot of mathematicians, including Newton himself, worried that calculus was not instantly in a shape of which Euclid would have approved. It is worth noting what Johnny, supposedly the stern axiomatizer, thought about this criticism.

He ridiculed it. He accepted the argument that "the first formulations of the calculus were not even mathematically rigorous. An inexact, semi-physical foundation was the only one available for 150 years after Newton." Johnny then pointed out that it was during this period (1730–1880), against this inexact and mathematically inadequate background, that the main takeoff into mathematically based industrial revolution took place.

Johnny had a surprising answer to those who debated whether the next technological advances would best be based on Euclidean mathematical rigor or Newton's dilution of it or Cantor's set theories. He thought they were much the same thing. Newton's principal work, he said, was "in literary form as well as in the essence of some of its most critical points, very much like Euclid." Johnny agreed that Newton based himself also on physical insight and experimental verification, but he thought intriguingly "that a similar interpretation of Euclid is possible, especially from the viewpoint of antiquity, before geometry had acquired its present bimillennial stability and authority—an authority which the modern edifice of theoretical physics is clearly lacking." That is why he passionately believed that there was never any case for excluding even unrigorous first-class mathematics from everyday use, which may be why he entered the frog-mouse battle (unlike his more successful later battles) leading with his chin.

It is true that in his early undergraduate writings Johnny was inclining to Hilbert's (and Leibniz's) Germanic assumption that mathematics could solve most of man's mysteries for him. English Newton did not. Newton never believed that he or any other mathematician was getting near to discovering the "great ocean of truth." Newton described himself as "only like a boy playing on the seashore, and diverting myself in now and then finding a smoother pebble or a prettier shell than ordinary." This was very close to Johnny's later-in-life self-appraisal that his own motives when exploring pure mathematics were "mainly aesthetic."

Newton eventually deserted pure mathematics to serve the British government lucratively as warden of the Royal Mint (i.e., controller of the currency), and also to write more than a million words of pro-establishment (in the end, disgracefully anti-Catholic) theology, trying weirdly by astronomical history to establish the literal truth of events in the Bible. Johnny would have said that, at this end, Newton had descended into the very high baroque.

Sadly Newton, despite his depth and adaptability of thought, was probably always liable thus to descend. His childhood had not left him stable in temperament. He was roundly and rightly disliked by almost everybody who intimately knew him. He got other people to sign papers accusing Leibniz of having plagiarized everything about calculus from him, although Newton had actually written these papers of accusation himself. As a result of his many insults, British mathematicians were to some extent alienated from mathematicians in mainland Europe through the eighteenth and even nineteenth centuries. This meant that British mathematics fell behind German mathematics, just when nineteenth-century British industry was going ahead of continental

European industry, but also when German professors were becoming nationalistically more xenophobic.

◄►◄►

By the early 1920s, when Johnny arrived in Göttingen, these German nationalist emotions were understandably in flow. He found it convenient to sign himself "von Neumann." Some of his popularity in Germany sprang from the fact that he was devaluing Englishmen such as Russell and Sir Arthur Eddington (who patronized Einstein while helping him experimentally to establish relativity theory, but who did not understand much mathematics thereafter). Still, Johnny's own description of his part as Hilbert's standard-bearer in the frog-mouse battle did not show himself, ex post, as an impassioned pioneer. He saw that he had been picking up pretty seashells on the shore. The convention used below is to put Johnny's own words about the frog-mouse battle in quotes, while the pieces outside quotes seem reasonable summaries of what he at some stage implied.

"In the late 19th and early 20th centuries," wrote Johnny in 1950, "a new branch of abstract mathematics, G. Cantor's theory of sets, led into difficulties. That is, certain reasonings led to contradictions; and, while these reasonings were not in the central and useful part of set theory, and were always easy to spot by certain formal criteria, it was nevertheless not clear why they should be deemed less set theoretical than the successful parts of the theory." In this situation Brouwer developed a system of mathematics in which "the difficulties and contradictions of set theory did not arise. However, a good 50% of modern mathematics, in its most vital—and up to then unquestioned—parts, especially in analysis, were also affected by this purge: they either became invalid or had to be justified by very complicated subsidiary considerations."

It is difficult to overestimate the significance of these events, said Johnny. As Johnny entered the profession of mathematician in the 1920s, Brouwer and Weyl, "two mathematicians—both of them of the first magnitude, and as deeply and fully conscious of what mathematics is, or is for, or is about, as anybody could be

—actually proposed that the concept of mathematical rigor, of what constitutes an exact proof, should be changed." The developments that followed, said Johnny, could be divided into four parts:

"First, only a very few mathematicians were willing to accept the new, exigent standards for their own daily use. Very many admitted that Weyl and Brouwer were prima facie right, but they themselves continued to do their mathematics in the old easy fashion."

"Second, Hilbert came forward and proposed what some mathematicians had to do to satisfy Brouwer and Weyl. . . . Various mathematicians made . . . a decade of attempts to carry out Hilbert's programme." Here Johnny was too modest. He himself, starting from his teenage years, made a main attempt.

After Russell escaped from his near nervous breakdown in 1901, the Englishman had sought to remedy the contradictions in his "class of all the things that are" by writing enormous tomes about them. The huge volumes of *Principia Mathematica* by Russell and Alfred North Whitehead (published in 1910–13) did largely remedy these contradictions, but in a way that was ponderous, partly unusable, and (thought xenophobic Germans just after the 1914–18 war) very English and absurd. This was the problem tackled by Johnny in his original "An Axiomatization of Set Theory" (published 1925 but written earlier) and then his fuller "The Axiomatization of Set Theory" (published 1928 but written earlier). Johnny's papers were a great relief to every German student who had not yet bought and struggled through Russell and Whitehead's tomes. In effect, said German and some American professors, Johnny had replaced Russell and Whitehead's thick volumes with axioms that could be set down on a single printed page of paper.

Johnny's system had no need of Russell and Whitehead's baroque structure of types and orders and hierarchies of propositions. Johnny replaced most of these by redefining two concepts: sets and classes. All sets are classes, but some classes (such as the universal one that worried Russell) are not sets. Johnny said that a set exists (this implies it does not lead to contradictions) if, and only if, the multitude of its elements is not of the same cardinality as the multitude of all things.

At the same time as presenting a peace treaty for the frog-mouse battle, some Germans hoped that young Johnny had thereby shown that Hilbert's program could be fulfilled. They wanted to think that the undergraduate was introducing new mathematical techniques, whereby all the regions previously abandoned to waffle could be conquered for analysis by precise formulas. Johnny never made any such claims. He was grateful that he did not, because of the third development in the frog-mouse battle.

In that third development, said Johnny, Gödel became the first man to demonstrate that certain mathematical theorems can never be proved nor disproved with rigorous methods of mathematics. Gödel did this, in effect, by expressing in mathematical form an assertion something like "The following statement is unprovable." Once he had said that in mathematical language, it clearly was no longer possible to prove everything by mathematics alone. Johnny instantly saw the truth and importance of Gödel's work, which a lot of other people did not.

There was some interest in how Russell would react to Gödel in his autobiography thirty-five years later. He reacted in what is sadly a typical way for mathematicians who were not sufficiently loved in childhood. He emitted one growl ("Gödel turned out to be an unadulterated Platonist, and apparently believed that an eternal 'not' was laid up in heaven, where virtuous logicians might hope to meet it hereafter") and one whine ("the followers of Gödel had almost persuaded me that the 29 man-years spent on the Principia had been wasted," he wrote to a New York lady in 1963, and he rejoiced she was not among them).

Johnny was much more relaxed in describing the fourth stage of the frog-mouse battle. He wrote: "Fourth, the main hope of a justification of classical mathematics . . . being gone, most mathematicians decided to use that [classical] system anyway. After all, classical mathematics was producing results which were both elegant and useful, and, even though one could never again be absolutely certain of its reliability, it stood on at least as sound a foundation as, for example, the existence of the electron. Hence, if one was willing to accept the sciences, one might as well accept the classical system of mathematics." Johnny said this showed a shocking lack of rigor among the majority of mathematicians, but he felt in no position to attack them "because I was one of them." He added that he had told the story of the four stages of the frog-mouse battle "in such detail because I think it constitutes the best caution against taking the immovable rigor of mathematics too much for granted. This happened in our own lifetime, and I know myself how humiliatingly easily my own views regarding the absolute mathematical truth changed during this episode, and how they changed three times in succession."

Some people have taken this admission as a sign that Johnny considered he had wasted the early years of his academic life. He felt no such waste. Nor should the world, because Johnny's early cold bath in mathematical logic helped later in the development of the digital computer. There, too, there was required an innate mastery of sequential operations.

Our version of the computer story (chap. 11) accords sympathy to the finer of the two engineers who felt they would have earned greater royalties if Johnny-come-lately had not looked at their pioneering wartime model of the computer—and then jumped ahead of it. By 1944 electronics had reached the stage where there was need of a genius who was accustomed to saying that this should follow from this. Computers needed the last great axiom-atizer. In Johnny they got it. He even borrowed with glee from "the greatest philosopher since Aristotle." There is a parallel be-tween Gödel's encoding of logical statements as numbers and John-ny's encoding of computer instructions as numbers.

This continuing glee explains why it is also untrue that Johnny felt any depression at some of his stumbles in the 1920s. He felt exactly the opposite.

In 1926, the youthful Johnny entered professional mathematics at a time of beautifully rising yeast. The world was in the process of profound conceptual change, in which the verities of the cen-turies were being dismissed by Einstein and the discoverers of quantum theory in the most exact of the natural sciences; by Freud and (some thought) Marx in the behavioral sciences. It was a world of enormous material change and extraordinary impetus for conceptual innovation. The telephone, the radio, the airplane, developments from the cathode ray tube, each added to the pace at which knowledge accumulated and could be put to work making new knowledge. On top of this, there was in 1926 a surge of political confidence. A war that had seemed endless, and that had been waged at enormous material and emotional cost, had come to an end. The postwar miseries, such as inflation and fear of the spread of militarism, seemed in 1926 to be ending also. Perhaps energies could be turned to other matters. Mathematics, closely associated with the ego as it must be, had always been a highly competitive enterprise. It promised to engage greater and greater numbers of intense competitors.

It was that kind of world that Johnny embraced at the age of twenty-two and that occupied the forefront of his attention until the resumption of world war in 1939 began to demand his talents for other matters. He also happened to arrive at Göttingen just when Werner Heisenberg was discovering quantum mechanics.

The Quantum
Leap, 1926–32

▶◀ **W**hen Johnny arrived in Göttingen in the early autumn of 1926, the university was in a happy ferment. In 1925 Göttingen's freckled twenty-three-year-old wunderkind Werner Heisenberg—who was still apt to walk about in the shorts of the German youth movement—had devised what his professors called "quantum mechanics." In 1926 Erwin Schrödinger, working from Switzerland, had appeared to say that Heisenberg's formulation was completely wrong.

In Johnny's early weeks at Göttingen in 1926 (although some say on a special visit a few months earlier), Heisenberg lectured on the difference between his and Schrödinger's theories. The aging Hilbert, professor of mathematics, asked his physics assistant, Lothar Nordheim, what on earth this young man Heisenberg was talking about. Nordheim sent to the professor a paper that Hilbert still did not understand. To quote Nordheim himself, as recorded in Heims's book: "When von Neumann saw this, he cast it in a few days into elegant axiomatic form, much to the liking of Hilbert." To Hilbert's delight, Johnny's mathematical exposition made much use of Hilbert's own concept of Hilbert space.

That last paragraph will require explanation of both quantum mechanics (straightaway, over these next few pages) and Hilbert space (tersely, later in the chapter). The story of quantum mechanics is the most arresting one in science in this century. It includes all the great names like Max Planck, Einstein, Niels Bohr, and a dozen others—a company that young Johnny was now about to join. A fine lay history of it appears in Richard Rhodes's book *The Making of the Atom Bomb*, to which this biography is several times indebted.

At the beginning of the twentieth century, scientists thought they understood many of the problems of electricity and magnetism, thanks to the equations of Britain's James Clerk Maxwell (1831 to a tragically early 1879). Maxwell showed how the wavelike disturbances in each electromagnetic field will travel outward at a fixed speed like the ripples caused by a stone thrown into a pond. When the wavelengths of these ripples (i.e., the distances between the crest of one wavelet and of the next) are a meter or more, they are what we now use as radio waves. If they are much smaller, anywhere between a 40,000,000th of a centimeter and half that, visible light will come from them. If they are shorter even than that, they can be ultraviolet rays or x rays or other useful or dangerous things. Einstein rightly called Maxwell's laws the "most important event in physics since Newton's time," but they did leave a lot of untidinesses still lying around.

One of these untidinesses was that Maxwell seemed to suggest that a hot object such as a star, or indeed anything that remained hot such as the inside of a kiln, should set its particles vibrating to send out energy at all frequencies (i.e., all wavelengths per second) equally. Because there are an infinite number of possible frequencies, this seemed to mean that the hot objects should be radiating infinite energy, which (*a*) would roast us all dead, and so (*b*) fortunately could not be true.

In 1900 the long-lived Berliner Planck (1858–1948) suggested that this must be because light, x rays, and other waves could be emitted only in certain packets, each of which he called "a quantum." In Latin, *quantum* is the neuter form of the word meaning "how much?" Each quantum has an amount of energy that varies with the frequency of the waves. At very high frequencies the emission of a single quantum traveling at near the speed of light requires more energy than is available, so there are not such waves to roast us dead.

Atomic physics, at this stage, was going into a state where the most learned atomic physicists were required to believe the impossible. The first splitter of the atom, the hymn-singing New Zealander Lord Rutherford, showed by his experiments that an atom operated like the solar system. It had a heavy nucleus (with a positive electric charge) around which electrons (i.e., particles with a negative electric charge) were smoothly circling. All normal physics said this could not be happening for long. Even in the case of the simplest atom—the hydrogen atom—the circling electron should emit radiation, lose energy, and fall into the nucleus.

In 1913 the young great Dane Niels Bohr, with considerable help from yet another of Johnny's fellow Hungarians, George de Hevesy, bounded in to solve the problem. Bohr saw that Planck's quantum discoveries must apply also to things with very small dimensions, such as the electrons circling around a nucleus. He calculated that the electrons had to make quantum jumps to different permitted orbits in ways that were controlled by Planck's arithmetic. That was why they did not fall into the nucleus.

Even at this stage Einstein thought that Bohr's quantum hypotheses were "insecure and contradictory." This was a pity because Einstein had himself contributed greatly to quantum theory, with his 1905 paper that explained photoelectric emission in terms of quanta. More important, Einstein's marvelous discoveries of the special and general theories of relativity (which explained the odd things that happen when something moves at near the speed of light) married well with what Bohr and others were discovering for things that are very small. Together they were pointing to new sorts of technology undreamed of in Newtonian mechanics.

132 ►◄ John von Neumann

Broadly, Newton's seventeenth-century laws of classical mechanics still hold true until something is moving very fast, when some of the rules of relativity begin to matter, or unless it is tiny, when quantum mechanics hold sway. That still leaves Newton ruling most of the field. Even if something is moving at ten times the speed of sound, it is affected by relativity rather than classical mechanics only in terms of less than one part in ten billion. Newton's laws also hold true for anything big enough for us to see. Even if a moving speck has a diameter of a thousandth of a millimeter, quantum corrections to its laws of motion are too small to measure. But, to quote Hendrik Casimir (born 1909), "Newton created a theory that enabled us to calculate the motions of planets and satellites, of thrown stones, of pendulums. . . . Quantum theory enabled us to describe the behavior of molecules, atoms and electrons." This allowed physicists of Casimir's generation to go forward into "the wonderful world of atomic physics" and to the electronic revolution. Casimir was later head of Holland's Philips Industries, which spread electronic wonders around the world. But—and this is why mathematical translators such as Johnny became important—from 1900 to the 1930s the intellectual giants of quantum theory were disagreeing with each other with academe's accustomed heat. This was partly because they were saying the same things in what looked like very different words.

Bohr spent the years of the 1914–18 war feeling "scientifically very lonesome" in Denmark. His forte did not lie in writing articles or books. He was the despair of his publishers because he ditheringly rewrote everything on proof, and usually toned it down so that it could mean practically nothing. His strength lay in talking with other scientists at seminars, getting them to redefine what they meant, sometimes greatly increasing their confidence but sometimes (as with America's poor Robert Oppenheimer) almost destroying it. Bohr, who won the Nobel Prize in 1922, remembered the early post-1919 years as a period when the lonesomeness miraculously passed away into the "unforgettable experience" of "unique co-operation of a whole generation of theoretical physicists from many countries."

Bohr's visitors to Copenhagen at this time included physicists from the new Soviet Union, a fact that caused Churchill to be worried about him in 1945. But Bohr's main cooperation in the 1920s was with the admirable team at Germany's Göttingen University. While Göttingen's mathematics department had Hilbert as an aging monarch and Courant acting as magnet for brilliant minds and money from all the world (especially from rich America), the physics department had become the best ever assembled in any university anywhere. Ten years before Hitler, and twenty years before the atomic age, this was rather terrifying, but nobody thought that at the time.

The head of physics at Göttingen was Max Born. He had been Hilbert's student as a mathematician. He kept rigorous mathematics and flighty physics sensibly together when at some other universities they were tending to be divorced. In addition to temporary grants for almost everybody later in the A-bomb's story (Fermi, Oppenheimer, Johnny, Wigner, and Teller), the permanent physicists at Göttingen in or just after 1926 included Wolfgang Pauli (a superb theoretician but in practical matters even clumsier than Johnny), James Franck (like Pauli a Nobel laureate), Pascual Jordan, and—as the youngest and perhaps most assiduous—Heisenberg, the son of a professor of classics. Brilliant Heisenberg was a man who really could have changed history and most dreadfully for ill. He was the leading scientific figure in Hitler's Germany through the 1939–45 war. His advice often went directly to the führer, whom he fortunately disliked. So Hitler did not pay full attention to him.

In 1922 undergraduate Heisenberg was brought by his professor at Munich (the great Arnold Sommerfeld) to hear a lecture that Bohr gave at Göttingen. He enthused about it for the rest of his life, as did many people who heard or met the Bohr of the 1920s. "Each one of [Bohr's] carefully formulated sentences seemed a long chain of underlying thoughts, of philosophical reflections, hinted at but never fully expressed. I found this approach highly exciting." But young Heisenberg was also percipient enough to disagree with one of Bohr's thoughts. He asked a question about it. Bohr, unlike Newton but like Johnny, adored students who made him rethink. He invited Heisenberg for a long walk with him that afternoon and urged that he come to see him in Copenhagen often.

Heisenberg came to Göttingen as a privatdocent (a lecturer who depended on students' fees, if he could attract them to his courses) after graduation from Munich. In May 1925 he wrote down what he hoped was a proper set of mathematical equations for the "strangely beautiful interior" of the atom, although he admitted that he was using some odd algebra of whose rigor he was uncertain. The mathematically minded Born assured him that the strange algebra was matrix algebra, of which Göttingen's own aging mathematics professor, Hilbert, had been a pioneer.

For the next three months Heisenberg, Born, and Jordan worked through the summer of 1925 together. By September they presented what Heisenberg hoped was "a coherent mathematical framework, one that promised to embrace all the multifarious aspects of atomic physics." Because they hoped that this formulation would make possible many things more marvelous than most people's frightened idea of atomic physics, they called the new subject they were conceiving "quantum mechanics." Heisenberg gave a lecture that summer in Britain's Cambridge, where Paul Dirac (the discoverer of antimatter) helped further mathematicize the new ideas. In Göttingen Pauli showed that the equations fitted the rather small experimental evidence available with a high degree of accuracy, and that they confirmed what Bohr had declared from his supposedly insecure and inconsistent assumptions in 1913. In Copenhagen Bohr, who habitually bounded up and down stairs three at a time, seemed liable to bound over the moon.

This formulation in 1925 won tumultuous applause from half of the academic world and a raspberry from the other half. The objections from physicists were initially most thoughtfully led by Schrödinger. The more ill-founded objections from some mathematicians were soon to be stilled by Göttingen's brand-new research student, Johnny. We should deal with Schrödinger's contribution first, which was admittedly much more important. Schrödinger was a charming Viennese then working in Switzerland. Like many other physicists, he was "frightened away by Heisenberg's algebra," so in 1926 he developed a theory based on physical properties of the atom that the usually polite Heisenberg at one stage called "disgusting." Schrödinger's view was that one could draw up wave equations for the electron that explained what was happening without necessarily having to bother with Heisenberg's or Bohr's or even Planck's quantum theories. The physicists at Göttingen and Copenhagen disliked that, but Schrödinger had some things on his side. He had worked through his ideas from a seemingly strange thesis by France's Louis de Broglie, which had the endorsement of Einstein. There was a direct line to his ideas from earlier work by Hilbert and Schmidt. Some mathematicians at Göttingen (who had disputed Born's assurance that Heisenberg was using orthodox Hilbert-invented matrix algebra) perked up their ears at this, although Göttingen physicists tried to flatten them.

It was soon shown mathematically that Schrödinger's equations fitted the experimental evidence—for example, correctly predicted the spectrum of the hydrogen atom—as well as Heisenberg's did. This mathematical proof was provided by our old friend from Zurich's ETH, "heiliger Hermann" Weyl, who at one stage had a friendship with Schrödinger's wife (the personalities were becoming as complicated as the mathematics). From Britain's Cambridge William Lawrence Bragg quipped amiably: "Here God runs electromagnetics on Monday, Wednesday and Friday by the wave theory; and the devil runs it by quantum theory on Tuesday, Thursday and Saturday." Sometimes it was easier to use Schrödinger's equations, sometimes Heisenberg's.

Once it became possible to put atoms and electrons to deliberate use, the world was going to change. It clearly was desirable that scientists should decide whether God was running the physical world one way or the devil another. Older physicists tended to prefer Schrödinger. Heisenberg went to question Schrödinger at a Munich seminar in the late summer of 1926, and the chairman (a Nobel laureate) told the uppity young Heisenberg "rather sharply that one must really put an end to quantum jumps and the whole atomic mysticism, and the difficulties I had mentioned would certainly soon be solved by Schrödinger." From Copenhagen Bohr and at Göttingen the newly arrived twenty-two-year-old graduate student Johnny reached a more logical conclusion. Because both the Heisenberg and Schrödinger equations were proving correct, they must actually be saying the same thing (as Schrödinger—to do him justice—early on nearly came round to agreeing, although not quite).

Rhodes recounts the next stage superbly. Bohr invited Schrödinger and Heisenberg together to Copenhagen, for a meeting that Heisenberg described with returned good humor. Although Bohr was a kind and obliging person, he was able in matters which he considered important "to insist fanatically and with almost terrifying relentlessness on complete clarity in all arguments." He was so relentless with Schrödinger that the latter sensibly retired ill to bed, but Bohr followed him. Sitting on the edge of the bed he would say, "But you must surely admit that . . . ?" "If one has to go on with damned quantum jumps," said poor Schrödinger, "then I'm sorry I ever started to work on atomic theory." Bohr was instantly obliging again, insisting that Schrödinger had made all physicists like Bohr think again, so the world was very grateful to him.

Bohr and Heisenberg then settled down together to see what points in both theories stayed weak: in particular, of course, the fact that both agreed with all the evidence, but that evidence was small. In February 1927, Bohr went on his annual skiing holiday. He undertook all physical exercise with a zeal that made Johnny shudder. Heisenberg went for a long walk through Copenhagen at night, by now no longer in leather shorts. He stumbled brilliantly onto what the world now knows as Heisenberg's uncertainty principle.

If you are going to study the velocity or position of something as tiny as a particle, you have to use some tool, such as shining light on it. If you do, as Planck had proved, you have to use at least one quantum of light. This is the tiniest possible quantity. But even one quantum of light will disturb a moving particle and change either its velocity or its position in a way that cannot be predicted. The more accurately you probe the position of a particle, the less accurately will you know its velocity, and vice versa.

A lot of intelligent people did not want to believe that anything as revolutionary as quantum mechanics does not enable one to predict a definite outcome from any measurement—that at best it tells us a number of different possible outcomes, and how likely each of these is. The objectors included Einstein with his cry, "God does not play dice." Bohr, as the guardian of Heisenberg's thinking, which now became known as that of the Copenhagen school, eventually replied sharply and in private to Einstein: "Nor is it our business to prescribe to God how He should run the world."

Johnny sailed into mathematical action in 1926 as an axiomatizer on behalf of the Copenhagen school. Critics of his writings on it, which culminated in the publication of his book *The Mathematical Foundations of Quantum Mechanics* (German edition published in 1932), say that dogmatic young Johnny far too often seemed to suggest that his formulation was "end of the road" and "complete." It should be said, deliberately and disarmingly, that Johnny agreed with these criticisms.

Nobody even now should pretend that the last word has been said on quantum mechanics. A modern system of visualizing them came later from the American physicist Feynman, whom Johnny regarded as tremendous fun. The tiniest of particles tries to get from point A to point B in space-time by every possible path. On a lot of the paths the way forward is blocked by whether the wavelets met are near crest or near trough. On some paths there are no blockages, and these are Bohr's permitted orbits. Since 1926, many other things have been discovered about particles. As Stephen Hawking said, a lot of Nobel Prizes (including by Johnny's later Princeton colleagues Lee and Yang) "have been awarded for showing that the universe is not as simple as we might have thought." It is likely that we will in time get a unified quantum theory—"a theory of everything," which Einstein was trying to grope toward in his last unproductive thirty years. But the critics misunderstand what young Johnny was rightly trying and managing to do sixty-six years ago.

◄►◄►

The twenty-two-year-old Johnny, at this birth of quantum mechanics in 1926, was a servant of the great but by then a bit obsolescent axiomatizing Hilbert. Johnny was also a young man who wanted to get on with the world. He saw at once, as did Bohr, that the similarity of the results of the apparently different arguments of Heisenberg and Schrödinger meant that they must really be saying the same thing. He was politer than Bohr in questioning people to confirm or refute this view, but more determined than Bohr to propagate the good news once his mind was made up. He saw that quantum mechanics could be used hugely for man's good. He did not want his own profession of mathematician to engage in another frog-mouse battle, with some mathematicians trying to block progress by saying that the great new discoveries were too unrigorous to use. Unfortunately, that is exactly what some mathematicians were starting to say.

Probably as a result of that first paper which he had written for Hilbert and Nordheim after Heisenberg's lecture in 1926, Johnny saw how Heisenberg's ideas could be made convincing to mathematicians. He felt that Schrödinger's scheme fitted readily into the same framework. Johnny's basic insight, which nobody else had, was (to quote Paul Halmos) "that the geometry of the vectors in a Hilbert Space has the same formal properties as the structure of the states of a quantum mechanical system."

This may sound appalling gobbledygook to the reader of this book. He or she (like the author) may have given up high school mathematics at about age fifteen. The following attempted explanation of Hilbert space is limpingly directed at him or her and me.

As a reasonably gross oversimplification, we may remember from before age fifteen that there were two ways in which one could solve such equations as $x + y = 12$ and $3x - y = 16$.

One way is to add the equations together. If you do this with these two equations—because I have chosen them that way—the y cancels out, so you get $4x = 28$, $x = 7$, and y (which is $12 - 7) = 5$. I trust you have now checked this back on the first two equations as you did early in high school. The advantage of mathematics as a science is that you can check whether you are right or wrong. You probably also remember that the second schoolchild way is to draw on any piece of graph paper the line joining the points where $x + y = 12$ (for example x at 11 and y at 1, x at 10 and y at 2, etc.). You will then find that the one place where that line crosses a line of points where $3x - y = 16$ is at the point where $x = 7$ and $y = 5$.

You can also perhaps imagine solving systems of equations with three unknowns—one, for example, beginning $x^2 + y^2 + z^2 = 29$, by going into three-dimensional space, through inserting a z axis by sticking a pen (or, better, something more flexible and wagglable into a sphere) through this piece of paper. You would then find that one of the possible answers is $x = 2$, $y = 3$, and $z = 4$, because those are the numbers of which I first thought. But when you want to solve an equation with more than three unknowns you need to envisage more than three dimensions. Hilbert wanted mathematicians to begin to tackle equations with infinitely many variables. So he called on them to visualize infinite matrices in a geometric space with infinitely many dimensions. *The Oxford English Dictionary* tells us that the first meaning of "matrix" was "female animal used for breeding." The mathematical meaning of a matrix in Hilbert space can be called a notation that breeds many offspring, and complicated children some of them are. Bluntly, although Hilbert had had the space named after him, the old boy in 1926 knew rather little of the mysteries that existed there.

Some people will feel that such an abstract space, largely unexplored by its inventor, is terribly theoretical and muddling. Others will find it enormously challenging fun. Johnny was the human being who found it the most challenging fun. He spent much of his next dozen years probing intellectually into Hilbert space, producing (sometimes in collaboration with other fine minds like F. J. Murray's) nearly sixty papers and over a thousand startling ideas. Each of these new ideas and discoveries was aesthetically pleasing to him because he was treading on ground that he thought rather few had reached before, and he was quick to think of useful applications for many of the things he found.

From his initial probing of infinite matrices and bounded matrices (which were the main things that Hilbert's previous disciples had considered), Johnny moved in quickening intellectual flow into the study of unbounded and self-adjoint matrices and then (when at Princeton) of operators and rings of operators in them. These last introduced dynamism into the concepts of what was happening there. He found that what really determines the dimensional structure of a space is the group of rotations that it permits. He moved to create axioms for spaces with dimensions that can vary continuously. These helped lead to a branch of mathematics now called "continuous geometries." Johnny's equations in these fields are called "von Neumann algebras." In the process he helped mathematicians not only to do sums in infinite dimensions but also to think (if they wished) in such weirdnesses as one-third of a dimension, or the square root of two as a dimension, or π as a dimension, or any other real number they wanted. It is just worth saying that some of this later thinking—the continuous geometry and so on—has not yet had as much significance as Johnny hoped. It may still do so, of course, or it may be that in these furthest depths of Hilbert space Johnny entered his phase of the high baroque.

As early as 1927–29, however, Johnny also helped extend spectral theory, which means a theory of vibration. Classical examples in spectral theory are the sounds emitted by musical instruments. Quantum mechanical examples are the vibrations emitted and absorbed by quantum mechanical systems. It was not possible to use atomic physics precisely until people had some idea what these vibrations were. Hilbert had a spectral theory for bounded symmetric operators, but this did not help explain much until Johnny unveiled the notion of symmetry for unbounded operators. He did this by creating a spectral theory for unbounded operators that are self-adjoint.

After those last three paragraphs, the ordinary reader (and this ordinary writer) may be staggering with incomprehension. We may desperately ask whether we need to understand all these things, about unbounded and self-adjoint matrices, in order to assess Johnny's impact on quantum mechanics. For reasons that will appear in six paragraphs' time, the happy answer is that we do not. We merely have to assess whether he brought aboard the boat of quantum theory those mathematicians who, until the late 1920s, even at Göttingen, were telling their students that the new Bohr-Heisenberg quantum mechanics were based on mathematical mistakes.

The best evidence comes from Professor K. O. Friedrichs, who was one of the original doubters: "When the basic formulae of the quantum theory were set up by Heisenberg, Born and Jordan," wrote Friedrichs as late as 1979, "some mathematicians in Göttingen claimed, somewhat sneeringly, that such formulae could not be valid. They claimed that they could prove this by using Hilbert's theory of infinite matrices," although it was on Hilbert's matrix algebra that Heisenberg's formulas were supposed to be based. Mathematicians "in the school around Courant" pointed out that the symbols P and Q in the Heisenberg-Born equations were infinite matrices, and they were required to do things that Hilbert had proved that no bounded infinite matrices could do.

"The mistake these mathematicians had made," continued Friedrichs in 1979, "was that they tacitly assumed that the matrices P and Q were bounded. They were not. Already Born had observed this, but he thought that the same rules would be valid for unbounded matrices as for bounded ones. That was not so. Some work on unbounded matrices had been done before, but it was not completely satisfactory. It was von Neumann who completely cleared up how to handle unbounded infinite matrices" and how to use Hilbert space.

This clearing up took time. Even in 1929–30, said Friedrichs, "we in the group around Courant were quite suspicious of the abstract work" that Johnny was known to be doing on quantum theory. But when "I studied these abstract papers, I was dumbfounded. In fact, I had just handed to Courant for publication a manuscript on spectral theory. I asked him to return the manuscript. I then rewrote the paper in von Neumann's abstract language. That was the origin of a substantial part of my later work" on both spectral theory and partial differential equations. Johnny thus set a lot of mathematicians on to new roads and was tickled rather than irked when more practical men did not notice this.

When Friedrichs met Heisenberg after the war, the refugee from Hitler said to Hitler's top scientist that mathematicians from Göttingen owed apologies to him for those misunderstandings long ago. Happily, mathematicians had repaid the debt, because it was a mathematician (Johnny) who had clarified the difference between an unbounded operator that was self-adjoint and one that was merely symmetric.

"Eh?" said Heisenberg. "What is the difference?"

Because the genius who discovered the uncertainty principle apparently did not understand what we have been talking about for the last page and a half, you and I are also excused from wading back through it. The essential point is that work like Johnny's was needed to get many mathematicians aboard the boat of quantum mechanics. Without them aboard it is unlikely that the boat could have moved so fast. Awkwardly, however, we now know that there is another vessel on which they could reasonably have clambered. This was Paul Dirac's.

Dirac—the Nobel Prize winner for physics in 1933 for his discovery of antimatter—published his mathematization of quantum theory in *The Principles of Quantum Mechanics* (Oxford University Press, 1930). From then on, most eminent physicists preferred his formulation to what the mathematicians initially insisted was the more profound formulation by Johnny. Johnny's book was eventually published in 1932 as *Mathematische Grundlagen der Quantummechanik* (Springer Press, Berlin), after considerable changes on proof. Johnny picked up a lot of last-minute new ideas from Marshall Stone and others in the United States.

Dirac explained quantum theory by playing an odd trick with elementary calculus. He said that in quantum mechanics the next possible change in x is infinite when $x = 0$ but is equal to zero when x equals anything else. Mathematicians were shocked by this use of sharp variations, instead of infinitely multidimensional ones, but physicists found them a convenient way of doing or avoiding their sums. One part of Johnny's book is a fierce attack on Dirac's delta functions, to general applause from mathematicians of the day, who might have remained divorced from quantum theory if Johnny's alternative formalization had not appeared. It is therefore awkward that fifteen or so years later France's Laurent Schwartz made Dirac's delta functions mathematically precise, respectable, and useful. Johnny felt that his prewar work on logic had run aground on Gödel, and to some extent his prewar work on quantum theory had run aground on Dirac.

Most mathematicians do not feel that way. Johnny provided them with fine new toolboxes as he wandered through Hilbert space, although he did feel embarrassed at starting with a now-fading Hilbert by his side. As Johnny's first attempt to translate Heisenberg to Hilbert had been via Nordheim in 1926, his first writings on quantum mechanics were in a joint paper with Hilbert and Nordheim published in 1927. But within a few months, in a paper also published in 1927, he had broken free into the field he made his own. Hilbert's rules about infinite matrices had been stimulating for a beginner in the subject (Johnny in 1926) but were cramping for the world's greatest expert in it (Johnny by 1927).

By the middle of 1927 it was clearly desirable for the young eagle Johnny to soar from Hilbert's nest. Johnny had spent his undergraduate years explaining what Hilbert had got magnificently right but was now into his postgraduate years where he had to explain what Hilbert had got wrong. This fact, plus the need to earn a living, induced Johnny in the autumn of 1927 to accept the post of privatdocent at the University of Berlin. He was the youngest privatdocent who had ever been appointed by that august establishment. In 1929 he moved briefly to be privatdocent at the University of Hamburg, partly because the prospect of becoming a full professor seemed less distant there, but also because it was by then desirable to soar from the nest of Berlin's mathematics professor, Erhard Schmidt.

Johnny remained loyal to Hilbert in all his writings, but the awkwardness by 1927 was explained to me by Wigner, Johnny's old schoolmate at the Lutheran Gymnasium. In 1927 Wigner was appointed to succeed Nordheim as Hilbert's assistant in physics. He says that he soon learned that it was possible only on a few occasions a year to meet Hilbert at all. Hilbert was by then very old, said the eighty-nine-year-old Wigner to your sixty-five-year-old author in 1989. "Actually," said your author, "Hilbert by 1926 will have been aged 64." "Well, people must have aged earlier in those years," said Wigner. Another contemporary describes Hilbert's reaction to the sacking of Jewish professors in his beloved Göttingen in 1933. Hilbert went to the railroad station and assured the departing ones that their emigration could not last long. "I am writing to the minister to tell him what the foolish authorities have done." Because the minister was the appalling Nazi Reichsminister Rust, the initiator of the expulsions, it may be almost comforting that Hilbert spent his last fifteen years (up to his death in wartime Germany in 1943) in such a daze.

Johnny, by the late 1920s, was the young lion rousing German mathematics out of any dazes, as some others of its grand old men faded. In the 1930s Berlin's Schmidt was running a seminar at which a student was reporting on the results of his own new research. The student started in the now-standard way: "Let H be a Hilbert Space and L a linear operator." Schmidt interrupted him: "Please, young man, say infinite matrices." With Schmidt's language, much of the mathematical exposition of modern science would be impossible, which may help explain Johnny's departure to Hamburg in 1929.

Johnny's stay in Hamburg was brief. His eyes were already on America. The years 1927–29 were also the busy ones of his colloquium period in Europe.

▶◀▶◀▶◀ 7

Sturm und Drang,

Marriage, Emigration, 1927–31

▶◀**B**y the end of 1927 Johnny had published twelve major papers on mathematics. By the end of 1928 these had risen to twenty-two, by the end of 1929 to thirty-two. They had established something of a cult among at least Europe's younger mathematicians, who through 1928–29 were avidly awaiting his extraordinary output of nearly one major paper a month.

All the 1927–29 papers were written in German in a uniform, orderly, rather Prussian style. The orderliness meant that other mathematicians could more easily grasp each paper's meaning even when it was abstruse, and use it in their own work. Some of the ideas he created were breathtaking to the few dozens of people who could understand them. They set other mathematicians, said one central European professor, to wondering aloud what they had been doing all through their mathematical lives.

Others of the 1927–29 papers had major effects on physics, but physicists are less inclined to enthuse. There was less excitement in the laboratories than expected about Johnny's success in making precise mathematics out of quantum theory, via his travels in Hilbert space. Physicists did him the compliment of accepting what he said as if it was obvious, which it certainly had not been. Some physicists enthused more about four papers he wrote with Wigner in 1928–29 on the spectrum lines of various atoms.

In the hydrogen atom the spectrum lines are simple (that was the basis of Bohr's theory), but in some other atoms there are thousands of lines. They had seemed rather random until the papers in 1928–29 by Johnny and Wigner. Sixty years later, in 1989, Hans Bethe was still calling these among the most remarkable of Johnny's works. Johnny supplemented the overmodest Wigner admirably. Although Johnny instantly leapt an average of five blocks ahead of most people who brought suggestions to him, he could leap only about one block ahead of Wigner. But he made Wigner's politely suggested possibilities mathematical, undeniable, emphatic, and precise. It is possible that he made them too emphatic. Wigner said sixty years later that some of their work was then unpopular, because it obliged physicists to learn new mathematics. The greatest joy of any physicist is to discover something new, but there is resentment at being told to go back to school.

A few of Johnny's 1927–29 papers were not immediately picked up by other people. These included his first paper (1928) on the theory of games. Rather more of them were grasped and extended by other mathematicians, so that some critics said that Johnny did not sufficiently follow his own ideas through. Some resentment was later expressed on his behalf about such filching. "There is hardly a young mathematician today who realises that such-and-such a familiar general proposition was von Neumann's discovery originally," complained some of his contemporaries in later years. Young Johnny was changing some of the shape of his profession, by flashing like a meteor through different colleagues' specialties and then leaving illumination rather than detailed work behind. Some colleagues resented this. Others took advantage of it, which he wanted them to. He himself was sometimes accused of "skimming off the cream," which is often what a superior mind should do.

The explanation for his lack of follow-through is surely that Johnny, although already, as in most of his life, taking only a few hours' sleep a night, had decided to enjoy himself in the twenty or so hours a day when he was energetically awake. His chief enjoyment was thinking, but he had a low boredom threshold. He would follow his ideas through when they were aesthetically amusing (in the case of Hilbert space, perhaps too far), but he did not mind when other people got the glory from extending what he had originally thought up. He was rightly and modestly unsure that he had always done all the original thinking anyway, especially in the colloquium period of his life, which now began. Some of the stories from his colloquium years 1927–29 shade into his later lecturing habits in America, but this chapter seems the right niche for them.

In the 1920s younger professors across Europe were energetic in arranging congresses and conferences and colloquia, which in mathematics come cheap. Mathematicians do not have to hike laboratory equipment or samples on their journeys—just bits of chalk. Johnny proved a willing participant at these meetings, partly because he did not work boringly in preparation. He just pondered on a train. He hardly ever lectured from a prepared text. He wrote equations on the blackboard at what seemed the speed of light. Sometimes he reached the end of the blackboard and erased to get more space at the top, before some of his audience had imbibed what he was now rubbing out. Among those who doubted him, Johnny's system of "proof by erasure" became an irritated joke.

A lot of other people's talks at colloquia were boring. Johnny did not mind because he could shut them off and mutter to himself while thinking up other mathematics, or even fall asleep. He had a hand-over-mouth sitting position that enabled him to wander away mentally while looking politely engrossed. Sometimes his colleagues had to nudge him as he sat in an emptying lecture room, still looking politely engrossed.

If he was interested, he would ask questions that a speaker would find penetrating and flurry-inducing but flattering because they generally extended what the speaker had first thought up. When really interested, he started walking round the room. Bethe told me that he rated seminars in ten grades. "Grade one was something my mother could understand. Grade two my wife could understand. Grade seven," said this Nobel Prize winner, "was something I could understand. Grade eight was something only the speaker and Johnny von Neumann could understand. Grade nine was something Johnny could understand, but the speaker didn't. Grade ten was something even Johnny could not yet understand, but there was little of that."

Unlike Robert Oppenheimer, Johnny did not ask put-this-fool-down questions. He never saw any point in that. There was allegedly an exception when one German professor praised the habit of asking Ph.D. students "unsolvable questions" at their oral exams. If the student instantly said, "That's unsolvable," he was deemed to have the right sharp set of mind. The professor put his favorite unsolvable equations on the blackboard as an illustration. Johnny muttered at the ceiling for a few minutes, and then solved some of them.

A more typical occasion was when one professor propounded a new discovery that was actually quite wrong. This wrongdoer handled all the questions at the seminar devastatingly well, and there was discussion of his discovery at a private dinner that night. Johnny demolished the whole discovery by saying that he should have been asked *a, b,* and *c.* "Why didn't you ask that?" said the seminar organizer desperately. Johnny intimated that he did not like to be publicly rude. There were echoes of this at the Moscow conference of 1935 (see next chapter) when a German professor presented a paper that purported to introduce the new concept of *Hauptvermutung* into topology. Johnny did not enthuse with the rest but merely said that the professor had handled well the questions that were asked. A year later the paper's proof was proved unconvincing, and twenty years later it was found to be simply wrong. The point of this story is that Johnny was in no way a topologist. Topology is the branch of mathematics that deals with materials that have not been altered (e.g., have not had a hole drilled into them) but that may have been twisted into shapes and knots. Johnny rather liked another Hungarian's euphemism for a near lie: a topological version of the truth.

All his life Johnny handled some of his personal relations awkwardly, but he blossomed at these 1927–29 seminars for several reasons. One was that he was clearly the best roaring young lion there. Another was that he resolutely and early decided not to argue insultingly with anybody. A third was that there were few women at these mathematical seminars. He could therefore use his inexhaustible store of unprintable stories to relax tension at any moment he chose, and he frequently did. Because of his facility in languages, said Teller to me in 1989, Johnny was the only man he had known who could tell jokes (including doubles entendres) in three languages simultaneously. Even at age twenty-three Johnny was suave at drawing on the most apposite of these when he wanted to avoid argument with a bore.

Because Johnny's other trick in that situation was to make intriguing analogies between the matter at hand and events in ancient history back to 500 B.C., he seemed extraordinarily learned for a twenty-three-year-old mathematical genius. The dirty jokes made him seem engagingly unpompous as well. He managed to help many a mathematician whose own work had run into a brick wall. Either Johnny muttered at the ceiling and then led the man straight through the wall; or he said, I would try a or b or c or d. This later made him popular in America as a referee for papers that had been submitted to learned journals. On at least one occasion he commended a paper but said it could be made much stronger by inserting the following dozen lines of figures and equations. The paper was thereby transformed into a major one, and the young author was rather embarrassed to keep in his own name even as a joint work.

One of the first conferences where Johnny appeared as a rising star was at Lwow in Poland in 1927. A Polish professor was sent to Germany to sound out whether Johnny seemed a suitable speaker and reported with breathless enthusiasm. He had discussed set theory, measure theory, and real variables with Johnny in a Berlin taxicab—and the youngster had explained to him more about these subjects in a few sentences than he had gleaned from correspondence and conversations over a decade with other mathematicians.

Lwow carried the tradition of coffeehouse mathematics to extremes. In many university towns across Europe in the 1920s mathematical teachers and their brightest students would gather in cafés at tables with marble tops. You can write equations on marble tops and then wash them off. In Lwow the mathematicians' favorite café was called the Scottish House, and the principal guru was Stefan Banach (1892–1945). The difficulty about Banach was that his sessions at the Scottish House were liable to last for up to seventeen hours with brief interruptions for meals. During these sessions Banach would smoke four or five packs of cigarettes and was scarcely less abstemious in his drinking. There was some debate just after the war whether Banach had been murdered in 1945 by the Nazis or the Russians. It seems that he had actually died of lung cancer.

Johnny never smoked, partly because he early suspected cigarettes were unhealthy, and his drinking was not as Rabelaisian as he liked to pretend. At one of his Princeton parties a three-year-old climbed on Johnny's lap, as three-year-olds were wont to do, and caused some consternation by gulping down what was assumed to be Johnny's gin; it was a soft drink disguised. But he survived a later Polish test when Banach deliberately spiked his drinks with vodka, to the point where Johnny had to dash to the lavatory to vomit. He returned from vomiting to pick up the equations he had been expounding at the exact point where he had left off.

These colloquia often ranged also over political debates, and Johnny's technique in these proved the same as later in America. He never argued with people who said anything emotional or politically convinced. He did not believe that public argument changed such people's views, and he thought preaching back at them simply brought boredom and bad blood. But he asked probing questions of anybody who said anything interesting, and "interest" was a word to which he gave a wide range. Johnny preferred people who laughed at the world rather than whined at it. He shied away from those who had adopted any ideology that blinded them to either mathematical fact or real events.

In America Johnny had the reputation for seeking the company of cheerful nuts rather than gloomy nuts. In Europe in the 1920s he was regarded as the good-natured, laughing pessimist. This was certainly true about the prospects in his own profession. In 1929 Johnny calculated that there were likely to be three vacancies for professors of mathematics in Germany during the next three years, but he knew forty privatdocents who felt confident that they would become professors in the next two. He therefore intimated early that he would be interested in any offer from America, particularly if it came while the 1920s economic boom still lasted. He was dubious about the last stages of the 1928–29 economic boom, although it is not true that he forecast the full horror of the 1930s depression.

He did not feel by 1929 that Europe had settled down to politics that would bring lasting peace. If pressed by those who feared Germany "might try to avenge 1918," he would recount the atrocities perpetrated in the island of Melos by the otherwise immensely civilized ancient Athenians. Even the music-loving and math-loving people of Germany, he feared, were capable in the near future of doing terrible things. Johnny had sad enough memories of the chopping of Hungarian territory to see why even his gently Göttingen-owlish Germans were boiling mad that countries like what he called "Tschechoslovakia" had been given so much German land. He wrote that France and Britain had imposed a settlement on central Europe that those two war-weary countries would not risk new horrors to maintain.

Johnny in 1928 had written his article on the theory of games (see chap. 10), which suggested that in group struggles it is logical to predict an eventual "saddle-point" outcome. This is reached where each antagonist feels he is attaining most of what he wants to attain while incurring the least risk. The saddle-point outcome to post-1919 Europe could be a nationalist Germany pushing east to grab back its old territories and then going on to war with Russia. When Hitler arrived, Johnny knew that there would be European war but intermittently hoped that the madman would have his war with Russia first. He agreed that this would put Hungary and Poland in an awkward position in between. He told friends that he feared that a territory-recovering Hungary might end up with a nationalist Germany and that he did not want to be "caught dead on that side."

It would be wrong to pretend that this prospect kept Johnny through all his youth very deep in the glums. But he did intend early that he should escape from Europe to America if he could, and he hoped his facility in languages could help toward this. He had devised a cunning way of getting the syntax in foreign languages, such as English, right. He read selected books in the language he wanted to get the feel of, very quickly but with enormous concentration, so that every word in the passages he chose was implanted in his mind.

Through this practice, he was able at age fifty in the early 1950s to baffle Herman Goldstine by quoting the first dozen pages of Dickens's *Tale of Two Cities* word for word. In English he had also chosen to browse through encyclopedias and pick out interesting subjects to learn by heart. That is why he had such extraordinarily precise knowledge of the Masonic movement, the early history of philosophy, the trial of Joan of Arc, and the battles in the American Civil War. In German in youth he had done the same thing with Oncken's *Allgemeine Geschichte*. He had learned all of ancient history from the German—which perhaps meant a too militarist—point of view.

His memory and feel for words, plus unsurpassed feel for mathematical symbols, had not extended to memory for faces. All his life he was embarrassed by not knowing people who clearly knew him. He had no sort of photographic memory. This imposed some limitations on his mathematics (he was not good at envisaging shapes) but probably also added to some of his strengths. It is difficult for anybody with a photographic mind to think in terms of more than three dimensions. Johnny had no difficulty in thinking in terms of a quarter of a dimension or of some minuscule fraction of a dimension or several hundred thousand dimensions or infinite dimensions. He just moved the algebraic symbols for these across the chessboard of his mind.

It may be that he also did not bother to record faces the first time he saw them. Committing faces to memory would be a waste of effort if they proved to be faces of people who would never have anything interesting to say. His relationship with women remained clumsy throughout his life. He was liked by all the women who really knew him, but those who merely encountered him sometimes thought him creepy. When he was preoccupied, he used to stare at women's legs unconsciously and rudely—just as, when driving an automobile, he might stare at but not see the road ahead. At Los Alamos the secretaries had desks that were open at the front. Some of them stuck cardboard there because, they said, Johnny had a habit of leaning forward, muttering, and peering up their skirts. Because his nightly four hours of sleep might interrupt his thinking, he devised a way to do some thinking during sleep. He thought of some problems before dropping off and would dart to a notebook with new notations at 4 A.M. because his subconscious had been working while his body was at rest. He joked that in one dream he was working through a proof that set theory really is consistent, if based on his axioms; he woke up before the proof was completed. The next night he dreamed again and got very near to completion. It is a mercy, he said, that he did not dream on the third night; otherwise he would have confidently proved what Gödel later showed to be untrue.

◄►◄►

At this stage there appeared the fairy godmother who was to whisk Johnny to America. Oswald Veblen (1880–1960) had been professor of mathematics at Princeton since 1910. In 1929 he was invited for a spell as visiting professor at Oxford, and set out on a safari hunt through Europe for mathematicians with whom to modernize the United States. Veblen was tall, slim, Scandinavian-looking, and the nephew of the Thorstein Veblen, who wrote that American classic *The Theory of the Leisure Class*. He possessed a delightfully caustic wit, rather akin to Johnny's own. He talked to Johnny at a meeting of mathematicians in Italy, and Mariette Kovesi says he also came to Budapest. He took to Johnny as a father to a son—at just the right time both for Veblen's own ambitions for American mathematics and for Johnny's career.

Veblen was worried that American mathematics were falling behind European ones, even though American universities had so much more money to spend. In the early 1920s he was telling every authority who would listen—including (see later) Abraham Flexner—that American professors of mathematics had too many administrative duties. They were expected to teach too many underclassmen instead of upperclassmen. This gravely impeded their opportunities for mathematical research. Veblen saw that mathematics in Europe had become an oral culture, bred in all those colloquia on all those blackboards and marble tabletops. He feared that America was becoming cut off from this. The solutions were to set up an American center of mathematical research, to entice some of the Europeans by offering large American university salaries, and to get those colloquia going. Veblen's aim was to make Princeton the equivalent of what Göttingen had been for mathematics in the beautiful years, and during the glum 1930s he partly achieved this.

The first European mathematician to be enticed to Princeton was Weyl, from Johnny's old ETH at Zurich. Weyl was professor of mathematical physics at Princeton in 1928–29, but it soon became clear that he was not going to stay. He had been told that he would succeed Hilbert as professor of mathematics at Göttingen when Hilbert became incapacitated as a professor, and that incapacitation was plainly advancing fast. Weyl left Princeton in 1929, and Veblen had to search anew.

There was a problem that some physicists at Princeton felt that the next professor should be more a physicist and less a mathematician than Weyl was. There might be objections to Johnny on the same score. After all, the physicists said, the main problem was that Europe had set alight a wider debate than America on the quantum revolution. This was more a matter of physics than math. But Johnny and Wigner had at this time just written their joint papers on the spectral lines of atoms, which physicists admired. This gave Veblen an idea. He suggested to Princeton that they should invite both Johnny and Wigner. Wigner's modest recollection of what happened is that a recommendation had been made to Princeton that they should

invite not a single person but at least two . . . who already knew each other, who wouldn't feel suddenly put on an island where they had no intimate contact with anybody. Johnny's name was of course well known by that time the world over, so they decided to invite Johnny von Neumann. They looked: who wrote articles with John von Neumann? They found: Mr. Wigner. So they sent a telegram to me also.

Some accounts suggest that the telegrams arrived in November on the same day. Actually Johnny had been sent a letter on October 15, 1929, offering him a lectureship in mathematical physics at Princeton for the term from February 5 to June 1, 1930: "The stipend to be offered for this term is $3,000, plus an allowance of $1,000 to cover travel expenses. The duties would be to deliver a course of lectures (2 or 3 lectures a week) on some aspect of the quantum theory. The lectures could be either elementary or advanced, according to your preference." The letter made clear that Weyl's return to Europe had left open the Jones chair of mathematical physics at Princeton. Johnny might be considered for this later, if things went well. There was agreement that he should return to Europe for the second half of 1930 to give a course of lectures in Berlin for which he had already contracted.

The letter mentioned that Dr. H. P. (Bob) Robertson was giving some lectures on quantum theory in Princeton but hoped that Johnny could fit in reasonably with him. It also specifically asked

whether Johnny would think it desirable for Wigner to be invited
to lecture at Princeton at the same time. Johnny accepted both the
offer and the suggestion about Wigner with alacrity, although he
told Veblen that he must go to Budapest first to "fix a family
matter." Then he would arrive in Princeton in January 1930. His
next message from Budapest was that he was being married to
Mariette Kovesi. The rest of this chapter is her story.

◄►◄►

Mariette Kovesi was born in 1909. She first rode into Johnny's
life on a tricycle at the age of two and a half because that was her
chosen entry when invited to a party for the four-year-old Michael
Neumann. Mariette's grandfather had prospered in Budapest's real
estate boom after 1866. He was a sporty and very rich old gentleman who owned the first automobile in Hungary. Mariette's father
was a doctor who was also a professor of medicine at the University of Budapest and, thanks to the grandfather, also comfortably rich. Her mother was a devoutly religious woman who, even
after Mariette was sixteen, insisted that she should go to parties
only when the chauffeur waited and brought her back at a fixed
time. When Cinderella broke curfew, as she sometimes did, the
mother was liable to retire to bed for a day or two in hypochondriac
huff.

Johnny was part of Mariette's set even in his Zurich days, which
means before she was seventeen. The Kovesi and von Neumann
summer houses in the country were near to each other, up a steep
hill. Grandmother Kovesi got out of the car at the bottom of the
hill. She had been told through most of her life to be kind to the
horses.

In the summers of 1927 and 1928, when Johnny had become a
privatdocent at Berlin, Mariette was disturbed because Johnny
suddenly became polite to her. She was by now an undergraduate
at Budapest University reading economics and very much the
center of her social circle. She was slight (she remains dazzlingly
slim to this day), witty, well-dressed, and vivacious. The word
applied by the many young men who fell in love with her was

"gay." Her present husband of the past fifty-four years regrets that the word no longer carries the meaning that it did then.

The reasons for Johnny's politeness became apparent at the beginning of the summer vacation of 1929, when he informally proposed to her. Or at least he said awkwardly, "You and I could have a lot of fun together, for instance you like to drink wine and so do I." Mariette did not find this very romantic. But Johnny was already world famous for his mathematics, and Mariette was a leader of Budapest's young society. Her father saw this as the proposed betrothal of a golden couple, and her mother did not retire in hypochondriac huff at all, especially as Johnny promised that he would be received into the Catholic faith. Indeed, at this stage, all Johnny's family was converting to Catholicism. Max had died earlier in 1929, and Johnny's letters of negotiation with Princeton were written on black-bordered stationery.

It was decided that Johnny should accompany the Kovesi family on a holiday to Paris, where Mariette fell in love with him partly because he was such a superb guide around the museums. He already knew more history than most professors of that subject, and he had presumably done his usual concentration trick on the guide books. He had read them with such intensity that he knew the best bits by heart.

He fell still further in love with Mariette, even after he had seen how much she spent in Paris on clothes. The engagement was formalized, although not yet announced. The plan was for a rather grand June wedding in Budapest in 1930.

In October 1929 Dr. Kovesi had a phone call from Hamburg. "It's Jancsi, he's been invited to America for a term, and wants you to go with him." Mrs. Kovesi retired to bed for several days. They were married on New Year's Day 1930 and left via Paris (with more shopping) for Cherbourg. The honeymoon was to be spent on one of the very early trips of the luxury liner *Bremen* to New York. Mariette had never been to sea before, but her frame was so slight that she felt she could not have much seasickness in her.

No seasickness was the first wrong forecast of the John von

Neumann family. As soon as the ship was out of Cherbourg harbor into the Atlantic's January gales, Mariette was confined to her bunk. ("What a honeymoon!" she laughs now.) She did not touch deck until near that first superb sight of the Statue of Liberty.

Veblen met them in New York, and at dinner Mariette committed her first American gaffe. Canned peaches were unknown in Europe, except in American movies, so she wanted those luscious-looking things for dessert. When the Roosevelt Hotel served natural peaches (all too familiar in Hungary), she asked for the canned sort. "Elizabeth Veblen plainly thought I was someone from the boondocks."

Mariette was thrilled by New York ("America, where have you been all my life?"), and Johnny had the same reaction. Wigner arrived a week later (not, as some of the histories say, by the same honeymoon boat). It was now that Wigner recorded, "Johnny fell in love with America on the first day. He thought: these are sane people who don't talk in those traditional terms which are meaningless. To a certain extent the materialism of the United States, which was greater than that of Europe, appealed to him."

Veblen took Johnny off on some mathematical business next day. What did Mariette, as a twenty-year-young European who had read about America from afar, want to do on her first lonesome early evening in New York in 1930? She naturally wanted to go to a speakeasy. She expressed this desire in a drugstore where she was practicing her governess-taught English. A man customer unsurprisingly offered to take her. He said he was employed building New York's bridges; it was a mercy he did not try to sell her the Brooklyn one. In Hungary she had drunk only wine, but in a speakeasy it seemed right to order her first Scotch and soda, a drink of which she had only heard. Outside the speakeasy, she shook the disappointed bridge builder firmly by the hand and said she must go back to her husband. Johnny did not appreciate this adventure. He had come to conquer the new world by conventional mien, and Mariette had not.

At Princeton she committed her second blunder when invited for dinner at the Comptons'. In Hungary, if your invitation said

8:00 P.M., you did not arrive before about 8:40 P.M. or you would find your hostess in hair curlers. Wigner had been invited along with them, but he was in an awkward state. He had read a paper on how to make his thinning hair grow thicker. He thought the notion of shaving it completely to get faster growth had some scientific plausibility. It had not, and his pate temporarily gleamed obscenely nude. Mariette had bought her clothes in Paris, and for this first party appeared in a gown that was dazzlingly backless, which was that year's fashion in Paris but not yet in Princeton. The improbable trio—bare-backed Mariette, gleamingly bald Wigner, and a formally overdressed Johnny—arrived at the Comptons' when the other guests were already eating their dessert.

There were no difficulties with the quantum-theory-lecturing Bob Robertson and his wife, with whom Johnny became friends for life. Mariette volunteered to baby-sit for them, and on one of her first evenings in America found herself confronted with a baby to bathe. The servant-employing classes in Europe did not do such things, and she was terrified of it. But the baby survived, and his younger sister is today called Mariette after her godmother. To Americans Princeton is a quaint old town. To Europeans it dates from something modern like 1776. It tries to be historic by keeping some of its plumbing and other facilities of that ilk. This awkwardness applied to much of the accommodation available for rent, and Johnny responded to Mariette's early house hunting with "How could I do good mathematics in a place like this?" They eventually rented from a Mrs. Frothingham, who furnished her apartment in a fashion that Europeans found gracious but Princetonians found odd.

Johnny was at this stage more involved with students than through most of his life. There was not the opportunity to meet them in cafés as in Europe. So Mariette arranged a sort of open house in the evenings at Mrs. Frothingham's, which people interested in discussing mathematics could attend. This was the origin of the von Neumann Princeton parties that later became famous and much more grand. The rapport Johnny established with the students was successful, although his letters at the time show that his English spelling was not. But the physicists at Princeton clearly did not want another mathematician in the Jones chair; he was not going to get that. This still let him fulfill his contract in Berlin for the summer term of 1930.

Although depression-hit Berlin in 1930 aroused some forebodings in Johnny, he was enjoying professional success there. Earlier in Berlin he had shared his seminars on quantum mechanics with Szilard, whom he had found irksome. Now his colleague at the seminar was the great Schrödinger, with Szilard merely seated in the front row. Mariette admits guiltily that she hugely enjoyed pre-Nazi Berlin. The women were better dressed than at Princeton and the intellectual company was livelier. She met the liveliest of all on a Berlin bus.

"Why did we not get a taxi when you are carrying such a large parcel, Albert?" a querulous voice sounded down the bus's aisle. "Everybody is looking at you." "Well then, my dear, I will sit on the parcel and they can look at me more closely," said Einstein—giving Mariette, in a neighboring seat, a dazzling smile. Mariette thereafter kept a soft spot for Einstein. Contrary to what is often written, she says that Johnny did too. Certainly, Johnny had exasperated reservations about Einstein's politics after 1945. In 1930 his main worry was that he did not want Mariette to see that Mrs. Einstein regarded the henpecking of a genius as good, cruel, feminine sport.

Matters were more romantic in 1935 when Mariette was eight months' pregnant with her daughter Marina. The von Neumanns dined with the Einsteins à quatre. Mrs. Einstein remarked that the party nearly had not come off because Einstein was supposed to be the guest of honor at a concert in New York. Einstein guiltily remembered this and said he must go to the concert at once. As there were two tickets, Mrs. Einstein was left à deux with Johnny (it was one of the days when he had deserved this), and Einstein and Mariette went to the concert. They arrived just in time for a last-minute entrance, scuttling through to the special front seats reserved for Einstein. As they did so, all heads turned toward them, as at a tennis match. The familiar old man bore on his arm this slight but enormously pregnant figure with reddish brown hair. There were press photographs and comments the next day, along the lines of Who would have thought the old man had it in him? From Einstein Mariette got a large bunch of flowers, together with a poem.

Back in Princeton in 1931, it was time for the von Neumanns to buy an automobile. "Everybody has to have a Ford in their lives some time," says Mariette. The difficulty was getting a licence to drive. Mariette had passed her driving test in Budapest, where the strict rules even obliged her to know how to fix a car. But, because of the chaperoning chauffeur, she had driven little. Johnny had driven a lot but had never passed a test anywhere. Everybody who saw his driving said that he would not pass one in America. Mariette had heard the best hope was a driving-test instructor under the Brooklyn Bridge. You offered him a cigarette. Then, if he admired your cigarette case, that was a sign that you could pass the test by paying him $10 in those depression days. Johnny took the test, and the driver said he admired the cigarette case very, very much. That is how Johnny was let loose on the roads of America.

There was one worse driver in Princeton—namely Wigner— but in a different mode. Johnny drove fast down the middle of any road. Wigner drove very slowly, keeping well to the right side—unfortunately, so far to the right side that his wheels generally moved down the sidewalk like a very slow steamroller, sweeping terrified pedestrians from the path. The most patient of the graduate students was deputed to teach Wigner driving. He was a lively young man, able to sit balanced on a Coca-Cola bottle while putting both feet behind his head.

He was called Horner Kuper, but Mariette nicknamed him Desmond because he looked like her favorite china dog of that name. In 1937 Mariette left Johnny for him, and she and Desmond lived happily ever after.

But the divorce came after the bequests of Louis Bamberger and Felix Fuld's widow to Princeton's Institute for Advanced Study (IAS) had changed life for the von Neumanns, the Einsteins, and perhaps—well, see next chapter—for science in America.

►◄►◄►◄ **8**

Depression at
Princeton, 1931–37

►◄ *I*n 1892 the then-thirty-eight-year-old Louis Bamberger opened a small dry-goods store in Newark, New Jersey—a place now renowned around the world as the town attached to the third airport of New York City. Bamberger had a fine entrepreneurial mind and found some expansion-minded partners. The ablest, Felix Fuld, married Bamberger's sister Caroline, who thus became Caroline Bamberger Fuld. The business prospered. The story is best told in Ed Regis's *Who Got Einstein's Office?*

By 1929, Bamberger's department store was the biggest in the city of Newark, and the fourth largest retail store in the United States: with an annual turnover rising excitingly through the 1920s boom. In 1929 Bamberger passed his seventy-fifth birthday, and Felix Fuld's death left Caroline Fuld a widow. Brother and sister sold the store to New York's thrusting R. H. Macy Company for $25,000,000 in early September 1929—at just the right time. They banked the money six weeks before the stock-market crash on Black Thursday.

Both were childless, and now had far more money than they needed for the brief remainder of septuagenarians' lives. They had become suddenly extraordinarily rich at a time when the depression was driving most other people poorer. They were philanthropic Jews in a great tradition. They wanted to give back some of their fortune to the people of New Jersey whose shopping at their store had created it. Their original intention was to establish a medical school in New Jersey that would give preference to aspiring young Jewish doctors. They believed (to a large extent rightly) that existing American medical institutions in 1929 discriminated against Jewish students and staff.

The conventional person to consult about starting a medical school in 1929 was the sixty-three-year-old Dr. Abraham Flexner. In 1910 Flexner had undertaken a study for the Carnegie Foundation of all the 155 medical schools in the United States and Canada. He reported without equivocation that 120 of them were so awful that they should be immediately closed and that many of the other 35 needed to be reorganized. This brought Flexner a flood of libel suits, at least one threat on his life, deserved praise when a lot of the quack schools did close, but also a reputation for great knowledge on how to found medical and other learned institutions (which he did not in fact have).

By the 1920s Flexner's interest had turned to founding learned institutions other than medical schools. He was keen on research but rather disliked students. He agreed with Veblen that America's mathematicians and physicists, in particular, needed a research center where the latest developments from near and far would be discussed around many visitors' blackboards, as in Europe. He considered it absurd that the minds of the greatest researchers should be increasingly distracted by "parental responsibility for an immature student body" in bureaucratic academe. He believed passionately that Darwin, Faraday, Einstein—and indeed all "the men who have, throughout human history, meant most to themselves and to human progress have usually followed their own inner light. No organiser, no administrator, no institution can do more than furnish conditions favourable to the restless prowling of an enlightened and informed human spirit, seeking its intellectual and spiritual prey. Standardisation, organisation, making trifles seem important . . . are simply irksome and wasteful."

Flexner was writing a book on this subject—called *Universities: American, English, German*—when two representatives of Bamberger and Fuld telephoned to ask whether they could come to see him. They said they represented two benefactors who wanted to give away a great deal of money to establish a medical school near Newark. Flexner said it would be folly to found a medical school among the paint factories of Newark. It could not be attached there to a good university, or a good hospital, or be in a place to which scholars would want to flock. It would be just across the river from New York City, whose medical schools had all these advantages. And the stipulated discrimination in favor of Jews would kill the very small competitive chances any medical school in Newark had. Schools could maintain their reputation only if they sought to recruit the best scholars without discrimination of any sort. To discriminate in favor of people against whom some medical discrimination already existed would make the prejudiced discrimination against graduates of the new Newark medical school even worse.

However, if Bamberger and Fuld really wanted to make their money shine through New Jersey's and America's future history, Flexner had a suggestion to make. He gave the representatives of the two philanthropists the first chapter of his new book—"The Idea of a University." Bamberger and Fuld nibbled, and Flexner began discussions with Veblen about the possibility of setting up, with Bamberger-Fuld money, what came to be called the Institute for Advanced Study (IAS) in Princeton, New Jersey. The plan that emerged during 1930–31 was that the institute should start in the October term 1933 with four or five mathematicians or physicists (including Veblen) as its first and exceedingly well-paid professors. The professors would be expected to stay at the institute from October to spring each year but could spend the summer lecturing anywhere. Professors at the institute would have no laboratories and no routine, but plenty of time to think. Temporary members, at much lower salaries than the professors, would be invited to it for one-year or two-year stays. Flexner told the thrilled Bambergers that these terms might attract to their institute, among others, the cleverest and most revered Jew in the world: Flexner was stalking Einstein.

In 1932 Einstein's main job was still in pre-Hitler though increasingly unpleasant Berlin, but he was being wooed by—among public-relations-oriented others—the California Institute of Technology (where he spent part of the winter of 1931–32) and Oxford University in England (which he visited more briefly in the early summer of 1932, between the spring and summer terms in Berlin). Flexner, although assuring everybody he was not trying to poach, just happened to arrive for conversations with Einstein in all three places that year. The conversation in Berlin in June 1932 was decisive. As Einstein, walking hatless in an old sweater through pouring rain, escorted Flexner to the bus back to Flexner's Berlin hotel, he announced that he was now "fire and flame" in favor of coming to Flexner's new institute unpolluted by students ("Ich bin Flamme und Feuer dafür"). Einstein intended at this time that the fire and flame should burn as a part-time winter offering only. "I have received leave of absence from the Prussian Academy for five months of the year for five years," explained his press statement in Berlin in July 1932. "Those five months I expect to spend at Princeton. I am not abandoning Germany. My permanent home will still be in Berlin."

The attraction had been the promise that in those five months a year Einstein in Princeton could just sit and think. It had not been money, about which Einstein (to whom money meant nothing) was indeed embarrassingly modest. When asked to name his own terms, he had suggested to Flexner a salary of $3,000 a year. Flexner had already decided that the professorial salaries at the IAS would be $10,000 for ordinary professors, and $16,000 for senior ones (including Veblen). Mrs. Einstein quickly arranged that Albert should get the $16,000.

These salaries of $10,000 or $16,000 a year in depression-hit 1933 were enormous sums—equal after taxes to a real living standard of somewhere between $100,000 and $150,000 today. As it was easy in the 1930s to hire full-time domestic servants, the domestic comforts of living at this standard were even greater. The first reaction of professors across the world was to say that this little IAS research institute, without traditions and infrastructure, was an Institute for Advanced Salaries that was going to lure a tiny number of greedy scholars into a dead end. The second reaction of many of them was to apply for such appointments themselves.

But appointments were in the hands of Veblen (he thought) and Flexner (he knew). Over Christmas 1932, Veblen recommended, and Flexner at that stage agreed, that the five inaugural professors should be (1) Veblen himself, (2) Einstein (who, with Veblen, was already appointed), (3) Weyl (who had seemed to telegram his acceptance from Göttingen, after overtures the previous August), (4) James Alexander (who had been Veblen's favorite collaborator at Princeton and who was regarded as the best forty-five-year-old American mathematician), and (5) the cherubic twenty-nine-year-old Johnny.

At the trustees' meeting on January 9, 1933, Johnny's appointment was not approved. Indeed it probably was not even discussed. Flexner that day wrote a tactful letter to Johnny to explain why he was not going to be appointed to the IAS and sent a copy to Dean Eisenhart at Princeton. The dean had presumably yelped that the new IAS had proposed poaching from Princeton its three leading mathematicians (Veblen, Alexander, and Johnny). Flexner had originally half promised that, in return for library facilities and so on, he would not poach from Princeton at all. Instead, he was going to bring glittering stars to the town of Princeton—Einstein and Weyl from abroad, plus attractive catches from rival universities to Princeton in the United States. Because there was none of the latter, Flexner felt by January 9 that he had to jettison one of the poached Princeton three. Johnny was the youngest—the one Flexner knew least. He told Veblen that two Germans

(Einstein and Weyl) and two Americans (Veblen and Alexander) seemed the right mix.

On January 11 a telegram arrived from the always-vacillating Weyl at Göttingen. "Can you give me my promise back?" Weyl decided in that January 1933 that Hitler was not after all going to become chancellor of Germany, so he wished to stay home. Between January 12 and 14 there were several fortunately amiable conversations between Flexner, Veblen, Eisenhart, and Johnny. Under pressure from Veblen, Dean Eisenhart was now saying that he had not strongly opposed Johnny's appointment at the IAS. He probably realized that Princeton itself could not long keep hold of Johnny anyway. It had gotten Johnny at a bargain price because this fitted with his desire to be a half-time American professor, spending the spring and summer in Germany. As part of the package deal, Wigner spent other parts of the year in Germany, and was also a half-time professor at Princeton. Johnny was sure that Hitler would soon come to power in Germany. The half-a-year job in Berlin would then become impossible for both Wigner and himself. On January 15, 1933, an offer was made to Johnny of a lifetime professorship at the IAS at a salary of $10,000 a year. On January 28 this was confirmed by a committee of the IAS trustees.

Two days later, on January 30, 1933, Hitler became chancellor of Germany. Weyl asked Princeton to let him give his promise to come again.

◄►◄►

While triumphant storm troopers paraded with torchlights through Berlin, Johnny left for his half-year in Europe on February 2, 1933. He now had a lush personal income for the first time in his life. He no longer needed subventions from his family (which, anyway, had not been so available since Max had died in 1929) or from Mariette's. The train journey to Budapest took him through Berlin, and he had a meeting with a desperately worried Schmidt beneath the fluttering swastikas at the railroad station. Just as Johnny's own affairs were advancing so splendidly, his Europe was—

as he told Veblen—"relapsing into the dark ages." Johnny wrote from Budapest to Princeton that he had not decided what to do with his Berlin lecture contract for the summer. He would like to see Berlin and beautiful Göttingen once more, but from the viewpoint of warmth and friendliness "a visit to the North Pole would be more attractive."

Between April 7 and April 11, 1933, the Nazi government promulgated the decrees implementing its Law for the Restoration of the Professional Civil Service. These stated that all civil servants "descended from non-Aryan, especially Jewish, parents or grandparents" must retire or be dismissed—with a few exceptions such as those who had fought at the front for Germany in the 1914–18 war. Universities were state institutions in Germany, and the decrees destroyed the livelihood of sixteen hundred of Germany's most prominent scholars on university faculties—especially in physics, mathematics, and medicine. Because frightened private employers were not likely to hire sacked Jews, by far the best course for the sacked scholars was to emigrate if they could.

There were fewer Jews to sack in the faculties of chemistry and literature and the arts because these were older established subjects. In consequence, older established German anti-Semitism—back before Bismarck's time—had made it seem wisest for the brightest Jewish scholars to go into the physical and mathematical sciences. You cannot easily disguise through your prejudices when one physicist or mathematician is better than another, but you can disguise whether an art historian is. The term "Jewish physics" was used in 1919–45 in Germany not only by Hitler but also by many a Herr Professor in what other countries called the liberal arts. It was a lunatically antiproductive prejudice. The physicists and other scientists driven to emigration from Germany in and after 1933 included eleven existing or eventual Nobel laureates, and more than a dozen scientists who helped America invent the A-bomb in 1945. The prevalence of the phrase "Jewish physics" possibly lost Hitler the second world war.

Johnny did not go to Berlin that summer of 1933. He returned to Princeton in September 1933 to take up his post at the new

IAS. A few months later he applied for naturalization as a citizen of the United States.

◄►◄►

This biography has to examine next either what happened in Johnny's personal life in 1934–37, or in his academic life, or what happened at the IAS. I will start briefly with his personal life— although I have not really found what went wrong. Johnny and Mariette were now earning plenty of money. They were big fish in the rather small Princeton pond that the depression was hitting quite hard. They realized that there was a danger of the institute becoming isolated from the mainstream, and that is one reason why they ran their famous parties. "The Alexanders," says Mariette almost defensively, "ran even better parties than we did."

Stan Ulam arrived at Princeton in 1935, and his autobiography captures the atmosphere of intellectual excitement, some disorganization, equations, roses, and white wine. Straight off the *Aquitania*, provincial Polish Ulam called Princeton. The woman telephone operator said, "Hold the wire." This was worrying to Ulam, who did not know which of the many wires in the booth to hold. He survived this problem to reach his shabby shared Princeton lodgings. He "went directly to visit von Neumann in his large and impressive house. A black servant let me in, and there was Salomon Bochner in the living room and a baby crawling on the floor." The baby was the present Dr. Marina von Neumann Whitman, who in 1935 vied with "almost periodic functions in a group" as the chief interest in Johnny's life.

Ulam settled into Princeton and immediately agreed with Johnny that isolation and loneliness were the things wrong with it. "I went to lectures and seminars; heard [Marston] Morse, Veblen, Alexander, Einstein and others; but was surprised how little people talked to each other compared with the endless hours in the coffee houses in Lwow. There the mathematicians were genuinely interested in each other's work, and they understood one another because their work revolved round the central theme of set-theoretical mathematics." Princeton in 1935 had "one of the greatest concentrations of brains in mathematics and physics ever to be assembled" anywhere. But they amazed both Ulam and Johnny by working in small separate groups—guarding each "separate racket like Chicago gangsters." "The topology racket," complained Ulam, "is probably worth $5 million, the calculus of variations racket another five." Johnny, who had helped advance calculus of variations, grinned, "No, that is worth only $1 million." This was a dig at that subject's guru, his fellow IAS professor Morse: the brilliant product of a one-room New England schoolhouse, whose parochialism often jarred Johnny.

Johnny was worried from the first both at the way practical Americans worked with patents in mind and with the way unpractical Americans got cross with each other on the irrelevant matter of who had thought or said something first. He believed the only way science could progress was by scholars picking up each other's work and improving it. This is what American scientists at last started to do in the war. It explained much of their progress out of provincialdom then. Johnny's views on this were to have marvelously welcome consequences for the postwar computer revolution, although they grieved patent seekers in it.

The IAS in the mid-1930s was becoming a station for European scientists fleeing from Hitler. After being temporary members at the IAS for a year, on tiny stipends compared to the rich professors, they were supposed to find other jobs. Unless they moved swiftly whenever a job appeared, and thus cut their time at the IAS short, they were liable not to get employment. This provided two other reasons for Johnny and Mariette's parties: to be a meeting place for some of the brightest scientific conversation in the world and to provide a place where poor but brilliant scholars temporarily at the IAS could find prospective employers.

Ulam described one of these parties in 1935 where a man who looked to him infinitely old (over fifty) was sitting in a big chair with a nice young lady on his knee. They were drinking champagne. Ulam asked Johnny who he was. Johnny replied, "Theodore von Karman." Johnny drove Ulam home to his lodgings and they were caught in a traffic jam in the rain. "Mr. Ulam," said

Johnny, "cars in America are no good for transportation any more, but they make marvellous umbrellas." Passing the Gothic university chapel Johnny explained, "This is our one million dollar protest against materialism."

A year later, however, Ulam realized that something was going wrong with Johnny's marriage. The 1934 trip abroad had been delayed to May. The von Neumanns landed from New York in Genoa because they no longer wanted to pass through Germany. The idea had been to hire a car in Genoa to drive all the way to Budapest, but the Kovesis remembered Johnny's reputation as a driver. The Kovesi family car was waiting on the harbor front at Genoa, complete with the chaperoning chauffeur of five years before. Johnny insisted on driving, fast through northern Italy and Austria, across the Hungarian border into wooded country in the driving rain. With his mind soon preoccupied with something else, he totaled the car against a tree. Mariette was pitched head-first onto the windshield wipers, which broke her nose in several places. This necessitated a lot of surgery. She wrongly believes to this day it damaged her good looks by putting her nose out of joint.

Baby Marina arrived in 1935. Johnny was a besotted father, enclosing details of her weight in letters to Veblen but with a capacity to laugh at himself the while. "Marina does not talk yet," he wrote when the child was six months old, but "this is for fear that Mariette's family would instantly make her play bridge." Johnny, scrambling as good company on the floor, treated small children in the adult way they often prefer. He would compete keenly with them in doing jigsaws or debate gravely whether he or they should have priority in playing with some construction toy. Some people even said that he chose colleagues according to whether he could play with their children. But Johnny was not a diaper-changing sort of dad. His contributions to housework were nil. He regarded housework as something for the women and the servants. Johnny's second wife, Klari, once asked him to get a glass of water quickly in some minor medical emergency. He came back worriedly and asked her where they kept the glasses. "We had only been in the house seventeen years," said Klari.

Mariette was with her parents during much of their 1935 trip to Europe. Johnny's lectures and seminars sprawled far afield to both England's Cambridge and a week's seminar in Moscow (September 4–10). It was a Moscow relapsing into the worst of Stalin's terror. All Johnny's views about the failure and horror of communism were confirmed. The Russian mathematicians who had called the conference had first-class brains, but the fear under which they lived surpassed even Nazi Germany's. The signs of the recent famine in the Ukraine lay across the ruined city, but left-wing Western mathematicians preferred not to notice them. It was a matter of mortification to Johnny that many of his generation of scientists, including some of his best friends, did not see that communism had led merely to tyranny and poverty.

As an intellectual who believed he thought clearly, Johnny agreed most with the economist John Maynard Keynes, who had called Karl Marx the author of an "obsolete economic textbook which I know to be not only scientifically erroneous but without interest or application for the modern world." An especial sadness was that James Alexander (a jolly, mountain-climbing mathematician) turned near-Marxist during the depression. He felt guilty because he had been born rich. Johnny was puzzled that even the brightest minds did not understand what was happening under Stalin, although it paraded before their eyes.

Despite the arrival of baby Marina, the itchy six-year gap between Mariette and Johnny probably gaped biggest in this 1935. She was a lively twenty-six-year-old and he was a respectable thirty-one-year-old professor of international renown. Johnny's temper burned on slow fuse into occasionally hurtful explosion. All his life his main recreation was thinking. If interrupted, his kindest and most frequent reaction was just to ignore the interrupter. When this habit spread to engulf most of her hours with him, Mariette felt she was not living the life that a bright, witty, much admired young dazzler should. Even at the Princeton parties Johnny would sometimes retire to jot down equations in his study and leave Mariette to host the throng. Desmond (né Horner) Kuper, with his contortionist tricks, was much more relaxing fun.

After the divorce Mariette complained that Johnny had been

"dull." This shocked some of his friends more than she knew, but it was probably Austro-Hungarian for "preoccupied." Klari, Johnny's second wife, always worried that she was way behind Johnny in intellectual brilliance, as indeed was nearly everybody in the world. Mariette was not in the least worried. She intended to be her own woman and through her life has managed to be so.

The breakup came during the 1936 trip to Europe. Johnny's first lectures were in Paris at the Institut Henri Poincaré. The intention was that they would go on from there to Budapest together. Mariette went on to Budapest alone. Johnny drifted around his engagements and came glumly home to the United States. Divorce proceedings were settled amicably in 1937. Baby Marina would live mainly with Mariette in her pre–high school years; and then mainly with Johnny when her education became more intellectual. Johnny's first letter to Ulam after the breakup thanks Ulam for his worries about "my domestic complications. I am really sorry that things went this way—but at least I am not particularly responsible for it. I hope that your optimism is well-founded—but, since happiness is an eminently empirical proposition, the only thing I can do is to wait and see." Unusually for Johnny, it is very unclear what this last sentence means. Like others of Johnny's letters at the time, this is the letter of a lonely and unhappy man.

He was not to remain lonely for long. During his 1937 trip to Budapest he met again with Klari Dan, who was then becoming divorced from her second husband in quick succession. Johnny married Klari in October 1938, and she enters our story from the next chapter on. The present chapter has to discuss how far Johnny's early years at the IAS were a professional, as distinct from domestic, success. My controversial judgment is: not much.

◄►◄►

The IAS has succeeded magnificently in all the respects about which there were originally the gravest doubts, but Flexner's concept did not work out for some of the finest minds originally assembled at it—as Flexner himself soon saw. At American universities then (a) the average teaching load was twelve or fourteen

hours a week, (*b*) research was an optional activity, and (*c*) professors did not have to spend so much of their time chasing grants.
The release from *a* did not always lead to a huge expansion in *b*,
so some IAS hopes as well as fears were confounded.

One wrong fear had been that the IAS might rob luster as well
as professors from Princeton University down the road. Princeton
has instead developed as one of the liveliest intellectual communities anywhere, partly because bright minds congregated to be
in the same town as the glittering early stars. In addition to the
permanent professors there were the regular distinguished visitors.
Dirac was invited from England's Cambridge for a year by Johnny
in 1934, as part of an exchange that gave Johnny a summer job in
Cambridge in 1935; Dirac returned at least once a decade to the
IAS ever after. As the man who deduced the existence of antimatter
by equations before anybody had discovered it from observation,
this silently thinking loner was a tailor-made IAS character. Pauli
was at the IAS in the war years 1940–46. Although the opposite
of a silent loner—he was apt to say "do not be foolish" even to
Bohr—he opened the way to knowledge about neutrinos and me-
sons. Bohr paid brief visits to the IAS, and other great minds paid
longer ones.

Another success has been with the one-year or two-year young
(and poorly paid) postgraduate members. This may seem odd
because the IAS, contrary to original intent, has never granted
even Ph.D. degrees. In the 1930s the IAS served as a waiting room
for brilliant new Ph.D.'s who could not get university posts during
the depression, particularly refugees from Europe. In the 1990s
the one-year or two-year freedom from teaching chores makes the
IAS a good place for young scholars who (to quote Ed Regis) are
"between jobs, perhaps, or trying for tenure at their home university, and the one thing they need most in life is to get several
important pieces of research out of the door and published." Note
that this is the opposite of Flexner's original intention. He thought
of his institute as a place that would not put fires under any scholar.
There were few fires under the Einstein-generation permanent
professors in the 1930s, and that is why some drooped cold.

Flexner insisted there should be no laboratories at the IAS.

Einstein and Weyl agreed that a theoretical physicist did not need such things: "It is enough that laboratories exist in the civilisation in which he lives; it is by no means necessary that he be associated with a laboratory at the place where he works." Einstein and Weyl wrote this in a paper recommending that Pauli be made a professor at the institute rather than Oppenheimer, at a time when neither wished to be made one. As early as 1935, Oppenheimer described the laboratory-less IAS in his favorite rude polysyllables as "a madhouse: its solipsistic luminaries shining in separate and hopeless desolation."

In the 1950s, by when Oppenheimer had become the IAS's third director, the Nobel laureate Feynman turned down a professorship at the institute. In his engaging and ungrammatical style, he was more convincing than Oppenheimer in explaining why. Said Feynman:

> When I was at Princeton in the 1940's I can see what happened to those great minds at the Institute for Advanced Study, who had been specially selected for their tremendous brains and were now given this opportunity to sit in this lovely house by the woods there, with no classes to teach, with no obligations whatsoever. These poor bastards could now sit and think clearly all by themselves. Okay? So they don't get an idea for a while. They have every opportunity to do something and they are not getting any ideas. I believe that in a situation like this a kind of guilt or depression worms inside of you, and you begin to worry about not getting any ideas. And nothing happens. Still no ideas come.

Feynman said that in his own infertile periods his students jerked his mind toward "a problem by asking questions in the neighborhood of that problem. It's not so easy to remind yourself of these things. I find that teaching and the students keep life going and I would never accept any position in which somebody had invented a happy situation for me where I don't have to teach. Never." From New York, Courant agreed with this assessment.

Flexner's two main mistakes in the 1930s were his beliefs that permanent professors would like to be freed from the burden of administration, and that all brilliant elderly scholars could create great ideas in vacuo. In vacuo means in a place that does not exist and into which hot air is constantly seeking to rise. By the time Flexner had filled the IAS in the 1930s with many "an enlightened and informed human spirit, seeking its intellectual prey," that prey was all too usually a colleague, especially Director Flexner. After the war Oppenheimer commissioned an official history of the IAS (1930–50) to describe the institute's contribution to the history of scholarship in the twentieth century. The manuscript was never published and was almost suppressed. Regis says that one professor described it as the story of twenty-six faculty members stabbing each other in the back with knives.

By 1939 most of the permanent professors (including Einstein, although excluding Johnny) were plotting Flexner's downfall, at a time when he had already decided to go. The spleen against poor Flexner thankfully did not reach that thirty years later (after Johnny's death) when Carl Kaysen, an economist and author of the classic antitrust study *United States versus United Shoe Machinery Company*, became the institute's harassed fourth director. That story is (once again) told best in Regis's book.

"I believe he wrote his thesis on a shoe factory," said one mathematics professor. "[He is] eager for power, but does not have the moral integrity or intellectual capacity to use it wisely," said another. Regis asked the right question: "Why do mild mathematicians turn into ogres, anxious to devour directors?" One good answer to him was that the IAS's powerful mathematicians did all the mathematics that anybody can bear "in a few hours of the morning, and then they've got the rest of the day to bug other people." Johnny was always thinking mathematics at midnight more relaxedly and usefully than some of his colleagues had thought it for two hours after breakfast, and he thus avoided this trap.

Kaysen eventually decided to "spend the next decade or two in more agreeable ways." There was similar bitterness in Flexner's farewell advice to his mild Quaker successor Frank Aydelotte in

1939. The intriguers against himself, Flexner told Aydelotte, had originally said they wanted to be scholars without administrative duties. They "did not mean a word of it. . . . They wanted opportunities for scholarship, with high salaries, but they also wanted managerial and executive powers. . . . You have to make them realise from the jump that you are the master."

Johnny hated this academic infighting, more than he politely let his colleagues know. His attitude on how to comport himself in Princeton was by now almost always the opposite of Einstein's, but both men derived amusement rather than enmity from the fact. After the Nazis' anti-Semitic decrees in April 1933, Johnny resigned in gentle German from his membership in various German academic bodies. He stressed in resignation letters that he would always be proud to have been a son of German science, associated with German universities in the past decade. He tied his resignations to Nazi monstrosities against particular named scholars, with some hope that German professors would do more to help them.

When the Nazis' anti-Semitic decrees appeared, Einstein was already out of Germany, in Belgium. He renounced his German citizenship with fire and flame, which brought the headline in the Nazi press "Good news from Einstein. He's not coming back."

Einstein sailed into New York harbor on the S.S. *Westmoreland* on October 17, 1933. At the pier where the *Westmoreland* was due to dock, New York Mayor John O'Brien (who was fighting an election campaign against Fiorello La Guardia) awaited him with banners, a parade band, and a speech to try to win the Jewish vote. Flexner had Einstein disembark at Quarantine Island and carried him in a launch to the New Jersey shore. This was to avoid O'Brien and other political involvement. Flexner's desire to keep Einstein out of politics was pushed to paranoia when Flexner turned down an invitation for Einstein to have dinner with President and Mrs. Roosevelt, although Einstein's secretary had intimated that he would be delighted to go. Einstein was understandably furious. He started heading his letters, "Concentration Camp, Princeton."

More mellowly Einstein wrote to Queen Elizabeth of Belgium that Princeton was "a quaint and ceremonious village of puny demigods on stilts. . . . Here, the people who compose what is called society enjoy even less freedom than their counterparts in Europe. Yet they seem unaware of this restriction since their way of life tends to inhibit personality development from childhood." Johnny, by contrast, believed that America's greater materialism saved it from being as childish as Europe. He could not see such emotional doctrines as Nazism or Marxism ever really gaining ground among the sensible, money-seeking masses of the United States. But he was worried by the childishness in American academic life, although usually up to the point only of chuckling at it.

Because Johnny was a cherubic twenty-six-year-old when he arrived in America as a professor, he took the trouble of always wearing a business suit. If he did wear casual clothes, he was apt to be mistaken for a student—which he thought was more embarrassing for the perpetrator of the mistake than for himself. At Princeton Einstein soon relapsed into his habit of not even wearing socks, and of donning more formal clothes only for show. He arrived at a dance at the institute in full evening dress. "This is what Mr. Flexner bought me for," Einstein said.

Einstein continued to work very hard. When his wife died in 1936 she said on her deathbed that the professor "believes his latest work to be the best he has ever done." Einstein's own attitude was expressed in his strange letter from Princeton to Born, who was now in Edinburgh: "I hibernate like a bear in its cave, and really feel more at home than ever before in all my varied existence. The bearishness has been accentuated further by the death of my mate, who was more attached to human beings than I." The brutal fact remains that at Princeton Einstein was not working successfully. He was trying to find inconsistencies in the quantum theory (which exist), but, after probing ninety-nine solutions, he comforted himself that "at least I know 99 ways that won't work." His success, he said, had been "to save another fool from wasting six months on the same idea."

Many of the early geniuses at the IAS were in the 1930s limping forward in the same way. A progress report from its school of mathematics in 1941—by Morse and Johnny—bravely fails (despite Johnny's usual desperate politeness) to disguise this. The report says that mathematics is "a language differing no little in its words, considerably in its grammar, and absolutely in its syntax, from any other language used by men." The contents of mathematical research cannot be described precisely, any more than the contents of a Chinese poem. Both should often be judged by aesthetic standards.

After these excuses for colleagues who were sometimes slipping into the baroque, the report had not too many new Chinese poems to offer. Among the nonprofessors, as one success story, Gödel had "found the (negative) solution of the famous continuum problem which had resisted all efforts for over 40 years"; it went back to Cantor. Gödel was a loner, who worked well in isolation anyway. Indeed, Mariette says Gödel used to wander into their house to borrow one of Johnny's books, sit down to read it on the spot, and then wander out without saying a word. This was awkward for a twenty-five-year-old woman, especially when Johnny left some of his books in the bedroom. The other great men at Princeton were more gregarious—less intense but sometimes less productive.

As the institute nears its sixtieth birthday in the 1990s, three of the main discoveries usually advertised as coming directly from it are still (a) Gödel's work on the continuum problem; (b) the Nobel Prize won in 1957 by Chen Ning Yang and Tsung-Dao Lee for overturning the law of conservation of parity (these were two Chinese physicists whom Oppenheimer brought in the 1950s to the IAS—in the 1930s Flexner had been accused of discriminating against "coloreds or Asians"); and (c) Johnny's work.

Johnny was at the IAS for part of each year from 1933 to 1955. He produced seventy-five papers in those twenty-two years, including thirty-six in the nine years 1933–42 when the institute was the main focus of his attention. How did he keep up this output, while the work of many other permanent professors at the institute ran toward the sand? The awkward answer is that Johnny might have produced even more somewhere else. Remember that in Germany he had been publishing nearly one new paper a month.

Ulam reported that, during his stay at Princeton in the 1930s, Johnny was showing some hesitation about what he was doing. "He was immersed in his new work on continuous geometries and on the theory of classes of operators in Hilbert Space. I myself was not so interested in [these] problems. . . . Johnny, I could feel, was not completely certain of the importance of this work either. Only when he found from time to time some ingenious, technically elegant trick or a new approach did he seem visibly stimulated or relieved of his own internal doubts."

Johnny, however, retained his capacity for following into fields that other clever people suggested, and soon going further than they. For pure mathematics, the most important of these collaborations in the 1930s was that with Columbia's F. J. Murray. For the future, the most important connection may have been that with Alan Turing.

In the spring of 1934 the young Murray got his Ph.D. from Columbia and (to quote a paper he wrote in 1990) "constructed various Hilbert spaces for partial differential operators and obtained what I thought would be useful results." Professor Marshall Stone suggested that he should look at a paper Johnny had written in his German days. Then Johnny himself suggested that Murray should read a second one. The result was that Murray discovered that one of Johnny's original conjectures was wrong and drew up various diagrams to prove it. "All the diagrams had algebraic equivalents, which von Neumann preferred. He was tolerant of my diagram procedures but certainly not enthusiastic," said Murray fifty-five years after 1935. Once the relevant algebra was written down, however, Johnny reacted with his usual incredible speed. Straightaway, said Murray, "von Neumann described the five types of ranges for the dimension function in a discussion of less than half an hour."

The two men's subsequent papers on rings of operators through the 1930s were the first to see that the factors with which Hilbert space theory is concerned are of at least three types. This required considerable imagination since at the time nobody could be sure that types 2 and 3 existed. Today infinite families of type 2 and type 3 factors have been revealed, and mathematicians deal in their subfactors and superfactors.

Because Johnny was a recognized expert on Hilbert space, other people's wanderings in it were referred to him. When B. O. Koopman in 1931 showed how to formulate the ergodic theorem in terms of Hilbert space, Johnny accepted this as "a challenge and a hint." The ergodic theorem was crucial for the foundation of statistical mechanics. When scientists in the nineteenth century sought to explain the behavior of liquids and gases on the basis of Newton's laws of mechanics, they did so by taking averages. Johnny's "naïve" ergodic theorem was briefly celebrated as the first rigorous mathematical basis for this sort of statistical mechanics.

Within a very short time, G. D. Birkhoff from Harvard had greatly strengthened and improved on Johnny's ergodic theorem. Some people thought Johnny was cross about this, especially because Birkhoff was able to dash into print faster than Johnny could. Johnny expressed pleasure rather than resentment, although he did kick himself for not spotting the next steps from his own calculations that Birkhoff saw. He also felt that the European system (where keen minds would gather together around blackboards to help forward each other's ideas) worked better than the American system of claiming personal priority for everything. His Princeton parties, with the drink flowing, did not make up for the European coffeehouses' communal math in this respect.

It was about this Princeton period that Ulam said Johnny "had this habit of considering the line of least resistance. Of course, with his powerful brain he could quickly vanquish all small obstacles or difficulties, and then go on. But if the difficulty was great right from the start, he would not knock his head against the wall, nor would he . . . walk around the fortress and knock here and there to find the weakest spots and try to break through. He would switch to another problem." This was not true of his papers on rings of operators. As Jack Schwartz said, "To carry out this work, he reached three or four stone walls, and in each case smashed right through them." But on some other matters in those 1930s he was accused of not following his most brilliant ideas right through. He won the Bocher Prize for his 1934 paper "Almost Periodic Functions in a Group." This had important consequences for what mathematicians called "abstract harmonic analysis," but he got rather bored by this. He was upset by the early death in 1933 of his fellow Hungarian Alfred Haar. He felt that Haar's discovery of the so-called group invariant measure had provided mathematicians with an important tool. Some critics said that if Johnny had stayed in Europe, with his 1927–29 rate of productivity, he might have discovered Haar's group invariant measure himself.

Some gluttons for this sort of language will say this book should probe deeper into Johnny's pure mathematics in his Princeton days, but the temptation can mercifully be resisted. He started or pushed forward many new roads in math from both Germany and Princeton, but other men since then have naturally gone much further down them. Also he did not belong solely to mathematics. One of my most interesting interviews when researching this book was with Professor (of philosophy) John Dorling of the University of Amsterdam. Dorling regards Johnny as one of the most important philosophers of the twentieth century. "In about six areas of philosophy, von Neumann made substantial contributions, mainly in turning vague problems into ones that could be precisely formulated mathematically." Dorling listed these six: (1) Johnny's contribution to the philosophy of mathematics (including set theory, number theory, and Hilbert space); (2) the philosophy of physics, especially quantum theory; (3) the philosophy of economics; (4) the philosophy of rational action (we will discuss both 3 and 4 in chap. 11); (5) the philosophy of biology; and (6) the philosophy of computers and artificial intelligence. Johnny started on the fifth and sixth areas with his meeting with the strange young Englishman Alan Turing, who came to Princeton in the 1930s. Johnny wanted to keep him as an assistant—in which case they would probably have progressed faster together to computers—but Turing went back home to become Britain's master decoder of German wartime ciphers, through something that was not called a computer but was one. When Turing's promiscuous homosexuality made British bureaucrats crassly regard him as a security risk, he committed suicide.

Turing had started his career in the same field of imagining that Johnny did. His first published paper was an extension of Johnny's and Gödel's work on logic. Turing proved that certain kinds of mathematical and logical problems could not be converted to algorithms, and therefore could not be solved even by advanced sorts of automatic universal computing machines if such things existed. Because they did not yet exist, Turing described how a universal machine could be created by feeding in a limitless tape. He thereby laid the theoretical foundations for much of modern computer programming.

I originally thought Johnny himself was not thinking much about computers at this stage, although some of his branches of mathematics in the 1930s had relevance to what was to come. He became interested in turbulence in hydrodynamics, including a study of how to make explosions more efficient. This was to be the most important part of his early war work. If he had not moved to the IAS, Veblen had asked him to lecture on this subject at Princeton in 1933–34. He did some preliminary research and immediately concluded that there would be need of a lot more number crunching than the 1930s' desk calculating machines could easily do. He started on the numerical analysis that would be needed if calculating machines became better. Also in this period came his proof that it is possible to build large systems with a bounded probability of deviation of error, provided that you build a sufficient number of "gates" around the system and that each gate's failure rate is sufficiently small.

The recent publication in Hungarian of Johnny's letters to Rudolf Ortvay in 1928–39 shows that Johnny was thinking past error theory to computing machines. The principal lesson from those letters is Johnny's extraordinary political foresight. "There will be a war in Europe in the next decade," he wrote in 1935. He feared Germany would rather easily overthrow France but cheered Ortvay by saying that America had a fonder special relation with England than central Europeans realized. "If England is in trouble, that will be for the US a *casus belli*. Perhaps even the suspicion of it." He was startlingly accurate in his fear for European Jews. He thought that during a war in Europe they might suffer genocide similar to the slaughter of Armenians in Turkey in 1916–17.

Interspersed with this, and with explanations that Roosevelt's New Deal was not as inflationary as Europeans thought, Johnny said that mathematicians must start to pay attention to "the anatomy of the brain." There was going to be an advance to computing machines that would have to work partly as the brain did. He and Ortvay agreed that such machines would become attached to all large systems such as telecommunication systems, electricity grids, and big factories.

It would be wrong to suppose that he yet saw this as the principal road down which his own career would go. Johnny's wide-ranging letters to fellow Americans in the 1930s contained references to his desire to write a book on the ergodic theorem, and to collaborate with Ulam or somebody else to write an up-to-date work on measure theory ("as much combinatorial and as little topological as possible, making extensive use of finite and infinite direct products, and—above all—interpreting measure work much more as probability and much less as volume"). He wondered whether it might be possible to move to a superset theory, and whether Gödel might not prove to have made possible a new approach to formalism in mathematics rather than having closed the subject. By 1937 he was preparing himself "to cause a scandal by making much noise about the non-distributivity of logics. I think I know how to handle the quantifiers in such a system. I should rather do honest work on the algebra and arithmetic of continuing rings— but after all, before God, one pastime is as good (or bad) as any other."

He never really followed these ideas through, and his exasperation ("before God, one pastime is as good . . . as any other") had something to do with his 1930s Princeton mood. He was depressed that his colleagues' great minds there were not proving as intellectually provocative as he had hoped. At one time he feared that the whole impulse toward scientific achievement might be slowing. "The interests of humanity may change. The present curiosities in science may diminish, and entirely different things may occupy the human mind in future."

What Johnny missed in Princeton in these depression years was the driving force provided at Göttingen when theoretical physics seemed to be changing every day. That driving force was soon to come from the approach of World War II. It is perhaps ironic that his entry into work on it came through study of the mathematics of artillery duels, which had been a more important part of the trench warfare of World War I.

►◄►◄►◄ **9**

The Calculating

Exploder, 1937–43

►◄***D***uring the 1914–18 war the Germans lobbed their shells from Krupp's biggest guns several thousand feet into the sky. They found to their delight that their range was nearly twice what their professors of mathematics had predicted. The main reason was not that the chemical propellant for the largest gun, called Big Bertha after a flattered fat Bertha Krupp, was designed by (you have guessed it) Fritz Haber. The reason was that the shells were going through thinner air far above the earth. A new science of artillery ballistics was born as they crashed down erratically on Paris and other places previously thought safely behind the lines, such as generals' GHQs.

Generals at GHQs became advocates of spending a lot of research money on this new science. They received unusually solid interservice support from admirals, who preferred that the battleships carrying their flags should fire on enemy warships from distances where these could not yet fire back at them. The mathematicians had red faces because they always had been bad at solving the nonlinear—that is, continuously changing—equations that rule the motion of anything passing through air of continuously changing density. That includes most explosions.

Linear equations are maps showing how to get home out of an ordinary forest. Nonlinear equations are required when the trees in the forest tiresomely change position with each step you take. Accordingly, as Johnny was relentless and early in pointing out, mathematicians were bad down to the 1940s at calculating what shock waves to expect from an explosion, what could be the result of turbulence around a projectile or aerofoil or propeller or rudder or in a nozzle, especially if any of these were moving through water or colliding with each other. Johnny thought that similar problems would lie ahead in assessing the elasticity or plasticity of various materials. He saw that nonlinear equations would have to be solved if he was ever to advance to his pet project of eventually controlling the weather. These were all reasons why he became so excited after 1944 by the possibilities roused by the computer, which might enable these things to be worked out. But he had turned himself into a calculator of shock waves and ballistic trajectories in 1937–43, which means in precomputer days. He was rather shocked at the mathematical rubbish he found there.

◄►◄►

In the distant precomputer 1914, the firing tables for guns on the western front proved to be based on equations that had been wrenched into a form that would be easy to solve rather than one that described what would actually happen. That sort of nonsense is still sometimes found in military and economic and some other "practical" mathematics to this day.

Because the Europeans in 1914–17 seemed to be firing big guns at each other inaccurately, the United States moved enthusiastically into the new post-1914 science of modern artillery ballistics, even before America entered the war. By 1918 the world's leading institution in the science was what became the Ballistics Research Laboratory (BRL) of the ordnance department of the U.S. Army.

It was eventually placed at the Aberdeen Proving Ground in Maryland. The commanding officer on the technical side in 1917–19 was Major Oswald Veblen, on wartime leave from being professor of mathematics at Princeton. The place of ballistics as the clever man's study in war was reemphasized when some of the other luminaries engaged in it during or just after 1918 included Princeton's Alexander and Morse, plus R. H. (Bob) Kent, who was to be Johnny's close associate early in World War II. One of the juniors working on the firing tables in 1918 was Wiener, then in revolt against the world because some plagiarizer at Harvard had refused to confirm him as an instructor.

In the twenty-five years after 1917 the firing tables for guns at Aberdeen grew in ever more daunting complexity. The main object of a firing table is to tell a gunner at what angle to poke his gun so as to get the right trajectory to hit his target miles away. By the time Johnny was interested in the subject in the 1930s, a typical gun was supposed to require a firing table showing about three thousand possible trajectories, with about 750 multiplications required for each trajectory. One then had to add a lot of other complications that would affect how the shell flew and where it landed—such as the type of fuse and shell, whether it was fired from hard ground or soft desert, the special wobbles to be expected as the speed of the shell dropped from muzzle velocity downward through the speed of sound, and several other matters that the armorers had not first thought of.

The complications grew when you were trying to hit a moving target. Because the well-equipped British army in 1914 had a mere eighty motor vehicles, only the sailors among the original compilers of firing tables had bothered to think of that. Very soon, almost everybody had to. In the 1930s some despairing people minuted that two years would be needed to do the several million mathematical calculations required before being able to calibrate at what angle each gun should be pointed in order to hit what size of target when.

It is worth pointing out that many of these calculations were not needed as assiduously as the deskmen then thought. The accuracy of artillery gun sights and even aircrafts' bombsights played a smaller part in World War II than soldiers and sailors expected at its beginning. The Japanese sank the American fleet at Pearl Harbor with hardly any bombsights at all. Germany's rockets landed on London erratically as they ran out of fuel. The problem became quite different in the deterrence of World War III, for which it has been important that every potentially aggressive Brezhnev should think that any multinuclear warhead intercontinental missile could be targeted (via Johnny's computers) quite instantly to land in the right place—namely, on top of himself. Witness also the accuracy of missiles in the 1991 Gulf War.

The expectation just before 1939 was that the coming war would be of the push-button-and-bayonet-charge variety. Instead it became one of tank blitzkriegs. The eastward guns of the Maginot Line and the seaward guns of Singapore were exhaustively calibrated, but the Germans on motorcycles and Japanese on ordinary bicycles appeared from the other side.

In the years after 1918, Veblen acted as an able recruiting sergeant for his old command. Money for it disappeared in the isolationist 1920s, but recovered as Hitler made war look more probable. In the mid-1930s, so as to do the sums to compile its ever more complicated firing tables, Aberdeen acquired one of Vannevar Bush's differential analyzers. It was because this was no longer adequate by 1943 that the laboratory made its historic contract with the Moore School of Engineering at the University of Pennsylvania in Philadelphia to build the first electronic computer. In 1937 the laboratory at Aberdeen was also building (under the supervision of nobody less than Hungary's now fifty-six-year-old Theodore von Karman) the first supersonic wind tunnel of unusual design.

In that year Aberdeen also acquired (through the recommendation of Veblen) the very part-time consultancy services of Johnny.

◄►◄►

Johnny had by this time (1937) decided that war was clearly coming. He was wondering what part in it he might most productively play for America. He modestly thought that his best role might be similar to that of Veblen in 1917–19. For this reason, at the end of 1937, as his American naturalization papers had just come through, but as his wife and baby daughter had just left him, he applied to sit for the exams to become a lieutenant in the reserve of the ordnance department of the U.S. Army. As a member of the Officers' Reserve Corps he could get more trouble-free access to various sorts of explosion statistics, and he had already begun some research in collaboration with Kent that suggested these could be fascinating.

The level of sophistication in these army officer's exams was rather below any to which he had stooped since the age of nine, but he tackled them in a good Johnny way. He read the relevant army manuals through in one concentrated gulp and remembered them verbatim.

He sat his first exam on The Organization of the Army in March 1938. Sample answers from Johnny: "The continental area of the United States is divided into nine corps areas. . . . The arms are Infantry, Cavalry, Field Artillery. . . ." His mark in the exam was 100%.

He got the same 100% in his exam in May 1938 on Military Discipline, Courtesies, Customs. Sample Johnny answer: "He should stand to attention, and salute." His 100% mark tickled him. He told Veblen that he was due to become the army's master of ceremonies. In his April exam on The Law of Military Offenses, he got only 75%. The army asked what charges should be brought against committers of various offenses, and here Johnny's gentle common sense came into minor collision with the army's brute formalism. "This man should be charged with absence without leave," he wrote to one question. He explained that any charge of desertion could be met with a defense that civilians would find convincing. "No, desertion," wrote the major in the U.S. Cavalry who was his temporary lord and examining master. But the 75% awarded to Johnny was still the sort of pass mark that was going to make him high on the list of lieutenants. The remaining exam in the early summer of 1938 was to be on The Organization of the Ordnance Department, but the paper was not ready, and three other considerations intervened for Johnny at the beginning of the universities' summer vacation for 1938.

One was that he believed there was going to be a European war in September or October. A second was that Klari Dan's divorce was due to be finalized in Budapest at about that time. He intended to marry her immediately after the divorce and get her on the next boat to New York. He hoped to persuade his mother and brothers to come away from Budapest at the same time because, he wrote, the "only sensible move now in Europe is out." He again told his family that it would be a mistake in this coming war to "be caught dead on the wrong side."

The third reason was that he had the usual clutch of lecture requests—to travel and to dip himself in Europe's cultural streams for what he feared might be the last time in a long while. One of these invitations came from the League of Nations' International Institute for Intellectual Cooperation—a body whose name he did not revere. "Nebbitch, if you remember your Middle High German," he wrote to Ulam. But the institute's draft program for its conference in Warsaw was to begin with a lecture by Bohr, specifically examining what Johnny delightedly called "one of my youthful indiscretions in Quantum Mechanics." Johnny was satisfied that he had helped mathematicians to accept quantum mechanics, but he did not believe in a frog-mouse battle about different ways of saying the same thing. He wanted to show Europeans how relaxed he was over this. A second lecture was to be given by Heisenberg on his latest views. Because Heisenberg would return from Warsaw to become Hitlerite Germany's most eminent scientist (perhaps a new Haber?) during what Johnny saw would be a war, it did seem rather useful to tap his views for a last time. A third lecturer was to be England's Sir Arthur Eddington, who still did not really believe in what he called "the theory of quanta." Johnny thought he would rather enjoy joining with future enemies such as Heisenberg to tell future allies such as the English that Eddington was daft.

Secure with an American passport in his pocket since his naturalization in 1937, he therefore traveled through the doomed Europe of 1938 in a very Johnny way. Although Hitler was clearly preparing to rape what Johnny still spelled in English "Tschechoslovakia," Johnny's views on the imminence of full Armageddon fluctuated as did many Europeans' in that Sudeten summer. At one stage Veblen had apparently suggested some program of negotiation through which war might be avoided. Johnny replied, with his favorite mathematical humor: "The world has become so complex lately that I don't see how this could be done, without an essential use of positive integers as ordinals." Yet by the time he reached Warsaw in June 1938, he was writing more optimistically: "I think that there will be war, although it may be at a distance of a half year or perhaps even one or two years." He did not now think that Sudetenland would be the issue on which it would break out because most Europeans seemed to feel that Tschechoslovakia (like Yugoslavia) should never have been created.

He stayed in Copenhagen with Bohr, for three reasons. First, he was completing the arrangements for Bohr to come to the IAS in Princeton for the opening semester of 1939, at the then rather large fee of $6,000 a term. If there was to be a war, Johnny saw early that Bohr was the European most needed on the American side of the Atlantic. Next, Bohr's Copenhagen in 1938 was an intriguing place in which one could meet many of the great scholars who had recently swarmed out of Nazi Germany, plus some who were still in touch with Berlin (where German scholars were making fearful nuclear breakthroughs in that Sudeten September). Third, Klari Dan's divorce proceedings in Budapest were at a delicate stage. Her lawyers had suggested that the man she intended immediately to marry should not be in the same city as her while—to facilitate her divorce in a Catholic country—his existence was still being partially denied. As the war clouds darkened in September 1938, however, he felt he had to hurry to Budapest to be at her side.

He therefore admitted he had guilty reason for welcoming the Anglo-French surrender at Munich on September 30. "I can only say that Mr. Chamberlain obviously wanted to do me a great personal favour," he wrote to Veblen from Budapest in early October. "I needed a postponement of the next world war very badly." The reason was that Klari's divorce was not yet through. But he now expected the war to start in 1939: "I can't see any reason why European politics should not be in the same mess six months hence as they were six months ago." In the last days of September 1938 he had seen what a European war would look like when it "gets started—which is very good for me since I hope and trust to look at it from the outside when it really starts. It was very lovely: air-raid drills, blackouts, a dearth of gas masks, pleasant meditations. . . ." Very Johnny-like, he reports that in this period of expecting imminent war:

Peculiarly enough I did some mathematics. I can make a unitary spectral theory for non-Hermitian matrices, which seems to be new even in two dimensions and looks quite amusing.

Johnny's definition of amusing often did differ from other people's.

Klari's divorce was finalized at the end of October. Johnny married her two weeks later. They sailed to New York at once. He had not persuaded either his family or Klari's to come during this post-Munich period of euphoria about peace in our time.

◄►◄►

In America with his bride in January of 1939, Johnny sat his final exam to become an officer in the army reserve: the paper on The Organization of the Ordnance Department. Once again his mark was 100%. "Generalship looms," he said to friends. If he had entered the army reserve then, he would presumably have disappeared into uniform when America joined the war. He could not then have made as many extraordinary wartime contributions to the free world's firepower as he did. A lot of history was changed for the better because an army clerk made a daft bureaucratic obstruction, and the topmost command felt obliged to back him.

The story is expostulated in a letter dated July 5, 1939, from Senator William H. Smathers to Harry Hines Woodring, President Roosevelt's secretary of war. John von Neumann, wrote Senator Smathers, "made application for a commission as lieutenant in the Ordnance Department of the army for the purpose of doing research work in ballistics. I understand that he took all examinations and passed, but during the exams he reached the age of 35 years and his application was turned down. Mr. von Neumann is internationally known as a mathematician, and I cannot understand how a man with so much potential value to the American armed forces should be turned down for a technicality."

Woodring's reply on July 27, 1939, carried all the bristle of a pompous ass. He said he had "carefully considered the interesting letter from Mr. John von Neumann, an assistant to Dr. Einstein in the Institute for Advanced Study at Princeton (sic)," but this application is "not favorably considered."

The age requirements for appointment in the reserve corps were adopted after a thorough study of all factors involved, and have been adhered to consistently since their adoption, many applicants otherwise splendidly qualified and in every way desirable having been denied solely on the basis of age. Should exception have been made in the case of Mr. von Neumann the position of the War Department in denying similar considerations in other deserving cases where the age limit has been exceeded by a brief period would be untenable.

The world therefore went into its first year of war from September of 1939 without having Johnny in even a reserve officer's uniform. The cause of freedom did not prosper during it. Partly because Johnny's effort to get a commission was still being fought through by senators, Klari von Neumann was dispatched in that summer of 1939 to Europe to play the Scarlet Pimpernel and to get her and Johnny's family out to America before war broke. In the month before war did break, most of the von Neumann and Dan families except anxious Johnny were still at sea, although all did arrive safely.

The safe arrival of Klari's parents proved a tragedy. Charles Dan had enjoyed being a rich man in Hungary, and he did not enjoy being a poorer one in New Jersey. At that first American Christmas, in 1939, he slipped to his death beneath a train, in what was clearly suicide. Today his body lies in a four-plot grave in Princeton cemetery, beside his daughter Klari (who drowned, probably also a suicide, in 1963 after Johnny's death). In the two other plots of the grave lie Margaret and John von Neumann, mother and son. Charles Dan's widow insisted in 1940 on going back to wartime Hungary. At one time Johnny and Klari feared she must have perished in the Holocaust. Actually she sat unharmed in her house under gunfire through the siege of Budapest in 1944, reading Klari's love letters from boyfriends in her various betrothals with some interest. Mrs. Dan went to live in England with Klari's sister after the war, until her death past age ninety.

Charles Dan's unhappiness in New Jersey is a reminder that not all of the emigrants from Hungary found America to be as congenial as Johnny did. Theodore von Karman brought his old mother to New York. "Today at last I saw a horse," she wrote after six months there. "It was riding in a car." She presumably meant a horse trailer. A sadder case was the composer Bela Bartok, who also arrived at this time. He complained that every second American seemed to be a ruminant (i.e., was chewing gum). He could not write music overflowing with joy because the noises of New York City were not the soft sounds of birds and insects he had loved in the Hungarian countryside. Also, he thought that everybody was trying to cheat him because he could not adapt to the American checkbook system. Columbia did not renew his appointment as a lecturer.

The free world's awful 1939–40 was therefore also a personally harrowing one for the new bridegroom Johnny. He reacted to the unpleasantness in his and his father's usual way by sounding excessively lighthearted about it. His one paper with military applications was that with Kent, published as report 175 for the Aberdeen Proving Ground in September 1940: "The Estimation of the Probable Error from Successive Differences." It calculated where to aim when you have several times missed. He was to write three additions to this report in the next two years, and they made him regarded as one of America's greatest mathematical experts on bombing patterns. But most of his papers in that 1940 continued to be about rings of operators in abstract Hilbert space (which by now were becoming too abstract), plus a paper, "Minimally Almost Periodic Groups," with Wigner.

Because trips to Europe were now out of the question, he started the summer vacation from Princeton by taking Klari out to the West Coast of America, which she had never seen. This was partly to stay with Fellner at Berkeley, but also to teach in a summer school at the University of Washington in Seattle. It was during this summer session that the incident occurred which later caused desperately anticommunist Johnny to be accused of having communist connections.

One of his favorite pupils (some say his only pupil) at Princeton in 1936 had been a young Canadian, with whom he later wrote a mathematical paper, "On the Transitivity of Perspective Mappings." These are not the sorts of mappings about which spy catchers need become excited; they referred to clusters of figures. The Canadian was a fellow lecturer at the summer school in Washington in that awful summer of 1940 as France fell. Johnny discovered to his surprise that the youngster's politics inclined, or perhaps had inclined, toward Marxism.

Six years later, in 1946, this mathematician was arrested in Canada's communist spy trial. Johnny signed a letter to the prime minister of Canada. It said, in effect, that he could well understand how a bad report could have been made about the youngster if anybody had been listening to his political spoutings, but he did not believe that the young man regarded politics as a central concern; he was much more intent on mathematics. Eventually the court did not think that the Canadian was guilty of anything. It acquitted him, and he has continued with a distinguished mathematical career to this day. Johnny thought that this proved his letter absolutely right, but at least one senator in Johnny's confirmation hearings for the Atomic Energy Commission (AEC) in 1955 called it "not the brightest thing that you have ever written."

There is a clash of evidence about how far Johnny was willing to argue about politics with friends. One of his then mildly left-leaning colleagues says he was a delightful man to argue with, because conversation flowed in a way where neither side could possibly get cross. Others say Johnny always avoided political arguments, usually by retailing a risqué joke and thereby changing the subject.

The connecting line is probably the proviso that "nobody could get cross." Johnny veered away from political arguments whenever he felt the person he was talking to might become either cross or boring. Johnny did not himself grow angry with those who desperately wanted to believe that communism could bring succor to the poor, despite all the evidence he had seen since 1917 that it is bound to do the opposite. He thought that those who believed in communism or socialism deserved the same sympathy as other simpletons who could not understand even linear equations. But he also did not believe that being a communist meant that anybody became a bad mathematician or bad scientist, and he was anxious to recruit into mathematics and science all the able brains he could.

On two other occasions he went to some risk to protect people who were being edged out of sensitive jobs for their left-wing opinions, and he privately did the same to protect one alcoholic. He thought that considerations of security were overdone.

The main event in the summer of 1940 was that the German army cut through France as through butter, very much as Johnny had predicted: he was not as surprised or horrified as most of his friends. France's ruling politicians, he wrote to Veblen as the Germans raced forward in May, "seem to expect a miracle, for which I sincerely hope and pray, but it would have been much better if they had been able to run the war on a less metaphysical basis." He had a low opinion of French and British military planning throughout (in January 1940 he had shrewdly hoped for some Dardanelles-type operation in Scandinavia). But he also thought that America should not overrate the intelligence of "Schickel-gruber's employees," which was becoming his favorite term for Germany's officialdom and officer corps.

In July 1940 he expressed the unfashionable view that Britain would be able to resist or deter a German invasion. But he felt it likely that some time in 1941 America would have to come into the war, as it had done in 1917. In Johnny style, he said that America would have to accept the unpopular advice given "by a court physician to a septuagenarian German prince and princess, on announcing the birth of a daughter: 'I regret that your majesties will need to move yourselves about energetically once again.' "

By contrast a letter from Ulam, on the day of Pétain's surrender in July 1940, plumbed into the depths of despair. "As regards the world situation," wrote Ulam, "my worst premonitions have become true. My faith in America has almost completely disappeared, and I suppose that you must have been greatly shocked by the spectacle of complete chaos, indecision and even some worse characteristics in this country. There is perhaps still hope that Russia will step in in Europe." Ulam believed that rearmament in America would take far too long even to "come out of the planning stage, and in a few months it may be too late. I think we both have had many false hopes and there may be further disappointment ahead. There is enough of experience now to teach us how to take it."

Johnny was not disposed to accept this criticism of America. He was cheered that whichever president was going to be elected in 1940, whether Roosevelt or Willkie, would probably bring America into the war in 1941. He thought that free mankind's two enemies (Germany and Russia) might by then "be doing the nice thing of fighting each other." He did not like Ulam's vision of Russia stepping in, but hoped for a German attack that would become bogged down in that vast Russia. He rejoiced when this attack happened. "Conceding that war is a fundamentally dangerous industry," he wrote to Veblen after Hitler's assault on Russia in the summer of 1941, "I feel that the world situation is not bad, much better than it might have been."

In this period he was doing the un-Johnny-like thing of bombarding his congressman with letters and cables in support of all of Roosevelt's actions that brought America nearer to war. "I would like to express my conviction," Johnny wrote to the Honorable D. Lane Powers in September 1941, "that the present war against Hitlerism is not a foreign war, since the principles for which it is being fought are common to all civilised mankind and since even a compromise with Hitler would mean the greatest peril to the future of the United States." Immediately after the sinkings at Pearl Harbor did bring America to war in December 1941, Johnny wrote almost exultantly to Ulam: "I think as before *qu'on les aura.* May take honorable 2–3–4 years."

It is unlikely that he had yet found any wider technical vision to back up his optimism, although one letter in the Library of Congress archives for the summer of 1940 almost suggests that he had. It is from another Canadian during France's fall—signed Erwin—and also begins by saying that the writer cannot understand Johnny's "optimism as to the world's situation. I recall that you were of perfectly sound mind when we met last, but your healthy pessimism seems to have left you since. Is this due to objective developments in the outside world or to changes within your subjective self?" This Erwin then asks about an article in the *New York Times* mentioning the isotope of uranium. "Part of the developments have taken place in your own Institute for Advanced Study, and I don't doubt that you know a great deal about this whole question which, though front page news, seems to be tremendously important. . . . Please set my heart at rest: tell me why and how we will win this war very soon and how the new discoveries will turn out for the best."

Johnny was not at this stage concerned with the isotope of uranium. But by the early autumn of 1940 he himself, although not the United States, was on a war footing.

◀▶ ◀▶

In his confidential report on his war work in 1945 to the IAS, Johnny listed his first important government appointment as being his elevation at Aberdeen, in September 1940, from being a mere consultant to being a member of the Ballistics Research Laboratory's scientific advisory board. On December 12, 1940, he wrote to a Professor Edward M. Earle, who wanted to list his military qualifications on a lecture program:

Dear Ed,

The exact definitions of my defense activities are as follows:

Member of the War Department's Scientific Advisory Board to the Ballistics Research Laboratory at Aberdeen Proving Ground.

Chief Consultant on Ballistics of the War Preparedness Committee of the American Mathematical Society and the Mathematical Association of America.

In the above I have sacrificed brevity to precision. Of course you may not want to print all these sea-serpents.

The scientific advisory board at Aberdeen consisted of about a dozen people, including the ubiquitous von Karman and other scientists such as George Kistiakowsky, I. I. Rabi, and Johnny himself. It met three or four times each year to review the functioning of this, the army ordnance department's most prestigious laboratory—and to suggest to the war department where it should and should not be going next. The original letter to Johnny in 1940 from Major-General Wesson said that "the main motive of members for joining the Committee would be patriotic, but the scientists would get a free railway pass and a stipend of $15 a day."

The program for one of these about-thrice-a-year meetings gives a flavor of what was done. From 1330 hours to 1430 hours on April 18, 1944, Johnny was to read a paper, "Experimental Methods of Studying Shock Waves"; von Karman was to be one of the four other scientists to comment on this paper and so were resident staff members at Aberdeen. Two other papers were being read simultaneously, on theories of fragmentation and the application of electronics to ballistics. From 1500 hours to 1600 hours Johnny and Kistiakowsky were to hear a report from staff members on the latest experiments in concrete demolition, and von Karman was to hear one on experiments in the wind tunnel. Next day

Johnny was to lead a discussion, "Methods of Integration of Differential Equations with Applications to Stresses in Guns and Shocks in Air," and to attend and comment on another talk, "Spin, Drag, and Other Aerodynamic Coefficients."

In 1940–42 Paul Halmos was Johnny's assistant at Princeton. The published works on rings of operators continued in cooperation with him. There was also a foray into astrophysics with a paper, "The Statistics of a Gravitational Field Arising from a Random Distribution of Stars," with S. Chandrasekhar, and in his spare time (see chap. 11) Johnny began to revolutionize microeconomics. But his main concentration was now on something completely different. In the year to September 1941—before America entered the war—Johnny became the master calculator of complicated explosions, such as colliding ones.

His route of entry was through the war preparedness committees. Some other war preparers felt these committees were too untidy to be properly bureaucratic, but Johnny regarded them with affection. He described them to Ulam as "sets, and sets of sets, of committees." He thought their work could bear good fruit "when The Day [of America's entry into the war] comes." After the war, Johnny was to say that—right from this beginning—America's organization of research had proved at least as good as any of the belligerents', and better than most of the other big ones'. A scientist with a contribution to make could see from the different offers before him where he could contribute most at any time, and in practice all these bodies worked together to win the war. Any planned top-down research program, allocating this scientist to that job for that number of years, would have failed to take advantage of changing knowledge and opportunities. The American research system provided the nearest equivalent that wartime secrecy could have allowed to a free market.

Bethe described to me how the initial 1940–41 system worked. In the summer of 1940 he, too, sent a request to one of these war preparedness committees to ask how, as a theoretical physicist, he could best help America prepare for the coming war. The most attractive answer that came back from on high—well, actually from von Karman—was, "We don't know how the equilibrium in shock waves is established. There is this sudden change of pressure in a shock wave. Surely it cannot go completely suddenly? Tell us how it goes." Bethe and Teller did some work on this, and soon found that Johnny was also interested. "Johnny was particularly intrigued with the next stage: to investigate what the equation of state of a gas or other substance is, and its relation to shock waves."

An equation of state is the equation that relates the pressure of a fluid (like water or air) to its density and temperature, and thus becomes a key to explosions. Intriguingly, the Soviet Union's Andrei Sakharov in his autobiography described the calculation of equations of state even in the 1980s as a nightmare, beside which "the physics of atomic and thermonuclear explosions is a genuine theoretician's paradise." "The equations of state of matter at moderate pressures and temperatures," wrote Sakharov, "cannot be calculated without introducing simplifying assumptions into the theoretical equations (otherwise the computations involved exceed the capabilities of the most advanced computers)." It was much easier for nuclear physicists to describe what happens "at temperatures of millions of degrees centigrade, resembling those at the center of a star" (which last had been broadly the research for which Bethe was to get his Nobel Prize).

In 1940–41 Bethe made some advances in calculating equations of state, particularly on the interesting things that happen when water grows colder. "Johnny von Neumann was doing research in a related field" and was characteristically taking wing from it. Bethe expressed eagerness to work with Johnny. By early September 1941 Johnny was writing to Kistiakowsky, one of the organizers of war preparednees committees. His letter is a good example of the octopus-like intellect with which Johnny was by now absorbing several senior people's areas of work:

You are familiar, from the discussions which Professor Kirkwood and I had with you and with Professor Wilson, with the directions in which our theoretical work on shock waves (connected with your research program on explosions) is progressing. We have made quite good progress so far. The theory of shock waves in gases should be investigated further. Almost all existing work deals with the elementary case of linear plane shock waves. . . . Here the powerful "integration method of Riemann" is an important tool, as you and Professor Wilson discussed in your report on the subject. . . . But . . . when the shock wave is in permanent contact with regions of variable density (e.g. on the back side of the shock wave of a gas explosion) and thereby becomes non-linear (i.e. of varying velocity, etc.), then the Riemann method gives scarcely any quantitative information and entirely new procedures have to be found.

Johnny said he had made some first steps in this direction with his new paper called "Shock Waves Started by an Infinitesimally Small Detonation of Given (positive and finite) Energy." He continued:

There are many ramifications of the subject which should be treated: generation of energy in the affected medium (detonation waves, particularly in the work of Chapman and Jouguet), weakening of spherical waves as they progress (three dimensional cases), deviation of the gas from the ideal state, etc. The last mentioned aspect of the problem leads to a consideration of general equations of state, and thereby establishes contacts with Professor Kirkwood's work on liquids.

He concluded by saying that he was going to ask for about $3,700 for two assistants plus expenses, but pointed out that he was also working energetically with Bethe and Bill Flexner at Cornell. Two months later Bethe sent Johnny his manuscript about a theory of shock waves, whereby "I believe I am on the track of an explanation of the Chapman-Jouguet condition, but I am not sure yet." Johnny conspired with Flexner that there should be a four-person "seminar of you, Kirkwood, Bethe and Kennard." On the vexed question of security, because some of the best professors had not

yet got American security clearance (indeed some were still officially Germans), Johnny advised Flexner

> not to discuss specifics of the confidential original work of the
> Kistiakowsky, Wilson etc. committee. Not to discuss subjects un-
> less they have been investigated in the generally accessible inter-
> national literature. Not to discuss the existence and the program
> of our committee. Apart from these taboos, I think that the training
> of competent workers in hydrodynamics in this country will do
> more good than the infinitesimal risk of a good exposition of the
> known theory leaking through to the enemy can do harm.

◄►◄►

Johnny reported to Princeton after the war that from September
1941 to September 1942 he was a consultant and then a member
of division 8 of the National Defense Research Council (NDRC),
and was also acting as the technical supremo ("official investigator") of a contract that the IAS itself had with the Office of Emergency Management. His main work with the NDRC was
concerned with the so-called shaped charges: "In these devices the
precise geometrical shape of an explosive charge is used to modify,
concentrate or limit the physical effects of detonations." This had
important implications for torpedoes and antitank weapons. When
American infantry surged into land battle after 1941, their most
startling new weapon was the antitank device known as the bazooka. Johnny never claimed that he contributed much to the
bazooka. Some of his colleagues at Los Alamos gave him credit
for versions of it, but it seems that his advice to the army on
shaped charges (although initially received with enthusiasm) did
not work too well in eventual practice.

Until 1941–42 Johnny had been known among exclusive pure
mathematicians as a prodigy in their subject, but political men
such as Secretary of War Woodring had thought it cheek to suggest
that this alleged assistant to Einstein should have rules stretched
to make him a lieutenant in his man's army. After America's first
few months of war, Johnny's fame as a practical calculator of

explosive weapons had been spread among all who needed to know, perhaps especially by the admiring Colonel (later General) Leslie Simon, the commanding officer at the army ordnance department's laboratory in Aberdeen, Maryland.

The result of this high reputation with the ordnance department of the army was that Johnny was soon pinched by the ordnance department of the navy. "Johnny preferred admirals to generals," said one libelous contemporary, "because the generals drank iced water for lunch, while the admirals when ashore drank liquor. And Johnny prided himself on his strong head." Apart from Simon, his private letters at this time do express a preference for admirals. On August 31, 1942, Johnny was scribbling by hand a letter to Vannevar Bush, head of the Office of Scientific Research and Development (OSRD)—and thus overlord of the part of America's defense research effort which was not run directly by the army or navy. On the notepaper of Washington's Lafayette Hotel, Johnny explained he had "accepted a contractual appointment in the Navy Department, Bureau of Ordnance, effective full time from 1st September 1942." This meant effective full-time from the next day. "I understand," wrote Johnny, "that as an employee of the armed services the regulations of the OSRD oblige me to sever my relationship with the OSRD and with the NDRC. It is therefore with regret that I resign my membership in Section B1B of the NDRC [this was the shaped-charges contract] and my appointment as official investigator of contract OEM Sr-218 [this meant the money channeled into a special project by the IAS, which also had relevance to complicated explosions]." "The final report on this contract," said Johnny, "is under preparation, and will be submitted in a few weeks."

The fresh opportunity that had inveigled Johnny from September 1, 1942, was to work for the navy's section of mine warfare in the new field of operational research. This meant, as Johnny told Princeton after the war, "physical, statistical and on-the-spot military investigation of the use of weapons under the jurisdiction of that section, and of counter-measures against them." One feature of his contract was that Johnny would work full-time in

Washington for the navy department for the last three months of 1942, and then from January to July of 1943 in England.

Because a trip to England at the beginning of 1943 was regarded as a sortie into a war zone, Johnny's first thought was to take out an insurance policy on his life: for the then-large sum of $20,000, for his seven-year-old daughter Marina. A somewhat stiff letter was dispatched to the Kupers' lawyers to see whether they had any suggestions to make about any consequent changes in the part of his divorce separation of September 1937 which referred to sharing of property after his demise. It is nice to report that this brought an instant "Dear Johnny" letter from Mariette which relieved his estate from any obligations to her while this insurance for Marina lasted. Second wife Klari had the problem that Johnny was allowed only limited luggage for his transatlantic trip in a bomber, and that the suitcase was supposed to contain a large navy-issue tin helmet. Johnny kept taking this out of the suitcase, so that he could put in the bulky volumes of the Oxford Histories of England. His intended recreation while abroad was to tour the old battlefields of England, as he had toured in America those of the Civil War. Klari kept taking the books out, and putting the helmet back in. When the bomber flew off, the histories were in the suitcase and the helmet at home.

The original reason for the navy's call to him seems to have been that German magnetic mines around England were becoming more sophisticated. These mines had originally been attracted to the first bit of metal they sensed and had exploded against it. This made it easier to trawl metal to find where they were and blow them up. Now the Germans were planting devices on the mines so that they did not explode the first time they sensed metal (which usually meant when a minesweeper was scouting to find if they were there). They lingered until perhaps the third or fifth or eighth time. There had to be some pattern that the methodical Germans were using to plant their mines along the convoy routes to Britain. Johnny was asked to work out mathematically what these patterns might be, and how best to counter them. He seems to have done this with ease and effectiveness and to have saved many seafaring lives thereby. There were pleased mutterings in the wardrooms of Britain's Royal Navy that "a major break-through has been made in the Battle of the Atlantic by a Dr. von Apfelstrudel or Something—yes, honestly, presumably an American Kraut."

The wider significance of Johnny's arrival in England was that the man who had become America's deepest thinker about explosions had now got into the free country that was then being most exploded against. Both the British and American war efforts gained from this. British scientists quickly realized that Johnny had done far more thinking than they about oblique shock reflection both in air and under water, and it is from oblique shocks that most damage comes. He had also devised equations for the tapering of explosions that were new to them. They hastened to conduct experiments in their supersonic wind tunnels at the National Physical Laboratory in Teddington and in what had in peacetime been called Britain's "Road Research Laboratory."

Contact with the antisubmarine department of the British admiralty was also good, and this more than repaid the U.S. Navy for their nine months' employment of Johnny. When postwar Johnny was awarded the U.S. Navy's Distinguished Civilian Service Award (July 1946) and President Truman's Medal for Merit (October 1946), the citation for the latter said that Johnny "was primarily responsible for fundamental research by the United States Navy on the effective use of high explosives, which has resulted in the discovery of a new ordnance principle for offensive action, and which has already been proved to increase the efficiency of air power in the atomic bomb attacks upon Japan." The press briefing at the time talked of his contributions both to antisubmarine warfare and to bombing theory. Some newspapers portrayed him as having discovered that "a miss was better than a hit" and as the man who showed that the A-bomb on Hiroshima would be most effective if exploded at well above ground level. In December 1947 Johnny wrote to the *New York Times*: "I did initiate and carry out work during the war on oblique shock reflection. This did lead to the conclusion that large bombs are better detonated at a considerable altitude than on the ground, since this leads to the higher oblique-incidence pressures referred to. The principle that is involved is better described as the high burst principle, rather than by saying that a miss is better than a hit." Johnny was already passing on some of these discoveries in England in 1943, and thus changing part of the war effort while on the hoof.

But Johnny was also reporting by March 1943 that he was learning a great deal from the British, "mainly from Marley at the Road Research Laboratory and Penney at the Imperial College of Science [London]. In fact it is most surprising that more of their work did not transpire to us earlier." Johnny believed the British had made real strides toward discovering what makes explosions escalate. He wrote to Veblen by secret diplomatic pouch:

The usual view of a detonation is that the flame, or rather the burnt gases, coming out of the detonated explosive, push the air outwards. So there are in this phenomenon—or rather in the blast which follows—always two dividing surfaces: the flame front (between the burnt gases and the air) and the shock proper (in the air, between two air layers of discontinuously different velocity, pressure, density, etc.). . . . It seems that the flame front is of a highly irregular spongy structure, and the air hides in its recesses. The whole area is best described as a mixture of the burnt gases and compressed hot air. And since the burnt gases are only burnt as far as the original explosive reaction is concerned, but still capable of slow burning, this mixture is still burning. The burning is not too slow either, since the air is very compressed and very hot.

B. Lewis, of the BRL Scientific Advisory Committee, has for a long time insisted on the possibilities and importance of such processes in slightly different connections—but the phenomenon seems to be absolutely universal with high explosives in air. Marley and Penney [in Britain] have shown experimentally that the shock contains (for TNT in air) more energy than the explosive reaction alone can provide. Hence the above mentioned after-burning is even energetically necessary. The blast of TNT in an atmosphere of nitrogen (which excludes this after-burning) is correspondingly weaker. . . . The whole matter looks also as if it were very interesting from the theoretical point of view.

He moved from this into the equations that should apply, in a way that few others had yet dared. Johnny then imbibed some information on wind tunnels from the British, and from a free Frenchman at Oxford about photographic techniques for checking explosions, and was allowed to dig into British research on shaped charges. He found that this latter had some useful x ray techniques but was otherwise behind the United States.

The part of the trip that was not going well was operational research to help the precision daylight bombing of the U.S. Eighth Air Force. Johnny reported that interallied operations research was efficiently organized both for antimine and for antisubmarine operations. But the supposed expertise of the British about the effects of bombing on land was nonexistent. The Britons' night bombing missions obligated their young aircrew to undertake twenty-five or thirty-five ops to a tour, where they were losing an average of one aircraft in five on each mission. These twenty-year-old Britons thus had huge odds of five or seven to one against surviving for another few weeks. They therefore simply released bombs whenever the pathfinders' target flares indicated they were in what seemed the right position. It was not really possible to work out scientifically when they were having an extraordinary effect and when they were having a minimal one. Your biographer was a nineteen-year-old under-training Royal Air Force (RAF) navigator at the time. Over the interval of nearly fifty years, Johnny's report seems to him total sense.

One of the Britons attached to Johnny in 1943 for his study of bombing patterns was the scientist Jacob Bronowski, who after the war became a British television personality. On postwar BBC television Bronowski gave one view on Johnny that was usual to most who met him: "endearing and personal . . . the cleverest man I ever knew, without exception . . . a genius." But he added that Johnny was not a modest man. When I worked with him during the war, we once faced a problem together, and he said to me at once: "Oh no, no, you are not seeing it. Your kind of visualising mind is not right for seeing this. Think of it abstractly. What is happening [on this photograph of an explosion] is that the first differential coefficient vanishes identically, and that is why what becomes visible is the trace of the second differential coefficient." As he said, that is not the way I think. However, I let him go to London. I went off to my laboratory in the country. I worked late into the night. Round about midnight I had his answer. Well, John von Neumann always slept very late, so I was kind and I did not wake him until well after ten in the morning. When I called his hotel in London, he answered the phone in bed, and I said "Johnny, you're quite right." And he said to me, "You wake me up early in the morning to tell me that I'm right? Please wait until I'm wrong." If that sounds very vain, it was not. It was a real statement on how he lived his life.

Actually, Bronowski did not really understand how Johnny lived his life. First, Johnny would have mildly resented the interruption because he would by ten have been working for some hours on something else less simple. After Johnny's death, Bronowski criticized the way that in his last years mathematical Johnny "became more and more engaged in work for private firms, for industry, for government. They were enterprises which brought him to the centre of power, but which did not advance either his knowledge or his intimacy with people—who to this day have not yet got the message of what he was trying to do about the human mathematics of life and mind." Bronowski assumes that in his researches into the computer and the brain Johnny was searching for the way "in which the different parts of the brain have somehow to be interlocked and made to match so that we devise a plan, a procedure, as a grand overall way of life—what in the humanities we would call a system of values." That is what planners such as Bronowski thought great minds should be doing. In both Hitler's and Stalin's day, Johnny was more concerned to save the world from dictators who were trying by brute force to impose a single system of values on us.

By around May 1943 there were suggestions from Washington to London that the Americans would like their best theoretical expert on explosives back home again, please. Johnny wanted to stay longer in Britain because he was now interacting with practical physicists who had something immediately interesting to do. "I think that I have learned here a good deal of theoretical physics," he wrote to Veblen, "particularly of the gas dynamical variety, and that I shall return a better and impurer man. I have also developed an obscene interest in computational techniques." This last probably meant that he had been seeing Turing (see chap. 13). At this time Klari wrote to Elizabeth Veblen, begging that Veblen should not encourage a recall because Johnny was still intellectually enjoying himself in England. If he was brought back, without being asked whether he wanted to come, he would be very mad. Klari did not want Johnny to be mad while he was alone. He often got mad when at home, but she knew how to handle him. The war effort of the allied powers owed a lot to this then calming, although eventually neurotic, lady.

Johnny was abruptly recalled to the United States in mid-1943 for the biggest of reasons in human history so far. That is the subject of the next, and nuclear, chapter. As we shall see, Johnny continued his habit—even when helping in the invention of the A-bomb and the computer—of doing lots of other things at the same time. In this chapter we will continue with the story of his expertise on conventional explosions until the end of the war.

◄►◄►

On his return to America the army ordnance department snaffled him and his learned-in-Britain-but-financed-by-the-navy new knowledge. From late 1943 to early 1944, he reported later, he was spending 25% of his time (and for a brief period all of it) on aerodynamics for the army and for its air force. He was expanding the theory and application of high explosives in the air—although no longer, as during his navy days, their explosion under water.

He was by now a member of a lot of different research organizations at once, a fact that caused coughs from the sidelines by those who were not getting so much of his time. In early 1944 Warren Weaver pointed out that Johnny was under contract to the Applied Mathematics Panel. Although Weaver did not want to interfere in any way with his magnificent wartime service— was he, er, actually giving that panel any of his time whatever? Johnny replied rather huffily that since returning from England he had spent about 40% of his time at Princeton. Nearly all of that was on the most important applied mathematical problem allotted to him. He had been examining "collisions of shocks with each other or with tangents of other media." When these "depart from the simplest head-on type the field was completely unexplored a year ago." Now he had explored it, and the results (he intimated) were exploding around the world.

In that early 1944 this correspondence led to another contract with the IAS from the Applied Mathematics Panel. It was to explore new methods of numerical analysis of explosions. From this eventually sprang a joint paper with his collaborators, Valentine Bargmann and Deane Montgomery, that started the story of new computer-oriented numerical analysis, on which much depends.

He was by now the source to which other army researchers into shock waves were being referred. A letter from Johnny to CalTech on April 14, 1944, perhaps best explains his state of play:

Dear Dr. DuMond,
    Please excuse my delay in answering your enquiry of March 30th. I was away from Princeton [he was actually at Los Alamos]. I have worked with several associates on shock wave problems; indeed they are now in the center of our interest. The theoretical work was done by a group in the Navy Bureau of Ordnance, and under a contract with the NDRC Applied Mathematics Panel. We are also developing computational methods, mainly for punchcard machines, for certain problems of this type. We had aerodynamical experiments done at the Ballistics Research Laboratory, Aberdeen, Maryland; at the Princeton Station of NDRC Division 2; and last year in two British laboratories.

We are concerned with shocks in air as well as in water; but mostly in air. In the experiments micro-explosions were used, also ballistic shocks and various wind tunnel arrangements; we got most information from 20 millimeter and 37 millimeter projectiles ballistic shocks and a rather unconventional non-stationary wind tunnel. The shock strengths with which we worked corresponded to pressure ratios of 1.1 to 6; mostly 1.25 to 3. Am I right in assuming that the region of your main interest . . . corresponds to shock strengths expressed very approximately by pressure ratios of 1.2 to 1.03? If this is correct, then the domains in which our two groups worked are unfortunately rather disjunct.

We were mostly concerned with the reflection and refraction of shocks in the unacoustic domain; we found that entirely new forms of these processes, connected with extraordinary pressures and production of vortex sheets, exist there. If I understand you correctly, your interest lies mainly in the nearby acoustic range.

I hope nevertheless that we might be able to give you some help. This will, of course, be considerably facilitated when your request comes in through the regular NDRC channels, and you can describe more precisely what your problems are.

Your observations on the form of shocks in the late decay stage are very interesting. H. Bethe did predict theoretically that for a three-dimensional blast wave the asymptotic form would be this, with the two legs of the N asymptotically equal to each other and . . .

Here Johnny dived into more of his equations.

Johnny had by now rejoined the NDRC and was a leading light of its division 2, the division concerned with the interaction and reflection of blast waves. His practical work for NDRC from late 1944 to the end of the war concerned the conditions under which large and very large bombs could best be detonated and their effects on various sorts of structure. In Britain he had been asked to inquire why some of the first experiments with large, 8,000-pound bombs had failed disastrously. One of these bombs had failed to blow up a wall that was little more than a foot thick. "Is it true that TNT would only go 16 inches? It is not true of course,"

Johnny had written. A lot depended on confinement and shapes and structures. His handwritten notes at this time include calculations about the relative amount of glass and concrete in typical structures in Germany and Japan; about the area of blast from bombs of particular tonnages according to the type of shelter in the way; and about some detailed reports on what happened when the Germans blew up much of Halifax, Nova Scotia, by exploding a munitions ship there in World War I.

In Johnny's papers for 1944 the words "kilotonnage" and "computer" began to appear quite often for the first time. The computer was to come into its particular form of existence because of his old connection with the BRL at the Aberdeen Proving Ground. Kiloton bombs (which mean little bombs mysteriously carrying more explosive power than would enormous bombs unimaginably carrying more than 1,000 tons of TNT) were his new concern. After September 1943—that is, after his return from England— up to 30% of his time was spent in Los Alamos as a consultant to the marvelously misnamed Manhattan District, United States Engineers.

►◄►◄ *10*

Los Alamos to
Trinity, 1943–45

►◄ *T*he history of the A-bomb has been near definitively told in Richard Rhodes's superb Pulitzer Prize–winning book, *The Making of the Atomic Bomb*. Many of the non-Johnny stories in this chapter are told better there. It is a surprise that Rhodes, probably rightly, starts his story with the weirdest of the Hungarians, Szilard, who foresaw the possible end of the world when taking a walk through London's Bloomsbury on a gray depression-era morning in September 1933.

In 1932 Cambridge's James Chadwick had announced the existence of the neutron, which had no electric charge. Many scientists mused that this might be made to slip past the positive electrical barrier of the nucleus of an atom, and create as much havoc within that nucleus as if the moon hit the earth. What "suddenly occurred" to Szilard in 1933 was the possibility of a chain reaction. If scientists could find an element that would be split by a neutron and that, because of that split, would then emit two neutrons, which would then instantly in chain reaction emit four, which would then—well, that could release in a few millionths of a second far more energy than had ever been known in a small space in the world before. This could create atomic power on an industrial scale, and produce an A-bomb.

When Szilard typically asked for a patent or patents for this idea of a chain reaction, to be assigned to the British navy, Churchill's favorite scientist, Frederick Lindemann, wrote to the British admiralty that the chances of anything coming from Szilard's notion might be a hundred to one against, but that the little Hungarian was "a very good physicist" and that humoring him would cost the government nothing.

In 1933–34 the world's three most imaginative senior physicists (Rutherford, Einstein, Bohr) were even more scornful of Szilard's thesis than was Lindemann. As Rhodes noted, Rutherford had already said that "anyone who looks for a source of power in the transformation of the atoms is talking moonshine"; Bohr, in one of the papers that he rewrote on proof virtually into meaninglessness, seemed on balance to say the same thing; Einstein was to joke later that research into atomic energy was like shooting in the dark at small and scarce birds. This was peculiar because, by late 1934, the world's most imaginative younger scientist probably had already shot the most important bird, and had not noticed it.

Beginning in January 1934, Italy's Enrico Fermi (1901–54) and his team in Rome began bombarding with neutrons almost everything they could think of—water, lithium, beryllium, boron, carbon, fluorine, aluminum, iron, silicon, phosphorus, chlorine, vanadium, copper, arsenic, silver, tellurium, iodine, chromium, barium, sodium, magnesium, titanium, zinc, selenium, antimony, bromine, and lanthanum. When they bombarded uranium, the neutron went through to the nucleus—and began to transform atoms. Fermi decided that he had discovered a new man-made transuranic (i.e., beyond uranium) element, never before seen on earth. Four years later he was awarded the Nobel Prize, partly for thus having made what some say was the only analytical mistake of his life.

Fermi had a mind with many of the same contours as Johnny's. The two men later found each other enormous fun. Oppenheimer once summarized Fermi: "Passion for clarity. He was simply unable to let things be foggy. Since they always are, this kept him pretty active." Oppenheimer would have regarded this as also true of Johnny, and Johnny would have muttered that Oppenheimer's habit of retreating into poetic fogginess (e.g., about whether and how to deter Soviet Russia) was what later made people at the postwar AEC unfortunately so cross with him. Like Johnny, Fermi was of conservative political bent. Although he made constant jokes about Mussolini, as about everybody else, he did not in 1934 regard the fascist buffoon as an ogre. He inclined to think all forms of authority pretty absurd but, said his wife the historian Laura Fermi, thought it better to accept than to argue with them. Fermi's patron in 1934–36 was Senator Orso Corbino, who would have passed on to Mussolini any military information emerging from Fermi's work.

An intriguing possibility emerges. If anybody around Corbino had recognized what Fermi's transuranic ventures meant—and in retrospect some physicists should have done—Mussolini's bombastic and inefficient fascist army might have become the first in the world to reach the A-bomb. What a mouse might then have roared, and with what strange results.

By 1938, when Fermi won his Nobel Prize, he no longer regarded Mussolini as a joke but as a man who had "gone mad and was crawling on all fours to Hitler." Mussolini had begun to promulgate anti-Jewish decrees, and Laura Fermi was the daughter of a Jewish officer in the Italian navy. The Fermis decided to use the Nobel Prize money as a means of emigrating to the United States. They proceeded from the 1938 prize-giving in Scandinavia on a Christmas boat to New York, landing on January 2, 1939, where Fermi told pressmen that "we are founding the American branch of the Fermi family."

While he was away from his laboratory and preparing to emigrate, and then on the boat, the most extraordinary things had happened in nuclear physics. They had happened in what looked the most dangerous time and place: in 1938 in the Kaiser Wilhelm Institute in Hitler's Berlin.

◀▶◀▶

Until the middle of 1938 the livest wire in the Kaiser Wilhelm Institute was the sixty-year-old spinster Lise Meitner. Small, intense, shy, an analysis-oriented experimenter, she (like Fermi but unlike Johnny) was the sort of person who would today go jogging. Even at sixty in 1938, she would march off on thoughtful 10-mile walks. When she was an x ray technician with the Austro-Hungarian forces on the eastern front in the 1914–18 war, she would time her leaves so as to get back to the Kaiser Wilhelm Institute at the same time as Professor Otto Hahn (then a German poison gas officer on the western front). Their idea of a wartime holiday was to work at the Kaiser Wilhelm Institute together.

Meitner was about as much a Jew as Johnny was. Her parents had been baptized into Christianity during the Austro-Hungarian empire. Until 1938 she was designated by the Hitler regime as a foreign (i.e., Austrian) Jewess and was therefore allowed to continue with her useful work. Absurdly the 1938 *Anschluss* of Austria with Germany made her officially a German Jewess. Although she was doing some spooky scientific research in Berlin, bombarding uranium with neutrons, the Gestapo intended to arrest her. Otto Hahn and some others, with courage, helped her illegally to escape via the Netherlands to Denmark, where Bohr had arranged for her to have a rather unsuitable job in Sweden.

Back in Berlin Hahn and an assistant, Fritz Strassmann, stayed on bombarding uranium with neutrons. They were bombarding them especially energetically in September 1938, as the Sudetenland crisis so nearly brought Europe to war. On January 6, 1939, they published a paper saying that their bombardment had brought some strange results. These had been sent to Meitner before the proof stage, with a request for analysis of what she thought they meant. Meitner and her nephew, Otto Frisch, puzzled about them over Christmas 1938. On the evening of January 6, 1939, Frisch took their conclusions to Bohr, who was leaving for the United States the next morning to spend the term at the IAS, which Johnny had helped arrange the summer before.

Bohr asked for a blackboard to be put in his cabin on the Swedish-American liner *Drottningholm*. He worked at it with another scientist on the journey over, despite being fearfully seasick the while. As the *Drottningholm* drew into New York harbor on January 16, 1939, the new immigrants Enrico and Laura Fermi awaited them on dockside.

Once he had confirmed that the Meitner-Frisch paper had been published, Bohr had news to spread through the physics community of America. George Gamow (who had escaped from the Soviet Union in 1933) phoned Teller and described many people's initial reaction best: "Bohr has gone crazy. He says a neutron can split uranium." Teller thought of the strange radioactivities revealed by Fermi's experiments in Rome, and "suddenly understood the obvious."

Fermi did, too, with a certain embarrassment. His Nobel Prize lecture had been delivered only a month before, and had not yet been printed. He added a quick footnote to it. The discoveries by Hahn and Strassmann, he said, "make it necessary to re-examine all the problems of the transuranic elements, as many of them might be found to be products of a splitting of uranium." Like many of the ablest physicists—Oppenheimer, Teller, Wigner, Szilard (although oddly not yet Bohr)—Fermi recognized something more. As Rhodes recounts, he stood in his new office in a New York skyscraper and looked down on the length of Manhattan. "A little bomb like that," he said, shaping his hands as if holding a football, "and it could all disappear."

◄►◄►

Like Johnny, Szilard had long believed that war was coming to Europe. He had declared his intention of moving from England to America one year before it broke out. He actually arrived as an immigrant on January 2, 1938, ostensibly to do some research into a cure for cancer, on which he had naturally tabled a patent. He turned instead to radiating bugs out of fruit, for which he held another patent, but he thought about nuclear chain reactions the while.

Szilard learnt Bohr's news in January 1939 from Wigner. He was soon urging Fermi that "if neutrons are emitted in fission, this should be kept secret from the Germans." Because it was the Germans who had discovered this process, that did not seem very hopeful. Szilard therefore moved to his next project: writing a letter for Einstein to send to Roosevelt, urging him to start research on a project for America to invent an atomic bomb. Because Szilard was no motorist, he was driven on one visit to Einstein by Wigner (who had been taught driving by Desmond Kuper) and on the other by Teller ("I entered history as Szilard's chauffeur"). The three of them—Szilard, Wigner, and Teller—became known as the Hungarian conspiracy. Einstein in later years called his recommendation to Roosevelt to make A-bombs "the one great mistake of my life."

For once, Einstein overestimated his own effect. Roosevelt delegated the problem to a committee run by Dr. Lyman J. Briggs, who decided that the matter sounded so terribly worrying and secret that few people should be told about it. He locked up almost everything submitted to him in a safe.

By September 1939 the British were at war, and were becoming more worried about it fast. Frisch had left his aunt and had come to Britain, where he teamed up at Birmingham University with the brilliant Rudolf Peierls. These two—still nominally Germans and therefore enemy aliens—calculated what would happen if a golf-ball-size of uranium-235 could be separated from the much commoner uranium-238, and if there was fast-neutron fission of it. Their answer was that in a few millionths of a second it would be possible to create pressures greater than those at the center of the earth, where iron flows as a liquid, breeding a greater explosive power than anybody had yet imagined. Their report suggested to the British authorities that this victory-achieving weapon could be achieved, at a cost insignificant compared with the cost of the war, either by Hitler's Germany (which could then destroy civilization) or by Britain (which might then save it).

In April 1940 the Germans captured Denmark plus Bohr, who was lecturing elsewhere in Scandinavia at the time but felt he had to return to Nazi-occupied Copenhagen and destroy a lot of papers there. That famous cable arrived in Britain from Frisch's aunt, Lise Meitner, in Sweden saying, "Met Niels and Margarethe [i.e., the Bohrs] recently. Both well but unhappy about events. Please inform Cockroft [the British nuclear scientist] and Maud Ray Kent." What did "Maud Ray Kent" mean? The British decided they were an anagram for "radyum taken," and thus gave warning that the Germans were moving fast to develop an A-bomb. Perhaps that was the reason the Nazis had occupied Bohr's Copenhagen, and were capturing Norway and its heavy water too?

Down in her home in Kent, Miss Maud Ray, the former English governess to Bohr's children, remained uncontacted because nobody had heard of her. She now entered history because the team of British boffins to examine nuclear prospects was named the Maud Committee, as a tribute to Meitner's supposedly brilliant anagram.

Lindemann (by then Lord Cherwell) summarized the Maud Report to Churchill: "People who are working on these problems consider that the odds are ten to one on success within two years. I would not bet more than two to one at most or even money. But I am quite clear we must go forward. It would be unforgivable if we let the Germans defeat us in war." Churchill had that week been in some danger under German bombing in the blitz on Britain. He minuted with his usual chutzpah: "Although I personally am quite content with existing explosives, I feel we must not stand in the path of improvement, and I therefore think action should be taken in the sense proposed by Lord Cherwell."

In reality, the British did not have the resources to create and manufacture an A-bomb. The right decision was therefore taken to send all the minutes and reports of the Maud Committee to Briggs in Washington D.C., who was supposed to be in charge of Roosevelt's project for perhaps making such a bomb. The British were bewildered that no response came back from him. In August 1941 Dr. Mark Oliphant, Peierls's and Frisch's nominal superior at Birmingham University, was sent to America to find out why. "I called on Briggs in Washington," he reported back, "only to find that this inarticulate and unimpressive man had put the reports in his safe and had not shown them to members of his committee."

Oliphant stormed around America's scientific establishment and leaked the gist of Maud to everybody he could (and maybe to some he should not have). He made first breakthrough by convincing Ernest Lawrence at Berkeley. It was also at Berkeley that Oliphant saw America's huge resources, in things like Lawrence's cyclotron, and knew that the bomb could much better be made in the United States. Lawrence did a lot to persuade the other organizers of America's scientific effort in late 1941. Once they were convinced—as so often happens in America when a government committee is ousted from the control of anything—America's by-then-brilliant community of physicists moved with efficient speed. It was on October 9, 1941, that Dr. Vannevar Bush carried the Maud Report to Roosevelt (how surprised Maud Ray in Kent would have been). He got the president's authorization to launch America on what—until then—was the world's most expensive scientific project: determining whether America could produce an A-bomb. Roosevelt made this $2,000,000,000 spending decision, without any reference to Congress, while America was not yet at war. He saw that America needed a weapon that could help it hold the political balance of the world even if the Nazis won the European war (which in October 1941 still looked rather probable). Bush called together the scientists most immediately concerned for a meeting in Washington, D.C., on the first Saturday in December 1941.

The next day the Japanese bombed Pearl Harbor.

◄►◄►

Johnny was not recruited into the A-bomb project at this early stage, although his three fellow Hungarians (Wigner, Szilard, and

Teller) were. One reason for Johnny's nonrecruitment was that the project was then regarded as one for physicists rather than mathematicians. Another was that both army and navy treasured Johnny as a scientific resource who should not be diverted from other things. A possible third reason was an awkwardness in the first few weeks of war between Bush and the IAS. In mid-December 1941—in that first fortnight of war and first month of the new A-bomb project—Bush asked the IAS director, Dr. Frank Aydelotte, for the services of the IAS's most glittering star. Could Einstein help with some calculations connected with the possible separation of uranium-235 from its chemically identical isotope? After two days the Quaker Aydelotte was sending back Einstein's answers, with expressions of enthusiasm that sat oddly with Einstein's and Aydelotte's original pacifist convictions:

> Einstein asked me to say that if there were other angles of the problem that you want him to develop . . . he would be glad to do anything in his power. I very much hope you will make use of him in any way that occurs to you, because I know how deep is his satisfaction at doing anything which might be useful in the national effort. I hope you can read his handwriting. Neither he nor I felt free, in view of the necessary secrecy, to give the manuscript to anyone to copy.

On December 30, 1941, Bush was replying to Aydelotte, with some embarrassment, that he would not be sending more work because "I am not at all sure that if I place Einstein in entire contact with this subject he would not discuss it in a way that it should not be discussed." Bush would like to tell Einstein all, but "this is utterly impossible in view of the attitude of people here in Washington who have studied into his whole history." Aydelotte was not enamored with this brush-off, and the IAS did not play as big a part as might be expected in the bomb until the call for Johnny in mid-1943.

Johnny's first letter on return from England in that July of 1943 was to Ulam from the Cosmos Club in Washington, D.C. "I am leading a poule de luxe life," he told Ulam, "I do not yet know whether I am to be bigamous or trigamous." The bigamy was with the army and navy ordnance departments. Each wanted him to be working full-time for it, on all he had just learned in England on blast waves. His original idea had been that he might be able to work full-time for both army and navy while also spending two days a week at Princeton.

The threat of trigamy arose because he had now been told that his expertise in high explosives would be required on a consultancy basis at a mysterious site Y in the Southwest, which was actually Los Alamos. This transfer to what other people would regard as four full-time jobs (navy ordnance, army ordnance, Los Alamos, Princeton) did begin to play havoc with his usually polite social relations. By September 1943 he was writing again to Ulam from "no address" and slightly apologetically: "Since I came back from England I have been in 3–4 different places each week. I am now in the south west [he was actually at Los Alamos]. . . . I may have to go to England once more before Christmas. . . . I don't know exactly when or how long. . . . Absolutely impossible to stick to any civilised schedule of answering your letters."

One question for this biography must be what Johnny contributed to the two Los Alamos bombs in 1943–45. Two others are how he fitted in with the place's odd management (Groves and Oppenheimer) and scientific atmosphere (gentle leftish seminar held regretfully on how to destroy the world). It will be convenient to discuss the last two questions first.

◄►◄►

Johnny disagreed politically with the majority of people at Los Alamos but adored the wartime atmosphere there. He fitted in with most of its warring characters like a glove. It was of this period that Laura Fermi was to write that "Dr. von Neumann is one of the very few men about whom I have not heard a single critical remark. It is astonishing that so much equanimity and so much intelligence could be concentrated in a man of not extraordinary appearance." Johnny extended this equanimity to both Groves and Oppenheimer.

In September 1942 the forty-two-year-old Brigadier General Groves had been appointed as military director of the A-bomb project. The best comment on Groves came from Louis Alvarez: "Almost everyone disliked him heartily except the men who worked closely with him. Both Robert Oppenheimer and Ernest Lawrence told me how much they respected him." Johnny was later to be among these cheerleaders for Groves, whose military flexibility snapped only in not being able to tolerate Szilard (which few could).

Groves's bravest first decision was to appoint Oppenheimer director of the Los Alamos laboratory, instead of Lawrence, the Nobel Prize winner whom many insiders had expected. Groves explained his choice in language that shows both why clever people appreciated him and why shallower ones thought him an arrogant blimp. "While Lawrence is very bright, he is not a genius, just a good hard worker," Groves said. But "Robert Oppenheimer is a real genius. . . . knows about everything . . . can talk to you about everything. . . . Well, not exactly . . . he doesn't know anything about sports."

Groves's choice of Oppenheimer unnerved the watchdogs in military intelligence. They were told (on the whole, rightly) that Oppie was the best man to run America's most secret and important project; that he would be skilled in picking the best people for it, best at guiding who should do what next. A later great historian called Oppie "the most captivating, commanding and worshipped teacher of theoretical physics of his generation," whose students "devotedly imitated his mannerisms, even his walk."

When the security men compiled a dossier on Oppenheimer, they then discovered that he had several times threatened to commit suicide in his moody youth; and that those whom he had both chosen and inherited as the nearest and dearest in his family all seemed to have belonged to the Communist party in Stalin's worst terror years. The one-time party members included Oppenheimer's first fiancée (Jean Tatlock), his hard-drinking wife Kitty Oppenheimer and her first husband, his brother and sister-in-law, and a colleague for whom he illegally covered up. Beautiful, unstable Tatlock was probably still a Communist in 1943, but Oppenheimer spent at least one adulterous night with her while he was director at Los Alamos. The watching security agents reported lasciviously on this, shortly before she committed suicide in 1944.

Johnny thought that Oppenheimer's political and economic beliefs were unscientific and therefore regrettable (poor chap). He opposed Oppie's appointment as director of the IAS after the war. When they were at Princeton, said a contemporary, the two men stalked around each other like alley cats. But Johnny always passionately supported Oppenheimer's wartime record, including to people who became Oppie's postwar persecutors, like Strauss, who was also Johnny's friend. "Robert at Los Alamos was so very great," Johnny insisted, "in Britain they would have made him an Earl. Then, if he walked down the street with his fly buttons undone, people would have said—look, there goes the Earl. In postwar America we say—look, his fly buttons are undone."

Bethe regarded Johnny as the superhumanly clever man at Los Alamos, but thought Oppenheimer was the ideal leader. It was not, said Bethe (and Johnny agreed), the primary function of the director of Los Alamos in 1943–45 "to make technical contributions. What was called for from the director was to get a lot of prima donnas to work together, to understand all the technical work that was going on, to make it fit together, and to make decisions between various possible lines of development. I have never met anyone who performed these functions as brilliantly as Oppenheimer."

In late 1942 Groves and Oppenheimer also pleased Bethe and Johnny by choosing the right environment. Oppenheimer had long said that his two great loves were physics and wilderness country. He combined these—and the 1943–45 need for secrecy —by getting Groves to buy the Los Alamos Ranch School. It had been founded so as to toughen up little boys by making them take exercise all year round—in shorts in an area where the winter temperature can be under $-10°$ F and the summer temperature over $90°$ F.

After military takeover in early 1943, cheap barrackslike build-

ings were constructed in Los Alamos at great pace, and Oppenheimer toured the universities of America to persuade top scientists
to come there. As educated people with a mission are apt to do,
they civilized it almost at once. Today (1992) half a dozen of the
top wartime or immediate postwar team have retired to live at or
near Los Alamos. Despite some lack of home comforts, Johnny
found the atmosphere the most exhilarating in his life. If he had
lived on to an age like seventy, he intended to make a home near
there himself.

One can see why. By the time Johnny was recruited as a consultant for Los Alamos in 1943, the greatest collection of scientific
talent had been assembled on the high tableland for the most
expensive scientific project the world had known. Even Bohr was
on his way, because of a historic misunderstanding.

After the occupation of Denmark in 1940, Bohr avoided contact
with most of the German invaders. His relations were better with
the brave Resistance. But in late 1941 his German former student
Heisenberg pleaded for a meeting "like in the old days." During
a walk together, Heisenberg talked about the possibility of a uranium bomb, and even gave Bohr a drawing of the experimental
heavy-water reactor he suggested it might be most efficient to
build. Bohr was terrified this was a hint that Hitler's Germany
was likely to get an A-bomb before the end of the war.

Heisenberg did indeed report shortly afterward to the associates
of Albert Speer, Hitler's minister of armament, that a uranium
bomb as small as a pineapple would be capable of destroying a
whole city; Otto Hahn was at that meeting as well. But when
Speer passed on this view to Hitler, the führer still was not eager
to plunge a lot of money into "Jewish physics." Said Speer in his
autobiography, "Professor Heisenberg had not given any final
answer to my question whether a successful nuclear fission could
be kept under control with absolute certainty or might continue
as a chain reaction. Hitler was plainly not delighted with the possibility that the earth under his rule might be transformed into a
glowing star."

However, Bohr did not know about Hitler's reaction. Nor did

he know that Heisenberg's heavy-water drawing was way below what even by 1942 was America's state of the nuclear art. Bohr worried about whether he should carry news of it to the West, as he worried lengthily about so many decisions in his life. If he deserted Nazi-occupied Europe for an enemy nation, he feared that retaliation against some of his friends would be bloody and vile. So it was not until October 1943 that Bohr escaped to nearby Sweden in a fishing vessel. He was flown by RAF Mosquito aircraft to Britain, and thence shipped to Los Alamos. He arrived there as part of the same extra recruitment drive that had brought Johnny to site Y in September 1943.

A party of British scientists—including Johnny's friend in England Bill Penney, plus Peierls and Frisch—were invited out at about the same time. An invitation was also made to Göttingen's old professor of physics, Born, who was now working at Edinburgh in Scotland. Born had decided he did not want to engage in war work, but one of his laboratory team at Edinburgh joined the party. His name was Klaus Fuchs, and he worked at Los Alamos as a devoted Russian spy.

◆▶◆

In the winter of 1943–44 a common mood of the scientists at Los Alamos was that (*a*) we are doing something sinful by inventing so murderous an explosive, but (*b*) we have to do so because otherwise Nazi Germany might get there first; so (*c*) after the war we must try to internationalize these weapons (which became official American policy). In private, Johnny disagreed with this "good guys' view" in almost every particular.

Johnny had no doubt that weapons would be made much more murderous. Murderousness is what people in wars try to achieve. After the advent of quantum mechanics (atomic physics) in the 1920s, he saw that "efficiency at killing people would make a quantum leap." An A-bomb would be invented as a result of this present 1939–? war. A hydrogen bomb, which Teller had adumbrated (to Johnny, convincingly) as early as 1942, would be ready to help (with luck) to deter the next one.

Johnny sounded callous, even at this early stage, about the deaths that would flow from nuclear radiation. These may have included his own death. It is plausible that in 1955 the then-fifty-one-year-old Johnny's cancer sprang from his attendance at the 1946 Bikini nuclear tests. The safety precautions at Bikini were based on calculations that were meant to keep any observer's exposure to radiation well below what had given Japanese at Hiroshima even a 1 percent extra risk of cancer. But Johnny, like some other great scientists, underestimated risks at that time. He was startled when radiation probably caused the cancer and death in 1954 at age fifty-three of his great friend Fermi, whose 1930s experiments with nuclear bombardment in Italy were not accompanied by proper precautions. Soon after a Soviet nuclear test in 1953 Sakharov and Vyacheslav Malyshev walked near the site to assess its results. Sakharov ascribed Malyshev's death from leukemia in 1954, and possibly his own terminal illness thirty-five years later, to that walk.

Johnny would have regretted all these deaths, especially his own. But now that an A-bomb could be made, neither the maintenance of ignorance nor reliance on dictators' goodwill seemed to him a tenable policy. Most previous scientific advances, from steam power and industrialization to the automobile, had ended some lives in accidents. They had enriched and extended many more by aiding mankind to escape from immobility, low productivity, tyranny, and early death. Johnny thought nuclear power would do the same. Given political calmness and proper commercial incentives (both of which have been lacking since 1945), he thought the nuclear age would mean that cheap energy could at last be released from its storage in matter.

It was a pity that the first such release was being plotted at Los Alamos in a way that would kill as many Japanese as possible per dollar spent. But the Japanese at this time were talking about resisting invasion with the "honorable hundred million deaths." Japanese generals were ordering Japanese soldiers to kill at least ten American soldiers each before they died. The overthrow of Japan with conventional weapons might cost as many Allied (mainly American) lives as the 1914–18 battles in France. Nuclear bombs should end the Pacific war less bloodily than that.

Even Johnny could not find similar consolation if the world later moved on to H-bomb war. But this led him to his next conclusion: that the horror of modern weapons could provide an opportunity to scare dictators out of starting wars, if free countries operated the concept of deterrence. In his book *The Theory of Games* (see chap. 11), he hoped that he had begun scientifically to develop that concept.

He saw that deterrence would not be achieved through endless committees of the United Nations, as some of his optimistic colleagues pretended. Logical Johnny felt that the only way forward for his generation lay through a pax Americana. By late 1943 he was fortunately confident that the United States would get to the A-bomb before "either of our two enemies" (Germany or Russia) did. He did not underestimate the efficiency of German scientists such as Heisenberg, but they clearly had not been given sufficient resources after Hitler's murders of the Jews. Germany by 1943 suffered aerial photoreconnaissance almost every day, and a German project as large as Los Alamos would have been spotted and obliterated forthwith.

By the time of his arrival in Los Alamos in September 1943, Johnny thought that the European war was anyway probably entering its last year. His stay in England had convinced him that the Allies would invade France in 1944, and he expected something like the German officers' rising of July 20, 1944. His letter to Ulam in September 1943 responded to an even more optimistic guess from Ulam himself. "I would still think," wrote Johnny, "that Germany may last well into 1944—say 10% probability for a political collapse before spring and the probable end summer or fall. I don't think that Russia will ever settle with Germany unless there is a revolution in Germany, but otherwise I am 100% pessimistic about Russian relations." The words "100% pessimistic" about Russia had the numeral "100" struck through with the mathematical symbol Johnny used for "infinitesimally less than." He liked using mathematical symbols originally. When Ulam's wife

Françoise was pregnant with her first baby, Johnny's sign-off to his letter was "greetings to the two of you and to the $\frac{1}{2}^2$ unknown from house to house."

Johnny's pessimism about Stalin's Russia was not shared by all at Los Alamos. He said sadly to his fellow Hungarians that some of the best and the nicest of the scientists misunderstood the nature of the Stalinism that was being allowed to engulf their Hungary and half their Europe. Many scientists did not understand that Stalinism was a mixture of terror, inefficiency, and secret police. But he was determined not to enter into political argument about any of this, because he was sure it would not do any good. He assumed even in 1943 that almost everything was likely to be leaking out to the Russians, although probably not from the people who talked the most communist tosh. With a project that by 1945 had ten thousand people on site at Los Alamos and elsewhere, the Russians were certain to have infiltrated agents, through construction workers if nobody else.

Johnny joined in the social life at Los Alamos, playing and generally losing at poker. He had just published his massive textbook on how to win at games like poker (see chap. 11), but he was not in fact very good at the game. He was generally playing while thinking of a dozen other things.

Bethe and Fermi organized Sunday walks and sometimes mountain climbs. Johnny had no intention of going on the latter. "If there is a 10,000 foot mountain near here, which nobody has climbed, then I am willing to consider climbing it," he said mendaciously, "but in walks as in physics, why do you want to go where lots of people have been before?" Johnny did go on one of the Sunday uphill walks, inevitably wearing a business suit—in a Los Alamos where almost everybody except Johnny wore informal western clothes. Ulam disliked climbing even more than Johnny. After Johnny recruited him to Los Alamos, Ulam usually spent his free Sundays calling unannounced on other colleagues to discuss (in Johnny's phrase) "this and that, and especially everything else." On the day Johnny went walking Ulam had nobody to talk to, so he joined the first part of the hike. Two hundred yards up the trail is the spot where Ulam stopped. It is known at Los Alamos to this day as "Ulam's landing."

Ulam had been summoned to meet Johnny at Union Station in Chicago, when Johnny was changing trains there in one of his earliest trips west. Ulam was impressed that Johnny was accompanied by two security men who looked like gorillas, thus suggesting that the Princeton mathematician was now an important national treasure. Johnny was able to say only that an important war job might be available at a western engineering project. Ulam replied that he knew nothing about engineering—indeed, gesticulating at the porcelain pissoir that they then faced—he was "not even sure how this toilet flushes, except that it is through some autocatalytic effect." As the word "autocatalytic"—meaning a chemical reaction through the presence of a substance that itself suffers no permanent change—was at the heart of some processes in making the bomb, there was a danger that the gorillas might suspect a leak. But by November 1943 Johnny was writing to Ulam, "I am very glad that Mr. Hughes and all he stands for came through." Mr. Hughes was the personnel officer at Los Alamos.

The recruitment of Stan Ulam was part of one of Johnny's two main contributions to the atom bomb: namely, finding short cuts that helped the mathematicization of Los Alamos. His second main contribution was to the implosion bomb. Consider the mathematicization first.

It is important not to exaggerate Johnny's part in that first atom bomb. "He contributed a lot," said one wise man who read my first draft of this chapter, "but not that much." Still, Johnny was the mathematician most respected among American physicists, and he arrived at the great physicists' laboratory at a time when there was urgent need to bring terser mathematics into the place. Most of the physicists were used to doing experiments, but it was not easy to do experiments on how to blow up the world. Johnny was therefore part of the team who invented modern mathematical modeling at Los Alamos. He showed that, in explosives as in many other things, numbers can be made to represent the physical elements in an experiment; and that often these numbers—properly manipulated—can constitute the whole experiment. Today we do not find which sort of bridge is best by building two bridges and then observing which does not fall down. We work the process out on computers, just as we also compute how men dispatched to the moon can arrive within a few yards of where they are meant to land.

In 1943 the scientists at Los Alamos needed that sort of mathematical modeling. They could not say, "Let's see whether this sort of nuclear explosion works best—ouch!" Johnny was the right mathematician to arrive among them, for reasons that Herman Goldstine later assessed: "Unlike many applied mathematicians who want merely to manipulate some questions given them by a physicist, von Neumann would go right back to the basic phenomenon to consider the idealisations made as well as the mathematical formulae. He possessed . . . a truly remarkable ability to do very elaborate calculations in his head at lightning speeds . . . especially . . . when he would be making rough order-of-magnitude estimates mentally."

The bomb at Los Alamos required a lot of rough order-of-magnitude estimates, both at top level (to introduce new concepts) and lower down (to save unnecessary hours of work, and thus get the bomb ready in time). It happened that the people already on site were very good at these order-of-magnitude suggestions (Bethe, Feynman, Teller, Weisskopf). Johnny's forte was to pick up the daring ideas of brilliant men and advance them.

Hans Bethe, who was head of the theoretical division at Los Alamos, told me of the effect at the top. "Johnny was so intelligent in general problems," said Bethe, "he taught me a lot of mathematics at Los Alamos, simply by explaining it. There were some differential equations which I couldn't solve. He always could, and there was no embarrassment in asking him. He just sat down, and did them." This covered such matters as mach reflection, problems where viscosity caused complications, and problems when the density of materials compressed.

A graduate student explained to me Johnny's usefulness at the bottom. "When Dr. von Neumann came out of a room, he would be besieged by groups of people who were stuck by some calculation. He would walk down the corridor, with these people around him. By the time he walked into a door for the next meeting he would likely have suggested either the answer or the best shortcut to getting it."

At Los Alamos in late 1943 most of the calculations were still being made on desktop calculators. By April 1944 Dana Mitchell had arranged for the theoretical division to be equipped with IBM punch-card sorters, the last step but two before computers. Old Los Alamos hands say Johnny was impressed by these sorters, and instantly started to think how to make them better. Mitchell had apparently had some contact with J. Presper Eckert of the ENIAC computer, which could help explain why Johnny leapt so enthusiastically when he first saw ENIAC. If so, this changed the world.

By the spring of 1922 Stan Ulam sat amid the punchcard sorters. In the part of his autobiography touching on 1944–45, Ulam is probably right in saying that this new half technology crucially mattered. A main task at Los Alamos by mid-1944 was to calculate the course of an implosion. Johnny and others had tried to work this out with intellectual rigor, but their ingenious shortcuts and theoretical simplifications were not always working. Johnny, said Ulam, did not have "a penchant for guessing what happens in given physical situations." Ulam felt it was necessary sometimes to tackle a problem "by simple-minded brute force. That is, by more realistic, massive, numerical work."

With the arrival of the punch-card sorters, this does seem to have happened. It needs to be remembered when turning to the next part of our story—how far Johnny shortened the war against Japan by helping to invent the lens for the Fat Man or implosion or plutonium or Nagasaki A-bomb.

◄►◄►

Two fissile materials were being made for Los Alamos: uranium-235 and plutonium. An atomic explosion occurs when fissile material in excess of a small critical mass (some tens of pounds) is assembled all in one piece. Early in the experiments it became clear that the uranium-235 bomb (the one dropped at Hiroshima) was going to succeed by the so-called gun method. Under this, one mass of uranium-235 is fired by a gunlike device into a cavity in another piece of uranium-235, and the two together then explode. The physics of this, said Bethe to me, "soon came to seem almost trivial."

The difficulty was that the uranium-235 was having to be separated atom by atom. Even if a bomb could be ready for explosion over Japan in the summer of 1945, Japanese scientists could tell their army that another bomb would not be ready for a long time. They probably did in fact tell their military that, which is why the Japanese did not surrender until after Hiroshima's bombing on August 6, 1945, had been followed by Nagasaki's on August 9. The plutonium bomb dropped on Nagasaki could be assembled much more quickly because plutonium was more easily available. It could be separated by chemical means. Uranium-235 could not, because the isotopes of uranium are chemically identical. The timetable by the date of Nagasaki's destruction on August 9, 1945, was that another plutonium bomb would be ready that August, and three more in September, with the rate of production rising to seven a month by December.

The awkwardness when Johnny arrived at Los Alamos was that the gun method was not going to work with plutonium. If you fire one piece of plutonium into a cavity in another piece of it, at the required velocity of 3,000 feet per second, the plutonium bullet and its target melt down and fizzle before the two parts have had time to join. Because a plutonium bomb was needed to make the murderous new weapon credible (plutonium was becoming available so much faster than uranium-235), a despairing Oppenheimer in July 1944 came close to resigning the directorship of Los Alamos. He ordered a discontinuation of research into a gun method for the plutonium bomb. He ruled that "an over-riding priority must be assigned to the method of implosion."

Under the implosion or squeezing method a subcritical mass of plutonium is surrounded by a fat mass of high explosive—hence the term "Fat Man bomb." The high explosive is ignited at all points on its outside surface simultaneously, and the inward shock wave from it causes the plutonium to be squeezed into a dense mass that then becomes supercritical and explodes.

When Johnny paid his opening visit to Los Alamos in September 1943 he became involved in the implosion controversy on his first evening. Teller took him to dinner, and the two men swapped their respective expertises on implosion. They were complementary and hopeful.

The experiments on implosion at Los Alamos were then being conducted under California Institute of Technology's Seth Neddermeyer, who had suggested the idea when Oppenheimer and most others (except Teller) had thought it stank. Even Fermi said you could not squeeze plutonium into a smaller ball because it would squirt out in every direction—as water would if you tried to squeeze it into a ball in both hands. Johnny had become an expert on implosion during his studies of shaped charges. Immediately after his first visit to Los Alamos in September 1943, he discussed the possibilities of implosion with Kistiakowsky, who was professor of chemistry at Harvard. They came to instant agreement that implosion should work. A joint recommendation from Johnny and Teller went to Oppenheimer that month: "Press on with implosion."

Neddermeyer was initially pleased to have the support of Johnny, whom he recognized as a genius on the subject, although Neddermeyer was slightly defensive still. Johnny, he said later, "is generally credited with originating the science of large compressions. But I knew it before and had done it in a naive way. Von Neumann's was more sophisticated." Actually, this was another example of Johnny picking up other people's work and leaping blocks ahead of them. The original idea of implosion seems to have come from Richard Tolman, aided by Robert Serber. Neddermeyer had attended lectures on the subject. Johnny's calculations showed that a Fat Man bomb would be hefty but still carriable in an aircraft. The eventual bomb dropped on Nagasaki was "a big egg with tail fins, a little over 9 feet long and just under 5 feet diameter at the fattest part." Neddermeyer proceeded with the more sophisticated methods Johnny had suggested, but they did not at first seem to work. When he ignited the outer surface, the high explosive crashed in on the metal cylinders he had put in the place where plutonium would eventually be, but the flash photos showed jets of explosion traveling way ahead of the main mass. The implosion picture in that early winter of 1943 was "terribly ragged; it looked like a model of the Alps."

Oppenheimer decided that Neddermeyer needed help and drafted in an unwilling Kistiakowsky from Harvard. This created personal problems. Navy Captain (later Admiral) Deke Parsons, the head of the ordnance division, was at constant odds with Neddermeyer. Parsons wanted his division to be run in a slightly military way. Neddermeyer certainly did not. Until January 1944 Parsons and Neddermeyer could not agree on most anything. After that January they agreed on one thing: they were not going to have Kistiakowsky interfere with either of them. At the same time a row brewed between Bethe and Teller. Said Bethe:

As soon as the implosion method was proposed by Neddermeyer, Teller advocated that the laboratory devote a major effort to its development. In 1944 he was given the responsibility for all theoretical work on the problem. Teller made two important contributions. He was the first to suggest that the implosion would compress the fissile material to higher than normal density inside the bomb. Furthermore he calculated, with others, the equation of state of highly compressed materials which might be expected to result from a successful implosion. However, he declined to take charge of the group that would perform the detailed calculations of the implosion.

Bethe later complained of Teller's "wish to spend long hours discussing alternative schemes he had invented for assembling the atomic bomb or arguing about remote possibilities for the failure of our chief design. He wanted to see the project run like a theoretical physics seminar and spend a great deal of time talking, and very little doing solid work on the main line of the laboratory.

To the rest of us, who felt we had a vital job to do, this type of diversion was irksome."

During this period Johnny showed his capacity for remaining friends with everybody. When people tried to hold conversation with him about personalities, he always returned the conversation to the job in hand. The need to bring in new scientists, after Teller's disagreement with Bethe, gave jobs in implosion studies to some of the Britons then arriving at Los Alamos. One unfortunately was Fuchs. A happier one was the tall and eccentric James Tuck, who tickled Johnny with his English drawl. It was Tuck who suggested the idea of an "implosion lens." This meant that the outer layer of high explosive around the plutonium core should be fast-burning. The inner layer—toward the thinner end of the lens pointing inward—would be slower-burning. This would allow the rest of the shock wave to catch up. In the final stage before hitting the plutonium, the whole shock wave would again be speeded up. The analogy was with an optical lens that directs light toward a focal point, because light that hits the thicker center (of, e.g., a magnifying glass) must follow a longer path than light that hits the thinner edges.

Bethe and Johnny both took an immediate liking to Tuck's idea, and both set about trying to devise such a lens. "I failed," said Bethe to me with his usual modest brevity, "and Johnny succeeded." In his interview with Rhodes, Bethe said that in the winter of 1943–44 Johnny "very quickly devised an arrangement which was obviously correct from the theoretical point of view." Kistiakowsky, whom Oppenheimer elevated above Neddermeyer in June 1944, spent several months turning this theory into practice.

After initial disappointments, the first really satisfactory lens worked in December 1944. In March 1945 Oppenheimer froze lens design, on a system close to what Johnny had proposed, but with a rider: however scarce plutonium might be, there would have to be a test explosion of Fat Man in New Mexico before it was launched as a weapon against Japan. The uranium-gun Little Boy would obviously explode and could be dropped on Hiroshima when ready. But nobody at that stage could be sure that these weird lenses from Johnny's fertile brain would really work.

At least one expert in the implosion group decided that they would. Fuchs passed details of Johnny's lens to the Russians as fast as he could. It was one of the main counts against him at his trial. The eventual breakthroughs that made the implosion bomb look ready for testing occurred in the month that Germany surrendered, in May 1945. Johnny's letter to Ulam on June 6, 1945, shows that he believed that Ulam's mathematics, rather than some of the quarrelling physicists, had contributed most to one of the final problems: "I was exceedingly glad to hear about the unconditional surrender of physics to set theory. I think it was only fair to settle the patent matter as it apparently will be settled. In spite of the intellectual promiscuity at Y, you are nearly as feasible the father of that idea."

◄►◄►

With both bombs now likely to work, Johnny became a principal Los Alamos calculator of the height from which to drop them and the other mathematics of delivery. He was therefore on the target committee in Washington to decide which four Japanese cities should be put on the list to die. Unusually his notes on the target committee's deliberations on May 10 (held in Los Alamos) are still available in the Library of Congress. They show a deadly cool and orderly mind.

There were eleven topics for the morning meeting to discuss, and Johnny listed them, apparently from Oppenheimer's agenda, with figures and squiggles beside each which no doubt meant something to him. The topics were (1) height of detonation; (2) report of weather and operations; (3) gadget jettisoning and landing; (4) status of targets; (5) psychological factors in target selection; (6) use against military objectives; (7) radiological effects; (8) coordinated air operations; (9) rehearsals; (10) operating requirements for safety of planes; and (11) coordination with twenty-first's program (the twenty-first U.S. bomber command was dropping conventional bombs on Japan).

Height of detonation was the initial subject on which Johnny was to speak (he had made a note to himself to check with Bethe and Wigner). There are two tables in his notes, with arrows between figures, at points where he felt satisfied. The advice was that, although a height could be recommended for each target, it would be better to go too low than too high. If the detonation was 14% too high, damage would be reduced by 24%; you would not get that reduction in damage even if you went an unlikely 40% too low. The right delays and fuses were tabulated, even though nobody knew yet what the explosive power of the bomb would be. Most of the experts were still judging that Little Boy's explosive power over Hiroshima could be anywhere between 5,000 and 20,000 tons of TNT equivalent; it actually proved to be 12,500 tons but Truman reported it at 20,000 tons before getting the full information back. Nobody knew the likely power of the Fat Man bomb, but that was to be fused after the Trinity test had provided the information.

Johnny put ticks beside the morning's other topics when they had been discussed, together with figures and signs of eventual approval. The afternoon meeting had then to make its recommendations on targets. The air force had listed which targets it preferred to attack by ordinary bombing. It suggested six as suitable for the A-bomb. They were (a) Kyoto, (b) Hiroshima, (c) Yokohama, (d) the imperial palace in Tokyo, (e) Kokura arsenal, (f) Niigata.

A second group of possible targets had been suggested by intelligence sources. Johnny's notes on each made it clear that he thought the air force's list was better. The intelligence people had underestimated the extent to which an A-bomb would destroy entire cities rather than individual factories. Johnny put Greek letters expressing disapproval against suggestions for dropping the A-bomb on the Yawata ironworks ("twenty-first prefers penetrating bombs"), the Asano dockyard at Tokyo ("will be burned by twenty-first"), Mitsubishi Airframes in Tokyo ("as with . . ." the symbol he had put beside Asano), a steel-rolling works in Tokyo (same symbol as Asano), Osaka arsenal (already "burned by twenty-first"), the Dunlop rubber factory in Tokyo ("poor target, leave for twenty-first"). The only target on the intelligence list that Johnny marked "O.K." was the large Kokura arsenal, which was also on the air force's list.

His pen returned to the air force's list, and he was clearly against bombing the imperial palace. If the air force insisted on still considering this, the matter must be "referred back to us." As the Japanese managed to surrender smoothly three months later, mainly because the emperor was still alive, those who sided with Johnny then probably saved many lives. From the air force's list he also deleted Niigata, saying, "wait for more information on."

Johnny's four eventual votes were therefore for A-bombing (a) Kyoto, (b) Hiroshima, (c) Yokohama, or (d) Kokura arsenal. These were also the suggestions put forward by the whole committee that day.

The idea of nuking Kyoto was fortunately opposed by seventy-two-year-old Secretary of War Henry Stimson, who had first been secretary of war in the administration of President William Howard Taft before becoming President Hoover's secretary of state. Kyoto is a holy center of the Buddhist and Shinto religions. A-bombing it would have been the equivalent of atom bombing Rome or Florence or Athens in Europe. It would have put America in appalling odor in Asia for the next fifty years of peace. The air force memo had persuaded Johnny that the treatment of Kyoto as a bomb-free city hitherto meant that "many people and industries are being moved there as other areas are being destroyed," but had also thought it a psychological "advantage that Kyoto is an intellectual centre for Japan, and the people there are more apt to appreciate the significance of such a weapon." This suggests the same lack of psychological good sense as had afflicted the public-relations nuts who suggested throwing the first A-bomb at the palace of the emperor.

Yokohama was taken from the list between May and August because it had been bombed so much already. Another port was substituted in Nagasaki, which had the advantage of being distant from Tokyo. By now it was seen that it was undesirable to kill off too many people in the capital because the decision to surrender would have to be taken there. The alternative targets eventually listed for the Little Boy bomb on August 6 were (*a*) Hiroshima, (*b*) Kokura arsenal, and (*c*) Nagasaki. The weather was clear and the primary target of Hiroshima was hit.

For the Fat Man bomb on August 9 the primary target was Kokura arsenal, with Nagasaki as the alternative. There was muddle in the time of arrival of the aircraft and mildly bad weather over Kokura. So the aircraft flew on to an equally cloudy Nagasaki and dropped it (supposedly through a gap in the clouds) above the steep slopes of the city, a long way from where it was meant to go. This was a botched bit of bad flying, after the Trinity test in New Mexico on July 16 had shown that the Fat Man implosion bomb did work.

◄►◄►

Johnny was always satisfied with the mathematics of the Fat Man bomb, but there is no record that he took a ticket in the sweepstake on what its yield in the Trinity test would be. Teller had made the most expansive guess at the equivalent of 45,000 tons of TNT. Down near the bottom Kistiakowsky had bet on only 1,400 tons equivalent, and the permanently doubting Oppenheimer only 300 tons. It is probable that Johnny would have guessed something like the 8,000 tons for which Bethe plumped. On the evening before Trinity the tension was increased two ways. One group of scientists logically "proved" that the implosion bomb could not work, so the right ticket to buy was nought. Fermi was jovially offering to take bets on whether the bomb would ignite the atmosphere and, if so, whether it would destroy merely New Mexico or the whole world.

The Trinity explosion actually achieved the equivalent of about 20,000 tons of TNT. The target committee was told that this was enough to reduce a city of 300,000 to 400,000 people to "nothing but a sink for disaster relief, bandages and hospitals." It would not have been wise to aim it only at a Dunlop rubber factory. As Trinity lit up New Mexico, General Groves was told by his second in command, "The war is over." "Yes," said Groves, "after we drop two bombs on Japan."

The news of the Trinity test was released to the world in the fortnight that brought Hiroshima, Nagasaki, and Victory-Japan (V-J) Day. Johnny, as always, was not inclined to overstate his own role. Some others were, including Lawrence (who had been responsible for separating most of the uranium-235). There was even a certain irritation at Los Alamos when Oppenheimer reached into the Hindu scripture of the *Bhagavad Gita* to mourn: "Now I am become Death, the destroyer of worlds." Johnny's comment: "Some people confess guilt to claim credit for the sin."

Ulam compared the jealousies to a Berlin boarding house where one man took most of the asparagus from the platter on the table. Another stood up shyly and said, "Excuse me, Mr. Goldberg, we also like asparagus." This "science of asparagetics" became one of Johnny's standby jokes. At one committee he chaired there was argument (not including Johnny) about who should claim most credit for something which—like the digital computer and the nuclear bomb—was wholly a joint effort. Johnny's summary of the meeting ran "Per aspera ad asparagetica"—dog Latin for "through bitternesses to asparagetics."

But that was long after the cold peace had begun—and with it Johnny's civilian achievements, not just his role as the master exploder.

►◄►◄►◄ **11**

In the Domain
of Economics

►◄**J**ohnny made two major contributions to economic science. One was the huge 640-page *Theory of Games*, coauthored with Oskar Morgenstern in 1944. From Maynard Keynes's Cambridge, Professor Richard Stone instantly called this "the most important textbook since Keynes's *General Theory*," although many economists have not understood everything in either of them still.

Johnny's second main economic contribution was a half-hour unscripted lecture, doubtless accompanied by speed-of-light blackboard scribbling, to a Princeton mathematics seminar in 1932, originally and unappetizingly called "On Certain Equations of Economics and a Generalization of Brouwer's Fixed-Point Theorem." He thought so little of this that he did not write down an English text.

In 1936, he had agreed to repeat it off-the-cuff to a mathematical colloquium in Vienna. That was the year when he discontinued his European tour because his marriage to Mariette broke down, both on the transatlantic liner and in the hotel in Paris. It seems probable that he just sent to the colloquium's organizer (Karl Menger) a nine-page German text that too tersely explained his beautifully terse mathematics. He may even have written it in the deserted Paris hotel after his miserable split with Mariette. It was published in German in the proceedings of the colloquium in 1937, but initially only a few very sharp-eyed economists noted it.

Around half a century later, in the 1980s, Professor E. R. Weintraub was calling it "the greatest paper in mathematical economics that was ever written." With it "von Neumann changed the very way economic analysis is done," said an admirable textbook in 1989, *John von Neumann and Modern Economics* (edited by Mohammed Dore, Sukhamoy Chakravarty, and Richard Goodwin). The eleven economists contributing to it came from three continents, and included two Nobel laureates in economics. The first part of this chapter draws heavily on what they (sometimes diversely) said.

Johnny's almost casual scribblings on that Princeton blackboard helped lead into the sciences of linear and nonlinear programming, of dynamic models of economic growth, and better future understandings of what both economic planning and the free market can and cannot do. They had a recognized effect on the work of at least six Nobel laureates in economics: Kenneth Arrow, G. Debreu, Paul Samuelson, T. C. Koopmans, A. Kantorovich, and Robert Solow. Johnny's paper enlarged economists' mathematical toolbox with many complicated new tools like convex set theory and mathematical programming. It sent some of the wisest of economic professors to search back through his previous mathematical work to see whether they could find new econometric weapons there, which they could. Said one of the aforementioned Nobel laureates in economics: "the Durbin-Watson statistic we all use in our econometric reports is based on von Neumann's derivation of the mean-squared-adjacent-difference for a time series."

Professor Richard Goodwin, who in 1938–39 had dismissed the Menger colloquium paper as "no more than a piece of mathematical ingenuity," was later to describe that as "the greatest mistake in my career." By the 1980s he was calling Johnny's Menger nine-page paper

one of the great seminal works of the century. . . . The beautifully spare architecture of its encompassing structure leaves one awestruck. Apparently without antecedents, it sprang full-blown from that fertile brain, demonstrating the existence of a solution to the economic problem wherein all goods could be produced at the lowest price and the greatest possible quantity, with price equal to cost and supply equal to demand for all goods, along with showing the necessity for maximal growth if dynamic equilibrium is to exist.

When I wrote my first book about the Japanese economy in 1962, I argued that Japan's economic policy of "trying to double real income in a decade"—which many Western economists thought was too inflationary—did seem to have jumped into a "virtuous circle" of growth, while some slower-moving countries were dropping into a "vicious circle" of stagflation. Japanese economists at the time cited Johnny's model as showing the need "for maximal growth if dynamic equilibrium is to exist." A lot of Western policymakers disagree with this conclusion, chiefly because even more do not understand it.

It is still too early to trace this 1932–37 paper's full effects, but it fortunately is now possible to trace its origins. When twenty-five-ish Johnny was lecturing at Berlin in 1928 and 1929, he spent his summer vacations back home in Budapest. So did a brilliant twenty-ish left-wing Hungarian economist then passing through the London School of Economics to Cambridge. This was Nicholas Kaldor, who had been at the Minta school during the last four years when Johnny was at the Lutheran. The two men took an instant liking to each other, although their politics were poles apart.

Kaldor was a lifelong socialist who later advised many of Britain's ex-colonies to go down the road of economic planning and supposed egalitarianism (into what people like me think became a terrible mess). Kaldor told the dictators of the new countries not to worry if they "enraged millionaires," which was awkward because the millionaires tended to be the only businessmen available to the country, or else tribal leaders capable of raising riots in the streets, or else the dictators' brothers-in-law.

As Lord Kaldor, Nicky was a principal adviser on taxation to Harold Wilson's Labour governments in Britain in the 1960s. He helped put the top marginal rate of income tax on unearned income up to 98%. Almost single-handedly, Kaldor devised the selective employment tax to tax Britons out of joining service industries, so that they would go back into manufacturing, just when we free-traders thought that the coming of efficient low-wage manufacturers like the South Koreans made it desirable for Britons to move the other way. Kaldor appeared to his critics (like me) to be a sparkling, amazingly perverse, dramatically original, and always likeable man. It is easy to see why Johnny enjoyed and respected him. Kaldor's opinion of Johnny was that of nearly all brilliant men. Johnny, wrote left-wing Kaldor in his last paper in 1985 before his death, was "unquestionably the nearest thing to a genius I have ever encountered."

On his summer vacation in probably 1928, Johnny asked Kaldor whether he could find a short book that gave a formal mathematical exposition of what economic theory thought it was currently about, particularly whether and how it sought to get maximum growth with minimum prices. Kaldor recommended a book that summarized mathematical economics from its near founding father, Léon Walras, in 1874 on.

That 1920s history of economic theory ran something like this: For the century after Adam Smith in the 1770s, Smith's disciples thought that prices were mainly determined by the cost of production. If a country wisely had perfect competition, production would be brought by that competition to the lowest cost possible, and all resources would then be diverted into the best possible uses and places because any less intelligent entrepreneurs would go bust. One difficulty was that this did not seem fully to indicate what should be demanded and thus produced. By the 1870s economists were teaching that consumers sought maximum extra satisfaction from the next dollar they spent. This "marginal utility" is necessarily a declining function for any particular good. If my refrigerator is overstuffed with cartons of milk, I would be crazy to spend my next dollar buying another. So I will spend it on one of several hundred thousand alternative satisfactions—or use it to increase my savings instead.

With Adam Smithian supply-side economics plus the concept of marginal utility, Walras in 1874 now had a supply and demand condition for each output and input. He therefore felt able to write down equations to show how an economy worked, although economic planners could not derive much joy from them. Walras seemed content to show that the number of equations equaled the number of unknowns, so there should be logical economic solutions, and he trusted that perfect competition should find them.

Johnny galloped through his reading of the textbooks Kaldor recommended at his usual speed. He reported back to Kaldor that, for three main reasons, he was not impressed with the Walrasian equations at all. First, the idea of marginal utility gives too much emphasis to substitutability and too little to the forces that make for mutually conditioned expansion. If every family in Peoria decides that it will get greatest extra satisfaction from buying a new car tomorrow, the Walras equations do not sufficiently point out there will be rather a jam on Peoria's roads. All modern economists agree with this, although the search for mutual conditioning has led many planned economies awry.

Second, and more novelly, Johnny said the Walras equations suggested that some goods could most economically be sold at negative prices. In that respect, the equations must simply be wrong.

Third, Johnny suggested that economics was probably driven as much by inequalities as by equations. If we are trying to maximize satisfaction or growth or anything else, we should remember that the maximum is a quantity with which other things are not equal, and planners' mathematics had better recognize that. In that 1928 Johnny was already devising the paper that led on to his future *Theory of Games*. In this he concerned himself, not mainly with equations, but with matrices of bargaining power. The right economic strategy for Ford Motors does not depend wholly on what is happening in the market, but on how the market will be changed by the strategies followed by General Motors, the Japanese, and other carmakers.

In or just after 1928 the economist Jascha Marschak was holding a seminar on economics in Berlin. The Nobel laureate Kenneth Arrow has quoted a letter from a correspondent who accompanied Johnny to it:

> Von Neumann got very excited when J. M. put production functions on the board and jumped up, wagging his finger at the blackboard, saying (approx): "But surely you want inequalities, not equations there?" Jascha said that it became difficult to carry the seminar to conclusion because von Neumann was on his feet, wandering around the table, etc., while making rapid and audible progress on the linear programming theory of production.

"The rapidity with which he made the connection and developed it," said Arrow, "is in line with many anecdotes of von Neumann's mental speed." Economics is often not well served by ordinary linear equations because what will happen next is affected in different ways by what you and I and other people do now.

This was the origin of his book with Morgenstern, the *Theory of Games*, but it lay behind the 1932–37 Princeton-Menger lectures as well. In 1939 Johnny sent Kaldor a slim offprint in German of the 1937 paper, marked "With apologies from the author." Kaldor admitted with his usual frankness that "unfortunately the paper was quite beyond me," except about three sections of it—one of which Kaldor thought chimed with something socialist that he had himself published in 1937, although it actually did not. Kaldor therefore got a refugee in wartime Britain to translate it into English. "Johnny," he reported, "agreed to this—indeed he was grateful for any efforts that would enable his model to reach a wider audience as he was much too preoccupied with whatever he was working on at the moment (I think it may have been the computer)." Johnny actually returned the paper's translation "with remarkably few corrections" from Los Alamos where he was indeed working on something else.

Kaldor arranged for it to be published in Britain's *Review of Economic Statistics* in 1945, with a fine commentary but some partly mistaken criticisms (see later) by the celebrated mathematical economist David Champernowne. In 1945 the paper was called "A Model of General Economic Equilibrium," but it is now more usually known as von Neumann's "Expanding Economy Model" (EEM). We will call it EEM henceforth.

◄►◄►

The EEM showed mathematically that the economic problem can indeed be solved in a way in which all goods are produced at the lowest possible cost in the greatest possible quantity. Happily, when you reach this maximum growth, a dynamic equilibrium will exist. This does not mean that any secretaries of the treasury following this model could create such a utopia, but the EEM does help to this day to show even to politicians (most of whom are not listening) which economic policies are the actions of an ass.

The EEM was initially greeted by economists with much genuine bafflement, some huffy resentment, and various detailed objections that were usually (not quite always) the product of misunderstanding of what it said.

The bafflement arose from the terse mathematics. When Johnny had said something in mathematics, he often preferred others to translate it into English unless the hearers could instantly go out of the room and make something work much better. Hearers of an English translation of the EEM could not do that. They tended to argue politics with rising emotion—the sort of argument Johnny disliked.

Some of the resentment from economists arose because a stranger to their profession had achieved in a nine-page wonder something that they had not been able to attain in all their lives.

It is fair to say that, sixty years later, this resentment has almost disappeared. The detailed objections to the model just after 1945 were a mixed bunch. Many arose from misunderstanding. Others were of the genre: it is unfair if economic logic says that. When a community consumes more of something, it will usually (not always) have to consume less of something else. Some economists do not like to be told this.

The EEM is a model in which everything is produced from everything else. To quote the Nobel laureate Paul Samuelson, maximum production is achieved because "all the fruits of production, above and beyond the costs of subsistence for horses, rabbits, looms and comfortably living men are ploughed back into the system for the growth of more horses, rabbits, looms, men." There has been misunderstanding and some mockery because the EEM's ideal growth rate is equal to the interest rate assumed in the model. That sounds crazy to a day-to-day analyst. When interest rates are bumped up to 12% in the real world, you do not expect growth to accelerate to 12% but instead expect it to go down.

This is a muddle about what interest rates in the model meant. Johnny was redefining interest rates in a way that classical economists knew. To quote Samuelson again, classical economists would not have been surprised with such a statement as "When the closed system is growing maximally in balance at say a 10% rate per period, with labour and land super-abundantly free and competitive goods having unchanging price ratios, the prices of goods at each period's beginning are exactly their respective prices and outputs at the period's end discounted at the 10% rate of interest set by the system's technological growth rate." Probably the loudest protests against the EEM came from the Left, some of whom assumed that Johnny was advocating a slave economy in which wages were kept near the lowest possible subsistence level. He was not. He was pointing out that growth is fastest when, as happened in countries such as Japan just after his death, labor can be absorbed from low-productivity work on the land into more productive jobs in new technology industries without too big a rise in the real wage. If Peronist trade unions insist on trying to push real wages on too fast a rising trend, they will actually bring real wages lower than they would otherwise be. That is one reason why Japan succeeded after 1945 and Argentina did not.

Another objection was that the EEM assumed that activities are closed completely when they cannot earn the market profit rate; Johnny was merely saying that growth is maximized when they are. The EEM assumed that prices of surplus goods decline toward zero, so producers flock out of those industries. This does not always happen, but mainly because politicians get in the way. In today's international trading system, America sells some of its surplus bread at subsidized prices abroad, while the EEC sells subsidized butter; Johnny's mathematics merely and rightly showed that both are silly when they do. Some people misunderstood the circular flow of the model and assumed it said that everything had to have in it some element of everything else. That would be awkward because most things bought or seen at random have no input from most other things at random. Jellybeans do not have much input from mamba snakes. All Johnny was doing was leading the way toward modern input-output tables. He was showing protectionists how growth is maximized when you get each input from the cheapest source.

Champernowne, perhaps misled by Kaldor's belief in class war, assumed that in the EEM the propertied classes saved all their incomes while the workers spent all theirs. Neither of them does any such thing. Champernowne also criticized what he regarded as Johnny's assumption that land and some other factors were available in unlimited quantities; the EEM merely said that growth was maximized when the next bit of any factor does not rise in price.

One criticism of the EEM that does ring true is that its nonmonetary character means that we cannot read from it how our prospects are damaged when erring politicians or central bankers create excess demand by overexpanding money supply or create recession by overrestricting it. It is in this respect that later dynamic economic models—sometimes derived from the EEM—are more useful today, although only after long controversies about which previous models led which political manipulators of economic policies awry. Johnny kept clear of macroeconomic policy (i.e., discussion of when politicians should artificially add to or subtract from demand) because he did not see any mathematical way into being helpful with advice on it. His private letters show that he had some fears in 1933 that Roosevelt's New Deal policies could bring inflation. Many people who had been in Germany in hyper-inflationary 1922–23 did. But his comments on this were never shrill. By 1935 he was writing (in Hungarian) to Ortvay in broad support of Roosevelt's expansion of demand. He thought it was desirable in order to offset contractionary influences through the crashing banking system, although he saw that Roosevelt's particular ways of trying to keep prices up were pretty odd.

Morgenstern was once asked how a scholar outside the mainstream of economic thinking could make a contribution to economics as original, innovative, and decisive as Johnny's EEM. Morgenstern replied that Johnny had an extraordinary capacity to pick the brains of a person whom he engaged in casual conversations. Once he saw from these that there was a problem of sufficient mathematical interest to warrant his spending of time on it, he homed on to that subject like a guided missile. On Keynesian macroeconomics in the 1930s, he did not feel either side was mathematically proving its case, so he turned to other things.

◄►◄►

In economics this meant he turned to decision theory, and particularly to how a businessman should operate when seeking a maximum of profit. Even in 1928 Johnny had produced a mathematical paper on how best to operate when you logically ask yourself what the other man is going to think you mean to do. In a two-person zero-sum game (i.e., one where anything I gain equals your losses and my losses equal your gain) you can in fact work out a best strategy that will maximize your potential gains or minimize your potential losses if I operate equally logically. And you will on average beat me hollow if I operate in any way illogically at all. It is always difficult to think of the least obnoxious way of explaining this "minimax theorem" of Johnny's to people who have not thought of it.

Start perhaps with the children's game of Morra, where you put out one or two fingers and shout "One" or "Two," to signify how many fingers you guess your opponent will simultaneously be putting out. If you are both right or both wrong in your guess, that hand in the game is void. If you alone are right, you gain points equal to the number of fingers held up. I here plagiarize the right strategy from a television program on the BBC that the mathematician Bronowski ran, but he indicated that it was his friend Johnny's strategy of which he talked.

You have four possible decisions in Morra:

Decision A. Hold out one finger and shout "One." If your opponent is indeed holding out one finger (and has not guessed right that you are holding out one), then you win two points—one for the finger you are holding out and one for the finger that he is.

Decision B. Hold out one finger and shout, "Two." If your opponent is indeed holding out two fingers (and has not guessed that you are holding out one), then you get three points—one for your one finger held out and two for his two.

Decision C. Hold out two fingers and shout, "One." If you have guessed right, the two of you are together holding out three fingers, and you therefore get three points.

Decision D. Hold out two fingers and shout, "Two." If you are triumphantly right, you then get four points.

Mathematically, as Johnny told his friends, you should never adopt Decision A or D. Instead, in each of the twelve games you should always go seven times for Decision B and five times for Decision C.

If you operate strategy A of proffering one finger and shouting "One" against a skilled opponent who is using the correct strategy, you will win on the seven times out of twelve when he is operating strategy B of proffering one finger and shouting "Two"; but because only two fingers will be shown by you plus him each time, your points on the twelve games will be seven multiplied by two, which means fourteen. On the five occasions when your opponent operates C and shows two fingers, he will gain five multiplied by three, which means fifteen points in the twelve games. In those twelve games you will therefore lose an average of one point, so do not ever use Decision A against an opponent who is using the right strategy.

If you employ Decision D against a skilled player, you will win five of the twelve games when he is operating Decision C. You will get four points each time, making a seemingly nice haul of twenty points in twelve games. But your opponent will get three points on the seven occasions out of twelve that he will on average win, namely twenty-one points. So you lose one point in twelve games on average.

If you are both following the right strategy, you and your opponent will eventually win or lose equally. If you alone follow the right strategy, you will over any large number of games of Morra win against somebody who does not know his mathematics.

◄►◄►

To ascend from this child's game to making millions for your corporation or saving the world, look at the matrix below. It is adapted only slightly from the way in which Johnny and Morgenstern's *Theory of Games and Economic Behavior* was described in Edwin Mansfield's admirable textbook *Economics: Principles, Problems, Decisions*.

In it, I set out a strategy to follow when something like my favorite brightly titled new product hit the market. It was a cat food with accompanying advertisement jingle: "So good that cats call for it by name." Have you guessed its name? The new catfood was called "Miaow," which is why my matrix is called the "Miaow matrix." Lines 1, 2, and 3 outline some alternative initial marketing strategies for Miaow. Columns A, B, and C outline the possible responses from other cat foods—which are here as-

TABLE 1

The Miaow Matrix

	OTHER CAT FOODS' STRATEGY			
MIAOW'S STRATEGY	A. Do nothing	B. Loud TV ads	C. Soft, other media ads	LINE MINIMUM
1. Loud TV ads	± 90	± 20	± 40	± 20
2. Do nothing	± 10	± 80	± 30	± 10
3. Soft, other media ads	± 70	± 60	± 50	± 50
COLUMN MAXIMUM	± 90	± 80	± 50 ←	SADDLE POINT

Note. All numbers represent millions of dollars.

sumed to be a monopoly on a static market that would lose every penny in profits that this interloper Miaow gains. All of the entries assume that the entry of Miaow onto the market would lose other cat foods some revenue and gain Miaow some. Otherwise, the newcomer would not be worth introducing.

Line 1, column A, suggests that market research tells Miaow that a blitz of full television ads will gain it $90,000,000 in net profits if the other cat foods do not respond. Line 1, column B, suggests net profits of only $20,000,000 if the other cat foods respond with loud television ads replying to Miaow. Line 1, column C, suggests $40,000,000 if the other cat foods respond with quieter ad campaigns that do not fill television screens every night. At first sight the other cat foods might deem it best to follow Line 1, column B, and respond to Miaow's expensive television campaign with loud television ads of their own. Their advertising agents may recommend this, saying that Miaow's net gain in profits (and their net fall in them) would be a measly $20,000,000.

But Miaow could respond to this in one of two ways. First, it might decide not to advertise. If it did not, and the other cat foods were crazy enough still to attack it through television ads, it could—according to line 2, column B, of our matrix—reap a nice cheap net profit of $80,000,000. The main reason for this is that any net loss to the other companies is assumed to be a gain for Miaow. By foolishly plumping for a bumper advertisement budget, the other companies would be forfeiting some of their capacity to compete in other ways, such as in price. Obviously, however, the other cat foods would be wise to respond to a Miaow policy of "do not advertise" by also deciding not to advertise, so—at line 2, column A, of our matrix—hardly anybody would hear of Miaow and it would make a tiny $10,000,000 in net profit.

Miaow will thus have an incentive to consider a softer and less expensive advertising campaign. This would again gain greatly ($70,000,000) if—at line 3, column A—the other cat foods did not advertise at all. If the others advertised stridently and expensively on television, the cheap ad budget of Miaow might still—at line 3, column B—bag it a nice net $60,000,000 profit, partly because the others were spending so much on ads that they could not compete so well on price and quality. The minimum gain to Miaow from running a cheapish advertising campaign would be $50,000,000—at line 3, column C; this would be the result if the other companies responded with a similar cheapish advertisement campaign.

This $50,000,000 is in fact the saddle point. If the figures in our matrix are right, it is the best gain that Miaow could feel certain of getting if the other cat foods adopted a sensible strategy. It is therefore this softer advertisement campaign on which Miaow would be wisest to embark (if market research suggests the figures in the matrix), unless it thinks the other cat food makers are silly pussies. If you look at the line marked "column maximum," you will see that $50,000,000 is the minimum figure on it; this means that, if the other producers operate sensibly, that is the most Miaow can hope to gain. If you look at the column marked "line minimum," you will see that $50,000,000 is the largest figure in it. If this infant Miaow is going to appear with the sensible policy of not-too-expensive ads, a policy of responding with softish ads is the policy that will lose the other cat food companies the least money. There will therefore be a tendency for the policy of both sides to settle on this one of meeting softish ads with softish ads, at the saddle point where Miaow will gain $50,000,000 net profit

TABLE 2

The Cuba Matrix

	U.S. STRATEGY		
	A. Do nothing	B. Invade Cuba	C. Blockade (but give ladders to climb down)
SOVIET STRATEGY	Absorb West Berlin, etc.	Probably absorb West Berlin, etc.	Probably climb down

at the others' expense. If either side does something different, it will (in this case) lose more to the cleverer other side.

It is often difficult for businessmen to believe that a matrix must have such a saddle point—on the improbable assumption that each side makes the same assessment of what the market will do. But there is in fact going to be a saddle point in any two-person zero-sum game, and shrewd assessment of the main chance, or fears of bankruptcy, will lead business strategists some way toward it. This can also, say enthusiasts, be important for saving the world.

An example of when thinking like this probably did help save the world was when Khrushchev planted nuclear weapons in Cuba in 1962. He was threatening to absorb West Berlin during a peace treaty with East Germany. Broadly, America had three possible responses to the nuclear weapons in Cuba (see Cuba matrix above). American policy in column A would be "Do nothing, pretend not to notice." That would show Khrushchev that he could painlessly take over West Berlin and raise Soviet infiltration in the Middle East, Africa's horn, Central America, and other trouble spots. We now know from some Russians themselves that this was their intention if (as they half expected) Kennedy played chicken.

The second possible American policy, in column B of the Cuba matrix, could be "React very aggressively, bomb the missile sites or invade Cuba at once." Opponents of this line whinnied that it could cause an indignant Khrushchev to press nearer to blowing up the world. Actually, Khrushchev never intended to blow up the world, particularly on behalf of Castro, whom he rather disliked. But his advisers in Moscow told him that an aggressive American reaction (which they also half expected) would fill the city squares of the world with protesting demonstrators. They would shout (and some politicians would listen) that America was wicked to bomb or invade Cuba. They would say it must not have European support next time it "reacted excessively" against a Soviet move and risked nuclear war. So either a chicken American response or a supertough one would probably make it easier to absorb West Berlin. That is why Khrushchev placed the missiles in Cuba.

The third possible American policy, in column C of the matrix, was to declare blockade against the Soviet ships approaching Cuba but to give Khrushchev ladders to climb down. This is the policy that wisely was chosen. It clearly gave maximum gain to America (which did not want either the enslavement of Berlin or genuine danger of nuclear war) and with luck gave minimum loss to Khrushchev (who would have to make a quick decision on whether to turn back the ships). He did not want to be humiliated in the eyes of his own politburo, but also did not want to be blown up with the world. He was in some way humiliated before his politburo, but was not sacked until two years later.

There is not as much enthusiasm among economists for game theory as there is for EEM. When you draw up matrix justifications—of the stumbling sort I have tried above—some of them always seem lame, as various parts of each matrix obviously do. Economists suspect that decision makers will veer off such matrix formulations toward surer-thing guesses and strive-for-independence strategies; they do not want to make decision making too complicated. There is circular reasoning involved in the assumption that every bluffer knows what every other bluffer will do. Forecasts that everybody knows about are forecasts that easily turn sour; if everybody sees that "the next generation of computers will be far better than present computers and will be particularly suitable for providing banking services," then too many people will probably produce new computers and banking services—with the result that computer makers and banks go into glut and go bust. In addition, very few decisions are really taken in a spirit of two-person zero-sum games. Later chapters of the huge von Neumann-Morgenstern textbook were concerned with *n*-person combinatorial games. They were even harder for any decision maker to visualize as applying to himself.

Consider two examples from Johnny himself: When he played poker he quite often lost because he felt it was boring during a relaxation to visualize too many matrices when there were better things to think about. He just stuck to the general rules that emerge from his mathematics in another paper specifically on poker play-ing (with many equations including the letter *n*). Those general rules are if you have a strong hand, always bid high; if you have a weak hand, sometimes bid high to bluff or sometimes bid low and pass; but never bid low and then see. Many thinking poker players do that anyway.

Johnny did feel he had contributed to decision theory. In his youth Europe had stumbled into the 1914–18 war partly because—as one historian has said—mobilization got entangled in railway timetables. Once troop trains had been sent off from home towns with flowers and bands, it was difficult to bring them steam-ing back again because the enemy had not climbed down (in con-ditions where nobody should sensibly have expected him to). During the cold war from 1945 to and beyond his death, policy was always more thought out, which is why there was no nuclear incineration of the world. Johnny believed that tougher behavior toward Russia would have stopped Stalin's grab of eastern Europe. Those who disagreed with him about his desire for toughness then spread the story that he was a mad strategist weaving matrices from his *Theory of Games*. Those who said this were usually people with whom he did not in fact discuss these matters. Herbert York, who (see chap. 15) did discuss them with him, told me: "Johnny never used *Theory of Games* language when discussing military or political options. He gave his views in the language used in newspapers."

But when there are debates about great matters, such as the Gulf Crisis in 1991, you will generally find that sense emerges from those who at least implicitly think in terms of matrix theory—and shallow rubbish can come from those who do not.

◄►◄►

I am among those who agree most strongly with the earlier pages of the *Theory of Games*. In these Johnny annoyed some economists by saying that much mathematics "had been used in economics, perhaps even in an exaggerated manner," but "had not been highly successful." Many social scientists have assumed that this is caused by the human element, by psychological factors, by the uncertainty about how different people will react to different incentives. Those social scientists, said Johnny, are "utterly mistaken." The main reason for the failure of mathematics in economics is that economic problems are "often stated in such vague terms as to make mathematical treatment a priori hopeless because it is quite uncertain what the problems really are. There is no point in using exact methods when there is not clarity in the concepts and issues to which they are to be applied." Johnny said economists should ponder how the mathematization of physics was achieved in the seventeenth century. The breakthrough by Newton and others into mechanics came because of previous developments in astronomy. These were backed by "several millennia of systematic, scientific, astronomical observation, culminating in an observer of unparalleled calibre, Tycho Brahe."

Nothing of this sort has occurred in economic science. Mathematical economists too often forget this. There are not sufficient scientific statements in economics saying that this has always followed from this, from this. "The underlying vagueness and ignorance have not been dispelled by the inadequate and inappropriate use of a powerful instrument [mathematics] that is very difficult to handle," wrote Johnny.

Johnny thought that mathematical economics probably needed a new mathematical language.

The decisive phase of the application of mathematics to physics—Newton's creation of a rational discipline of mechanics—brought

about, and can hardly be separated from, the discovery of infinitesimal calculus. . . . [Today] the importance of the social phenomena, the wealth and multiplicity of their manifestations, and
the complexity of their structure, are at least equal to those in
physics. It is therefore to be expected—or feared—that mathematical discoveries of a stature comparable to that of calculus will
be needed in order to produce decisive success in this field.

This, incidentally, is one reason why Johnny himself was less
satisfied with the *Theory of Games* at the conclusion of the book
than he was when he and Morgenstern set out on it.

Most mathematical economists did not like these strictures on
their science. It is not nice to be told that you are working out
your guts pushing on a piece of string, or using the wrong tools
in the wrong field. This biographer's guess is that these paragraphs
of Johnny's—saying proper economics will need a new mathematics—will prove dramatically true in time. That is probably
one reason why economic forecasting models by computers have
not generally proved successful. Another has been the commercial
push to produce too many of them.

Almost every bank and finance house and sometimes university
wants to be able to say that it has the forecasting model that has
proved most correct. Sometimes the forecasts themselves make it
impossible for them to prove true. If there is universal forecast of
a grave shortage of oil, people dig for oil in the far Arctic, and
install mechanisms that use less oil, so the forecast grave shortage
turns ineluctably to glut. Most important, in the first forty years
of computers, economics has continued to have far too few fact-
gathering Tycho Brahes. Its forecasting models have had too much
inconsequential garbage fed in, and enthusiasts have too fetishis-
tically worshipped some of the consequent garbage out. This has
been especially true of the stock market.

It is therefore the earliest of Johnny's essays into economics, the
EEM, which at present does most to buttress his high place in the
annals of the science. Because Johnny's collected works were published in 1963, economists have browsed enthusiastically through

them to find new mathematical tools to wield. They have found them in such exotica as "A Numerical Method to Determine Optimum Strategy," which Johnny contributed to the *Naval Research Logistics Quarterly* in 1954, and in some of his work on probability.

The golden opinions continue to grow. The Nobel laureate Samuelson is one of the economists who disagrees with Johnny's view that economics might need a completely new mathematics. In a critique of *The Theory of Games*, Samuelson wrote that the "respective scientific personalities" of Morgenstern and Johnny "led to resonance of minor faults—some tendency towards nihilism combined with Napoleonic claims." But Samuelson had no doubt that Johnny was "a genius (if that 18th century word still has a meaning)," the fastest mind he had encountered—"a man so smart that he saw through himself." "He was," wrote economist Samuelson, "the incomparable Johnny von Neumann. He darted briefly into our domain, and it has never been the same since."

▶◀▶◀▶◀ *12*

The Computers

at Philadelphia, 1944–46

▶◀ "*T*he history of computers," says Herman Goldstine, one of that history's heroes, "is littered with Australopithecanes, the deviant apes that anthropologists keep finding: little evolutionary lines that don't lead anywhere." All our lives changed because in the 1940s a mainstream line of computers emerged. The reasons for success lay in pure academic research of twenty years earlier, which was then mixed with wartime impatience, plus a fine young engineer, then aided by the participation of one of the cleverest men in the world (but, importantly, only part-time).

The pure research was Göttingen's breakthrough in quantum mechanics in the 1920s, which ushered in the electronic age. The most brilliant wartime innovators were Turing in England (with a development which was born Australopithecane) and J. Presper Eckert in Philadelphia (with the Moore School's Electronic Numerical Integrator and Computer, or ENIAC, which innovated superbly). The ENIAC proved the true father of the tribe, although Eckert sadly felt ever after that Johnny robbed him of his birthright. Any such robbery benefited the rest of us. Electronic computers by 1944 needed the presence of a top mathematician with insight into the most logical design for computers, publish-to-the-world public spirit, understanding that one more layer of scholarship was needed before computers could profitably turn competitive in free markets, sufficient scientific reputation to raise research funds to implant that extra layer of scholarship, although also with lots of other things to do. These were among the roles Johnny played in 1944–53. He could see both backward to how computers had turned Australopithecane before and forward to the new opportunity. Let us look briefly backward first.

◄►◄►

After physics was mathematized by Newton (1642–1727), there arose a need for reams of tables. Some were tables for mass consumption (such as logarithms, cosines, navigation tables). More had to be worked out by inquiring scientists themselves, as they noted down their observations and drew up tables to test hypotheses. The compiling of each table was dead boring. Wailed Leibniz, (1646–1716), "It is unworthy of excellent men to lose hours like slaves in the labor of calculation which could safely be relegated to anyone else if machines were used."

That is why Leibniz devised what would yesterday be called a desk calculator, or perhaps a mildly mechanized abacus. You could multiply and add figures by cranking its wheel around. Leibniz's wheel was better than the desk calculator built by the French philosopher Blaise Pascal (1623–1662), but perhaps a little behind one devised in 1624 by an obscure German professor of astronomy, mathematics, and Hebrew, who died in one of the many plagues of the Thirty Years' War.

The next top mathematician to share Leibniz's impatience was England's Charles Babbage (1791–1871). While he was a Cambridge undergraduate in 1812, Babbage expostulated that logarithm tables (then often error-ridden) should be calculated by machines, preferably driven by the new go-go technology of steam. Babbage got a large grant from Britain's chancellor of the Exchequer in 1823 to build a computing machine, in one of the first such research contracts to a scientist from a government. It had the same result as many subsequent contracts where governments pay scientists to try to do something, instead of scientists trying to produce something to prove salable on the market. It was almost wholly disastrous.

From 1827–39 Babbage held Newton's old chair as Lucasian Professor of Mathematics at Cambridge. He rarely turned up to lecture. He buried himself in London trying to build his computing engine, while suffering from overfunded academic scientists' all-too-common lack of will to bring his project to a close. Whenever he drew near to completing a machine that could in some degree work, he "hit upon an idea of doing the same thing by a different and far more effective method," and thought "this rendered it useless to proceed on the old lines." Babbage's biographer subtitled her book on him "Irascible Genius." His main phobias were against Italian organ-grinders and British chancellors of the Exchequer who would not persuade the House of Commons to give him even more money. "I should like a little previous consideration," explained the ablest of these chancellors, Sir Robert Peel, "before I move in a thin house of country gentlemen a large vote for the creation of a wooden man to calculate tables for the formula $x^2 + x + 41$."

Yet irascible Babbage was also a genius, breeding startlingly original ideas for digital computers. "Digital" means machines that add up digits, doing sums in the way the human brain would. Babbage spotted that the mechanization of mathematics could best follow on from what in 1805 had been Joseph-Marie Jacquard's mechanization of embroidery.

Jacquard, a Henry Ford of a man in the age of the French Revolution, dashed his invention into commercial production so quickly that by 1812 it dominated the upmarket sector of the textile industry in Napoleon's blockaded continental Europe. Jacquard attached to ordinary steam-driven looms a series of cards with holes punched in them to depict a particular pattern. These holes allowed hooks to come up and pull down threads of the warp so that the moving shuttle could go over some threads and under others.

Mr. Babbage's analytical engine, enthused the poet Lord Byron's daughter by the 1830s, "weaves algebraical patterns just as the Jacquard loom weaves flowers and leaves." In language useful to computer designers more than a century later, Babbage said that his analytical engine should consist of two parts: the store (which is nowadays the computer memory) and the mill "into which the quantities to be operated on are always brought" (nowadays the central processing unit).

Like Johnny, Babbage recognized that computers had to be based on logic rendered into a precise and mathematical form. He delayed his invention as new forms of mathematics—especially those of George Boole (1815–64) came along. "Pure mathematics was discovered by George Boole in his work published in 1854," exaggerated Bertie Russell as usual, and Babbage was of a temperament to agree with him. As we will see, one of Johnny's virtues in 1944–54 was that he did the opposite. He saw that the arrival of the computer and other automata would make new methods of numerical analysis important. He started striving to develop (instead of wait for) them.

Although Babbage's logic and arithmetic and computer architecture were sophisticated, his steam power was not. It is doubtful that even today any computer could be driven by steam, and certain that nobody should want to try. At their peak Babbage's prototype engines worked out equations only about as quickly as a human mathematician could, although with the advantage that they did not get tired. After Babbage's death in 1871, a friend bewailed, "the verdict of a jury of kind and sympathetic scientific men who were deputed to pronounce on what he had left behind him, either in papers or mechanism, was that everything was too incomplete to be capable of being put to any useful purpose."

That jury was wrong. Only nine years after Babbage's death there emerged the next great leap forward in digital or counting machines, springing from Babbage's work. Its early hero was a very entrepreneurial American civil servant, Herman Hollerith (1860–1929). He introduced electricity into Babbage's punched cards, and became the penurious grandfather of IBM.

As a teenager employed in the 1880 U.S. census, Hollerith saw it was nonsense that hundreds of clerks were tabulating the details of all the fifty million Americans by scratches of their quill pens. This meant that the census's interesting figures became available only after several more years of surging immigration had made them completely out of date. There must, thought Hollerith, be a better Jacquard-loom-like system of using a punched card for every respondent to the census: with different holes showing whether male or female, immigrant or native born, black or white, ability to speak English, parent of how many children.

For the census of 1890, Hollerith invented precisely such a machine. Each of the by-then sixty-three million Americans was allotted a card that had 288 places through which a hole could be punched. These were then sent under contact brushes that completed an electric circuit whenever holes appeared. The superintendent of the 1890 census was thereby enabled to announce the total population of the United States just a month after all returns arrived in Washington, D.C.—and then follow up with far more detailed pictures of America's social statistics than any country had ever had before. Officials rejoiced that with Hollerith's machines "complex aggregations can be evolved at no more expense than simple ones."

Officialdom was not pleased with Hollerith for long. He established his private-enterprise Tabulating Machine Company in 1896. He started charging the Census Bureau and other domestic and foreign clients a rental for using his machines. The U.S. government said he was charging too much, and Hollerith had a period of seeing his company (like many later computer companies) on a knife edge between lush prosperity and imminent bankruptcy. The eventual tilt toward prosperity came in 1914 when the financier acting as savior of the stockholders' last few cents hired an able executive from National Cash Register, Thomas J. Watson,

Sr. Before Hollerith died in 1929, Watson had renamed the company International Business Machines (IBM), and was running it very rich.

When the Bureau of the Census tried to undercut high-charging Hollerith in 1904–7, the job of devising a new machine fell to an engineer named James Powers. He went off to found his own private-enterprise company in 1911. It merged with Remington-Rand in 1927 and Sperry Gyroscope in 1955, thus giving birth to Sperry-Rand, which became one of IBM's main competitors. Whereas Britain's approach to computers in the nineteenth century had been to pump out government money to an academic genius in Babbage, America's approach in the early twentieth century was to wax furious when government civil servants deserted to set up privatized ventures of their own. The strength of America's early twentieth-century business-machine industry, and the weakness of Britain's, shows which road worked best. But I will argue later that, after about 1960, America has not learned as well as it should from some of the business lessons that in 1944–55 Johnny taught it—certainly not as well as did Japan.

◄► ◄►

The direct descendants from Hollerith were the IBM punch-card desk calculators that Ulam and Johnny were using in 1943–45 for the implosion A-bomb. By January 1944 Johnny was asking the authorities if any more modern methods of mathematizing Los Alamos were available. Warren Weaver—who was what might be called America's registrar-guardian of mathematical secrets during the war—recommended that Johnny make approaches for Los Alamos to use the new IBM-Harvard Mark I computer and the Bell Laboratory computer. Both of these were appearing amid hype and high hopes in 1943–44—just as the electronic computer was about to make such electromechanical devices completely redundant.

The Harvard Mark I—described by Thomas J. Watson, Jr., as "pretty much two tons of IBM tabulating [i.e., punch-card] machines synchronized on a single axis"—and the Bell did not look like lame ducklings at the time. A human being multiplying two sets of ten figures (like 1,234,567,809 by 9,087,654,321) with pen and paper takes about five minutes to do the sum. The IBM punch-card desk calculators in 1943 could do this in ten to fifteen seconds, which made some people proclaim they speeded matters more than twenty times. The Bell computer took about one second for each such calculation, and the Harvard by 1944 was in the same league. These two therefore seemed ten to fifteen times faster than a clerk with a desk calculator.

Because the machines did not need to sleep like a human, and further improvements in printing and other functions could be confidently foreseen, it seemed right in 1944 to hype their results as being higher. By running twenty-four hours continuously, it was said that new versions of these machines might soon do in a day what could take a human with a desk calculator six months. Indeed, enthusiasts for them feared they would run too fast for their commercial good. One of the Harvard's inventors allegedly warned that America could not have use for more than about five of his machines. This was an intriguing forecast in view of the several hundred million computers in the world today, with the most advanced running over two billion times faster than the Harvard did then.

Johnny did try out the Harvard and intended to use the Bell, for one Los Alamos calculation in 1944. He found such machines quite useless. The punch cards at Los Alamos solved the problem in three weeks. After five weeks, the Harvard reported it was halfway through it. This was partly because the Harvard tried to calculate each figure to an unnecessary eighteen decimal digits, partly because for security reasons the Harvard operators had not been told exactly what they were trying to do, and partly because of teething troubles at the IBM-Harvard baby, which was never going to grow up to bite anyway. All the attractions of the Harvard and Bell and their contemporaries paled into insignificance with the arrival of America's first real electronic computer, the ENIAC.

Starting from 1944, the electronic ENIAC was set for a speed about a thousand times faster than any electricity-driven computer like the 1944 Harvard or Bell could attain. That sounds odd because electricity flows through wires at very nearly the speed of light. But the contacts at the end of electromechanical relays have to weigh probably a gram, so in those days it took perhaps five-thousandths of a second for a relay to open or close. In the vacuum tubes of the ENIAC—or later in transistors—the elements being moved are electrons, which have masses equal to less than one trillionth trillionth part of a gram.

There is thus essentially no resistance to be overcome, and a vacuum tube can be said to operate almost simultaneously. In the original ENIAC, the time taken to activate other parts of the circuit was around five-millionths of a second, which was a thousand times faster than the 1944 Harvard's or Bell's five-thousandths of a second. It is true that the first ENIAC batted out only about 333 multiplications a second, while the Harvard on best behavior managed one, but everybody saw that the electronic wizard would be able to go faster and faster still.

Soon after seeing the ENIAC, Johnny guessed that electronic computers in our lifetime would go more than a billion times faster than the one calculation a second that the best of the calculators had given to scientists theretofore. This biographer sat in a bathing suit in October 1990 and pondered one of the surprise fruits of how right Johnny was, and yet how clumsily we still use his discoveries. In October 1990 the British Meteorological (Met) Office had taken delivery of a computer capable of two billion calculations a second. This was due to replace its old Cyber 205 computer (bought about 1981), which had run at only about four hundred million calculations a second. On the first Wednesday of its tests, when barely out of its wrapping, the Cray forecast appalling gale damage over western England the following Monday. Fearful that its new toy might have a bad habit of forecasting disaster from nil evidence, the Met Office did not announce this until Thursday, by which time its old Cyber was saying the same thing. Actually, "both metalheads had seized on the same wrong mid-Atlantic blip," explained next week's London *Sunday Times*. Monday dawned bright, clear, and calm. Tuesday's delighted morning papers showed scantily clad models strolling along sunlit beaches. Running at two billion calculations per second, the new Cray in 1990 was wrong twenty-four hours earlier than the old Cyber 205. It is occasionally worth pondering whether, had Johnny lived, we would have ridden his fast horses more sensibly than into the stampedes that they now sometimes attain.

◄►◄►

That was not the question for 1944. One question for the new year was, Why did Warren Weaver in January 1944 not draw Johnny's attention to the possible advance of the ENIAC? A main reason is that Weaver at the time did not think the ENIAC would conceivably work. Another is that Johnny was looking for computers to which some Los Alamos problems could immediately go, and the ENIAC was not yet available for that.

Paradoxically, though, Johnny was probably one of the few Americans who knew that the electronic computer would come. In his correspondence with Ortvay in Budapest, the two men had discussed during the late 1930s the possibilities for early breakthrough to understanding of the human brain. By 1940 Ortvay was discussing whether "a computing system consisting of electronic valves" might learn lessons from this. Also, there must be a chance (though there is no proof) that, while Johnny was in England in the first half of 1943, he learned at least something about the very secret machine that preceded America's ENIAC as the first big electronic computer.

Britain's tightest war secret had been its capture, or rather reconstruction in 1939–40, of the Germans' Enigma coding machine. This had enabled Churchill to learn the Germans' secret plans through much of the Battle of Britain. By early 1943 the Germans were playing more cleverly. They were changing their key to the Enigma code three times a day. There were about a trillion combinations of codes they could use. Hitherto the British had scoured through intercepted German Enigma messages with various electric decoding machines, which rearranged the numbers in the coded German radio signals until something appeared that made sense in German. In January 1943, just as Johnny was arriving in England, his prewar Princeton choice of an assistant (Turing) and a prewar Cambridge friend from 1935 (M. H. A. Newman) were two of the main three men who turned the decoder at Bletchley Park—halfway between Oxford and Cambridge—electronic.

By December 1943 Turing sent electrons racing without resistance along eighteen hundred vacuum tubes, so that a tape—which carried into the machine some five thousand characters a second —could be jiggled on permitted Enigma guidelines until near-German appeared. Then the operator could adjust his controls to home in more precisely on that. Although this was an Australopithecane machine, which was never going to be useful for anything else, Turing will have seen the implications for computers. We know that Johnny wrote to Veblen from Britain in 1943 that he had developed an "obscene interest" in computing. In wartime Britain the word "obscene" meant something you were not supposed to talk about, and anything to do with Enigma in 1943 was mortally secret. There have been arguments that Johnny was merely referring to a clever way of utilizing a National Cash Register calculating machine in a Nautical Almanac Office in western England—which he visited in 1943 because different ways of compiling naval almanacs meant that either Britain or America was behind the other one in getting its ships to know where they were (particularly important when radioing for help if under U-boat attack). It is true that Johnny wrote a program for this ingeniously modified cash register on his train back to London, but he is unlikely to have been "obscenely interested" in that.

What is clear is that Johnny was not told in early 1944 of the contract for the electronic ENIAC, struck in spring 1943 between his old stamping ground the Ballistics Research Laboratory (BRL) at Aberdeen and the Moore School of Electrical Engineering at the University of Pennsylvania in Philadelphia. He learned about that on a railroad platform in August 1944.

◄►◄►

At the time of Pearl Harbor in 1941 the BRL at Aberdeen owned one of Vannevar Bush's differential analyzers. The war gave it immediate control over the Moore School's ownership of another. These differential analyzers have been called forerunners of the computer, but they were in no line of paternity. They could be called the last elephantine types of mechanized slide rules. Each eventually weighed a ton, included 150 motors, 200 miles of wires, several thousand relays, and complicated printing machinery dependent on photoelectric cells. Each shaft and wheel had to be set very precisely for each problem. To change the nature of the calculation tackled was a long and finicky manual job, at which some of the professors attending the analyzer in Philadelphia were not good.

Despite its operation of these two monsters and a roomful of punch-card calculating machines, the BRL started the war in a ghastly mess. It was soon in a ghastlier one. Even by the third year of war its 180 or so statistical staff, pounding two shifts a day at their desk calculators and using their two differential analyzers, were taking three months to complete some of the complicated sums placed before them. The laboratory was then taking in orders for new firing or bombing tables at about six per day, so it was running gaspingly fast without often managing to keep its backlog standing still. In the early months of war the situation was worse. It was only after mid-1942 that the Aberdeen laboratory began recruiting statisticians at wartime pace.

The army ordnance department asked for a sifting through of the first wartime conscripts to see whether any promising mathematicians were among them. One of those gathered in through this sifting in the summer of 1942 was the twenty-nine-year-old Goldstine (born 1913). He had moved from a Ph.D. in mathematics at the University of Chicago into the faculty at the University of Michigan. Indeed he had been invited by Marston Morse to be his assistant at the IAS.

On September 1, 1942, the new Lieutenant Goldstine went with army ordnance's best technological colonel, Paul Gillon, to find out why the differential analyzer at the Moore School was working even less well than could be expected. They recommended various improvements, including the transfer to Philadelphia that same month of Lieutenant Goldstine to insert some military zip, and the replacement of several elderly academics as instructors for the differential analyzer by some brisker young women (such as Goldstine's wife). One of Philadelphia's advantages was that it could draw in so many personable female graduates from Bryn Mawr and all the other women's colleges around. Of the first six women programmers whom Goldstine appointed to the ENIAC, four married senior staffers in the project. Some lived happily ever after.

Goldstine's injections speeded operations, especially as he early discovered the finest young (then-twenty-three-year-old) graduate engineer at the Moore School—Eckert, who was let loose on the differential analyzer each night to improve it. He hooked a couple of hundred radio tubes into it, plus amplifying generators and some electromagnetic and electronic paraphernalia. He soon got "the old mechanical analog machine about ten times faster, [and] about ten times more accurate," but it was groaning protestingly as it ran. Eckert and Goldstine both realized that attempts to conquer the backlog of firing tables by differential analyzer were never going to work. At this stage, there entered into the story the more tragic figure of John William Mauchly.

In 1941 the mild, shortsighted, leftish, eventually bearded Mauchly taught mathematics at Ursinus College, a small school in the environs of Philadelphia that had no real budget for doing research. Eckert was an engineer of the very front rank; Mauchly was a mathematician who never got anything notable published, despite keen attempts. Goldstine and later Johnny found it difficult to regard Mauchly as a valued colleague, although their admiration for Eckert was great. In 1941 at Ursinus, Mauchly—ever pecking for new research subjects—had contacted the then-unsung John V. Atanasoff, who was an associate professor of mathematics at Iowa State College from 1926 to 1945. Atanasoff was one of several people who realized how much better computers could become if electrons were sent through vacuum tubes, rather than relying on electromagnetic relays. Atanasoff had indeed begun to construct an electronic computer with three hundred vacuum tubes in Iowa. It never got far because, says Goldstine, it "was somewhat premature in its engineering conception and limited in its logical one."

In the autumn of 1942 Mauchly—who had been recruited to the Moore School shortly after meeting Atanasoff—suggested that an electronic computer might be the answer to Aberdeen's backlog of firing tables. (That backlog grew worse when the American army landed in North Africa and found the backs of its guns sank into the sand.) Eckert was immediately interested in Mauchly's idea. He noted that an electronic computer might calculate the trajectory of a shell faster than the shell itself took to fly through the air. In March and April 1943 Goldstine persuaded Colonel Gillon and a committee (incidentally including Veblen) that the army should fund the attempted development of what Gillon named the Electronic Numerical Integrator and Computer (ENIAC). Work on it started in May 1943. It was quite well advanced before most of the top scientific advisers to the army sent in (fortunately unsuccessful) memos declaring that the ENIAC project was absurd.

One can see why they thought so. At the say-so of a colonel and a lieutenant, this small team of about twenty people at the hitherto dilatory Moore School had gotten themselves financed into building a U-shaped monster called an ENIAC that was going to be 100 feet long, 10 feet high, and 3 feet deep. It was to include 17,000 vacuum tubes, about 70,000 resistors, 10,000 capacitors, and 6,000 switches. Its priority to these parts was fairly low, at a time of grave wartime shortage. Many of the parts that did arrive were other army units' rejects or otherwise defective. Because the 17,000 vacuum tubes had to operate at a clock rate of 100,000 pulses per second, and because errors could spread through the whole machine when one of these tubes failed at one pulse, pessimists pointed out that the machine would have 1.7 billion chances of failing every single second. Fermi, who knew how vacuum tubes operated in Italy, was only one of those who thought electronic computers would be lucky if they ever managed to keep going for more than ten seconds flat. By November of 1943 the principal developer of the Bell relay computer was writing to Weaver that he was "very sure that the development time for the electronic equipment will be five to six times as long as that for relay equipment." Weaver probably believed this, which may be why he did not inform Johnny about the ENIAC two months later.

By the time that letter from Bell was written, it was a forecast of the past that had already proved wrong. Even by the autumn of 1943 it could be seen that ENIAC was surging to success far faster than computer ventures before it, although it did not actually start working until after the end of the war. How did this small pre-Johnny team on the ENIAC go as fast as it did?

Most of the credit lies with Eckert, and some with Goldstine. In the earliest stages, Mauchly was also useful. Besides being the man with the original courage of Atanasoff's ideas, Mauchly knew how the IBM-Harvard and other nonelectronic computers had tackled various problems. He was able to say, "at this stage IBM did this." Later Mauchly busied himself rather sinisterly with drawing up patent applications.

Eckert's contribution has been enthusiastically summarized by Goldstine, despite the later split between them: "Eckert's standards were the highest, his energy almost limitless, his ingenuity remarkable, and his intelligence extraordinary. From start to finish it was he who gave the project its integrity and ensured its success." Eckert demanded that the tubes should be preserved by seeing that the plate voltage be kept at no more than 50% of the rated maximum voltage, and by setting similar exigent standards for resistors, condensors, wiring boards, tube sockets, and every other component. Failures of vacuum tubes were soon kept down to about two or three per week. The mechanism for finding which had blown worked well—except during what Johnny later called the "battles of the bulge" when more than one tube failed simultaneously.

The other advantage for infant ENIAC was that Goldstine knew of Babbage's history of never finishing anything on time. Goldstine was determined to push the project through to operational prototype even though everybody kept finding ways to make it far better—if only he would permit some extra delays. These proposals for making ENIAC better were stored for implementation only in ENIAC's successor, which was to be called the Electronic Discrete Variable Computer (EDVAC).

By late summer of 1944 ENIAC was away in the hands of the construction engineers, and the more design-minded people at the Moore School were turning their minds to EDVAC. In what was probably the first week of August 1944 Goldstine was waiting on the railroad platform at Aberdeen for the train to Philadelphia. Johnny appeared on the platform, also waiting for a train. Goldstine had never met him but had attended some of his lectures. He recounted:

It was therefore with considerable temerity that I approached this world famous figure, introduced myself, and started talking. Fortunately for me von Neumann was a warm, friendly person who did his best to make people feel relaxed in his presence. The conversation soon turned to my work. When it became clear to von Neumann that I was concerned with the development of an electronic computer capable of 333 multiplications per second, the whole atmosphere of our conversation changed from one of relaxed good humour to one more like the oral examination for the doctor's degree in mathematics.

On what was probably August 7, 1944, Goldstine took Johnny to see the ENIAC at Philadelphia. Before this visit Eckert told Goldstine he would be able to "tell whether von Neumann was really a genius by his first question. If this was about the logical structure of the machine, he would believe in von Neumann, otherwise not. Of course this was von Neumann's first query."

The age of the modern computer began.

◄►◄►

There was to be bitterness about what happened immediately after August 1944. This biographer's view will not surprise: it is that Johnny picked up Eckert's brilliant ideas, and jumped blocks ahead of them. Both the judgment of the market and a long judgment in court eventually went the way Johnny would have wished. But it is easy to understand that Eckert and Mauchly felt they had been cheated.

Eckert was an inventor with drive, quick mechanical touch, and superbly innovative ideas. He had helped finance his way through college by inventing improvements to cinema organs. Then, during a radar project, he introduced a device for a mercury delay line. Because pulses travel through a liquid at a much slower pace than electricity travels through a wire, a mercury delay device could slow some pulses when it was desirable that other pulses should go on before them. Eckert's contribution to the ENIAC had been the outstanding one, but he was early aware of the ENIAC's defects.

The principal (although not sole) of these defects was ENIAC's lack of an adequate stored memory. Every time the machine needed programming to tackle a new problem, operators had to scuttle around to replug cables, throw switches, change dials, move equipment. This did not matter while the ENIAC stuck to firing tables, so that the same program could run for weeks. But it would matter as soon as a computer was required to move from one problem to another by key tap. Eckert had proposed several ways into a stored memory for the next generation of computers. One derived from tone generating in cinema organs. Another (incorporated in the EDVAC) used his mercury delay line.

There were two opposite initial mistakes from able men about the ENIAC, as contrasted with Johnny's weird mixture of an ultimately visionary yet immediately practical view. The mistakes were the inventors' dreams of avarice, and the businessmen's initial contempt. Eckert and Mauchly hoped they could become rich by taking out patents on the ENIAC first and the EDVAC after. They hired patent attorneys who encouraged them, instead of instilling caution. When anything as innovatory as the computer appears, the first models nowadays usually will not make money. Customers know that the next models a few years down the road will be much better.

In 1944–46, businessmen were inclined to disbelieve even in those next computer models down the road. When IBM's Tom

Watson, Jr., went to see the ENIAC ("acres of vacuum tubes in metal racks"), he was amused that the impressive Eckert and less impressive Mauchly thought they were "going to push IBM aside pretty quickly"—with an ENIAC that Watson regarded as "a gigantic, costly, unreliable device."

Johnny's reactions to his first sight of ENIAC, and to his first discussions on EDVAC, were very different. The visionary part of his mind soared to imitating the brain with the 17,000 radio tubes with which they were sharing that August room (because there was no air conditioning, they must have pulsed hot). The practical part of his mind came straight down to the nitty-gritty. These two young men (by which he meant Eckert and Goldstine) had produced a most commendable monster which could do fast mathematics logically. Because Johnny was the world's leading mathematical logician, he could clearly improve its logical design. Every moment that he looked at the proposals for EDVAC, ideas to make them better spilled out of his mind.

His musing about a machine like the brain had been fevered by his admiration for a 1943 paper on a mathematical model for the human nervous system (including a mathematization of psychology) by W. S. McCulloch and W. Pitts in the *Bulletin of Mathematical Biophysics*. Anybody who rereads it now sympathizes with a friend of Johnny's who will stay nameless: that the McCulloch-Pitts model was "immensely naive," but Johnny was "enormously impressed" with it.

Still, his excitement about McCulloch-Pitts helps explain why, when shown an electronic computer, Johnny mentally hit the ground running. Goldstine was an academic mathematician who thought that his team of electrical engineers had successfully started something important. Now the world's leading mathematician was confirming quick ways to make it even more important, with mathematical symbols that Goldstine was best able to appreciate and understand. Goldstine's book, *The Computer from Pascal to von Neumann*—from which many things in this chapter have been drawn—reprints part of two letters that he sent to Gillon on August 21, 1944, and then on September 2, 1944.

In the August 21 letter Goldstine says that Johnny was already conferring with him weekly and was working on how the computer might help with the aerodynamical problems of blast. The main needs ahead were to avoid wasting valuable time in resetting programs and to find an instrument in which to store data that was more economical than the computer's accumulator. "As the accumulator is so powerful an instrument, it seems foolish to tie up such tools merely to hold numbers temporarily. Eckert has some excellent ideas on a very cheap device."

In the September 2 letter Goldstine reports on a tough problem triumphantly overcome. The ENIAC could compute the equations suggested by Johnny far faster than the IBM-Harvard, but it took far longer to set the ENIAC up. "To evaluate seven terms of a power series took 15 minutes on the Harvard device of which 3 minutes was set-up time, whereas it will take at least 15 minutes to set up ENIAC, and about 1 second to do the computing." The marvellous news was that the team now knew how to remove this disparity. "We propose a centralized programming device in which the program routine is stored in coded form." The "crucial advantage of central programming is that any routine, however complex, can be carried out whereas in the present ENIAC we are limited."

"In the fortnight between the two letters," said Goldstine's postwar book, "the idea of the stored program seems to have evolved. Indeed in the September letter the concept already appears in quite modern guise, whereas in the August one the author was trying to evolve an emendation of the ENIAC's central controls to make it a little more useful." Goldstine's implication was that, in this fortnight, new team member Johnny led the leap across the chasm into proper stored-program computers, with amazing speed of mind. Others in Philadelphia thought Johnny's and Eckert's ideas ran more in tandem. A letter from Dr. J. G. Brainerd (director of the Moore School) to Gillon on September 13, 1944, said the ENIAC did not have sufficient storage capacity to handle nonlinear partial differential equations, which is what scientists wanted. The Moore School now knew "of two principles which might be used as a basis. One is the possible use of iconoscope tubes, concerning which Dr. von Neumann has talked to Dr. [Vladimir] Zworykin of the Radio Corporation of America (RCA) Research Laboratories [we will return to this Zworykin in chap. 13], and another . . . is the use of storage in a delay line with which we have some experience [Eckert's scheme]."

Some writers who think Johnny appropriated other people's ideas on the EDVAC, rather than pumped in his own in full flow, assume that he met the ENIAC only on September 7, 1944. That was the day when he was given security clearance, with another Princeton colleague, to see it. As the above quotations show, he was already a live wire in the EDVAC debate in the month before that. Indeed Johnny (unlike Eckert and Mauchly) was a participant at the BRL board meeting in Aberdeen on August 29, 1944, that virtually agreed to fund the EDVAC. The board was given a list of the subjects that EDVAC would handle more efficiently than the ENIAC. Most of them were the subjects in which Johnny was especially interested.

Johnny's detractors have also assumed that his only contributions to EDVAC came when he visited Philadelphia. One of the main lessons of this period is that, importantly, he was not hired to work on EDVAC full-time. You cannot hire one of the cleverest men in the world full-time and say, "Sit at a desk thinking where this project might most sensibly progress." But Johnny did let his mind pore over EDVAC's most pressing problems, pretty fancy-free, on his train journeys across America to fulfill his four other full-time jobs at this period, 1944–45.

As just one example of detail, a letter from Johnny to Goldstine on February 12, 1945, shows the tone:

I want to add something to our discussion on feeding data into the machine, and getting results out. As you may recall, in feeding in, two types of numbers occurred: binary integers x,y which denote positions in the memory: other binaries . . . [which] ought to be typed by a human operator and absorbed by the machine as decimal numbers, and also printed as such. . . . As to the x,y we had doubts. Since they had logical control functions, it is somewhat awkward to have to convert them. I argued for having x,y always in binary form, but we finally agreed that binaries are hard for handling and remembering by humans. I think that we overlooked an obvious solution: that is, to handle x,y outside the machine in the octal (base 8) system. . . .

By the spring of 1945 Johnny was asked to draw up a report on the logical framework for EDVAC. Goldstine said this would be particularly useful because nobody drew up anything of that sort for ENIAC—"and as a result the ENIAC is full of gadgets that have as their only raison d'etre that they appealed to John Mauchly."

Johnny wrote this "First Draft of a Report on the EDVAC" in March 1945. It was issued as a 101-page mimeograph by the Moore School on June 30, 1945, and has been described by Goldstine and others as "the most important document ever written on computing and computers." Johnny's language in some ways imitated Babbage's, as he explained the need for a central arithmetical (C.A.) part of the computer, a central control (C.C.) part to provide a proper sequencing of operations, and a memory (M.). He continued, "The three specific parts, CA, CC (together C), and M correspond to the associative neurons in the human nervous system. It remains to discuss the equivalents of the sensory or afferent and the motor or efferent neurons. These are the input and output organs of the device. . . ."

◄►◄►

Goldstine went into eulogies. Johnny, he wrote, was the first person "who understood explicitly that a computer essentially performed logical functions, and that the electrical aspects were ancillary." Johnny's First Draft "served as a model for virtually all future studies of logical design" of computers. Goldstine even had kind words for the use of McCulloch-Pitts notation: an "essential way for describing pictorially how computer circuits behave from a logical point of view." Johnny (said Goldstine) became the first to work out a detailed programming "for a sort and merge routine": a milestone because it was "the first elucidation of the now famous stored program concept together with a completely worked-out illustration." He set the EDVAC on a serial mode of operation (i.e., one instruction at a time is imparted and then executed). Johnny suggested that modifications of television camera tubes could provide a valuable memory device. "He was," says Goldstine, "among all members of the group at the Moore School the indispensable one. Everyone there was indispensable as regards some part of the project—Eckert, for example, was unique in his invention of the delay line as a memory device— but only von Neumann was essential to the entire task."

Eckert and Mauchly disagreed with this encomium for Johnny, with a bitterness that increased over the years. Even in September 1945 they (or their patent lawyers) described the First Draft as a summary of "physical structures and devices proposed by Eckert and Mauchly," which Johnny had then translated into McCulloch-Pitts language that they plainly regarded as pretty weird. "Johnny learned instantly, of course, as was his nature," said Mauchly. He was "rephrasing our logic, but it was still the same logic. . . . He was introducing different but equivalent symbols, nevertheless the devices still did the same things. Johnny did not alter the fundamental concepts which we had already formulated for the EDVAC."

Joel Shurkin, whose book *Engines of the Mind* argued that Eckert and Mauchly deserved the main credit for the EDVAC, said Johnny made his real contribution to computers in his IAS project after 1946. At the IAS, Shurkin thought,

von Neumann's technical contributions are manifest and beyond controversy. The machine he designed would be faster than anything else in the world. . . . While all the other computer makers were generally heading in the same direction, von Neumann's genius clarified and described the paths better than anyone else. . . . Many of the developments in programming and in machine architecture at the institute profoundly influenced future computer development. . . . While others were using crude digital instructions for their machines, von Neumann and his team were developing instructions that would last, with modification, through most of the computer age.

Johnny would have succeeded faster in his Princeton computer project if Eckert had joined him as chief engineer, which Johnny wished. But that last phrase from Shurkin—instructions that would last "through most of the computer age"—explains the difference between the two sides. Eckert and Mauchly thought that the EDVAC could lead on straight to commercial success. Johnny did not. His eyes were fixed on bringing in a new computer age.

Intellectually, it is difficult not to be more excited by Johnny's concept. Financially, it is easy to see why Eckert and Mauchly grew cross, although this really was not Johnny's fault.

Goldstine was thrilled at Johnny's First Draft in mid-1945. He saw instantly that these 101 pages of typescript were a historical document. He generously gave copies to people who asked for them, from all corners of the world. The only name on the title page was John von Neumann. Johnny did not give credit to others who had contributed ideas to his First Draft, but for the simplest of reasons. He thought this was a working document to those people themselves, clarifying the way he and they should move ahead in what in March 1945 he still regarded as a crucial wartime project. "Through no fault of von Neumann's the Draft was never revised into what he would have considered a report for publication," wrote Goldstine. "Indeed, not until several years later did he know that it had been widely distributed."

Part of the problem came because the war ended so soon after First Draft was being written in March 1945. Johnny in the four months after that was helping to create the implosion bomb for explosion at Trinity, deciding in Washington whether Hiroshima or other cities should die, calculating the height from which the bomb should be dropped, and collating the figures for destruction from Hiroshima and Nagasaki. He was living in the center of world events and had no real sense of being demobilized.

Eckert and Mauchly knew that their war work had consisted of helping brilliantly into existence a thing called the electronic computer, which would now come off the secret list. It would be the most important machine of the second half of the twentieth century, and they hired attorneys to try to harvest their share of the fruits.

The result of this unpleasantness was that the drive to develop computers split up—which is a pejorative way of saying it fortunately became very competitive.

◄►◄►

We had better tidy up the strands of the computers from Philadelphia. Because the final engineering took too long, ENIAC did not become available before war's end. It did its first useful work for the Hippo calculations for Los Alamos at the end of 1945. ENIAC was formally accepted by the Philadelphia Ordnance District of the army on June 30, 1946. It was meant to be sent to Aberdeen immediately, but it was by then still engaged in abstruse calculations for Los Alamos. Johnny used his increasing influence behind the scenes to see that this series of calculations was completed before ENIAC was switched off in Philadelphia on November 6, 1946. It was good that he did because the moving and reassembly of all those 17,000 vacuum tubes in Aberdeen took nine months of difficult rebirth.

ENIAC was restarted on July 29, 1947, at Aberdeen. Soon after that, Johnny gave the dying dinosaur a new lease on life. He programmed the entire machine into a new and somewhat primitive stored program computer and thus made it in its old age a stored program computer itself. This slowed ENIAC's speed of operation but speeded the programmers' tasks so enormously that ENIAC was never used under its old pre-1947 mode of operation again. By adding that stored program facility, Johnny extended ENIAC's useful twenty-four-hour-a-day existence to October 2, 1955. Its thousands of switches were then turned off, and parts of it—with flashing lights and other showpieces—were made a museum exhibit at the Smithsonian in Washington.

◀▶◀▶

The EDVAC lost both its quarreling teams of conceivers before its birth. Indeed it was preceded into existence by one of its own children. At the end of the war Johnny and Goldstine left for their own computer project at Princeton (see chap. 13), and Eckert and Mauchly left the Moore School because they would not agree to sign a university declaration about patent policy.

The Moore School in 1945 was left with a contract to complete the EDVAC computer for the army and a nest from which all the birds had flown. It carried through this contract loyally rather than enthusiastically. The school brought in new engineers to complete the contract, and they actually proved rather good. The EDVAC was delivered to Aberdeen in 1950, very much in the state that Johnny had recommended in his First Draft in 1945. By then, however, it was not even the firstborn son of First Draft. That honor fell to the Electronic Delay Storage Automatic Computer (EDSAC) set on stream at Cambridge in England in June 1949.

Half a dozen Britons had been among the lucky recipients of Johnny's First Draft in 1945. They included Turing, who tried to improve on First Draft to build a computer that would be mechanically simpler than Johnny's but more complex in its logical design and thus would require more complicated systems of coding. It did not flourish. This illustrates another facet of Johnny's genius: his First Draft's instructions could have been made more logically complex, but he wrote with deliberate simplicity to fit the engineering and programming facilities likely to be available at the time. The constructors of the EDSAC at Cambridge followed closely on Johnny's First Draft. They regarded it as an advantage that many computers appearing around the world had a common ancestry in that temporarily almost holy document. "Anyone familiar with the use of one machine will have no difficulty in adapting himself to another." Later, as we shall see in the next chapter, even more computers around the world were born as a result of the papers Johnny and Goldstine and their team published from Princeton.

◄►◄►

Eckert and Mauchly left the Moore School in 1946 to set up a private-enterprise Eckert-Mauchly Computer Corporation. It got a contract from Northrop Aircraft to build a Binary Automatic Computer (BINAC), which was operating by August 1950, and then a Universal Automatic Computer (UNIVAC) for the Bureau of the Census, which was operating by March 1951. Both looked successful machines for their era, but by then a flow of ideas for a newer era was emerging from Johnny's intellectually brilliant, if slow-coach engineering, computer project at Princeton.

Mauchly had a tragically tempestuous time after the war. In 1946 he and his wife went skinny-dipping in the Atlantic at midnight, and Mary Mauchly was sucked away to her death. Mauchly had to run naked through the neighboring village to get help, when he could not see well even under the lampposts because he had lost his spectacles. He remarried one of the ablest young women from the ENIAC project, who proved an admirable supporter, but he then had difficulty with defense contracts because he was persecuted by MacCarthyite slurs arising from some left-wing connection in the 1930s. Mauchly was not a good salesman anyway. When the Eckert-Mauchly Computer Corporation ran out of money in 1949, the two approached Watson, Sr., to try to be taken over by IBM. Wrote Watson, Jr., Mauchly was "a lanky character who dressed sloppily and liked to flout convention. Eckert, by contrast, was very neat. When they came in, Mauchly slumped down on the couch and put his feet up on the coffee table—damned if he was going to show any respect for my father." The Watsons said that antitrust considerations made it impossible for IBM to take over any computer companies. Eckert "understood perfectly. . . . Mauchly never said a word: he slouched out the door after an erect Eckert."

In 1950–51 the Eckert-Mauchly Computer Corporation was acquired by Remington-Rand, and by 1955 was merged with Sperry Gyroscope. It was Sperry-Rand which later became involved in litigation about how many Eckert-Mauchly ideas, right back to 1944, had been pinched by other computer companies. The judgment in 1973 was that the publication of Johnny's First Draft in 1945 had put these matters into the public domain; and that the original ideas for an electronic computer had not come from Mauchly but from Atanasoff.

Much of the task of leading the post-1945 computer revolution therefore evolved into another part-time job for Johnny. The papers he produced were more important than his machine. His First Draft for EDVAC in 1945, put straight into the public domain, was already helping people around the world to produce sons of EDVAC, each carrying modifications thought up and experimented with by each project's director and team. Johnny thought that was the right way to achieve progress. But he was also certain that, after a little more thought by himself, these sons of EDVAC would quickly be obsolete. He decided to do such thinking, and to put that, too, into the public domain.

When he did, most designers of computers who stayed unbust flitted from making EDVAC clones to making modified IAS clones. If you are trying to catch up with world markets, it is better to drive tomorrow's car than yesterday's. EDVAC had emerged after a very short span of thinking by a tiny and rather haphazard group of a dozen or so men, operating under conditions of wartime secrecy, although they were fortunate after August 1944 to have their thinking restructured, reassembled, and then codified by such a mathematician as Johnny. But Johnny had done only a few hours' thinking about EDVAC, much of it on uncomfortable wartime railway trains. He saw that, under proper conditions of research and experimenting, he could improve the logical design of computers by the length of several blocks. He could do this just by sitting and thinking, even if the engineering resources he assembled did not quite work (and they did not). This fact explains his attitude to Eckert and Mauchly and their commercialism. He wished them and others luck with trying to meet the demands of the market, although he thought the technology would be improving so fast that their models would be out of date before they were completed.

He resisted Eckert and Mauchly only if they were going to try to get restrictive patents: ones that would block him from using EDVAC technology when experimenting toward the post-EDVAC technology that was going to be so much more important. He wrote some fairly tart letters on that. He did have visions whether automata could in Darwinian evolution create better automata, and so on. But he wanted to stimulate computers better than EDVAC first.

Even in its simplest aims, this was an unusual Western approach to technology. Most big American corporations today do not send blueprints of their best intended innovations to their competitors, in the hope that they might think up complementary ideas that could make the innovation even better. In hiring patent lawyers to safeguard what they thought was their own intellectual property, Eckert and Mauchly were acting in a more American way.

In about a dozen visits to Japan since 1962, this biographer has persuaded himself that Johnny's approach to technological development was much more akin to the modern Japanese way. Japan has far fewer lawyers than America, including fewer patent lawyers. The first broad knowledge about any industrial opportunity tends to go quickly into the public domain. Then after a certain stage—but only after that—lots of companies try competitively to produce the salable models emerging from it. In early days a main player was Japan's famed or feared Ministry of International Trade and Industry (MITI). Many Americans presumed that MITI gave big subsidies to Japanese manufactured industry and were puzzled when search of the Japanese budget accounts revealed few direct ones. Although MITI is far less powerful than in the 1960s, its continuing mode of operation is shown by what happened when video recorders appeared. These were invented in the West, originally as very expensive machines used by television channels for instant replays, to confirm that the umpire had made a mistake when calling "Strike three" against any batter on your own team.

All the seven or eight big Japanese consumer electronics companies then attended meetings at MITI and initially put some of their own researches about videos into the pool. From these meetings emerged a target for the rival Japanese firms: "If we can devise a video recorder which sells for under $1,000 within such-and-such a timetable, we will have a consumer good with potential for hundreds of millions of worldwide sales." This became a slogan, rather like President Kennedy's in the 1960s: "Put a man on the moon in this decade." In one big Japanese corporation I knew, the video recorder project was only one of 128 target-oriented and date-oriented research projects under way at that time. A small ENIAC-like team of ten to twenty people worked on each project. It was assumed that all would have a prototype ready within the timetable. If the prototype looked like being worse than rival firms' ones, the company's top technologists were called in as part-time rethinkers at that stage. When "our company's video recorder ran into problems near the point of launch, all our top experts came in over the weekend and worked in shirtsleeves to solve them."

In target and timetable, this resembled America's research projects during World War II. In the placing of initial private knowledge into the common domain, it resembled Johnny's 1945–55 drive for computers. I do not find that restless spirit running through most research projects in the West now. This difference did not come about because Johnny was a collectivist sort of person. He believed in free markets far more than most academics. Perhaps he put his view most clearly at the launch of a project to which he had contributed while working somewhere else. At the dedication of the NORC computer built by IBM for the U.S. Navy in 1954, Johnny said he believed that

in planning anything new . . . it is customary and very proper to consider what the demand is, what the price is, whether it will be more profitable to do it in a bold way or a cautious way, and so on. This type of consideration is certainly necessary. Things would very quickly go to pieces if these rules were not observed in 99 cases out of a 100. It is very important however that there should be one case in 100 where it is done differently . . . to do sometimes what the United States Navy did in this case, and what IBM did in this case: to write specifications simply calling for the most advanced machine which is possible in the present state of the art. I hope this will be done again soon and that it will never be forgotten.

Johnny's post-1945 computer project at Princeton's IAS was an example of precisely this sort. It was a project in possibly the wrong place, with inadequately wrong engineering resources, but at exactly the right time. The next chapter will examine how far it worked.

►◄►◄►◄ **13**

The Computers

from Princeton, 1946–52

►◄**J**ohnny understood by V-J Day in 1945 that he would still have to work some months a year on military business, including at Los Alamos. He foresaw the need to deter Stalin's Russia and maybe wage preventive war against it. But, provided the world was not blown up, he recognized that his most important other work would be with large computers. He knew that he could help advance the next stage in them in ways that nobody else could.

There were four groups of computer decisions to be made. First, he had to decide where to operate from, how to raise funds, how to generate enthusiasm. As the first part of this chapter will argue, he managed the funds and enthusiasm splendidly.

Second, he had to devise and explain the changes that needed to be made to the logical design of computers, before computers could take off. As the second part of this chapter will argue, he and his team spread the von Neumann architecture for computers with amazing speed around the world.

Third, he set to work building a computer of his own, which he hoped would be especially useful for big scientific projects. As the third part of this chapter admits, this was—by Johnny's standards—rather a laggardly flop. His computer was important mainly because of the imitations it bred, sometimes before it had itself started to work.

Fourth, Johnny had a wider conception of where computers could lead than anybody before him—or, much more surprisingly, than anybody since. He did not envisage these machines as today's glorified typewriters. He hoped that experimenting scientists could use computers to start scientific revolutions that would change (in his favorite word "jiggle") the planet. In meteorology, the first great scientific subject to which he turned computer power, he helped bring what he would regard as a disappointingly unfinished revolution, although it has transformed that science. Bluntly, he hoped that by now we would be controlling the weather, to make it next day nearer to whatever in each location we wanted it to be. The conventional view of chaos theorists and environmentalists in 1992 is that any attempted jiggling of the planet would be grossly irresponsible. By 2012 the conventional view may be that in 1957–92 we lagged because we temporarily had not produced (or in the TV age of five-second sound bites had not allowed to enter into the opinion-forming classes) anybody as mathematically clever as Johnny.

The fifth section of this chapter will leave that issue in the biographer's own poetic doubt.

◄► ◄►

The first decision in 1945 was: where to operate from? The steam had gone out of the Moore School. The only puffs now coming up there were about patent rights. The disadvantages of taking a computer project back to Johnny's own IAS were that institute's smallness and snobbery against practical ventures. "Cavalry officers entering balloons are required to remove their spurs," proclaimed a sensible message board on the western front in 1914. That was the attitude of some people in the rarefied air of the IAS to sharp-edge research projects like computers, although it was not the attitude of the IAS's director Aydelotte.

Other American universities looked much more welcoming. As Ulam reported about a later meeting on Johnny's sort of computers at the University of California, "the atmosphere reminded me of the meeting of the Gun Club in Verne's Trip to the Moon, with exponential enthusiasm toward the project." Several universities were angling to recruit Johnny in late 1945, specifically to work on computers. He received formal offers of professorships from Chicago and MIT, and feelers from Harvard and Columbia. From MIT Wiener asked shrewdly how research into computers could "fit in with the Princetitute? You are going to run into a situation where you will need a lab at your fingertips, and labs don't grow in ivory towers."

Johnny turned these approaches from big universities down because Aydelotte at the IAS had responded to a tentative inquiry most generously. In October 1945, Aydelotte recommended to the IAS board of trustees that they contribute $100,000 of the estimated $300,000 needed for Johnny's computer project. Aydelotte also recommended—which was important—that the money could be drawn on at once. Such a computer, minuted Aydelotte, would be "the most complex research instrument now in existence. . . . Its construction would make possible solutions at which man at the present time can only dream. It seems to me very important that the first instrument of this quality should be constructed in an institution devoted to pure research, though it may have many imitations devoted to practical applications."

The second dollop of the $300,000 initially required was to come from RCA, whose laboratories at Princeton were turning over in 1945 to research on cathode ray tubes for what seemed bound to be the huge postwar boom in the new television industry.

Johnny had spotted that cathode ray tubes would be the most likely technique for his computers' memory. By storing information on a cathode ray tube, he could attain faster and more random access to a memory than via Eckert's mercury delay lines. Johnny had ignited enthusiasm in the RCA's prestigious Vladimir Zworykin, whom the company regarded as one of the coinventors of modern television. Johnny thought he could make RCA's attitude to patents sufficiently loose to allow him to publish to all the world whatever he found about computers. He realized there was more likely to be a clash on patent views between RCA and Eckert, whom in 1945 he rightly still wanted in his Princeton project as chief engineer. He accurately told RCA that he thought Eckert was brilliant, although with equal care he obscured that view from Eckert.

RCA busied itself producing a special cathode ray tube for Johnny called the Selectron. It contained grids of bars at right angles to each other, in a way which formed many "windows" —only one of which might be open at one time. That could allow a selected beam of electrons to flow through to the familiar television-like screens that were to be a feature of post-Johnny computers.

The Selectron was a tube of great ingenuity and complexity and fidelity—and really pretty disastrous. Almost simultaneously Professor F. C. Williams, working on a shoestring at Britain's Manchester University, discovered that the normal techniques used for switching the beam of a cathode ray tube were accurate enough for computers. Johnny's computer at the IAS was to be delayed before full operation partly by the nontechnological attitude of his IAS, and partly by the overly high technology of RCA. He had more luck with his next two sponsors. They were the armed services: sponsors who allowed him to operate most internationally and liberally, although they had been opposed by colleagues at the IAS on the ground that they would bring in secrecy and nationalism.

Because funds were not going to come from the traditional academic research foundations (the Rockefeller Foundation said it was too tied up with war-ravaged Europe), Johnny early saw the advantage of drawing in money from both the U.S. Navy and the U.S. Army. He attracted them—and made them enthusiastic

and cooperative partners—by one of the most skillful and visionary one-man lobbying campaigns seen even in multilobbying
America. It is worth summarizing not only for the millions of
people who more pedestrianly try to get billions out of governments today—but also because it shows the things that Johnny in
1945 wanted computers to do, many of which have still (in 1992)
not been done.

His first contact in the navy was wartime Commodore (later
Admiral) Lewis L. Strauss, who as a Wall Street banker had
brought Szilard to America in 1938 to study cancer and who was
to play an important part in Johnny's last dozen years—mainly
because Johnny knew how to make use of the efficient and rational
public-figure side of Strauss's personality, and also how to placate
the small-minded and vindictive personal-relationships side of it.

◄►◄►

All existing methods of approximation in mathematics, Johnny
wrote to Strauss in late 1945, had been conditioned by the speeds
of calculation that were possible. Now those speeds were going
to become at least ten thousand times quicker. In ascending order
of importance, this multiplier meant (1) that a single researcher
could do calculations in a morning that would have taken him a
working lifetime heretofore, (2) that research teams could do one
hundred times more research projects one hundred times faster,
and (3) that unimagined new fields of research would open.

In order to tackle certain nonlinear partial differential equations,
a mathematician might have to do a million more calculations than
when he tackled a problem ruled by linear equations. Few scientists
wanted to do a million sums, and then find out by age ninety they
had spent their lives on something that then might not exist. It
was therefore no coincidence that simple linear equations had ruled
in the subjects where scientists had recently been assiduous and
successful: in quantum mechanics, in radar, in television, in almost
all the fields where great technological progress had been made
just before or during the war. By contrast, in all problems that
had to be tackled by nonlinear equations, said Johnny in another

document in late 1945, the "advance of analysis has long been stagnant along the entire front."

Those damnably complicated nonlinear equations apply when a change in anything instantly leads to a change in all things around it. In his study of shock waves (especially in water) during the war, Johnny had found particular difficulty because with each stage of each shock "the character of the equations changes simultaneously in all respects." Nonlinear problems include most calculations about movements of air and water, some involved with friction (which varies as the speed of anything increases), various problems connected with elasticity and plasticity, and most organizational problems (a lot of economics and business planning is nonsense because once you have deployed resources to meet some particular problem, the very deployment of those resources means that the market situation and therefore the problem itself changes). Johnny believed that nonlinear problems would prove to lie ahead in meteorology (which he early regarded as an obvious first subject to tackle), biology, chemistry, and the probing of the human brain—as well as lots of other things nobody had dared to talk about yet. Johnny confessed that even his own imagination could not conceive what could come within reach.

To the narrower constituency of his fellow scientists, he tended to be more explicit and to sound more academically upmarket. His new computing machine was

likely to extend quantum theory to systems of more particles and more degrees of freedom than heretofore. . . . It may render [possible] a computational approach to the decisive phases of incompressible viscous hydrodynamics . . . , to the phenomena of turbulence and to the more complicated forms of boundary layer theory. It is likely to make the theories of elasticity and plasticity much more accessible than they have been up to now. It will probably help a great deal in three-dimensional electrodynamical problems. It will certainly remove many very critical bottlenecks in the computing approach to ordinary and electron optics. It may be useful in stellar astronomy. It will certainly open up a new approach to mathematical statistics: the approach by computed statistical experiments. . . .

These were partly far-flung pleas to special interests. But in talking to the narrowest constituency of his fellow mathematicians, he also stressed how completely their own jobs should be changed.

Our present mathematical methods, he said, were developed for slow and purely human procedures of calculation. The electronic computer would alter the possibilities, difficulties, emphases, boundaries. It would transform the whole internal economy of computing so radically, and shift all procedural options and equilibria so completely, that the old mathematical methods would have to give way to fresh ones, based on "entirely new criteria of what is mathematically simple or complicated, elegant or clumsy."

This warning to fellow mathematicians was the least tactful part of Johnny's crusade. He was telling very eminent fifty- or seventy-five-year-old dogs that they would have to learn new tricks. He was almost saying that the decades of great thought they had given to some orthodox mathematical conceptions were now to be rendered out of date by this collection of vacuum tubes in the Princeton institute's basement. As we shall see later, he did stir resentment among some mathematicians at Princeton, although he washed some of it away by his brilliance, bonhomie, and cocktail parties (in that order).

By contrast, Johnny's approach to generals and admirals in 1945–46 was setting their enthusiasm alight. To both he was giving examples of nonlinear problems that could transform the armed services. To the army he could say that nonlinear problems would need to be solved in aerodynamics for both faster jet aircraft and future rocket missile flights. When the design of new aircraft could be tested by computer simulation, only a few especially promising ones, selected on the basis of those computer simulations, would need to be carried into the hardware stage. Without these simulations, air force generals would be allowed by the budgetary authorities only the same few shots at devising new aircraft. They would use up available funds in launching new aircraft and other weapons that computers could show to be nonsenses. Such nonsenses would bring a great loss in America's military effectiveness and to the relevant generals' face.

Because the nonlinear calculations for the nuclear bombs on Hiroshima and Nagasaki had been devised rather crudely, nobody had known within many kilotons how powerful they would be. The smaller effect of the bomb at Nagasaki had shown that scientists had not yet worked out the right shapes and conditions for explosive charges, having regard to the differing elasticity and plasticity of the structures in the way. Radiation from nuclear explosions was a fearful and emotional new weapon of war. Without computer simulations, nobody (including the pacifist scientists now sounding off) really knew much about it. If America was to advance from a Hiroshima bomb to a superbomb (presumably a hydrogen one), a lot of nonlinear equations would have to be worked out.

Johnny's pitch to the navy could use all these arguments, and some more. Calculations of explosive power in water were even more in need of computing than explosions in air because of "the gas bubble that forms in an underwater explosion, and the inhomogeneities and boundary conditions that are necessarily introduced by the existence of the surface and of the bottom of the water mass." Computers could make oceanography and the study of terrestrial magnetism into proper sciences. Johnny said that "the liquid core of the earth is in a very complicated state of motion, where mechanical and electromagnetic forces both play about equally important roles." He thought that the navy should know when tidal waves are coming. He pointed out the advantages of computers to operational planning. If you are organizing a naval operation against an enemy, you need to allow for different possible responses by the enemy, for uncertainties like the weather on D day, for logistical problems if some shipments do not arrive at the right time.

With computers one can go through the calculations perhaps

one hundred times, each time assuming the accidental factors differently. If you get the computer to distribute them appropriately, then in one hundred trials you could obtain the correct statistical pattern. This sort of planning, said Johnny, has been done on a moderate scale in certain naval operations before, by rehearsals and the like. But rehearsal is a very difficult art. It has not been done more often and on a larger scale mainly because each single trial takes so much time and is so expensive in terms of equipment and patience, although the penalty for being clumsy is so high.

Johnny told the admirals that their problems in this had a wider application. In private conversations with admirals he tut-tutted about how much slower than the U.S. Navy American businessmen had been in waking up to it: "Nobody in planning a research programme, or an investigation, likes to commit himself to a particular plan which may not work, if this involves tying up the whole organisation for half a year. If, on the other hand, one can do these things rapidly, one will be bolder and find out more quickly how to do it." Similarly, Johnny argued to the admirals that computers could revolutionize meteorology and even bring in possibilities of weather control. It would be undesirable if Stalin got first to the possibility of inducing climatic change as a threatened weapon of war—maybe threatened to impose a new ice age over North America.

These arguments proved convincing to the admirals and generals. Available funds were never a factor that impeded Johnny's computer project at the IAS. The sponsors' different contributions kept altering in a heartening way, with equal numbers of generals and admirals and others seeking to clamber aboard collaboratively, instead of trying to cut each other's throat. This is what Johnny had intended from the start to achieve, by operating as a cunning old fox.

In his early memos to Aydelotte Johnny had expressed his concern that no sponsor must be able to claim title to the machine or priority for its use. Above all, nobody should be allowed to impose secrecy on whatever Johnny discovered to be the next best course for computer development around the world.

Johnny shrewdly said early that the IAS must not agree to one form of contract for the navy and another for the army. This was not because of abstract ideas of fairness, but because the federal budget authorities would then say, Let's choose one of these. Congress would pick the one that read as if it contained the more bureaucratic controls on behalf of the taxpayer, and therefore the worse one for the project. Johnny did run into some early difficulty with the navy in this regard. There was a tendency to say, Because the navy is putting up one third of the money for this part of the project, the navy must be allowed to use it one third of the time. One unfortunate navy captain assured Johnny that the navy appreciated "these things in a scientific spirit, and would even employ a Ph.D. in mathematics to deal with such matters." "It is difficult to continue the discussion, frankly," sneaked Johnny in a letter to Admiral Strauss, "once it has shifted to such a terrain."

He worked as craftily on the army. In an earlier memo to Aydelotte—admittedly while pushing the case that the IAS should be pioneering a computer for scientific research—Johnny had said that the government would certainly soon be commissioning electronic computers for specific federal laboratories, but he guessed they might then assign them to ridiculously specific tasks. Commercial concerns such as IBM would also enter the field but "would be influenced by their own past procedures and ventures, and would therefore not be able to make as fresh a start as is desirable." Johnny seems to have persuaded the army that it would get more specialist computers from the federal authorities in future if his early researches could be published to the world. His contract W-36-034-ORD-7481 with the army ordnance department imposed on him, at his own request, an obligation to issue reports on what he was finding out. The first of these reports, in June 1946, was sent to about 175 institutions or people in several different countries. It was later accompanied by a legal deposition that the authors desired that any material that might be of patentable nature be placed in the public domain.

These IAS papers from 1946–51 helped breed high-speed computers in almost every civilized country. They were the real achievement of the IAS Computer Project.

◄►◄►

Several institutions—with Johnny's approval—started to make Chinese copies of the proposed IAS computer while it was still being built, sometimes working faster than the small team at the IAS could. Each resident genius in each project around the world introduced his own modifications as his project went along. This proved a triumphant way of starting a new technology. It is a pity it has not been adopted more often for other technologies since. Once again the widest modern equivalent is probably the way the Japanese handle new technologies: with fierce competition between Japanese companies—but often only after they and perhaps MITI have established a broad common consensus about the best way some mysterious new things (like selling to America or producing consumer electronics) can be done. The difference in the computer revolution just after 1945 is that the consensus was created largely through blueprints and lectures emerging from one coruscant brain, working part-time out of a small American academic institution. In the early days Johnny had two important assistants, Goldstine and Arthur W. Burks.

In volume five of Johnny's collected works, the original IAS papers are listed as being by these three men. Goldstine's account is that Johnny would suggest the subject matter of a paper in conversation or briefing by blackboard. Then Goldstine, at one stage with Burks, would put it into writing. Then Johnny would suggest some amendments, and Goldstine would change the draft to include these. At this stage Johnny might quite extensively rewrite the paper, into a form that Goldstine would then leave alone: except for corrections in spelling (always necessary with Johnny), grammar, and sometimes requests for elucidation (for the sake of the already-expert people who would be reading the paper, because Johnny's were excursions into a very new land).

There were originally meant to be two early IAS papers, but the second appeared in three separate parts. After each paper was published, Johnny was apt to give lectures or informal talks that jumped several blocks ahead of them. For this reason, it is not possible to set up a snapshot of what at any instant he was trying to do. This was a period of extraordinarily rapid thinking about computers by the fastest mind in the West. The purpose of the simplest parts of the published papers—and they were not very simple—was to advise scientists, engineers, mathematicians, and logicians across the world how to marry together the ideas spilling daily from Johnny about the best new forms and combinations for the main organs of a computer: its memory, its arithmetic organ (later called central processing unit), its control, and its input-output.

The memory was to be the most innovative of these. Johnny was intent on producing the first all-purpose fully automatic computing machine controlled from its inside by a stored memory. Most previous machines of any kind had been controlled by people doing things (such as pushing buttons or moving switches) from the outside. In computers like the ENIAC the user had first to set switches and plugs before attempting any task; after this lengthy setup, the ENIAC would do any calculation at electronic speed. In other computers like the Harvard-IBM the user could feed in new instructions on a paper tape, so setup was quicker. But the calculation would then take up to a thousand times as long as the electronic ENIAC did. Goldstine and Johnny, says William Aspray, "suggested a design that incorporated the best features of each approach, based on storing instructions as numbers in the computer's internal electronic memory."

The ideal memory would be one with unlimited capacity and unrestricted random access. This would never be achieved, but Johnny stressed that each improvement should strive to be an advance toward that goal. The arrival of electronics meant that calculation was going to be unimaginably cheaper than ever before, so the cost of storage in memory had become relatively more expensive. The Princeton decision was to meet that by having a hierachy of memories. The primary memory would be fairly small, with rapid random access. Behind it would be a secondary memory. It should be able to transfer information into the primary memory automatically as needed. The computer should be able to move back and forth through the secondary memory. Individuals should be able to enter information directly into the secondary memory. The hierarchy of memories should stretch back to a dead memory. An individual would have to take action to transfer information from this into the primary memory if it was required.

Eckert's mercury delay line would not allow really random access and would not be fast enough for this architecture, so cathode ray tubes had to come into play. Initially, even these tubes did not work in creating hierarchical memories. Hierarchies became possible only when a magnetic drum was inserted to replace magnetic tape. The ENIAC had taken seventy times as long to print a calculation as to make one. The IAS team therefore minimized printing. Their aim was to make printing available on final demand but to keep the screen readable for calculations before printing took place. Most such improvements sound obvious now, as do others proposed in the IAS papers on input-output, the control unit, and the central processing unit.

One determination was that, if complicated things were happening inside the computer, then the computer must translate them into a simpler message before the user had to read it. Another was that, in future copies of this suggested prototype, different project directors should feel free to be more complicated or more simple as required. The second set of three IAS papers dealt with computer programming. They taught that programming would not be mechanical translations of mathematical problems, but must become a "technique of providing a dynamic background to control the evolution of a meaning" and thus be "a new branch of formal logic."

These papers from this tiny team developed a clear logical design for computers. They established the "von Neumann architecture" that—despite many marvellous changes in technology and components and potentialities since—provides the logical basis of most computers built even today. The same rapt admiration has not surrounded the engineering achievements of the IAS Computer Project. Bugs got into those.

◄►◄►

Johnny at one stage thought that the IAS computer could be built by ten people working for three years. Earlier he had hoped to dash through to a prototype before that. He minuted that there should then be two years when the machine "should not be assigned solely to immediate practical tasks." It should remain available for the testing of new computing methods, for scientific experimenting, and "for such further modifications" as by then seemed desirable.

Because of the machine's high speed, Johnny thought that much more elaborate computing methods would have to be discovered. He had hoped to be busying himself on these with his new toy by probably 1949. Proper use of computers may have been delayed because he never really got much chance. Between its fifth and sixth years of development, in 1951–52, the IAS computer was still only operating with what might be called hair curlers on. The IAS computer was hurried into its final stage in 1952 because some users—particularly Johnny with calculations needed for the H-bomb—did not want further dillydallying.

We had better turn to the reasons for relative slowness, while emphasizing that the success of the IAS computer lay in the fact that it bred so many children—some of which were in or near to full operation before it itself was.

A small reason for relative slowness at Princeton lay in problems with personnel. Johnny had wanted to get Eckert as chief engineer because he regarded him as brilliant but not to get Mauchly because he thought he was disruptive. Johnny and Goldstine recognized there would be some temperament clashes with Eckert (who in later litigation said of an opponent "he lies like a rug"), but both thought that with Eckert the Princeton project would be more efficient and rather fun. The offer to Eckert was eventually withdrawn because Eckert wanted to run a patent-protected commercial operation.

Johnny then appointed Julian Bigelow as chief engineer after an interview that caught some of the mood of the project. It is recounted in Ed Regis's book, and Bigelow confirmed it to me. Bigelow came down from Massachusetts in an ancient jalopy that arrived at 26 Westcott Road two hours late. There was a Great Dane dog prancing on the lawn, and it squeezed in past Johnny and Bigelow when Johnny opened the door. During the forty-minute interview the dog licked both men and wandered all over the house. Bigelow thought that Johnny should restrain his dog better but did not like to say this. When Johnny eventually saw his visitor to the door, he inquired politely whether Bigelow always traveled with the dog. "But it wasn't my dog," said Bigelow later, "and it now turned out it wasn't his either." Johnny, being a diplomatic type, refrained from making any remarks about this odd interviewee's behavior until the end. This jolly spirit among the team helped the project along, although it did not help with the staider watching scholars at the IAS.

There were later some clashes in approaches between Bigelow and Goldstine plus Johnny. Bigelow was more of a perfectionist, more of a Babbage who was willing to delay a workable scheme if a better one turned up, more apt to be "on the Julian calendar" (Johnny's phrase). When the computer project had lagged into 1951, and Los Alamos wanted calculations for its H-bomb, please, it was agreed that Bigelow should go on a Guggenheim Research Fellowship. He was succeeded by James Pomerene as chief engineer. Pomerene had come to the project in 1946 from the Hazeltine Company of New York, and his more commercial practice probably did drive the computer to faster completion in 1951–52. Bigelow says Johnny told the engineers at blackboard briefings what he wanted the machine to do and then let them get on with constructing it. But Goldstine was sending nonprogress complaints on the engineering problems even when Johnny was in Los Alamos, and a certain tension was building up.

A second and larger reason for delay was that the contracting out of some components to big business corporations failed. The corporations were asked to work at the leading edge of technology—sometimes without being entirely sure what they were seeking to do, at a time when the postwar boom made most firms concentrate on their own products rather than on odd orders from academe. A kindly comment from Princeton was that these private-sector contracts "saved us from researching into things that eventually would not work."

A third alleged reason for slowness was that the computer project was unpopular among the rest of the IAS. As we shall see, some of the attitudes among Johnny's fellow mathematicians were crabby. But the top IAS authorities never were. The computer project was housed first in what is today the institute's boiler room. It then moved to a small outbuilding that today looks like an equipment dump. When it moved, there were complaints from residents that it would be a horribly noisy industrial venture. Bigelow explained that when the door was closed, you could not actually hear whether the computer was on, and that the electricity used would be less than that of two domestic stoves. One of those who hurried the Los Alamos computer into operation faster than the IAS computer told me "it was probably easier at Los Alamos than in Princeton to find somebody who could mend a fuse." But Pomerene told Aspray that, by the end, the IAS laboratory was as good as any engaged on computers except IBM's. The lack of bureaucracy at the IAS allowed Johnny and Goldstine to run the project with efficient lack of formality, and the many world scholars coming to look at it found Princeton an enormously attractive place.

The main reason for relative slowness was that the tiny engineering team in that small outbuilding had to do a vaster job than Johnny at first realized. New technology was zigzagging forward in those postwar years of erratic supplies. Today's bright suggestion was liable to be tomorrow's joke. At the start in 1946 some people had considered that the computer's memory might best be embossed on wax, like an old gramophone or Dictaphone record, The technology of magnetic tape recorders had been greatly improved in Nazi wartime Europe. The team worked smartly in absorbing this news about magnetic tapes, then in redesigning magnetic heads and eventually magnetic drums. But it heard rather late about some European improvements.

The original notion for the input-output mechanism derived from Teletype. By 1947 it was found that the Teletype would take two hours to load the then-planned memory, but typing through a modern keyboard to a magnetic wire would take only thirty seconds. Johnny had expected Selectrons to flow instantly from RCA. In early 1948, after two years' striving, no Selectron tube was yet working. The small engineering team at the IAS darted through outsiders' original mistakes to considerable internal achievements, and passed on knowledge of both the mistakes and achievements to the score of IAS clones that by 1950 were sprouting around the world.

The first seven American sons of the IAS computer reached full operation in the same year (1952) as the IAS, or in the eighteen months afterward. Some got there earlier, although how many depends on your definition of what full operation meant. Those that approached or passed the IAS computer before the finishing tape usually had bigger engineering facilities for the final push. All paid tribute to the IAS papers as the blueprints that helped them start. These first American seven were the MANIAC (masterminded by Nick Metropolis and Jim Richardson at Los Alamos), the Rand Corporation's jovially named JOHNNIAC, the Argonne National Laboratory's AVIDAC (an acronym stemming from "Argonne Version of the IAS Digital Automatic Computer"), Aberdeen Proving Ground's ORDVAC, Oak Ridge National Laboratory's ORACLE, the University of Illinois's ILLIAC, and (most important) the IBM 701. The 701 led IBM into its dominance of the world market. IBM signaled its gratitude to Johnny ever after, but some features of its 701 in its birth year of 1952 were already superior to the IAS computer that started operations at much the same time.

The sons of IAS in foreign countries stayed too stuck in universities and did not move so swiftly into commercial improvement. But by the early 1950s IAS clones were starting around the world—stretching from the University of Sydney's SILLIAC, through Israel's WEIZAC, and Munich's PERM, to Sweden's BESK and even the BESM in the Academy of Sciences in Moscow.

The papers from the IAS in 1945–49 launched the part of the computer revolution that worked. It is less clear whether Johnny succeeded in his efforts to puzzle out how computers should be used.

◀▶ ◀▶

Johnny wanted his new computer to hit the ground running into the first of the great scientific achievements that he thought these machines could bring in. He decided that the first such epoch-changing project should be to try to invent meteorology as a science, instead of leaving it as an art.

As early as May–July 1946 Johnny negotiated a meteorological contract with the U.S. Navy. Enthusiasts say his prospectus then was the beginning of modern meteorology. Detractors say it was originally a suggestion that five graduate students should sit in Princeton for two years and try to work out why the Englishman Lewis Fry Richardson had got his models so wrong about International Balloon Day 1910. The Princeton team were meant to be ready to test their own new models on Johnny's IAS computer, if the computer reached its target date of operation in 1948–49 (which it did not).

Meteorology in 1942–45 was a subject about which theoretical physicists had terrifyingly optimistic dreams, while practical meteorologists (as in the chaos school now?) were too pessimistic. At Los Alamos Ulam and others had mused on the possibility of attacking hurricanes with A-bombs. The violent energy of hurricanes lies on top of a mass of air (the weather) that itself moves only gently and slowly. Perhaps one could place nuclear explosions in hurricanes' paths, so as to push them to somewhere less expensive than Florida? It is fun to contemplate what today's environmentalists would say about that. Even 1946's underdeveloped environmentalists did not like it much. RCA's Zworykin also wanted to change the world's bad weather. He said in an interview to the *New York Times* in January 1946 that Johnny's new electronic computers might lead toward that. Although Johnny had tried to stop this interview, Eckert at Philadelphia was furious about it; he interpreted it as Johnny's opening bid to grab public relations credit away from Eckert-Mauchly machines. Mauchly was crosser still; he had ideas about using computers to predict the weather from sunspot cycles, a project that set Johnny snorting.

Johnny had his feet nearer to mainstream meteorologists' ground. In 1942, when engaged in his research about undersea mines, he had consulted with America's most famed meteorologist, the University of Chicago's Carl-Gustav Rossby (most American meteorologists at the time seemed to have come from Scandinavia or Belorussia). Johnny was mildly shocked that meteorology still seemed to be a matter of individuals' guesswork rather than orderly physics. Meteorologists assembled data to draw isobar and isotherm maps of frontal systems, but equally competent meteorologists could then disagree completely about what might happen to those patches of bad or good weather next.

At Normandy D day in 1944 the equally competent Allied and German meteorologists did disagree. German professors on June 5 told Rommel that the weather was fortunately set to be so foul that he could forget about Allied invasion for a while. This helped to give the Allies tactical surprise. As the storms soon beat in on the supply beaches, there were fears the German professors might be right. The jettisoning of the Nagasaki bomb through a cloud gap also made Johnny worried about bad meteorological forecasts. He asked Rossby some such question as, If we know all about the weather at one particular moment in some particular place, surely we can work out the continuing physical process by which that translates into the same or a different sort of weather at a different place later?

Rossby gave the usual meteorological answer, about poor Richardson's fiasco. The British mathematician and World War I pacifist Richardson had published a book called *Weather Prediction by Numerical Process* in 1922. Richardson had gathered in—after the event—the extensive weather data compiled at the beginning of International Balloon Day in May 1910. He had then applied conventional contemporary physics and hydrodynamics to suggest what should logically happen to those data in the next six hours. He then checked this by the data that balloonists had gathered in at the end of their day. Partly because his algorithms were unstable, the two sets of figures showed no correlation whatever. A discouraged Richardson had said that you could calculate the world's weather only if you had about sixty-four thousand people doing the required sums while the weather was happening.

Johnny by 1945 was about to create a machine with the calculating power of one hundred thousand people. He himself had become one of the leading mathematical experts in the numerical calculation of hydrodynamic shocks, and he knew how much other physics had advanced since Richardson's day. Meteorology seemed to him to present problems that were nonlinear, multidimensional, time dependent, with arbitrary initial and boundary conditions. These were exactly the sorts of problems his computers were designed to solve. When they had solved them, perhaps he could make Iceland a tropical Hawaii.

In a letter to his naval contact Strauss in May 1946, as part of his plug for navy support, Johnny guessed that high-speed computing "would open up entirely new possibilities for studies of the stratospheric circulation and of atmospheric turbulence, and . . . would make weather prediction a week or more ahead practical. If such a program were carried out successfully, it would also be the first step toward weather control—but I would prefer not to go into that at this time."

A month after getting the navy's money in 1946, Johnny held a conference of leading meteorologists to ask for advice, which he hoped would be encouraging and uplifting. It was almost universally damping and depressing. Rossby said that the mathematical problem for meteorology was not yet defined; there were more unknowns than equations; computation could not succeed until there had been a lot more observation, experiment, and analysis.

The team of meteorologists at the IAS did not take real shape until Jule Charney (1917–81) arrived in 1948. Charney, whose parents had immigrated to America from Belorussia shortly before World War I, had different political views from Johnny; he was active in antiwar movements. But his praise for Johnny was unstinting: "Von Neumann was an eminently approachable god. . . . [He] thought so fast that he very often anticipated what one was going to say. . . . a pleasant agreeable person . . . the amazing logic of his thought processes." Charney's postgraduate work had led him into inquiring where Richardson's equations in 1910 had gone outlandish. Among other things, Richardson had not made sufficient allowance for the fact that the earth was revolving around the sun. Charney saw that the approach to a consistent set of prediction equations for meteorology would need to move through "a hierarchy of atmospheric models of increasing complexity." His aim was to try the simplest equations first by using them to predict the past: see how you would have predicted the weather on January 30 two years ago, and then check against what it was. If the simplest equations did not work, start introducing complications into them.

The main differences were between a nice simple "barotropic" model and a nasty complicated "baroclinic" one. A barotropic model would include only the generally two-dimensional figures you could gather on terra firma. It would assume that kinetic energy was being conserved within today's weather system. Conceivably, most forecasts for the day ahead could legitimately assume this. But it would be impossible to get away with such a simple model on days which saw the formation, intensification, or damping down of big storms. Then the mathematicians would have to study baroclinic conversions of potential energy far up into the sky.

Charney had simple barotropic equations nearly ready when he came to the IAS, and hoped these could be tested on the IAS computer if it was ready as promised in 1948–49. It was not. So the ENIAC—now running in Aberdeen with Johnny's addition of a stored memory—was hired for thirty-three days from March 6, 1950. Johnny both arranged for this and swiftly did some of the complicated math needed to enable ENIAC to understand some of the partial differential equations (PDEs) involved. The original intention had been to use the equations to forecast what should have happened to the weather on four widely separate days in January and February 1949—and then see whether it really had.

ENIAC limped through only two and a half of these four days' forecasts. One of the completed forecasts (for January 31, 1949) was excellent, but the other clearly was not. It took ENIAC thirty-six hours to do a twenty-four-hour forecast. Scoffers said this meant chirping at Wednesday noon "we can now tell you the computer was right in guessing what Tuesday's weather was." Still, as these thirty-six hours of sums would have taken eight years on a desk calculator (which Richardson in 1922 did not have), the experts could now see why poor Richardson had been in the wrong ballpark. Because Charney knew the IAS computer, when ready, would be far faster than the ENIAC, the thirty-six hours did not worry him. But the failure of one of the two full forecasts meant the barotropic model still looked worse than many conventional weather forecasts, so the team would have to insert much more baroclinicity into the models for next time. They did so, with Charney now being aided by his able new associate Norman Phillips, and with Johnny joining in with some of the heavy math as well.

It was an advantage that an appalling and unpredicted storm swept over the eastern United States on November 25, 1950, and ruined the Thanksgiving weekend. The team now had a classical baroclinic problem to examine. They did so in tests that put 296,000 calculations on the IAS computer in the summer of 1952. They were remarkably successful.

The printouts showed that the twenty-four-hour forecasts could be done in ten minutes, instead of the ENIAC's thirty-six hours, especially after improvements in the new IBM 701 computer were added to the pioneer path the IAS computer had blazed. By August 1952 Charney could report that "the barotropic forecasts are perhaps not as good as the best conventional forecasts, but the indications are that baroclinic forecasts will be much better." The

U.S. Weather Bureau and the armed forces clubbed together to buy an IBM 701 computer. Numerical weather forecasting began on May 15, 1955. It has continued ever since. It has been imitated in all advanced countries around the world, with erratically improved models and steadily faster computers.

The computer project did not move forward to longer-term weather forecasting as Johnny had hoped. Phillips produced a remarkable paper, "The General Circulation of the Atmosphere: A Numerical Experiment," in the summer of 1955. Johnny called a conference on it in October 1955 and as a result helped secure funding for what is now Princeton's Geophysical Fluid Dynamics Laboratory. In his last words on the subject at this conference Johnny said he thought short-term weather forecasting on computers was now set as a permanent feature; the computer could be fed the variants on today's weather map, and could make better forecasts than human experts usually could for twenty-four hours or perhaps forty-eight hours ahead. He thought that studies (like Phillips's) of the general circulation of the atmosphere should be extended to become "infinite forecasts." These would show what weather patterns would usually obtain, unless there were special disturbances, which there always would be unless man could somehow get them under control.

But Johnny also said that intermediate forecasts, say beyond the short term and up to three months, would be much more difficult. Tiresomely, any such intermediate forecasts "would have to be performed for the entire earth, or at least for an entire hemisphere. . . . The spread of meteorological effects is such that, already after 2 to 3 weeks, every part of the terrestrial atmosphere will have interacted with every other—except for the relative weakness of the interaction between the northern and southern hemispheres." The chaos school has extended this point by saying that the movement of a butterfly's wings over Beijing today can cause a storm over the eastern United States next month—and we really cannot impose a police watch on every butterfly.

The key fact about this meeting in October 1955 is that Johnny—although not his audience—had known for two months that he probably had terminal cancer. This was part of his last desperate rush (see chap. 15) to tidy up his legacy to the world. In meteorology he wanted to set long-term modeling in place. By then he recognized that intermediate forecasting (still more control of the weather) would be very difficult. But he did not think it would be as impossible as the chaos school now says. History will tell whether the checked advance of meteorology since October 1955—as compared with its sprint in the five years before that—springs from the fact that Johnny has not been with us.

◄►◄►

The arrival of the computer meant that arithmetic was suddenly cheap, and would therefore be more used. But arithmetic had long not been in fashion, especially numerical analysis. Johnny set about reviving it and giving it new shapes.

Computers were now going to speed through long calculations, without humans butting in. This meant a change in errors to be feared: fewer errors through doing insufficient calculations but more because of accumulation of errors that nobody had noticed at the start. It meant new sorts of problems: calculating how many equations would be needed with how many unknowns spread over how many happenstances. It meant new research into the qualities of randomness in numbers, and fresh probability theories. Johnny was interested in all these. As mainframe computers proliferated, there were people working on these problems at each of them. Many had been briefed by Johnny.

The computer opened a wider road for linear programming. America's pioneer in this, George Dantzig, visited Johnny for what he started as a too-leisurely chat. Annoyingly, Johnny told him to "get to the point." A slightly piqued Dantzig tried to faze Johnny by slapping the geometric and algebraic version of what he was saying on to the blackboard, in a way that he thought might be too terse for any newcomer to the subject to understand. Johnny said, "Oh, that"—and gave a ninety-minute lecture that taught Dantzig many things.

Apart from the Los Alamos and meteorology calculations, the

range of problems put on the IAS computer in its brief life was rather disappointing. Other computers were moving past it fast. The IAS computer proved to need too many hours of calculation to tackle problems such as shock waves, so Johnny turned his deepest thoughts to another opportunity in the computer age. This was what some call his greatest piece of unfinished business and others consider his spookiest dart off the rails.

He occupied some of the scarce spare hours in the last decade of his life with his musings on "cellular automata." By the time of his Vanuxem lectures in 1953 (a sponsored set of lectures in Princeton), he envisioned that by some date (not necessarily these 1990s) we might be making automata composed of mechanical cells. Each cell would act on the others near it and (by the 1953 state of his musings) would be able to go into one of twenty-nine states: an unexcited state, twenty quiescent but excitable states, and eight excited states.

A pulsar (or construction arm) would pass over these cells and help get them into the state that the automaton wanted. With these twenty-nine states for the cells, it would theoretically be possible to do anything logical or constructive or operative that was required, although Johnny said that it would be desirable to go further—into what he called excitation-threshold fatigue models. He mused that man can define (and so might eventually reach) a class of automata able to do everything logical that can be performed with finite means. These automata would be able to construct other automata, certainly including automata like themselves.

By the 1990s we have not really reached anything very like this. It is not true that Johnny was just pointing to the sorts of things modern software can do, or that computers do within so many modern machines. It is clear that his descriptions included many engineering and other inaccuracies. Yet his 1953–56 musings were merely the stage his thoughts had reached by the time he died. He had gotten to these thoughts by a darting process of mental development, each new stage including modifications but also usually advances on what he had thought before.

Johnny was involved in the two sets of conferences that led up to Wiener's 1948 book *Cybernetics: Or Control and Communication in the Animal and the Machine*. The first of these sets in 1944–45 did not really work because every scholar attending was supposed to pour out his latest intelligence and thoughts, but most of those scholars' latest intelligence and thoughts were deep military secrets (e.g., Johnny had come straight from Los Alamos). Johnny joined in the 1946 postwar conferences but at that stage pessimistically regarded the complexity of the brain as too "overawing." "After the great positive contribution of Turing-cum-Pitts-and-McCulloch is assimilated," he wrote to Wiener, "the situation is rather worse than before. . . . These authors have demonstrated in absolute and hopeless generality that anything and everything Brouwerian can be done by an appropriate mechanism." For us to try to understand the brain, said Johnny, looked about as hopeful as somebody trying to understand the ENIAC "who had never heard of any part of arithmetic."

At this time Johnny was beginning to think about mechanisms based on cells. Instead of mapping humans' complicated brains, perhaps we should try x-ray analysis of colonies of bacteria. They could not have complex brains, yet they knew how to find and get food, how to reproduce themselves, how to orient themselves in an unorganized milieu.

In the next years Johnny had extensive contacts with experts in the biomedical sciences. He wanted to integrate more of biology's good points into computers, including pondering on instructions to computers that could model the functions of a gene—leading to self-reproduction and much more. He was talking before Crick and Watson had uncovered the working of the genetic code, but his thinking was in line with what was to occur.

Johnny had been invited to give the Silliman lectures at Yale in the spring term of 1956. By that date he lay in hospital, immobilized by his cancer. Two of the prepared lectures, partly written on his deathbed, were published as *The Computer and the Brain*. They included his discussion of the possibility of finding new sorts of mathematics (discussed way back in chap. 1).

Since Johnny's death, the world has moved into automation in ways that would have been regarded as extraordinary in 1956. His visions of cellular automata are still regarded by some people as rather too extraordinary. He had not had time to lay the infrastructure for them—in the way that he had lain the infrastructure for the worldwide revolutions in computing power and short-term numerical weather forecasts, during the years of the computers from Princeton.

◄►◄►

Those years were to die soon after him. The IAS's welcome to its most famous project had always been underwhelming. The School of Mathematics at the IAS held a meeting in late 1945 to discuss it. The minutes explained:

> The discussion considered the effect of such activities upon the progress of mathematics and upon the general atmosphere of the Institute. The personal views expressed ranged from that of Professor Siegel, who in principle prefers to compute a logarithm which might enter into his work rather than to look it up in a table, through that of Professor Morse who considers the project inevitable but far from optimum, to that of Professor Veblen who simple-mindedly welcomes the advances of science regardless of the direction in which they seem to be carrying us.

The minutes were signed by Veblen, who liked to put in his own digs.

It is wrong to exaggerate any tensions while Johnny was still in the beautiful place. He was ever more admired at the institute's seminars, especially in harness with the new director Oppenheimer. He and Oppenheimer were the two best men in the world at explaining what visiting speakers at seminars had actually said and at making it seem interesting and sometimes important. There were political disagreements, including with Oppenheimer, because Johnny was known as an anti-Soviet hawk, who (especially after Eisenhower's inauguration in January 1953, see later) eventually had more influence in Washington than any other professor. But the camaraderie of very clever men continued, and so did Johnny's cocktail parties.

At first the computer was being built in the boiler room of the main building at the institute. It had funds to put up a small one-story building a short walk away. When this was built, there came some rift between some of Johnny's team and some institute professors, by distance as well as by habits of mind.

The meteorologists were not a settled bunch until Charney came in 1948. There were the weirdest rows, including literally one in a teacup: an accusation that a junior meteorologist had taken too much sugar for the computer building's tea breaks. This had to go up to Aydelotte for arbitration. Charney was capable of a few rows himself. At first there was a feeling among the IAS staff that the meteorological project was not working. It was known that the engineering of the computer was behind schedule, but the papers written from the computer project were attracting world fame. Goldstine and Bigelow were made permanent professors at the institute, but the top meteorologists Charney and Phillips were not.

By October 1954, with Johnny moving away to Washington, the rumbles came out. Some of the letters sent then are in the John von Neumann papers at the Library of Congress. Freeman Dyson, who was actually more procomputer than most of the older men around him, sent out letters to some of the great and good of the scientific world, explaining the IAS's predicament:

The [IAS] School of Mathematics has a permanent establishment which is divided into three groups, one consisting of pure mathematics, one consisting of theoretical physicists, and one consisting of Professor von Neumann. Von Neumann originated in 1946 and has since directed our Computer Project. The Computer Project built and operates a fast digital computer, the cost of the machine and almost all of the staff being paid by government money and not by the Institute. Rather by accident it has turned out that the most active users of the machine have been meteorologists.

The letter added that "naturally, the meteorologists would prefer to be on the Institute establishment on the same footing as the physicists and mathematicians, in order to be free of any sort of obligation to produce results useful on a short term basis." The faculty was divided on whether to incorporate the meteorologists—or (although this was not said) to get rid of them, and, it was hoped, be shot of Johnny's computer project altogether.

The replies from science's great and good around the world showed that Johnny was now a prophet with great honor outside his own small community. From Britain's National Physical Laboratory, Sir Edward Bullard stressed "the crucial point: in Dr. von Neumann the Institute has perhaps the cleverest man in the world, and the really deciding factor in the end should, I am sure, be what he wants to do." From Chicago, Chandrasekhar said:

So long as von Neumann was actively associated with the Computer Project one needed to have no doubts as to the soundness or the worthwhileness of the problems which were studied with the computer. Even though at a given moment one thing instead of another may occupy the centre of his attention, von Neumann has the flexibility to re-align his interests as the need and the occasion arise. All these are so obvious that it is not necessary for me to labor them.

But with Johnny away other scientists were not slow to suggest that it would be better to bring their favorites to the institute rather than those meteorologists. Oceanography "is at the moment a somewhat more mature branch—i.e., somewhat more past the zoological stage—than meteorology." Another choice was for "a man working on the mechanics of the deformation of the Earth's crust."

The professors at the institute did not respond eagerly to these suggestions. After Johnny's death in 1957, they closed the Computer Project. They passed a general motion that they would henceforth have no experimental science—no laboratories of any kind at the IAS. Charney and Phillips departed to MIT, Goldstine later to IBM.

When Johnny was in hospital in 1956, with what proved to be his terminal cancer, he wrote to Oppenheimer and explained, although not yet for publication, that he was not in fact going to come back to the IAS. He had privately accepted an offer to be professor at large at the University of California: he would live near one of its campuses (it had not been quite decided which) and proceed with research on the computer and its possible future uses, with considerable commercial sponsorship. We cannot know how much he would then have enriched our lives, with cellular automata, with totally new lines for the computer, with new sorts of mathematics.

But between 1952 and 1956 Johnny was even more busily engaged in saving the planet.

▶◀▶◀▶◀ *14*

And Then

the H-Bomb

▶◀*B*y the time of Japan's surrender in August 1945, Johnny still felt nearly 100% pessimistic that there was likely to be a future war with communist Russia, unless America kept very tightly and therefore internationally and therefore improbably on guard. Some later libelers have portrayed him as a fire-eating advocate of a first nuclear strike on Moscow, but he actually again showed his equanimity like a cherub. He remained on good terms with those whose opinions (if they prevailed) would help lose what he saw as the coming battle to save America from being nuked or enslaved or both. He felt merely that some of the cleverest men in American science did not "understand the world in which they lived." These included Einstein.

Einstein was proclaiming in 1945 that "the secret of the bomb should be committed to a world government . . . [which] should be established by the United States, the Soviet Union and Great

Britain, the only three powers which possess great military strength." Einstein wanted this world government to intervene militarily to overthrow fascism in Spain and Argentina, which he somehow regarded as 1945's main immediate threats to peace. Einstein also wanted Germany to be turned into a largely agricultural country without industrial power: "If the Ruhr is left to the Germans the terrible sacrifices of the English-speaking world will have been in vain." "The Germans," gentle Albert had said near the end of the war, "can be killed or contained, but they cannot be re-educated to a democratic way of thinking and acting within a foreseeable period of time."

Einstein's views were not exceptional. They were widely shared in the scientific community, including by some men whom Johnny recognized as his closest intellectual peers and otherwise jocular friends. They were also touted by many entertainers and literati and newspapermen, with whom Johnny did not so much mix. As late as 1947 the Foreign Press Association in Washington, D.C. gave Einstein its annual award "in recognition of his valiant efforts to make the world's nations understand the need of outlawing atomic energy as a means of war."

There is no evidence that Johnny waxed cross in any of this period. He was rather pleased that America presented to Russia the Bernard Baruch proposals for international control of nuclear energy, which had been largely devised by the respected scientists Oppenheimer and I. I. Rabi. He was pleased because he knew that Stalin's Soviet Union would rudely reject them. Stalin was hellbent on acquiring the largest possible nuclear armory himself. When Russia did rudely reject the Baruch plan, and even termed Einstein's proposals for a world government "nothing but a flamboyant signboard for the world supremacy of the capitalist monopolies," Johnny noted that more of his fellow scientists were at last letting pro-Russian scales fall from their eyes.

Johnny took it for granted that Stalin was going to break every treaty commitment so as to fasten hated communist government on eastern Europe, including Johnny's native Hungary. To the question, Which is worse, Nazism or Bolshevism? Johnny was ready to grant that communism had a much higher standard of deluded admirer than Nazism had. But a real difference was that in the late 1930s Nazism had been more dangerous and stronger. In the mid-1940s Stalin's battered Russia was not as strong as some fearful Americans supposed, but Johnny believed that within five years Russia would have discovered how to make nuclear bombs.

When it did, new problems would arise in enforcing a pax Americana. Johnny hoped this would be enforced more thoughtfully and resolutely against communism than deterrence had been enforced against Nazism in the 1930s. Johnny's military activity and political opinions in 1946–49 were determined by these considerations.

◀▶ ◀▶

His military activity consisted partly of spending about two months a year at Los Alamos. He was there in the autumn of 1945, throwing himself into analysis of the paths that had been taken by the atomic explosions at Hiroshima and Nagasaki. He concluded from these "Hippo" calculations that nuclear bombs could be made horribly more efficient rather easily. This meant that nuclear fission and later fusion would provide the overwhelming weapons for keeping the peace. He also thought that fission and then fusion would eventually bring the cost of electricity and thus energy down to virtually nil—or, rather, to being very nearly as free as water.

He recognized that radiation and accidents in the era of nuclear fission would cause deaths, but thought that (provided there was no war) they would be fewer than those caused by the automobile revolution—and he was glad that the world had automobiles, even with drivers as dangerous as himself. He had respect for other scientists' views that the free world would have to move to something more like world government. Projects such as changing the world's climate, which he regarded as becoming feasible, could hardly be decided by single nations alone. But meanwhile there was the problem whether the free world was going to exist much longer.

◄►◄►

The Hippo calculations confirmed his belief that nuclear weapons would not remain an American monopoly for long. A dozen or so Is-it-possible? questions had been answered at Los Alamos. Now it was known the answers were yes, it seemed to him easy to make a nuclear bomb. Johnny knew that the Soviet Union had a vast spy network in the United States. It could hardly have failed to notice that Los Alamos existed, so it had probably been aided by espionage. Anyway, Johnny did not regard secrecy as the main point.

Up to 1941 the Soviet Union had some tens of respectable scientists working on atomic energy, including Igor Kurchatov and Peter Kapitza. After the German invasion in 1941, these scientists were taken off nuclear research for more urgent war work. From mid-1945 a big new Soviet nuclear research effort had begun. Most of the German nuclear scientists in Russian-occupied East Germany had been taken into the Soviet Union, where they were being held in quite comfortable laboratory conditions, not in prison camps. So were captured German scientists who had worked on the V-2 rockets, which posed an awkward double threat. The Soviet Union's nuclear research efforts were under the direct control of Lavrenty Beria, the chief of the secret police. Johnny passed some wry jokes on how Beria might handle some of Los Alamos's prima donnas—more apposite jokes than he knew. Beria did indeed have a flaming row with Kapitza and temporarily locked him up. But Johnny guessed early that Russia was likely to get at least a crude A-bomb by about 1950.

Johnny's military objective was therefore to help America get a more powerful bomb—fast. The scope for this seemed large, even though most scientists were disappearing from Los Alamos. They were returning to teach at their home universities as the GIs came back from the foxholes, to what was a huge university boom. By late 1946 there were only eight theoretical physicists left at Los Alamos, augmented by visits for a month or so at a time by such wartime stalwarts as Johnny (who was rapidly becoming the most admired figure on the mesa) and Teller (who was not).

Teller was urging that there should be twelve nuclear tests a year, and high concentration on developing a hydrogen super-bomb (which we will discuss after this story passes 1949). It would have been practically and politically impossible for Los Alamos's small staff to carry out twelve tests a year. Teller was therefore thwarted in most of his proposals. He regarded 1946–49 as wasted years.

Johnny did not regard them as wasted, and at Los Alamos he was rather enjoying himself. The evidence emerging from Hippo, and from a test of the existing bomb at the South Seas island of Bikini in 1946, showed that the efficiency and reliability of A-bombs could be greatly increased. He attended this test at Bikini as an observer, and many think his eventually fatal cancer was contracted there. Hippo had revealed that the explosion at Hiro-shima had been the equivalent of 13,000 tons of TNT (or 13 kilotons). The implosion at Nagasaki had released 21 kilotons. The bomb at Nagasaki had done much less damage, but from Hippo Johnny learned where to place the bombs, what secondary factors to take into account. By the time of the Sandstone tests at Eniwetok Atoll in spring 1948, the biggest implosion bomb reached 49 kilotons. Before the superbomb took over, an ordinary fission bomb dropped from an aircraft probably reached about 500 kilotons in the King shot at Eniwetok in 1952—that is, potentially some forty times as murderous as the Hiroshima bomb.

Although the detailed work for these tests was done by the full-time staff at Los Alamos, Johnny's visits were welcomed as those of a chief problem solver. On arrival, he would listen to questions and then sit muttering at the ceiling, before handing out wisdom. He weighed in with some calculations from his early computers. He was also starting to think toward the day when nuclear bombs would have to be lighter so that they could be carried by rocket missiles—or be made into tactical weapons by being compressible into mines, artillery shells, and torpedoes.

As so often, Johnny found it easier to work with a small team in Los Alamos than in the huge team he had known there in the war. Herbert York has written that "those who chose to stay on in deserted Los Alamos in 1946 did so because some liked life on the bright mesa, some were intellectually interested in the problems suddenly due to be solved, and some were responding to the first chill winds of the cold war." Johnny was moved by all three. He liked New Mexico sufficiently for Klari and him to discuss seriously with Françoise and Stan Ulam whether they should build neighboring houses there for when their retirements came. He found post-Hippo problems to be intellectually fascinating, partly because he felt solutions were coming quickly within grasp. He was also reacting to chill winds of the cold war.

When the fighting ended in Europe, more of Johnny's relatives and acquaintances emerged from the Holocaust than he had dared hope. Klari's mother came chirping out of Budapest. The long-lived Alcsutis came to Manhattan, where Lily Pedroni (née Alcsuti), who helped greatly with this book, lived intermittently until her death in 1990. The massacre of rebaptized Jews did not reach as brutally into the upper middle classes in wartime Hungary as it did in the rest of Hitler's Europe. Admiral Horthy was a savior here; the hopeful gossip among frightened Jewish Budapesters was that Horthy's own wife's family had some Jewish blood. But, although Hitler's tyranny had been softened by Budapest conditions, Stalin's had not. All the refugees out of Hungary said that.

Johnny believed that American resistance to Soviet expansion should have started further east. It could thus have saved Poland, Hungary, Czechoslovakia, and the rest from suffering their slavery from 1945 to 1989. His critics said this was irresponsible talk that would risk war with the Soviet Union. His answer in 1945 was that "if we are going to have to risk war, it will be better to risk it while we have the A-bomb and they don't." This was one half of the reason why he acquired a reputation as an advocate of first strike and preemptive war.

The other half was that he undoubtedly did believe in the principle of deterrence. There were few comforts to be derived from the horrors of modern weapons, but one stood out. Johnny's aim was always that the Soviet leaders should be in no doubt what a nuclear war would bring to them. All those sitting around the

Soviet decision-making tables should know that in the first few minutes of a nuclear war, a bomb would arrive where they were and personally kill all of them. He saw the period of maximum danger as coinciding with Stalin's last few years and then immediately after. It was important that Stalin should not be succeeded by Beria.

◄►◄►

During the first three postwar years Johnny had no real influence in Washington. The Red Terror spread across eastern Europe, indeed after Mao's victory in 1948 across communist Eurasia. In 1948 Johnny became surprisingly enthusiastic for Truman, at a time when most right-wing Americans were not. The resistance to Stalin's blockade of Berlin, and then the Truman Doctrine guaranteeing Turkey and Greece, suggested to Johnny that the long tide of retreat had turned. When Truman unexpectedly beat Dewey in the November 1948 presidential election, Johnny wrote to Ulam: "I . . . am agreeably surprised by the election results. I don't think that the practical result is very overwhelming, but Dewey did represent an unknown quantity and a serious risk. It is a good thing that this is out." He was admittedly not a fan of the Republican candidate. He had snorted that one turgidly inconclusive scientific paper submitted to him "read like a speech by Governor Tom Dewey." His enthusiasm for Truman grew with the Marshall Plan and with the prompt response to North Korean aggression in 1950.

In this period around 1948–50, Johnny held half a dozen consultancy posts with the military and the same number of more lucrative consultancy contracts with private industry—in his spare time from developing the world's computer revolution and being an ordinary professor at the IAS. In March 1949 he was dictating a letter through his secretary, Louise, which arrived at the recipient saying, "I am delayed by a siege of work, which I hope will last only for a few days or so. At this point there was a considerable burst of hilarity from Louise. Can you interpret it?"

His main military consultancies in these years were with army ordnance at Aberdeen, with naval ordnance now at Silver Spring, with the Research and Development Board at Washington, with the Oak Ridge National Laboratory in Tennessee, as well as with Los Alamos. His main commercial contracts were with IBM, Standard Oil, and Rand. At Rand he displayed the talent that Strauss was later to note in his committees at Washington: "the invaluable faculty of being able to take the most difficult problem, separate it into its components, whereupon everything looked brilliantly simple, and all of us wondered why we had not been able to see through to the answer as clearly as he."

At Standard Oil, the research and development department could fortunately understand the reams of mathematical symbols he wrote on yellow paper for them. One such collection of symbols, apparently written on a train journey back from seeing them, led to a patent for an improved method of getting oil out of cavities in nearly dried-out wells. "Most of the residual oil will ordinarily be left near the dead corners of a pattern such as a 5-spot. By drilling wells in these corners . . ."

He was especially productive when traveling on or to trains. "I must have been feeble-minded when we were talking," runs one note apparently written on a train, "because of course . . ." There follow a dozen pages of mathematical equations, cut off when the train arrived at Lamy, the nearest railhead to Los Alamos. It was in a chauffeured government car from Los Alamos to Lamy that Ulam suggested the Monte Carlo method. Opinion pollsters were getting rather good forecasts of elections from polls of very small weighted or even random samples of voters. Would it not be possible mathematically to work out how to use similar small samples of the millions of figures becoming available to them on subjects such as the A-bomb—not in order to get exact answers but so as to say that the answer seems to be so and so, within a such-and-such margin of error, with such-and-such probability?

As so often, Johnny was initially skeptical of this suggestion from somebody else; then, after time for thought, he jumped several blocks ahead of him. After getting off his train back in Princeton, Johnny posted a dozen handwritten pages, saying, "I found the Monte Carlo procedure to treat a typical parabolic differential equation." Klari became a computer operator skilled in Monte Carlo procedures, but usually had to ask somebody else (not ungallant Johnny) for permission to sit in on meetings where they were used.

A conversation at a mathematics symposium centered on how one of czarist Russia's mathematicians had conceivably worked out a theorem from what seemed inadequate data, while without access to reference books on a six-day journey on the Trans-Siberian Railway. On his next train journey, Johnny covered fifty-three pages of yellow foolscap paper to get from the data to the equations. He sent them back with a note: "Train's running time to Chicago 5 hours 32 minutes." He once traveled ten hours across several time zones on a journey, and booked a seat back on a train that left from the same station twenty minutes after he got in. The travel agent naturally booked him back on the train twenty-four hours and twenty minutes after arrival. This annoyed Johnny, who had looked forward to twenty hours of uninterrupted work on the two trains.

When thus engrossed on one train journey, he asked the ticket collector to tell the sandwich seller (who had passed earlier) that in his seat in the first carriage, number whatever, he would like some sandwiches after all. "I will tell him if I see him," said the ticket collector huffily. "This train is linear, isn't it?" asked Johnny half politely.

He was once returning by train to Lamy with some Los Alamos companions, and explained that he meant to complete some work both on the train and in the car from Lamy to Los Alamos. There had been flooding on the road below Los Alamos. One of the party pretended that arrangements had been made for them to proceed by mule train. He still remembers Johnny's face when, on arrival at Lamy, they coincidentally were greeted by the braying of a jackass. In postwar years the journey from Los Alamos to the railhead could be made by light aircraft. Johnny one day arrived with a party for one light aircraft, just as Teller arrived for another. As the two Hungarians wanted to discuss something, they went in the second aircraft. The others went in an aircraft that took off just before it. One of the party in the first aircraft lost a scarf out the window. The group worried momentarily over what were the odds that it might catch in the propeller of the plane behind—and destroy so much Hungarian brainpower. After a safe landing, they jocularly described their worry to Johnny. "We were such-and-such feet above you, such-and-such yards ahead, the air speed was . . . ." "The odds against it hitting the propeller were such-and-such millions to one," said Johnny, citing a precise figure that later proved right. As with so many Johnny legends, I have to add that this was the most pro-Johnny version of the story; there were others less dramatic.

Most of the time up to 1952 Johnny did not have many contacts with major politicians. He was still used by some because of his extraordinary quickness. One example in 1952 came when a tornado occurred in Massachusetts shortly after a nuclear test in Nevada. Johnny was contacted by telephone by the office of a politician in that state, and he sent the following note back the same day. He often sent such notes covered with equations, but here he was writing to a public servant who needed plain English:

(1) A tornado is the result of the coincidence of a number of improbable circumstances, all of which are necessary: suitable initial updraft, suitable vertical layer structure in the atmosphere to continue these updrafts, immediate availability of humid air, availability of condensation nuclei. The compounded probability of all these in Massachusetts is such that Massachusetts had 16 tornado[e]s in 35 years (1915–50), i.e., the probability of a tornado in Massachusetts in any one year is 16 divided by thirty-five, which equals 45%. The distribution of these tornado[e]s in these years is according to Poisson's law: 22 years with none, 10 with one, 3 with two. So the Worcester tornado needed no A-bomb. Any one season has an almost even chance to produce a tornado in Massachusetts.

(2) The A-bomb can contribute little to a tornado: its energy is trivial and nucleation centres are abundant in the Massachu-

setts atmosphere. An ordinary weather front, producing rain all over Pennsylvania, at the rate of one tenth of an inch an hour, releases energy equivalent to one 50 kiloton A-bomb per second.

(3) Of the 30 or so A-bombs so far exploded only one caused demonstrable rain. This was the underwater shot at Bikini, and this by an interaction of the aerosol spray and the humid tropical atmosphere. These conditions are entirely unlike anything in the continental U.S., and they only produced a 30 minute tropical rain. Please let me know if you want more details on any aspect of this.

Johnny was asked in 1947, with two other professors, to describe how Congress could best obey its own law by having a fair apportionment of congressional seats. He explained succinctly that there were at least five different mathematical measures that the word "fair" could have in this context. He called them the methods of smallest divisors (S.D.), harmonic mean (H.M.), equal proportions (E.P.), major fractions (M.F.), greatest divisors (G.D.). All were different from each other. He could merely recommend which method offended against other definitions of fairness least, and which would or would not help sitting members most. Some congressmen did not much like this.

Strangely, Johnny's closer integration into the political world came with an appointment to his own IAS that he had tried to avert. By 1947 Aydelotte had decided to retire as director of the institute. The ubiquitous Admiral Strauss, who was by now on the board of trustees of the IAS, asked Einstein and Johnny what sort of successor they would recommend. Einstein replied, "You should look for a very quiet man who will not disturb people who are trying to think." Johnny recommended the forty-nine-year-old Dr. Detlev W. Bronk, who was a distinguished physiologist (a professor in the field between medicine and physics) who had managed to direct foundations and institutions without annoying everybody. When told that the most likely director of the IAS was Los Alamos's wartime chief Oppenheimer, Johnny wrote to

Strauss with (for him) unusual ambiguity: "Oppenheimer's brilliance is incontestable and he would seem to be a most desirable addition to our faculty—if we can interest him in this respect. I have some misgivings as to the wisdom of making him director of the institute, and so have others. I think these matters are better suited for an oral discussion if you would wish me to go into the details."

Oppenheimer nonetheless arrived at the IAS as director, carrying a large safe with very secret documents into his study. He had come to Princeton partly because it was near to Washington, where he intended to be on a great many committees, propagating very determinedly his left-of-Truman political and scientific views. The most important of these committees was Oppenheimer's chairmanship and dominance of the general advisory committee (GAC) of top scientists who were to advise the new Atomic Energy Commission (AEC). All matters concerning atomic energy, including Los Alamos, had been put by Congress under this AEC, because nuclear bombs were now regarded as too-serious matters to be run only by soldiers.

Many of the scholars at the institute objected that Oppie was carrying the cold war into their academe with that large safe, Johnny's fear was that Oppie's views on the cold war were too dreamy by half. In institute affairs, though, the two men proved a marvellous partnership. Benoit Mandelbrot, the discoverer of fractals, and a pioneer of the chaos school of mathematics, was first invited to talk to the institute by Johnny. Mandelbrot recalled to Regis that, because he was nervous in front of such great minds, he stammered through a lecture that was pitifully bad. "But the day was saved by a very marvellous summary by Oppenheimer and by von Neumann. Oppenheimer and von Neumann re-gave my lecture, each of them in turn, but much better than I could do it, and so finally it was a triumphal event, and it turned out very much to my advantage." Both Oppie and Johnny felt intellectual excitement at new scientific ideas and united in friendship about them.

Sadly, as Johnny had foreseen, the relations between Strauss and Oppenheimer went much less well. Oppenheimer treated those whom he regarded as fools with the cruellest sort of cutting contradictions, and Strauss did not like to be treated as a fool. Strauss suggested that the export of something to a Scandinavian country should be banned. The technology would then be out of American hands, and did not the scientists think the Soviets might have use for it when trying to make an A-bomb? Yes, indeed, said Oppie, as they might also have use for a hammer, a screwdriver, and a paper clip.

Then came the Soviet nuclear explosion of August 29, 1949. It blew up a lot of entrenched positions.

◄►◄►

High in the skies around the Soviet Union, American aircraft had long been on patrol, with protruding filters to pick up any Soviet nuclear debris. Old Los Alamos hands said they were in direct descent from planes that had sniffed the air over Germany in the war to see if there were any reactor by-products there. Some of the postwar establishment said they had been placed on patrol by Admiral Strauss, after discussions with scientists including Johnny. In late August 1949, their filters picked up what they did not want. After three weeks of examination in Washington and elsewhere, Truman announced that Russia clearly had exploded its first nuclear device, nicknamed Joe 1. This had been expected by some experts such as Johnny, but was a shock to most politicians and voters.

An immediate, although at first badly reported, debate started on what should be done about this. It was a doomsday debate between only about two hundred oddly haphazard and diverse people. The question was whether America should proceed to develop the superbomb or H-bomb, which (even in droppable form) promised to be a thousand times more destructive than the atom bomb at Hiroshima.

It had been recognized since 1942–43 that if the 100,000,000° temperature created in the center of a nuclear bomb could be used to burn up deuterium (a heavy natural isotope of hydrogen), perhaps laced with tritium (a still heavier but artificial and therefore very expensive isotope of hydrogen), then an explosion about a thousand times more powerful than Hiroshima's could result. Indeed, the explosion might be made limitless, in the sense of becoming ever bigger when ever more deuterium was added to it. It was theoretically possible to work out how much you would have to add in order to destroy the planet.

The most ardent advocates of the superbomb were Teller and Lawrence. Teller had wanted to prepare such a superbomb even during the war; he had originally thought out much of the physics behind it, and it was very much his pet project. Oppenheimer had told him firmly in 1944 that Los Alamos must concentrate on the project that it could complete first, which was the ordinary nuclear bomb. There was anyway a difficulty—some people thought it a fortunate difficulty—about the superbomb. Nobody could know whether a fission bomb really could burn up deuterium. The operation was rather like holding a match to a piece of coal in hopes that the coal would catch alight.

In early 1946 Teller had presented his proposed design for the superbomb to a secret committee of thirty-one scientists, including Johnny. The committee concluded that Teller's design—later to be called the "classical super"—probably would work, but it would require a lot of resources. Most of them did not much want to spend billions to get a bomb a thousand times more murderous than that which had killed one hundred thousand people at Hiroshima. The thirty-one scientists at the 1946 meeting included Klaus Fuchs. He passed Teller's suggested (but fortunately wrong) design straight to Moscow.

After the news of Russia's fission bomb in Joe 1 in August 1949, Teller barnstormed through Washington. He argued that work to create a superbomb must now be given the highest priority. Most scientists, including those led by Oppenheimer on the GAC, opposed this. Eloquent Fermi and Rabi said that the superbomb "is necessarily an evil thing considered in any light." It would destroy millions of innocent human lives; it could not possibly be applied to military targets only; the consequent great release of radioactivity would render large areas of the earth unfit for habitation for a long time to come.

Oppenheimer also "recommended strongly" against proceeding with the superbomb but said his arguments were technical rather than moral. "I am not sure that the miserable thing can work, nor that it can be gotten to the target except by oxcart," he wrote to a friend. In any case, he thought that the improvement of America's ordinary nuclear weapons should be given priority. He did not think that computers would be ready in time to do the sums needed to test whether the H-bomb would work, and he said (Oppie-like) that hit-and-miss research into a weapon that could destroy the planet appeared "to be singularly proof against any form of experimental approach." He doubted whether the Russians were close on the Americans' heels. To those who said the Russians might succeed in developing it, he said, "We would reply that our undertaking it will not prove a deterrent to them." His main worry, he told a friend, was that the superbomb in America "appears to have caught the imagination, both of the congressional and the military people, as the answers to the problems posed by the Russians. . . . That we become committed to it as the way to save the country and the peace appears to me full of dangers."

Johnny and Teller happened to be at Los Alamos in the week when news of Joe 1 broke, and Johnny instantly agreed with Teller that "if the super can be made, it should be made by America." He knew better than Oppenheimer that computers in America would be able to work out what happened in the one millionth of a second when an A-bomb is linked to deuterium, so there would not have to be all those environment-destroying tests. But Johnny's main argument was the mirror image of Oppenheimer's. If in America the superbomb had "caught the imagination, both of the congressional and military people," then the same thing would have happened with their nastier equivalents in Russia. Although Oppenheimer doubted whether the Russians would quickly start research on the H-bomb, Johnny was sure that they would have started already. We do now in fact know that Sakharov was researching on Russia's H-bomb by 1948.

For the Russians to get first to a bomb one thousand times more effective than Hiroshima's, thought Johnny, would have many awful effects not dreamed of in Oppenheimer's philosophy. In Europe there would be a drift in favor of surrendering to Russia's might. Any swing to weakness made Johnny ever more fearful of war. In Russia it would be a great victory for Beria if a project under his command reached a superbomb before America in Stalin's last years, and Johnny regarded the fight for Stalin's succession as one that Beria must not win.

Johnny's main propaganda activity in the few weeks after Joe 1 was to "argue the ear off Robert Oppenheimer" in Princeton. Oppie's ear remained in place, but in Washington he was losing his battle. Dean Acheson represented the politicians' view most accurately. He said that people like Oppenheimer understandably felt that scientists had brought "enough evil into human life" but they somehow assumed that if America did not research into how to produce the next evil, then nobody else would.

In January 1950 Truman announced that, as commander in chief, he had directed the AEC to continue its work on all forms of atomic weapons, including "the so-called hydrogen or super bomb." Within four weeks the relieved Joint Chiefs of Staff had dubiously but perhaps fortunately interpreted this to mean "all-out development of hydrogen bombs and the means for their production and delivery."

The scientists began to flock back to Los Alamos—including two original opponents of the superbomb, Fermi and Bethe. Fermi felt that, once legitimate political authorities had decided a question, it was not for scientists to go on intruding their personal opinions. Bethe admitted frankly that he went back to Los Alamos hoping to prove that H-bombs could not be made. He was taken aback that everybody at Los Alamos seemed gung-ho to create them. This swing of opinion could be attributed partly to the enthusiasm for the superbomb by such leaders of opinion as Johnny but perhaps even more to the outbreak in mid-1950 of the war in Korea.

It soon began to look as if Bethe's hopes about the impossibility of creating the superbomb might prove right. During 1950 it became clear that Teller's original project for a superbomb would not work. The A-bomb would not ignite the deuterium. The match would not light the coal in that required one millionth of a second. It would simply fizzle.

There were three steps to this initial disillusion. Some of the calculations suggesting the fizzle originated from Ulam, now back at Los Alamos as leader of the department called Group T-8. Actually Group T-8 consisted mainly of Ulam and his University of Wisconsin associate Dr. C. J. Everett. Ulam never concealed his dependence on Everett: "I had some general, sometimes only vague, ideas. Everett supplied the rigor, the ingenuities and the details of the proof, and final constructions." In these Ulam-Everett calculations, sometimes miscalled the "debunking of Teller's super," Everett virtually "wore out his slide rule." Ulam's admirers said that at this stage he was working single-handedly; his critics said that the single hand was that of Everett.

The second stage of the debunking was some more fundamental work carried out by Ulam with Fermi. The third stage was the runoff of the calculations on Johnny's computers. Johnny had at one time thought these calculations of what happened in that one millionth of a second would require more multiplications than had ever been done before in human history. This guess proved exaggerated, partly because he had underestimated the number of multiplications done by schoolchildren each week. But it was fortunate that he could now use two computers: the ENIAC and his Princeton prototype with its clip leads on. Even the early runs showed that Ulam was proving right and that Teller (who Johnny had hoped would win the argument) was mistaken. "Icicles are forming," Johnny reported to Los Alamos dejectedly after his first computer tests.

In consequence of these calculations, wrote Bethe, "Teller himself was desperate between October 1950 and January 1951." Bethe continued too cruelly, "Nine out of ten of Teller's ideas are useless. He needs men with more judgment, even if they be less gifted, to select the tenth idea which is often a stroke of genius." Because

Ulam and Johnny were two of the four men who proved that this one idea of Teller's was half wrong, it is worth scouring their letters to see how they regarded him.

The answer is that they had huge respect for Teller's scientific imagination but were able to giggle (where others grew furious) at some of Teller's mistakes in personal relations. There are references in the letters to the way Teller rejected a suggestion by a distinguished scientist, by saying, "If it came from that quarter it is certain to be 180 degrees wrong." He burst in on Everett at one stage of the Ulam-Everett calculations, saying, "There is a mistake here by a factor of ten to the power of four"; Everett, who did not make mistakes, was cross, but Ulam laughed. "Edward is now here," wrote Ulam one January, "but some of the Yule spirit still remains." "I am so glad that Edward is going to meet the Romans at Los Alamos," wrote back Johnny. "Edward has now at last got a committee established on this," wrote back Ulam, "where he will talk essentially to himself." Although some of the dislikers of the H-bomb, specifically including Oppenheimer, enjoyed Teller's momentary discomfiture in late 1950, Johnny and Ulam specifically did not. It was thus that what later became known as the Teller-Ulam invention was concocted between January and March 1951, which led on quickly to the real superbomb.

This is still partly classified because all holders of the thermonuclear bomb, including both Russia and America, do not want Colonel Qadaffi and others to know how to make any atom bombs they get a thousand times more murderous. But the Ulam breakthrough harked back to the implosion lens on which Johnny and he had worked for the A-bomb in 1944–45 and then added more stages in. Textbooks talk of Ulam's concept of a two-stage implosion design: of a redesigned detonator that would compress to a very high density a second fissile core composed of deuterium and tritium. The eventual joint paper by Teller and Ulam was awesomely called "On Heterocatalytic Detonations in Hydrodynamic Lenses and Radiation Mirrors," which evokes memories of that flushing toilet in Chicago.

It is not true that Teller and Ulam disagreed in any way at this stage. Ulam's account is that, after he had discussed his idea with some senior people at Los Alamos,

> The next morning I spoke to Teller. I don't think he had any real animosity towards me for the negative result of the work with Everett so damaging to his plans, but our relationship seemed definitely strained. At once Edward took up my suggestions, hesitantly at first but enthusiastically after a few hours. He had seen not only the novel elements, but had found a parallel version, an alternative to what I had said, perhaps more convenient and generalised. From then on pessimism gave way to hope.

Ulam also says that a more detailed follow-up report was written by Teller and Freddie de Hoffmann (who died in 1989, after having helped me considerably in fixing up interviews for this book). Teller's version was that, after the glumness in early 1951, "two signs of hope came within a few weeks: one sign was an imaginative suggestion by Ulam: the other sign was a fine calculation by de Hoffmann."

One survivor from those days says there were about six steps to the hydrogen bomb. Teller made them all, except half of the penultimate one. That is why Teller can still justly be called the father of the H-bomb. Bethe's view was that it was better to call Teller the mother of the thing. He carried it around with him such a long time and had many pains during its pregnancy.

After the Teller–Ulam breakthrough around March 1951, everything proceeded smoothly at Los Alamos except personal relations.

The so-called George shot in May 1951, which "lit the first small thermonuclear flame on earth," really had little to do with all this. The George shot was a successful attempt to light a very small bit of deuterium with a very large A-bomb. By putting a blowtorch to a very small amount of coal you can no doubt set it alight; but that does not solve the problem of lighting a large bit of coal with a match and then getting a bigger and bigger fire whenever you add more coal to it.

Once the Teller–Ulam configuration had been proposed, every-

body agreed that Los Alamos should proceed with the superbomb. Oppenheimer recorded his own views: "The programme we had in 1949 was a tortured thing that you could well argue did not make a great deal of technical sense. It was therefore possible to argue also that you did not want it even if you could have it. The program in 1951 was technically so sweet that you could not argue about that." Matters therefore went full speed ahead to the Mike shot at Eniwetok in November 1952. It exploded with a force equivalent to over 10,000,000 tons, or 10 megatons, of TNT—nearly a thousand times as large as the 13,000 tons or 13 kilotons exploded at Hiroshima. The Mike device admittedly needed a building full of refrigerating devices to keep the liquid deuterium in proper shape before being exploded. It would not have been possible to carry it around on an airplane. But a 15-megaton device that could be dropped from an airplane was ready by the Castle shot in March 1954.

In between Mike in November 1952 and Castle in March 1954, the new Soviet leader, Georgy Malenkov, announced that the United States had not only no monopoly on the A-bomb but no monopoly on the H-bomb either. On August 12, 1953, the Soviet Union fired its first thermonuclear device, partly fathered by Sakharov. It was a tiny thermonuclear explosion as such things go, probably under 500 kilotons, less than one twentieth the size of Mike. One reason for its failure was that Fuchs had been able to report only on Teller's original ideas in 1946, before it was discovered that they did not really work. Until about 1955 Russia had no equivalent of the Teller-Ulam invention. Then Sakharov produced Russia's equivalent of Teller-Ulam.

By the time of the Mike shot on November 1, 1952, Johnny was therefore satisfied that America had won the race to the superbomb. He was happy that one great disaster—the attainment of terrifying Soviet military supremacy while Stalin was still alive—had been averted, with considerable help from his infant computers. He was still a relative pessimist about nuclear war. As late as 1952 he was still writing to Strauss that confrontation between the Soviet Union and the United States remained very probable. That is why the United States had to be, at every moment, in a state where one message was flashed to Soviet leaders: if you dare engage in war, then you personally will be nuked to death in it, and the war is one that an admittedly shattered America is certain to win.

In the week after the Mike explosion in November 1952, Dwight Eisenhower was elected president of the United States. He appointed Strauss first as his special assistant for atomic energy matters, and then as chairman of the AEC. He also brought in Donald A. Quarles first as assistant secretary of defence for research and development, and then as secretary of the air force. By Quarles's side was the very busy Trevor Gardner as special assistant to the secretary of the air force. All three of these men—Strauss, Quarles, and Gardner—thought that America's technology for war could best be advanced by the man whom they regarded as America's quickest-thinking scientific genius.

All three were fans of Johnny.

►◄►◄►◄ *15*

With Astonishing
Influence, 1950–56

►◄**A**lthough Johnny had welcomed
Truman's reelection in 1948, he had been politically to the right
of most of the scientists who were advising the Truman administration in 1945–49. Until Truman plumped for the superbomb
in January 1950, Johnny's main military ties were with the bodies
like Los Alamos that had found him so useful in the war. After
January 1950 the military began to recruit hard nuts such as
Johnny, instead of gentler poets such as Oppenheimer. Johnny
accepted these recruitments with criticized alacrity. Some friends
said this was because he was privately chuffed by the "thump of
helicopters on the lawn." Another said he liked "dining and drinking with Admirals, especially after he found that he had a stronger
head than they." His own papers suggest a more potent reason.
He was horrified by the inefficiency of military bureaucracy. He
thought it important to introduce scientific method into it, so that
he could help save the peace and the world.

In the first go-for-superbomb year 1950, Johnny's two new

military appointments were as consultant to the Weapons Systems Evaluation Group (WSEG) and then to the Armed Forces Special Weapons Project (AFSWP), both in Washington, D.C. He was recruited to help the WSEG at a lunch in April 1950 with the wartime victor in Europe General Omar Bradley, plus the army's top technologist Lieutenant-General J. E. Hull and the distinguished wartime relic Vannevar Bush.

The letter to Johnny from Hull before the lunch said the WSEG had just sent to Truman its first massive (but actually ineffective) study on how strategic bombing should be planned in the nuclear age. For its next studies it wanted greater liaison with "the best scientific minds in the nation." The letter from Bush after the lunch oozed the opinion that "this chance to work with some of the keenest military minds" would allow Johnny to introduce "scientific methods of attack" into problems "where the results are being seriously regarded by military men in positions of great responsibility"—an appointment under "almost perfect auspices.
. . . The satisfaction of being a member of a group which has accomplished in such definite way real things in the interest of the defense of this country must be very great indeed." Johnny was asked to be a consultant to the WSEG and to help urge full-time work for it from Professor H. P. Robertson (by then of the California Institute of Technology, but in an earlier chapter the father of the baby that new-immigrant Mariette tried to bathe).

In a letter to Robertson starting, "Dear Bob," Johnny set about such urging, but was not as sweet as Bush in his appreciation of "the keenest military minds." Instead he was in near despair about them. He felt that the AEC had not got through to the military the sea change that nuclear technology had brought into the future of war, perhaps partly because his fellow scientists had not liked to explain to the brute soldiery how horridly easy it was going to be to kill millions of people with effective new weapons. But Johnny told Robertson:

I am quite certain that there is no organisation this side of eternity, other than WSEG, which can produce order in the chaotic relations between the Atomic Energy Commission and the services, and develop reasonable criteria for what AEC policy in its relationship to military matters should be, what its weapon development should aim at, how this should be integrated with the services, and how the AEC and services should exchange information. The lack of information in the places where it should have been available, and the misunderstandings and misdirections of effort which resulted from this in the past, have been fantastic, unbelievable for anyone who has not seen them. To be more exact: you may have seen such snafus, but it certainly rates with the worst of them. Some extreme mistakes are now being corrected, but plenty remain and there doesn't seem to be any organisation except WSEG which is properly positioned to correct this systematically and intelligently. I suspect that if you look into the matter (which you may have done already), you will find that the same thing is true for many equally decisive and equally expensive phases in the set-up and in the development of each of the services. There can be no doubt that WSEG needs a man of your calibre. . . .

In the AFSWP, Johnny was soon coldly shooting down some of the more exorbitantly expensive ideas. "On the Pelican Report," the commanding general wrote to him, "I will make known your additional minority opinions; but please stay on as consultant."

In 1951–52—still during Truman's administration—Johnny received four more military appointments: (1) as consultant to the CIA; (2) as member of the GAC to the AEC; (3) as consultant to Lawrence's and Teller's new rival-to-Los Alamos laboratory at Livermore; and (4) as member of the scientific advisory board (SAB) of the U.S. Air Force.

The last three of these appointments put Johnny's diplomacy under strain.

◄►◄►

Johnny was made a member of the AEC's GAC—a post that was a direct presidential (i.e., Truman's) appointment—just as Oppenheimer left it. As Oppenheimer had been the GAC's chairman for five years to the summer of 1952, he reluctantly tendered his half-resignation then. It was accepted with rude alacrity.

Some of the secret papers from Oppenheimer's Princeton safe were removed immediately, although Gordon Dean (Truman's appointee as head of the AEC and Oppenheimer's friend) left some there on the grounds that Oppenheimer was going to continue as a consultant to the GAC. In Truman's last year this was a mistake. McCarthyism foully filled the air, and persecution of anybody with distant past communist connections had become a congressional frenzy. Oppenheimer's close past family connections with the Communist party, in the worst days of Stalinism, looked like signs of instability. In personal, though not state secret terms—thought our Johnny—they probably were.

Johnny played no part in McCarthyism. He annoyed friends both on the indignant right and on the appalled left by treating the witch-hunt as mainly a vulgar bad joke. He wrote letters urging that the best men should always be chosen for any scientific post or grant, irrespective of past or even present communist leanings. True, he did urge friends with past communist associations not to apply for jobs where witch-hunts would certainly arise. He felt that there were still many good scientific jobs in which they fortunately did not. Those who had flirted with Stalinism in the 1930s depression were embarrassedly telling lies even to themselves about what they had said and wanted then, so they were in natural danger of committing perjury before congressional committees.

The spread of the persecution to Oppenheimer presented Johnny with problems. When Dean retired as Truman's chairman of the AEC in 1953, one of his last acts was to extend Oppenheimer's GAC consultancy for a year, so that those secret documents could remain in Oppenheimer's Princeton safe. When Strauss became Eisenhower's chairman of the AEC on the next day, one of his first acts was to remove them. As tempers flared, one tiresome congressional staffer published his own "exhaustively considered opinion" that "J. Robert Oppenheimer is an agent of the Soviet Union." The AEC held an inquiry in 1954, which concluded by the insulting majority view that Oppenheimer should have no further access to secret material.

Most of the witnesses against Oppenheimer were those who had opposed his recommendations to delay development of the superbomb. These hostile witnesses half included Teller. They would have fully included Lawrence had he not been ill. Johnny organized an important group of the witnesses for Oppenheimer: those who had disagreed with Oppenheimer's opposition to the superbomb but who knew that he was in no sense a security risk. Indeed, Johnny incurred some expenses in organizing them and refused any reimbursement from Oppenheimer's lawyer. He thus played an honest role in the middle of the road, and so was apt to be kicked by friends who were charging indignantly down both sides of it.

On the one side, Strauss—who was one of Johnny's main contacts with the Eisenhower administration—was hopping mad with Oppenheimer, who treated him with personal rudeness and contempt. On the other side, Johnny's colleagues at the IAS were massed in favor of IAS director Oppenheimer and against former IAS trustee Strauss. Johnny dashed back at dangerous speed by car to one faculty meeting, where Goldstine was playing Horatio and holding the bridge, so as to get some of the unnecessary bitternesses crossed out of one proposed anti-Strauss round-robin. Johnny remained reasonably friendly with everybody during this, although he hated joint statements of any kind. Everybody came under pressure to sign them, including one or two of the younger staff who privately disagreed. One of Johnny's personal definitions of a scholar was a person who did not sign manifestos that tabled joint emotions. In any complicated situation any thoughtful man should want to express his opinions in his own words, instead of baying in a pack like hounds.

◄► ◄►

The second office that Johnny accepted during the Truman administration in 1952 also required him to walk a tightrope over a chasm, where intelligent scientists among his friends were shouting at each other. After the Teller-Ulam breakthrough opened the way to the thermonuclear bomb in March–April 1951, Teller had a flaming row with director Norris Bradbury and other senior staff at Los Alamos about how to charge down it. Teller wanted faster progress than the others thought possible. Teller flounced out and lobbied in Washington for a second AEC nuclear laboratory to compete with Los Alamos. Bradbury and initially Oppenheimer strongly opposed a second laboratory. They thought it would divert resources from Los Alamos, which by now was progressing toward the Mike thermonuclear shot in November 1952 with great efficiency.

It did not help that Teller was finding support in Washington in 1951–52 from Senator Brian McMahon's congressional joint committee on atomic energy, one of whose staffers was later to accuse Oppenheimer of being an agent of the Soviet Union. It did help that Lawrence told Teller and Congress that the new laboratory could be built rather cheaply on land next to one of his own laboratories on a former naval air station at Livermore, California; and that it could be mainly staffed with people already on the University of California's payroll.

Interestingly, Teller told this biographer that two people whom he deeply respected advised him against joining with Lawrence. "They were Enrico Fermi and Johnny von Neumann," he said. Johnny argued that Teller might lose influence by being associated with as shrill a political hawk as Lawrence. Because some people alleged that Johnny was advocating preventive war against Russia at this time, it is intriguing that, compared with Lawrence, he cooed like a dove.

The Livermore Laboratory was established in the summer of 1952. It was immediately immersed in another row. The Mike shot in November 1952, the explosion of the world's first large thermonuclear device, had been wholly arranged from Los Alamos. Some newspapers, and later a book, attributed it to Teller's walkout from Los Alamos in 1951, into this new laboratory at Livermore (which at the time of the Mike shot was still wholly occupied in getting itself started). The annoyance about this at Los Alamos turned to huge horse laughs when the first Livermore test explosions in 1953 and 1954 simply fizzled. One of its nuclear devices failed even to destroy the flimsy tower in Nevada in which it had been placed.

How and why, then, did Johnny agree in 1952 to become a consultant at Livermore, while still remaining a consultant at Los Alamos? The answer is that his experience in developing computers had shown him that, once an initial breakthrough had been made, competition was the best way of carrying any new technology forward. Johnny fully agreed with Teller's wisest statement of the case for Livermore. Teller wrote:

I knew that science thrives on friendly competition, and the fostering of different points of view, and on the exchange of ideas developed in different surroundings. I knew too that a single group of scientists working together can easily become fascinated by special aspects of a development—to the neglect of other hopeful approaches. My conviction grew that the safety of our country could not be entrusted to a single nuclear weapons laboratory, even though that laboratory were as excellent as Los Alamos.

History was to prove every word of this. Because of the philosophy of Livermore's first director, Herbert York, the laboratory set out "to construct nuclear explosive devices that had the smallest diameter, the lightest weight, the least investment in rare materials, or the highest yield to weight ratio, or that otherwise carried the state of the art beyond the currently explored frontiers." When the navy needed a lightweight warhead for its submarine-launched missiles, Livermore's contributions helped bring Polaris into being. The safety of the free world from the late 1950s to the end of the cold war was better secured by not keeping all the eggs in Los Alamos's basket.

The third of the military appointments that Johnny accepted in the Truman administration's last two years—actually in 1951— was as a member of the Scientific Advisory Board (SAB) of the U.S. Air Force. He joined it out of loyalty to that old "native of the same village" von Karman. In his California days in the 1930s von Karman's advanced ideas on aeronautic design especially interested a young pilot in nearby March Field, Major Henry H. Arnold. When Arnold ended the war as head of the U.S. Army Air Force, he asked von Karman to chair an SAB to plan the air force's technological way into the future. As von Karman reached his seventieth birthday in 1951, he recruited his fellow Hungarian, Johnny, to the SAB. Johnny joined it and was almost immediately appalled at how bureaucratic the management of technology had become even in the air force. Then in November 1952, in the same week as the Mike thermonuclear shot, came the event that gave Johnny his extraordinarily influential last four years—the landslide election victory of Eisenhower.

◄►◄►

Eisenhower's election gave the United States its first real change of administration in twenty years. It brought to Washington a team of Republican businessmen determined to review and radically repair what they regarded as the Democrats' relapse into bumbledom. The new secretary of state, John Foster Dulles, pinned his speeches, and perhaps his policy, to the doctrine of "massive retaliation." The Korean war had suggested that the communists were going to probe the free world at places and times of their own choosing. The Dulles doctrine meant that any Russian decision makers who planned to start a war anywhere were to be given notice that they themselves could be killed within a few hours of its start. The new teams in the defense departments were to devise ways of making credible that possibly incredible policy of nuclear deterrence.

Johnny's first admirers in them were Gardner (the special assistant to the secretary of the air force) and Quarles (who soon became secretary of the air force himself). Quarles had been chief executive of the Sandia Corporation, which had been set up in New Mexico near Los Alamos to do the final engineering jobs when making nuclear weapons. This Sandia Corporation once sent Johnny a long consultant's contract that specified what he would be required to do, but then declared on the last page that the fee paid for this would be nil. Johnny had replied with humor and central European politeness, before discovering that the contract had to be signed so that Sandia could tell him some things he already knew (indeed had in part invented). Quarles liked Johnny and told Gardner to pay especial heed to him.

Gardner was a live wire, determined to make the Republican review of defense policy electric. The style of the Quarles-Gardner reviews was admirably described by York, who was drawn into them from his post as director of what we have called the Teller-Lawrence laboratory at Livermore. Wrote York:

> The reviews themselves were carried out at first by a number of committees working separately in each of the military services and reporting to different levels of programme management. These committees had a strongly interlocking membership, a feature of the apparatus which then, as now, allowed information to travel both up and down within agencies and laterally between agencies and thus to pass over and around the various barriers of secrecy, propriety and bureaucracy, which would otherwise cripple technical progress. This style of organisation and operation, of course, also allowed a few strong-minded individuals to dominate a broad part of the scene.

York continued:

> After about a year [i.e., in 1954], in the interest of making more rapid progress and more profound changes, the originally large number of committees were regrouped into a much smaller number and John von Neumann became the chairman of the most important of them. The "von Neumann Committee" (under different formal names) advised the Secretary of the Air Force on the projects that were under the direct control of that service, and it advised the Secretary of Defense on all large military rocket programmes. . . . Von Neumann was extremely intelligent, and curious about everything. He looked like a cherub and sometimes acted like one; my three and five year old daughters delighted in climbing on him when he came to call at the house. He was very powerful and productive in pure science and mathematics and at the same time had a remarkably strong streak of practicality. . . . This combination of scientific ability and practicality gave him a credibility with military officers, engineers, industrialists, and scientists that nobody else could match. He was clearly the dominant advisory figure in nuclear missilery at the time, and everyone took his statements about what could and should be done very seriously.

◄►◄►

Johnny's first appointment under the new order came in the Eisenhower administration's first week in January 1953. Gardner asked him to be chairman of the nuclear weapons panel of the SAB to the air force. This panel seemed liable to experience some explosive fission itself. Its members were Teller, Bradbury, Bethe (both of whom were seething with Teller), York, two scientists from the Rand Corporation, and one from the Pentagon.

Probably only a man of Johnny's temperament could bring such a committee to such quick conclusions, which helped turn American defense policy and (with it) foreign policy right around. His method was to emphasize new technical facts and to turn the discussion directly to their implications. Johnny stressed from the beginning that

> there has been a complete change in the underlying economic-political-strategic position. Nuclear weapons are no longer expensive, they are no longer scarce, and they are no longer a monopoly of the U.S. These things are known, but they still need to be repeated—I do not think that our thinking has assimilated them. . . . One must no longer consider the nuclear components as the hardest part of the problems involved in weapons systems of which they form part. They are now among the least difficult and most flexible parts of such systems.

The first question put to Johnny's nuclear weapons panel was, What would be the maximum power of a hydrogen bomb that could be carried by a B-52 bomber? The B-52s then (1953) on the drawing board would be able to lug weights between 30,000 pounds and 50,000 pounds into the air. Although the only thermonuclear device just exploded at the Mike shot had been quite impossible to carry in any aircraft, Johnny's panel confidently forecast that a thermonuclear bomb carriable in a B-52 could "quite conservatively" be expected to reach the extraordinary explosive power of 20 megatons or 20,000,000 tons of TNT. The Livermore

Laboratory in fact examined proposals of how to build and test a bomb bigger than that, thus suggesting a weapon that would be over two thousand times more powerful than the one at Hiroshima. Eisenhower rightly minuted: "Absolutely not; these things are already too big."

The second question put to Johnny's nuclear panel was whether it would be possible to get a bomb weighing only about 3,000 pounds and thus perhaps carriable on an Atlas missile, which would destroy everything within 500 yards. The panel coolly replied that "these two questions do not belong together." It would be possible to get a 2-megaton bomb which would weigh under 3,000 pounds. That 2-megaton bomb would be able to destroy everything within 3.2–4.5 miles. So planners should seek an optimum compromise, which gave an Atlas missile less weight to carry (this would make it much easier to build), but perhaps carry only a 1-megaton bomb (which could destroy everything within 2 miles).

The policy of threatening massive retaliation was thereby put into hard figures. A delighted defense and political establishment asked Johnny to chair the committee for evaluation of strategic missiles. Johnny and his colleagues caused a shock when they did. They also introduced a whole new management style into defense procurement.

Missiles did not seem a very effective military option in the ten years down to 1954. In the last year of the 1939–45 war the Germans shot off just under ten thousand unmanned missiles at Britain, of two sorts. Rather over eight thousand were V-1's. These were pilotless aircraft, and hopelessly inaccurate. Fewer than half hit the London at which they were aimed. Most were interrupted by British air defenses or went completely astray.

The other fifteen hundred or so German missiles in 1944–45 were V-2's. These were ballistic (or big bullet-shaped) rockets; they were called ballistic because, once launched, they follow a trajectory determined by the interaction between their momentum and gravity, as bullets do. None was intercepted before landing in Britain, but the fifteen hundred of them killed only twenty-five hundred people, nearly all civilians. This kill rate of only just over

one person per enormously expensive rocket was hopelessly un-
economic, like the Scud missiles that Saddam Hussein's Iraq fired
off in the 1991 Gulf War. The V-2's could not really be targeted
more accurately than "try to hit greater London." In 1944–45 one
ton worth of conventional explosive, which was all a V-1 or
V-2 could carry, had a destruction radius of only about 30 yards.
The Western Allies never attempted to build the equivalent of
V-1's and V-2's, for an entirely logical reason. So long as they
had command of the air (which by 1944 the Allies did), bombers
could deliver far more bombs far more accurately over much
longer distances than the 200 miles that most V-1's and V-2's could
stutteringly reach.

When the war ended in 1945, the Americans brought back to
the United States, under the absurdly named Operation Paper
Clip, most of the leading German rocket scientists from Peenemünde. The Russians got only a few rather junior Peenemünde
men, but they were possibly a better bargain. The junior German
scientists could pass on to the Russians German know-how about
building V-1's and V-2's, which was not in fact very complicated.
The senior German scientists in American hands had ideas about
the future of space programs, which were often not in fact very
good.

The Russians probably understood earlier than the Americans
that their military and political planning should be ruthlessly
geared to the three huge new strategic facts after 1945: (1) even if
nobody was going to dare to explode either a nuclear or a thermonuclear bomb, the side that most credibly threatened to do so
might surreptitiously conquer the world; (2) aircraft were going
to become more and more vulnerable; so (3) the future of nuclear
deterrence would lie with long-range rockets, which would not
just—like a V-2—carry a fairly harmless one ton of TNT equivalent, capable of killing just over one person each, across 200 miles.
The new missiles would carry several million tons of TNT equivalent per small rocket head, capable of destroying whole regions,
accurately targetable (eventually to within a few square inches)
after traversing one-fourth of the earth.

Between 1945 and the arrival of the von Neumann committee in 1953, America was not geared to such thinking. Its rather unimaginative research on missilery was tied up in interservice red tape.

The U.S. Air Force tried to develop three V-1-type pilotless aircraft that were all pretty obsolete before they were due to come into operation. The air force also started development of one ballistic missile but slowed it because of shortage of funds. The U.S. Navy and Army had separate rocket programs with rather little coordination or chance of success.

After its meetings in early 1954, the von Neumann committee reported (1) that it was possible to build a rocket-powered ballistic missile that would carry a nuclear warhead across a quarter of the world and deliver it with accuracy; (2) that the Soviets might be some years ahead of America in this field; and (3) that new management techniques would be needed so that America could catch up.

By 1954 the von Neumann committee on strategic missiles had members who (at Johnny's insistence) were go-go rather than talk-talk. An unexpected member was Charles Lindbergh, the hero of the first solo transatlantic flight; he was in place to tell senior service officers that they should not defend their own patches in a new pioneering age. The other members were two future scientific advisers to the president in Kistiakowsky and Jerome Wiesner, two industrialists in Simon Ramo and Dean Wooldridge (who were soon to leave the committee to form the Ramo-Wooldridge Group with important results), the founder of the Rand Corporation, the future head of Hughes Aircraft, two CalTech professors, a representative of Bell Laboratories, and representatives of both Los Alamos and Livermore.

The report that a strategic nuclear missile was possible followed partly from the work of Johnny's nuclear weapons panel, but it is possible that Johnny was aided here by his consultancy at the CIA. He coolly placed technicians with the services' various separate projects; so as to report back which parts could be relevant and which were not.

Johnny foresaw "unusual urgency for a strategic missile capability" for two reasons. The first was "a rapid strengthening of the Soviet defenses against our normal strategic air command bombers"; he thought this was to be "expected during the second half of this decade"—that is, the Soviets might be able to shoot down any Moscow-bound B-52's by the end of the 1950s. His second fear was "rapid progress by the Soviet in its own development" of missilery. He thought that this was already in train. There was going to be a brief but dangerous missile gap in the Soviets' favor sometime in the 1950s.

Some people thought Johnny's assessment in 1953–55 that the Soviets might be moving ahead in rockets was both tentative and pessimistic. Actually, it proved entirely right. The Russians had rather strangely allowed some of the technicians they had taken from Peenemünde to return home to Germany after about 1951. Johnny sought evidence from them and other intelligence sources. He then moved to action that proved decisive.

From the recommendations of the von Neumann committee came the six American missiles that were to guard the peace from the 1950s to the near-end of the cold war. Three were intercontinental missiles (Atlas, Titan, and Minuteman). Two were intermediate-range (Thor and Jupiter). Polaris was submarine-launched. All six programs were set afoot by decisions taken in the three years after 1953, although even the earliest flew only after Johnny's death in 1957.

Many people say it was wasteful that at one stage all six rocket programs were being carried through concurrently. Johnny had intended that they should be. He had learned from his experience in computers that it was better if forward-looking development of different programs continued in part competition and part collaboration with each other. Broadly, this was how Japan's eight big electronic companies carried Japan into the lead in the civilian microelectronic industry in the generation after Johnny's death, although he could not know it. What he did know was that the competition in rocketry should be between the most promising available emerging models and must not be based on rival air force or army or navy amour propre.

Strangely, his mixture of competition plus collaboration actually saved money. That can best be seen by giving numbers to each of the six programs. Broadly, Atlas (1) was devised as the first American intercontinental missile and met the performance goals and schedules laid down for it. Thor (2) was son of Atlas, using Atlas components and technological fallout. Because it would have a range of only around 1,500 miles it would have to be launched from the territory of European allies, and its advantage (apart from locking Europeans into the alliance) was that it would probably be ready before Atlas itself.

Titan (3) and Minuteman (4) both incorporated technology that was not ready at the time the Atlas program was set afoot. It was right not to delay Atlas but to continue with these.

Jupiter (5) was less excusable. It was the army's equivalent of Thor. Jupiter was originally lauded because it was narrow enough to get through Swiss railway tunnels and because Hitler's space pioneer von Braun was by now in the army's program. A better interservice argument then emerged. Narrow Jupiter could be adaptable for shipboard and possibly submarine use. The navy therefore originally supported it but immediately sought another missile under its own control. As Livermore Laboratory was finding that a bomb with a million-ton explosive power could be made lighter and lighter, the navy proposed the Polaris (6), only 4.5 feet in diameter. This meant that sixteen Polaris rockets could be fitted aboard a nuclear submarine, and Polaris would have a range of over 1,000 miles. These were deployed at sea by the 1960s. They became a credible nuclear deterrent against Moscow some time before the Soviet heavy missiles were a real threat to the United States.

The dangerous period of Soviet lead, or missile gap, lasted for sixteen months. It began in August 1957, six months after Johnny's death, when a test of a Soviet intercontinental ballistic missile sent it the length of Siberia. An American Atlas missile did not reach that range until December 1958.

Much less importantly, although more dramatically, this heaviest of Russia's rockets was modified to send the 183-pound Sputnik 1 into orbit in October 1957. The Americans reacted by sending the 3-pound Explorer into space in January 1958, using a rocket booster bootlegged from the army's and von Braun's Jupiter C. One of the jokes at the time ran, "Said Explorer to Sputnik—now we're alone, let's speak German." One of the realities was that the Russians had used their heaviest rocket to send a fairly insignificant radio transmitter into space, and the Americans had responded by sending a much smaller ball there with one of their lightest rockets.

President Kennedy was elected in 1960, when Americans were fearful of a missile gap that had actually closed two years earlier. There was reason to be scared in the sixteen months between the trans-Siberian rocket of August 1957 and the Atlas of December 1958. By Kennedy's inauguration, however, the American Atlas and its successors on the road were more credible, more usable, more accurate, lighter, and more flexible than the Russian missiles that had been started so much earlier. The Russians never really had a long-range missile lead over Kennedy's America. That is why they tried to put intermediate-range missiles into Cuba in 1962. Kennedy was able to tell Khrushchev to take the things away because both men knew that America by then had a credible deterrent against Moscow itself. This crucial peace-saving moment in the cold war was largely due to the crisply successful labor ten years before, in 1953–54, of the two committees chaired by Johnny.

Those committees' first reports also brought in a new sort of program management for defense and other projects. Because so many new technologies that could affect defense programs were now converging, the Americans in charge of racing the Russians to effective rocketry had to find some mechanism to coordinate the different technologies (which were usually only half understood by different people) and to conduct concurrently the development, production, and deployment of the weapons springing from them. No such mechanism existed. Two Johnny-inspired innovations were set afoot to find one.

The air force established its so-called Western Development Division (WDD) of the Air Research and Development Command

(ARDC) under General Bernard Schriever, who had worked closely with the von Neumann committee. Says York, a member of that von Neumann committee, "Much of what we now take for granted in methodology of systems development and systems management was pioneered under his [Schriever's] direction." It is not easy to recruit experts in fields which do not yet exist, but are clearly going to, and which will soon become more important than those managed by people higher up an existing hierarchy. Yet that is what the committee did.

Johnny's second innovation, to get the missiles rolling, might have been regarded by some fainthearts as improper. Ramo and Wooldridge of the von Neumann committee were induced to set up the new Ramo-Wooldridge Group to provide (says York) what the weapons trade now refers to as general systems engineering and technical direction (GSETD). After merger with Thompson Products, the Ramo-Wooldridge Group became TRW, which later grew into an important and more general defense contractor. Said York, who was an outspoken opponent of what he and Eisenhower called the "military-industrial complex": "There was absolutely nothing improper or wrong about this arrangement. . . . History can't be run by twice in order to check out alternatives, but I believe that without either WDD and General Schriever or the Ramo-Wooldridge Group, the Atlas project would have taken more than a year longer to complete and would have cost much more as a consequence." The year that was thus saved for Atlas was one of the most important in history.

◄►◄►

The work Johnny took up with the arrival of the Eisenhower administration was piled on top of a load that would already have exhausted an ordinary man. In addition to masterminding the revolutions in computers and meteorology, and to doing other IAS work, he was commuting from Princeton to Washington, New York, Los Alamos, and back to Princeton again all the time.

He returned from his January at Los Alamos in 1953 in time

for Eisenhower's inauguration. This was the calendar originally
laid on him:

JvN CALENDAR (A)

Thurs., Jan. 29—	9:00 a.m. AFSWP-sponsored TUMBLER Symposium, Wash.
Fri., Jan. 30—	9:00 a.m., TUMBLER Symposium
	12:00 noon, lunch with Gen. Simon and Mr. Davies (Simon's office)
	2:30 p.m., Height of Burst Panel meeting, Wash.
Mon., Feb. 2—	11:00 a.m., Dr. M. White
Tues., Feb. 3—	10:00 a.m., Math. Fac. meeting
Wed., Feb. 4—	11:00 a.m.–4:00 p.m., Nat'l Security Agency, Wash.
	4:30 p.m., meeting with Rabi, Whitman,
	AEC bldg., GAC offices, Wash.
Thurs–Sat., Feb 5–7—	AEC-GAC meetings, Wash.
Tues., Feb. 10—	Endicott, New York
Wed., Feb 11—	10:45 a.m., talk at IAS Seminar
	2:00 p.m., E.P. Wigner
	6:30 p.m., dinner at IAS with G. Ritter
Thurs., Feb. 12—	2:00 p.m., Mr. Johnson (McGraw-Hill)
	2:15 p.m., Dr. Richardson
	2:30 p.m., Bill Carlton (PU)
Fri., Feb. 13—	11:00 a.m., Physics meeting
	12:30 p.m., Full fac. meeting
Mon–Tues., Feb. 16–17—	Strategic Air Command meetings, Aberdeen
Thurs., Feb. 19—	11:00 a.m., talk at IAS Seminar
Fri., Feb. 20—	9:30 a.m., Mr. Russell (Esso Labs.)
Mon., Feb. 23—	10:45 a.m., talk at IAS Seminar
	1:30 p.m., Dr. White

Tues., Feb. 24—	3:30 p.m., N.Y. (Mr. Strauss)
Wed., Feb. 25—	7:30 p.m., Supper Club, Nassau Tavern
Thurs., Feb. 26—	11:45 a.m., Mr. Merle M. Andrew (ARDC, Baltimore)
Fri., Feb. 27—	10:00 a.m., Messrs. Russell, May (Esso Labs.)
Mon., March 2—	a.m., Wash. (GAC)
	8:00 p.m., Vanuxem Lecture
Tues., March 3—	3:00 p.m., Mr. Allott (RCA, Camden)
	5:00 p.m., Vanuxem Lecture
Wed., March 4—	10:45 a.m., IAS Seminar
	3:00 p.m., Mr. de la Torre
	5:00 p.m., Vanuxem Lecture
Thurs., March 5—	10:00 a.m., Meeting at IAS of Steering Comm., Numerical Weather Forecasting Proj.
	10:45 a.m., Mr. Abel (Wash.)
	5:00 p.m., Vanuxem Lecture

In practice, his work load was doubled while this calendar was being worked through. Gardner asked him to take up his new panels and committees.

By the summer of 1954 Strauss decided that Johnny was being asked to be in too many places at once. In August 1954 he therefore proposed that Johnny should accept direct appointment, from Eisenhower himself, as one of America's five atomic energy commissioners. The job would require ratification by a joint committee of Congress and was supposed to last from March 1955 to June 1959.

Why did Johnny accept this nominally full-time job, the first in his life: going to an office at a set hour, returning in the evening, with a secretary and staff to organize his affairs? One reason is that he did like the importance of being a commissioner. Another was that he did not regard it as a full-time job.

By that August 1954 Johnny knew that he could take most public servants and politicians in his galloping stride. Strauss wrote letters to coach him cautiously what to say during the ordeal of interrogation by the joint congressional committee. Johnny's replies to Strauss showed that he was positively looking forward to arguing with populists such as Senator Kefauver about the logical case for commercializing nuclear power. Johnny's mind at this stage was racing forward to the belief that nuclear fusion would become possible and make energy for all the world almost as cheap as water. He thought it important that America should handle this huge development in a world-embracing way when it came. He even hoped that this might happen during his period to 1959 as an atomic energy commissioner.

On world politics he had become more optimistic by late 1954. He believed the battle for Stalin's succession had been won by Russians who could be scared into being reasonable. He wanted to be one of the brains behind the negotiations that could begin with what was to be the Khrushchev regime. He thought that individual nations would decide that they could not now start wars. He believed that we might soon need something like a world government to deal with nuclear and some other inventions. He was seriously interested in the possibility that by spreading dyes on the Arctic and Antarctic ice fields we could regulate the amount of energy they reflect away from the earth. Unlike modern abhorrers of the greenhouse effect, he assumed that people would regard some warming—heating the world the few degrees necessary to turn it into a semitropical planet—as rather nice, but agreed that it could hardly be left to decisions within one country. "In the past we have always had new territory into which to carry new inventions," Johnny said in a press interview. "Now we have run out of real estate. With some new ideas we could jiggle the entire planet." As he peered forward to such a period, Johnny wanted to be near to decision-making power. He had quickly become a decisive voice on the Atomic Energy Commission, with chairman Strauss (Eisenhower's intimate) his devoted admirer.

If nuclear matters for the half decade down to 1959 did not

prove as dramatic as Johnny hoped, he did not feel that the AEC need detain him. He had other irons in the hot fires. With Congress's permission, even after it had confirmed him as an atomic energy commissioner, he stayed on as chairman of the von Neumann committee on missiles. With his usual capacity to work twenty-four hours a day, he was also carrying out a lot of other projects. He and Klari had moved into a yellow frame home in the Georgetown area of Washington, D.C. Klari discussed their life there with Samuel Grafton of *Good Housekeeping* magazine in 1955. "During the day," she said,

Johnny works in his office at the Atomic Energy Commission. At night, scientists in the many other fields he is interested in come to visit him. I am his night secretary. I entertain his visitors and pass them into him, one at a time. Then comes the hour when people normally go to sleep. Johnny goes to sleep too. But to him sleep is part of his work. He believes much of mathematics is done sub-consciously. He will go to sleep serenely with an unsolved problem and wake at three in the morning with the answer: his mind has done it for him while he has slept. Then he goes to his desk and phones his associates. One of his requirements for an associate is that he not mind being awakened in the middle of the night. Johnny will work until morning—half his books are in his bedroom—and then go to his office as chipper as a lark.

Klari was right about Johnny's main reason for attracting a pilgrimage of other scientists at this time. Many other scientists were speculating freely and brilliantly about new possibilities in the 1950s. Johnny's speciality was that he carried mathematics with him into these fields. He made other people's dreams suddenly concrete with precise figures. This was also a period when he was devising some heroic ideas about what he would next tackle, if his interest in his job as an atomic energy commissioner did fade. He thought that the mechanism of computers and the intricacies of numerical weather forecasting could now best be left to competitive forces, which he had helped set on stream. He was not as thrilled with his ideas on automata as he had been two years before. In the first preparations for his intended 1956 Silliman lectures, "On the Computer and the Brain," he had stumbled on the idea that he set out at the end of that deathbed book.

Johnny was fascinated in his last year by the contrast between his new computing machines (then with about ten thousand vacuum tubes, going down) and the human brain with so many billion neurons. The brain was much slower than his machines in doing multifigure sums, but the brain had so many other capabilities like visual recognition and imagination and ability to think laterally and make caring judgment, which his computers did not begin to have. How were these capabilities programmed on the brain? Whatever language the brain and central nervous system are using, he wrote, "it is characterised by less logical and arithmetical depth than we are normally used to." The multiplicity of languages spoken by different peoples shows that language is largely a historical accident. "Just as languages like Greek and Sanskrit are historical fact and not absolute logical necessities," he wrote, "it is only reasonable to assume that logics and mathematics are similarly historically accidental forms of expression. They may have essential variants, i.e., they may exist in other forms than the ones to which we are accustomed. Indeed the nature of the central nervous system and of the message system that it transmits indicate positively that this is so."

Johnny therefore believed at the end of his life that "when we talk mathematics we may be discussing a secondary language built on the prime language truly used by the central nervous system." He wanted to make some advances to finding what this prime language might be. He recognized that he could transform the whole prospect for mankind if he could. He wondered whether his computers could be jiggled so as to help in this search.

He felt he could not easily rewrite the old mathematics while remaining at the IAS in Princeton. That was the little community where sat a lot of the finest minds with the greatest vested interest in the old mathematics. Some people there had attacked even his swift and silent computers as noisy and polluting things. He also thought it possible that the rearrangement of computers to fit any new mathematics would best be accomplished by larger teams, paid for by somebody else. It was therefore in 1955 that he half arranged the post-AEC job about which he informed the IAS only from his hospital bed in 1956. He was going to be a professor at large at the University of California, living near one of its campuses but with support and cooperation from the giant commercial firm IBM. Because he had lost income by going into government service, IBM aimed to bring him additional funds by taking out patents in his name for various things he had suggested to them.

In these last Washington months in the summer of 1955 he continued to treat life as childish fun. Klari's description to Grafton of his driving technique suggested only a few changes from the Johnny who had got that first driving license under the Brooklyn Bridge in 1930. Said Grafton, "Dr. von Neumann's driving reflects his mathematical interests. He loves traffic jams because they present a problem: how can so many different bodies get through the same space at different rates of speed? He will twist and manoeuvre through a crowded street ('too fast,' says his wife) and just make it, delighted that he has calculated correctly. On the open road where nothing is in his way he drives slowly—with no problem to solve, his interest lapses."

It is probable that this statement to the press—that on the open road he drives slowly—had some elements of a built-in courtroom defense. Johnny, his interest lapsing at the wheel from driving and pondering deeper mathematical problems, was still rather apt to run into trees at 70 miles per hour. The traffic police had shown interest in this habit. "When we undertake a major project like buying a house," said Klari, "he is very good. He discusses all the factors very clearly and makes an excellent decision. Then his interest lapses. He has never touched a hammer or a screwdriver; he does nothing around the house. Except," Mrs. von Neumann smiled, "for fixing zippers. He can fix broken zippers with a touch. Apparently there is something subtly mathematical about the position of a snagged slider or a row of embittered zipper teeth that appeals to Dr. von Neumann. He studies it for a moment and sets it free."

He still had his old absent-mindedness, attached to one of the finest memories in the world. "He won't remember what he had for lunch today," said Klari, "but he will remember everything on a page in a book he read fifteen years ago." He was beginning to forget even some of the mathematics he had himself invented, because his mind was working with ferocious concentration on the next things he wanted to do. He never noticed the weather, even though he had just invented numerical weather forecasting. He would go on wearing a vest until July, then doff it and forget to return to it until February. "I go with him to buy his clothes," said Klari. "Otherwise, out of kindness, he would buy everything a salesman wants him to buy. If an aircraft was late taking off, he would try to find out the reason by buttonholing anybody in uniform within sight. Astonished porters, telegraph messengers and newsboys would be asked the cause of the delay."

Now that Klari and he were important folk in Washington, D.C., it was a bit worrying that he did not show undue politeness toward hackneyed minds. On first meeting, he would seem shy and polite, gauging the person he met. On the next meeting, he could by the mid-1950s rather pointedly avoid even important bores, preferring "to discuss screenplay composition with a Hollywood writer, or prescription compounding with a druggist, rather than the old questions on which everything interesting has been said long before."

He was not careful of his health, even though he never smoked. His pockets contained little except an increasing number of government passes, and some complicated Chinese puzzles to amuse him. "He can count everything," said Klari, "except calories." Klari did not get up for breakfast because of her job as Johnny's night secretary. Johnny would breakfast alone, dieting rigorously on yogurt and boiled eggs. Then he felt he had done enough dieting for the day. He would lunch and dine on the rich dishes and creamy sweets that he had liked since Budapest in about 1910. He sometimes added up the calories in the evening but always cheated in his own favor. When Klari was not there, he cheated against her dieting suggestions even at breakfast, gulping down English muffins. Overweight Johnny therefore had some medical warnings about his heart. But it was not for this reason that the blow struck.

◄►◄►

In August 1955 Strauss was in Switzerland for an international meeting to discuss the radiation diseases which the nuclear age might bring forth. A cable arrived from Johnny on August 11, 1955, running:

TODAY THE ORTHOPEDIC SURGEON AT BETHESDA [HOSPITAL] DIAGNOSED, ON THE BASIS OF SOME PAIN AND X-RAY, THAT I HAVE A VERY PROBABLY BENIGN "GIANT CELL" TUMOR ON LEFT SHOULDER CLAVICULAR BONE. RECOMMENDED OPERA-TION NOT ABSOLUTELY NECESSARY BUT WITHOUT UNNECES-SARY DELAY!

Strauss's first reply did not live up to the enormity of what this meant. He asked Johnny to "try to accept Admiral Radford's lunch invitation Monday August 22nd, but with leave to cancel if President wishes me to report to him in Denver Monday, which I should know tomorrow or Thursday." Strauss was still thinking that he would need advice from Johnny before reporting to Eisenhower on whatever Eisenhower wanted to talk about.

As the conference in Switzerland concerned radiation diseases, Strauss had some of the greatest world experts on cancer with him. They soon alerted a horrified Strauss to what Johnny's cable meant. A giant-cell tumor on the left-shoulder clavicular bone was very likely to be cancer. Grimly, it was unlikely to be primary cancer. It is likely that Johnny's primary cancer was in the pancreas, and certain that by that August he had cancer pulsing through his bloodstream and bones. He must by then have been in considerable pain. While concentrating, he had perhaps not noticed it. The exploratory operation that August grimly confirmed this. Johnny kept this from his friends and from some family. He dashed into

the last frenzy of activity as he tried to clear up the main things
he had started. His diary for the following two weeks, as of October 3, 1955, ran:

JvN CALENDAR

OCTOBER:

Wed., Oct. 5—

4:00 p.m., JvN speaks at National
Science Foundation (Auditorium)—
Colloquium Computer Research,
"High-Speed Computing & Com-
puters." (Talk: 40–45 min; Discus-
sion: 15–20 min.)
5:30 p.m., Dr. Killian of MIT—
Cosmos Club, Downstairs Lobby.
[Killian, the president of MIT, was
to become chairman of Eisenhower's
Science Advisory Committee]
8:00–10:00 p.m., JvN speaks:
Co-operative Forum, 1110 "F" St.,
NW

Thurs., Oct. 6—

5:30–7:00 p.m., JvN: cocktails for
Rand Trustees—at Cosmos Club.
6:00–8:00 p.m., Dr. & Mrs. JvN:
cocktails (to meet M. de Heens),
2501 Foxhall Rd. (DE-2-1286).

Sat., Oct. 8—

Tentative: breakfast with Dr.
Wheeler of Princeton.

Mon., Tues., Oct. 10–11—

Sc. Adv. Com. Meetings—Aberdeen. (JvN will definitely attend
Oct. 10; uncertain about Oct. 11)

Oct. 13

10:00 a.m., Report by Contractors re
ICBM-5C-1040.

Thurs.–Fri.,
Oct. 13–14—

Trip to Sandia:
Lv Wash.—UAL #611—4:30 p.m.
(Thurs.)

	Ar Denver—9:35 p.m. (Hotel Reservation: Brown Palace, Denver)
	Lv Denver—Cont. #320—8:00 a.m. (Fri.)
	Ar Albuquerque 10:28 a.m.
Sat.–Sun.,	Los Alamos
Oct. 15–16—	Lv Albuquerque—Cont. #323—9:00 p.m. (Sun.)
	Ar Denver 10:54 p.m.
	Lv Denver—UAL #730—1:30 a.m. (Mon.)
	Ar Washington 8:05 a.m.
	NOTE: JvN may return on an Air Force plane.
Mon.–Tues.,	WADC 8c. Adv. Com. (JvN's
Oct. 17–18—	Panel)
Tues., Oct. 18—	9:00 a.m., SAB Com. on Nuclear Propulsion of Missiles (Pentagon—5E-997).

While these two weeks were proceeding, his schedule sped up again. As of October 17, 1955, the calendar ran:

JvN CALENDAR B

Mon., Oct. 17—	9:00 a.m., ICBM Meeting, Rm 4C-1052 Pentagon
	6:00 p.m., AEC Committee meeting (at least two hours)
Tues., Oct. 18—	9:00 a.m., ICBM, Sc. Adv. Com. Rm 4C-1052 Pentagon
	3:45 p.m., Lv Wash.—AAL #752; Ar La Guardia 6:00 p.m.

	6:30 p.m., JvN: Sloan-Kettering Dinner in New York (Starlight Roof, Waldorf-Astoria) BLACK TIE 9:30 p.m., Lv La Guardia—AAL #337; Ar Wash: 10:50 p.m.
Wed., Thurs., Fri., Oct. 19, 20, 21—	Sc. Adv. Bd. (USAF) Meetings— Rm 5C-1040, Pentagon.
Wed., Oct. 19—	7:30 p.m., JvN: Reception (Stag) by Gen. Twining for Sc. Adv. Bd—at Bolling Officers Club—informal.
Wed., Oct. 26—	8:00 p.m., Dr. & Mrs. JvN: Dinner by Mr. & Mrs. Strauss for Mr. Sengier and Mr. & Mrs. Robiliart—at "F" Street Club—BLACK TIE
Thurs. Oct. 27—	Princeton: General Circulation Study Group (meteorology) 6:15 p.m., JvN: Dinner of NSF Divisional Com.—(Tally-Ho Restaurant; 812 17th St., NW) 7:30–9:30 p.m., Meeting of Natural Science Foundation Divisional Com. (NSF Board Room) (1520 "H" St. NW)
Fri., Oct. 28—	9:00–4:30 NSF Divisional Com. Mtg. (9th Floor Conf. Rm. at Natl. Adv. Com. for Aeronautics—1512 "H" St., NW)

All this by a cancer patient in considerable pain.

By November he was in a wheelchair. He told his friends that "it was the result of my operation in August, but is probably psychosomatic." York said of this time:

He was determined to continue his role in the work of the von Neumann committee, and the air force authorities were at least as anxious for him to do so. I recall several more meetings of the committee in which, after the rest of us were present and seated, Johnny arrived in a wheelchair propelled by a military aide. At first he seemed his normal self, smiling and cheerful, and the meetings proceeded in the customary way with Johnny dominating them intellectually without being at all argumentative or overtly domineering. Later when he came to see that his condition was hopeless he grew more despairing and turned back to the Roman Catholic Church for solace.

In January 1956 Johnny went into hospital again. He came out still in the wheelchair to receive a special Medal of Freedom personally from Eisenhower. "I wish I could be around long enough to deserve this honor," said Johnny to the president, in one of his first confessions even to his friends that he had known for some time that he was going to die. "You will be with us for a long time," replied Eisenhower, "we need you." This was possibly just an Eisenhower bumble, but in many senses Johnny's work did live on—and has been one of the reasons why the second half of the twentieth century has been nicer than the bloody first half of it.

The twenty-year-old Marina von Neumann had decided to get married straight from a brilliant college degree. Johnny was not pleased. He liked her chosen husband well enough but thought that early marriage would damage an academic career (a reasonable fear for a woman in 1955). He would have been pleased that the fear proved unfounded. Dr. Marina von Neumann Whitman was invited by President Nixon to be the first woman on any president's council of economic advisers. Johnny turned up in a wheelchair for Marina's engagement party in early 1956, but was back in the hospital before her marriage.

The great and the important now flocked to his bedside at the Walter Reed Hospital in Washington, D.C. Strauss was frequently there, together with much of the defense establishment, hanging on Johnny's words like black crows. It was known that Johnny's illness might lead to him talking in his sleep, and Colonel Ford was told to place soldiers to ensure that he did not shout out military secrets. This was not entirely successful. When Johnny started hallucinating in his sleep, he did so in Hungarian, which the soldier on guard did not understand. At least once Johnny summoned the soldier so that he could ring through a mild new idea he had for the air force in the middle of the night. His old associates on scientific subjects would have found this familiar, but the air force feared he was saying something very important with his last gasp.

These midnight calls probably led to the story that he sent screams from his deathbed through the dark, and that "Johnny von Neumann, who knew so well how to live, did not know how to die." He did admit his despair to some visitors. He could not visualize a world which did not include himself thinking within it. Some visitors say he was rude to Klari at this time. She was inclined to want to quiet those who would try to make him think while he was dying. He wanted to think as long as he could.

As the cancer had sent lesions near his brain he could not long continue with this. He had the draft of the Silliman lectures beside his bed, posthumously published as *The Computer and the Brain*. A few parts of that book, especially the end, are superb. Sadly there are other parts that are not up to the usual Johnny brilliance. These were the passages written when the cancer was advancing. "We could never keep up with the speed of his thinking," said one famous American scientist who is not a modest man. "Until sadly in that last year in the hospital we could."

The family gathered round the bedside. Michael Neumann read bits from Goethe's *Faust* in the original German. Johnny broke in when Michael reached speeches by his favorite characters and proclaimed them with gusto and total recall. In the summer his mother, Margaret von Neumann, was diagnosed as having cancer also. She died of it within two weeks. Johnny had eighteen months from diagnosis to death.

In this period Johnny returned to the Catholic faith that had also been significant to his mother after the family's conversion in 1929–30. There are those who say he took instruction from the

Catholic priest at the hospital mainly because the priest was an educated man, to whom Johnny could talk of classical Rome and Greece better than he could to the soldiers on guard. But Johnny had earlier said to his mother, "There probably is a God. Many things are easier to explain if there is than if there isn't." He also admitted jovially to Pascal's point: so long as there is the possibility of eternal damnation for nonbelievers it is more logical to be a believer at the end. His memory of old Latin was still perfect, and he astonished one deathbed visitor by reciting the Latin declamation that begins: "Judex ergo cum sedebit," and ends, "Quid sum miser tunc dicturus? Quem patronem rogaturus, cum vix justus sed sicurus?" (When the Judge His seat hath taken . . . What shall wretched I then plead? Who for me shall intercede when the righteous scarce is freed?)

All his friends, and some who had been a trial to him, were sending messages. Marston Morse's sounded a bit guilty: "We have stood shoulder to shoulder for two decades. There have been crises in which we had to take unwelcome positions prompted in each case, I believe, by considerations sometimes inevitable, sometimes very difficult to arrive at. . . . The conclusion of my mathematical colleagues with regard to the computer took into account the fact that your historic role of design and initial use of the computer had been magnificently finished." Gödel sent a letter of condolence about the illness in German, but soon wafted off on to mathematical symbols, asking Johnny's view on some impossibly abstruse problem. After about September the messages had rather little point, although Klari was gallantly replying to them. Her letter to Veblen on November 13, 1956, was in a mode she used to several correspondents at the time:

Dear Oswald

This is to acknowledge your recent letter to Johnny. I read it to him and he seemed to enjoy hearing from you, although by now it is very hard to tell about his reactions. He hardly speaks any more and the only way you can tell is by the expression on his face or the motion of his eyes. However, as well as I could tell, I

think he enjoyed just the fact that he received a letter from you—
and for this, I want to thank you.

On February 8, 1957, Johnny died. A large congregation arrived
at the funeral. He was buried in Princeton cemetery in a plot beside
his mother and the 1939 suicide, Charles Dan. The later suicide
Klari (who walked into the sea in November 1963) has since then
been laid beside them.

The old friends from Los Alamos crowded into a funeral car.
York remembers that Bradbury, the postwar director at Los Alamos, spoke a rather better epitaph than the Catholic priest had
during the ceremony. "If Johnny is where he thought he was
going," said Bradbury, "there must be some very interesting conversations going on about now."

Acknowledgments

The Alfred P. Sloan Foundation generously supported this book, and my first thanks must be to it. Arthur Singer and his colleagues at Sloan have helped bring into being biographies and autobiographies of the liveliest scientific minds of this century. My own level of scholarship is much lower than that of some of the other authors, so my highest hope is that I have not let the foundation down.

The Sloan Foundation had earlier commissioned a biography of John von Neumann from Steve White and the late Stanislaw Ulam. This slowed because of the difficulty of writing a book in both English and math, and had stopped before Professor Ulam's death. I have inherited some of the research, interviews, and notes from that intended book, and also the first-draft chapters down to 1926 which Stephen White had sketched. Many of the best sentences down to my chapter 4 are (with permission) White's.

I was able to put more flesh into these earlier chapters mainly because of help from three senior members of the von Neumann clan. These were Mariette Kuper (Johnny's marvelous first wife), the late Catherine

381

Pedroni (née Alcsuti), and Nicholas Vonneuman (Johnny's brother). Nicholas's perceptive book—*John von Neumann As Seen by His Brother* —appears in the Bibliography. I thank him for permission to use material from that book without being required to indicate in a footnote the citation applicable to each passage so used. He read my first draft for the earlier chapters, and removed many factual errors. Dr. Marina von Neumann Whitman, the distinguished economist who is Johnny's daughter, read the whole of the first draft and removed many more. Lots of errors will remain, and it is important to explain why they are all my fault.

Although Johnny was extraordinarily precise when explaining himself either in print or to his fellow scientists, he did like to gossip when he was switched off—with the aim of not intimidating anybody to whom he talked. Several times I heard jovial stories by people who said they had them directly from him, but in slightly different versions. Even his mannerisms changed according to the company he kept. I have probably sinned in choosing the versions that are most relaxed fun. The man was a legend in his lifetime, perhaps even more than he has become in the thirty-five years since his death. Everybody I met admired him, and nearly all liked him. The privilege from writing the book has been the entrée it provided to interviewing so many immensely distinguished people in or connected with American science.

They included (in alphabetical order) Hans Bethe, Julian Bigelow, the late Frederick de Hoffmann (who arranged some of the other interviews for me), Foster Evans, Herman Goldstine, Cuthbert Hurd, Carson Mark, Nicholas Metropolis, Joseph Smagorinsky, Edward Teller, Françoise Ulam, Eugene Wigner, and Herbert York. Professor Peter Lax read the manuscript, arranged the Los Alamos interviews, and deleted some of the mathematical mistakes. Once again, mistakes that remain are all my own fault. I had a distinguished editor in Michael Bessie, who wanted every sentence to be understandable to the ordinary man. This meant writing in English some passages that could have been written more deeply in math. I owe special thanks to the Library of Congress, the Library of the American Philosophical Society, the Library of the Institute for Advanced Study at Princeton, and the London School of Economics.

An embarrassment is the debt I owe to published sources, Whenever I found any really good point in the archives, somebody writing on one of the many subjects that were Johnny's seemed to have got to it first. I include in the Bibliography all those from whom I have learned; thank them for their permissions to quote; and hope I have not gone beyond the permissions kindly granted. Among the friends in the Bibliography to whom I owe special thanks are William Aspray (who has delved in more scholarly manner than I into many of the von Neumann archives) and Herbert York (who was a strong source for the final chapters). Among the works in the Bibliography by people whom I have not met (or only barely met), I learned especially from the book edited by Mohammed Dore (and his ten distinguished contributors) and the books written by Herman Goldstine, John Lukacs, Ed Regis, Richard Rhodes, and Joel Shurkin. Also from the articles cited in the Bibliography by Clay Blair, Samuel Grafton, and Paul Halmos. And from all the other people mentioned above.

In the Notes (see page 385), I make these acknowledgments again.

Permissions Acknowledgments

Notes

Chapter 1
Much of this chapter came from Steve White's notes, and from Stanislaw Ulam (both 1958 and 1976). Also from conversations with (inter alia) Hans Bethe, Peter Lax, Nicholas Vonneuman, Eugene Wigner. Published sources (see Bibliography) include Bell, Blair, Burks, Dore (especially Samuelson's chapter), Fermi, Gleick, Goldstine, Grafton, Halmos, Nagy, Rhodes, Shurkin, Strauss, Taub, Wigner (including the Quantum History Archives). The extended quotation from Lewis Strauss is from his speech at a von Neumann memorial dinner in Washington, D.C., in 1971.

Chapter 2
The two main published sources from which I drew (see Bibliography) are John Lukacs and Nicholas Vonneuman. Other points are from the books by Churchill, Heims, Rhodes. The late Catherine Pedroni (née Alcsuti) had the most encyclopedic memory, and helped me rewrite the second draft of this chapter. Earlier, Nicholas Vonneuman had kindly

385

removed many mistakes from the first draft. Steve White did the main research in and around Budapest; I drew heavily from his notes.

Chapter 3

Once again, much of this came from Steve White's notes, especially on his Budapest researches and his interviews with William Fellner and Eugene Wigner. By the time I saw the eighty-nine-year-old Wigner in 1990, his memory was less sharp. Much came from my conversations with Vonneuman, Pedroni, Lax. I drew especially on published work (see Bibliography) by Halmos, Nagy, Rhodes, Ulam, Vonneuman, Wigner.

Chapter 4

Steve White's notes. Published work (see Bibliography) by Bell, Clark, Heims, Reid, Taub, Ulam, Wigner (including the Quantum History Archives). I must thank the rector of the Eidgennosische Technische Hochschule at Zurich for responding so kindly with Xeroxed material from his records.

Chapter 5

It will be clear that I differ in opinions from Professor Steve Heims (who found Norbert Wiener a far more attractive character than Johnny) and from Bertrand Russell, but have gratefully quoted from their books (see Bibliography). Much of my summary of the history of math came from books by Carl Boyer and particularly Daniel Boorstin. The extensive quotations from Johnny's own views on the history of math, and on how to set about the subject, are in his collected works as edited by A. H. Taub. At this distance I assumed it was more convenient to cite this source rather than the various publications or seminar meetings at which they appeared. Other published works helpful in this chapter were (see Bibliography) Casimir, Dore (again, Samuelson's chapter), Regis, Wiener.

Chapter 6

Published sources again include Casimir, Dyson, Halmos, Hawking, Heims, the Quantum History Archives. Discussions with Peter Lax of New York's Courant Institute produced the reminiscences from K. O. Friedrichs. Other conversations with Bethe, Dyson, Wigner.

Chapter 7

The opening part of this chapter includes the many stories told about young Johnny, with the selection made from the ones that seem most likely to be true, though maybe with a bias to the jovial. Probably the most frequently cited published sources are Ulam and the *Collected Works of John von Neumann*, edited by A. H. Taub. But this is also the last part of the story to which Steve White's notes stretched. And it is the point at which both the von Neumann and Veblen files in the Library of Congress begin to be very useful. Other valuable conversations included those with Bethe, Dyson, Lax, Teller, Françoise Ulam (Stan's widow), Marina von Neumann Whitman (Johnny's daughter), and Wigner (including his interview in the Quantum History Archives). But, as the end of the chapter makes clear, the most marvelous interviewee was Mariette Kuper, née Kovesi, and in 1930–37 the first Mrs. Johnny von Neumann. My talks with her in 1990 set the book alight.

Chapter 8

The first part, and some of the middle part, of this chapter owe much to the lively history of the Institute for Advanced Study by Ed Regis (see Bibliography). Other published sources on which I drew include Clark, Feynman, Nagy, and especially Ulam. Reminiscences from Mariette Kuper abound through the chapter, as well as material from mathematical conversations with Lax. The librarians at the Institute for Advanced Study and at the American Philosophy Library in Philadelphia (guardian of the Ulam papers) were very kind to me. However, as this was a period during which Johnny kept his papers more methodically than at most other times, the main sources were again the von Neumann and Veblen files in the Library of Congress.

Chapter 9

Once again the main sources were the von Neumann and Veblen archives in the Library of Congress. The ballistic problems at Aberdeen are described (see Bibliography) in Goldstine and Shurkin. Other material (see Bibliography) from Grafton, Sakharov, Taub. Conversations with Bethe, Goldstine, Lax.

Chapter 10

I hope I express adequately in the text what any writer on Los Alamos owes to Richard Rhodes's superb *The Making of the Atom Bomb*. I drew facts and quotations from it. Other material is from (see Bibliography) Alvarez, Clark, Ulam, York. Peter Lax took me to his old stamping ground of Los Alamos, and I met the lively colony of those connected with the bomb who have retired there or near there, including Carson Mark, Nick Metropolis, Foster Evans, Françoise Ulam. Other interviews with Bethe, the late Frederick de Hoffmann, Sam Goldman, Lax, Teller, York. Again, a lot from the von Neumann archives in the Library of Congress.

Chapter 11

When I returned from being an RAF navigator to Cambridge University in England in October 1945, I took the economics tripos and got first-class honors in economics in 1947. I stayed on doing research and some teaching in economics at Cambridge until 1949, just as both *The Theory of Games and Economic Behavior* and Johnny's Expanding Economy Model were attracting attention. I therefore wrote the first draft of this chapter early, because I thought I had some competence in the subject. I soon discovered how wrong I was. Johnny's reputation as an economist has multiplied astonishingly since his death. I rewrote some of the first part of this chapter after the publication in 1989 by Oxford University Press, of *John von Neumann and Modern Economics*, edited by Professors Mohammed Dore, Sukhamoy Chakravarty, and Richard Goodwin (see Bibliography). The eleven contributors to it included two Nobel Prize winners (Paul Samuelson and Kenneth Arrow), as well as Sidney Afriat, Andrew Brody, John Harsanyi, the late Lord Kaldor, Lionello Punzo, Gerald Thompson. I have quoted views from the book, with I hope proper acknowledgment. I knew the late Lord Kaldor, and had very briefly discussed Johnny with him, but his introduction to the Oxford University Press book fills in the story much more fully. Other published sources drawn on (see Bibliography) include Bronowski, Mansfield, Nagy, and of course *The Theory of Games* itself.

Chapter 12

The two great published sources are Goldstine and Aspray (see Bibliography), and I have drawn from both. Much of the first and historical part of the chapter comes almost wholly from Goldstine, both his book and the interviews he kindly gave to me in Philadelphia. Other published sources (see Bibliography) include Nagy, Shurkin, Watson.

Chapter 13

Once again Goldstine and Aspray are the important sources (both their books in the Bibliography and interviews). Other published sources mentioned in the Bibliography include Burks, von Neumann's *The Computer and the Brain*, Taub (the IAS computer papers appear in the *Collected Works*), Kemeny, Regis, Smagorinsky, Ulam, Watson, Wiener. Interviews included Julian Bigelow, Cuthbert Hurd (of IBM), Joseph Smagorinsky, Françoise Ulam. The Library of Congress archives are especially useful in the period when Johnny was lobbying for funds and approval of his IAS computer project, and therefore detailing what his objectives were.

Chapter 14

Herbert York's books (see Bibliography) become especially important sources in these last two chapters. That includes the 1989 second edition of *The Advisors*, which has an appendix by Hans Bethe. Other published sources include Clark, Regis, Rhodes, Sakharov, Ulam. Interviews included Bethe, de Hoffmann, Lax, Pedroni, Teller, York, and the lively retired community at or near Los Alamos (including Carson Mark, Françoise Ulam, and others) with whom I had a memory-storming joint afternoon and long dinner in 1989.

Chapter 15

Herbert York's three books are again the best source. I have drawn heavily on them. Other published sources include Vonneuman, Heims, and newspapers at the time. By 1951–56 I was in the United States for *The Economist* once or twice a year, including four months swapped on to *Time* magazine in New York in 1952. I became intrigued that everybody in the know said that John von Neumann, who to me was an economist and author of *The Theory of Games*, was drawing near to the center of American defense strategy. I made requests for interviews, but they were never acceded to—although the rest of Washington, D.C., was amazingly open then to young assistant editors of *The Economist*. I talked casually about Johnny's 1952–55 influence to many people at the time and in my next thirty-five years as a viewspaperman. But I think the picture only fitted into place when (as Johnny's biographer) I read Herbert York's books. I am also grateful for conversations about Johnny's last years with York, Marina von Neumann Whitman (Johnny's daughter), and Nicholas Vonneuman (his brother), and with others who gathered at his bedside in 1956. In his last decade Johnny had fuller secretarial assistance than a professor usually has. His papers in the Library of Congress (including his daily lists or appointments) reflect this.

In writing this book, I have become very much aware that my training is as a viewspaperman rather than a scholar. A viewspaperman when in full employment publishes perhaps one thousand words a day, and is anxious to have his views considered and words used, with or without attribution, so as to keep discussion going. If others use my words, whether or not they agree with me, that gives me a feeling that the topics I have raised in that day's article are worthwhile. Scholars (unless they are a Johnny) publish far fewer words a year, and can become very cross if somebody repeats them without attribution. Johnny did not belong to this company. He wanted the ideas pulsing each moment through his mind to get quickly into the public domain, although preferably not through journalists. I believe the world can grow richer fastest and cheapest if we can have many more of his like again. I hope that in this book I have not offended against either his or other scholars' traditions, and have not trodden on toes.

Bibliography

Alvarez, Luis W. *Alvarez: Adventures of a Physicist*. New York: Basic Books, 1987.

Aspray, William. 1990. *John von Neumann and the Origins of Modern Computing*. Cambridge, Mass.: MIT Press.

————, and Arthur W. Burks, eds. 1987. *Papers of John von Neumann on Computing and Computer Science*. Cambridge, Mass.: MIT Press.

Bell, E. T. 1937. *Men of Mathematics*. New York: Simon and Schuster.

Blair, Clay, Jr. 1957. "The Passing of a Great Mind," *Life*, February 25.

Boorstin, Daniel. 1983. *Discovering the World*. New York: Random House.

Boyer, Carl. 1968. *A History of Mathematics*. Princeton, N.J.: Princeton University Press.

Bronowski, Jacob. 1974. *The Ascent of Man*. Boston: Little, Brown.

Burks, Arthur W. 1966. *Theory of Self-Reproducing Automata*. Urbana: University of Illinois Press.

Casimir, Hendrik B. 1983. *Haphazard Reality: Half a Century of Science*. New York: Harper and Row.

Churchill, Winston. 1930. *My Early Life: A Roving Commission*. New York: Charles Scribner's Sons.

Clark, Ronald W. 1971. *Einstein: The Life and Times*. New York: Avon Books.

Dore, Mohammed, Sukhamoy Chakravarty, and Richard Goodwin, eds. 1989. *John von Neumann and Modern Economics*. New York: Oxford University Press. Includes papers from these three editing professors, plus contributions from Sidney Afriat, Kenneth Arrow, John Arsanyi, Andrew Brody, Lionello Punzo, Paul Samuelson, and Gerald Thompson.

Dyson, Freeman. 1979. *Disturbing the Universe: A Life in Science*. New York: Harper and Row.

————. 1988. *Infinite in All Directions: An Exploration of Science and Belief.* New York: Harper and Row/Bessie Books.

Fermi, Laura. 1961. *Illustrious Immigrants*. Chicago: Chicago University Press.

Feynman, Richard. 1984. *Surely You're Joking, Mr. Feynman! Adventures of a Curious Character*. Ed. Edward Hutchings. New York: W. W. Norton and Company.

Gleick, James. 1988. *Chaos: Making a New Science*. New York: Viking Penguin.

Goldstine, Herman H. 1972. *The Computer from Pascal to von Neumann*. Princeton, N.J.: Princeton University Press.

Grafton, Samuel. 1956. "Married to a Man Who Believes the Mind Can Move the World." *Good Housekeeping*, September. Interview with Klari von Neumann.

Halmos, Paul R. 1973. "The Legend of John von Neumann." *American Mathematical Monthly* 80.

Hawking, Stephen W. 1988. *A Brief History of Time: From the Big Bang to Black Holes*. New York: Bantam Books.

Heims, Steve J. 1980. *John von Neumann and Norbert Wiener: From Mathematics to the Technologies of Life and Death* Cambridge, Mass.: MIT Press.

Kevles, Daniel J. 1987. *The Physicists: The History of a Scientific Community in Modern America*. Cambridge, Mass.: Harvard University Press.

Kemeny, John G. 1955. "Man Viewed as a Machine." *Scientific American* 192.

Keynes, John Maynard. 1963. *Essays in Persuasion*. New York: W. W. Norton and Company.

Lukacs, John. 1988. *Budapest 1900: A Historic Portrait of a City and Its Culture*. New York: Grove-Weidenfeld.

Mansfield, Edwin. 1974. *Economics: Principles, Problems, Decisions*. New York: W. W. Norton and Company.

McCagg, William. 1973. *Jewish Nobles and Geniuses in Modern Hungary*. New York: Columbia University Press.

Nagy, Ferenc. 1987. *Neumann Janos and the Hungarian Secret*. Letters to Rudolf Ortvay and others, published in Hungarian. Budapest: Orszagos Muszaki.

Philip, Miklos, and Tibor Szentivanyi. 1973. *Neumann Janos*. Interviews with some of Johnny's friends in America, published in Hungarian. Budapest: Tarsasag.

Regis, Ed. 1987. *Who Got Einstein's Office? Eccentricity and Genius at the Institute for Advanced Study*. Reading, Mass.: Addison-Wesley Publishing Company.

Rhodes, Richard. 1986. *The Making of the Atom Bomb*. New York: Simon and Schuster.

Reid, Constance. *Hilbert*. New York: Springer-Verlag, 1970.

Russell, Bertrand. 1967–70. *Autobiography*. 3 vols. Winchester, Mass.: Unwin Hyman.

Sakharov, Andrei. 1990. *Memoirs*. New York: Alfred A. Knopf.

Shurkin, Joel. 1984. *Engines of the Mind: A History of the Computer*. New York: W. W. Norton and Company.

Smagorinsky, Joseph. 1983. "The Beginnings of Numerical Weather Prediction and General Circulation Modeling: Early Recollections." *Advances in Geophysics* 25.

Strauss, Lewis. 1962. *Men and Decisions*. New York: Doubleday and Company.

Taub, A. H., ed. 1961. *Collected Works of John von Neumann*. 6 vols. Elmsford, N.Y.: Pergamon Press.

Ulam. Stanislaw M. 1976. *Adventures of a Mathematician*. New York: Charles Scribner's Sons.

Ulam, Stanislaw M., ed. 1958. "John von Neumann, 1903–57," *Bulletin of the American Mathematical Society* 64. Contributions from Garrett Birkhoff, F. J. Murray, Richard Kadison, Paul Halmos, Leon van Hove, H. W. Kuhn, A. W. Tucker, and Claude Shannon.

Von Neumann, John, with Oskar Morgenstern. 1944. *The Theory of Games and Economic Behavior*. Princeton, N.J.: Princeton University Press.

———. 1958. *The Computer and the Brain*. New Haven, Conn.: Yale University Press. See also Taub, above, for the collected works of von Neumann, and Aspray and Burks, above, for von Neumann's papers on computing.

Vonneuman, Nicholas A. 1987. *John von Neumann as Seen by his Brother*. P.O. Box 3097, Meadowbrook, Penn.

Watson, Thomas J., Jr., and Peter Petre. 1990. *Father, Son and Company: My Life at IBM and Beyond*. New York: Bantam Books.

Wiener, Norbert. 1964. *Ex-Prodigy: My Childhood and Youth*. Cambridge, Mass.: MIT Press.

Wigner, Eugene P. 1970. *Symmetries and Reflections: Scientific Essays*. Cambridge, Mass.: MIT Press. See also Wigner's recorded interviews in the Quantum History Archives in the American Philosophy Society at Philadelphia.

York, Herbert. 1970. *The Race to Oblivion*. New York: Simon and Schuster.

———. 1976. *The Advisors: Oppenheimer, Teller, and the Superbomb.* New York: W. H. Freeman and Company.

———. 1987. *Making Weapons, Talking Peace: A Physicist's Odyssey from Hiroshima to Geneva.* New York: Basic Books.

Archives drawn from:

Library of Congress. Mainly John von Neumann papers, Oswald Veblen papers.

American Philosophical Society Library, Philadelphia. Mainly Stanislaus Ulam papers.

Institute for Advanced Study, Princeton. Historical Studies–Social Sciences Library.

Index

Macrae on Macrae

Born 1923. RAF navigator 1942–45. Went up to Cambridge 1945. First-class honors in economics tripos, 1947. Did research and some teaching in economics at Cambridge in 1947–49, but left before completing Ph.D. because was already getting stuff published and wanted to get married. Joined *The Economist* in 1949, and apart from sabbaticals to write eight books and do a little consultancy was there until retirement in 1988. Assistant editor after 1954, and deputy editor after 1965. Have written over three thousand articles, mostly anonymous ones in *The Economist*, but have also lectured on five continents and written for other magazines around the world. The books published in America were *The Neurotic Trillionaire*, then *America's Third Century* (these were originally my two surveys on the United States in *The Economist*, but Harcourt Brace Jovanovich reprinted them in the United States as paperbacks), and *The 2025 Report: A Future History of 1975–2025* (published in America by Macmillan in 1985). I was a co-author of General Sir John Hackett's two books on World War III, which sold over three million copies worldwide; I wrote the chapters starting and ending the war, while the generals and admirals wrote the chapters fighting it.

Three surveys I have written on Japan, starting with one in 1962 which prophesied that they were the only country to have got economic policy right, have been published as books in Japan. In the Japanese emperor's birthday honors in 1988 I was given the Order of the Rising Sun with Gold Rays. In the same retirement year I was made a Commander of the British Empire in Queen Elizabeth's birthday honors.